Oxford
Children's
Thesaurus

OXFORD

UNIVERSITY PRESS

OXFORD
UNIVERSITY PRESS

Oxford University Press is a department of the University of Oxford.
It furthers the University's objective of excellence in research, scholarship,
and education by publishing worldwide. Oxford is a registered trade mark of
Oxford University Press in the UK and in certain other countries

Paper used in the production of this book is a natural,
recyclable product made from wood grown in sustainable forests.
The manufacturing process conforms to the environmental
regulations of the country of origin.

*The publishers would like to thank Shutterstock and Wikipedia for permission to use their material.
Every care has been taken to trace copyright holders. However, if there have been unintentional
omissions or failure to trace copyright holders, we apologize and if informed, endeavour to make
corrections in any future editions.*

Contents

Introduction
and how to use this thesaurus

The **Oxford Children's Thesaurus** helps children aged 8+ discover a wide range of words and shows how they can be used in writing.

---

guide words
The first and last word on a page are given at the top of each page so that you can find your way when you are searching for a word.

headword
The words you look up are in blue and in alphabetical order.

synonyms
Words that mean the same, or nearly the same, are given for each headword.

word web panel
Words that are related to the headword, or are types of the headword, help to give you more information which you may include in your writing.

overused word panel
Lots of alternatives are given for words that are used over and over again.

A B C D E F G H I J K L M N O P Q R S T U V W X Y Z

best *adjective*
1. *She is our best goalkeeper.* • top, leading, finest, foremost, supreme, star, outstanding, unequalled, unrivalled **opposite** worst
2. *We did what we thought was best.* • most suitable, most appropriate, correct, right

betray *verb*
1. *He betrayed us by telling the enemy our plan.* • be disloyal to, be a traitor to, cheat, conspire against, double-cross • Someone who betrays you is a **traitor**. • To betray your country is to commit **treason**.
2. *The look in her eyes betrayed her true feelings.* • reveal, show, indicate, disclose, divulge, expose, tell

better *adjective*
1. *Which of these books do you think is better?* • superior, finer, preferable
2. *I had a cold, but I'm better now.* • recovered, cured, healed, improved, well

beware *verb* beware
Beware! There are thieves about. • be careful!, watch out!, look out!, take care!, be on your guard!
beware of
Beware of the bull. • watch out for, avoid, mind, heed, keep clear of

biased *adjective*
A referee should not make biased decisions. • prejudiced, partial, one-sided, partisan, unfair **opposite** impartial

bid *noun*
1. *There were several bids for the painting at the auction.* • offer, price, tender
2. *His bid to beat the world record failed.* • attempt, effort, try, go

big *adjective* bigger, biggest
The giant owned three pairs of big boots. • large, huge, great, massive, enormous, gigantic, colossal, mammoth, *(informal)* whopping, ginormous, humungous **opposite** small, little, tiny

(!) OVERUSED WORD
Try to vary the words you use for big. Here are some other words you could use.
FOR A BIG PERSON OR BIG CREATURE
• burly, giant, hefty, hulking, mighty, monstrous, towering
The mighty robot clanked as it moved.

FOR A BIG OBJECT
• bulky, heavy, hefty, weighty
What could be inside that bulky envelope?

FOR A BIG ROOM OR BIG CONTAINER
• roomy, sizeable, spacious
Inside, the spaceship was surprisingly roomy. **opposite** cramped

FOR A BIG DISTANCE
• immense, infinite, vast
A vast stretch of ocean lay before them.

FOR A BIG AMOUNT OR BIG HELPING
• ample, considerable, substantial, generous, abundant
We each got an ample helping of porridge. **opposite** meagre, paltry

FOR A BIG DECISION OR BIG MOMENT
• grave, important, serious, significant
Yesterday was the most significant day in my whole life. **opposite** unimportant, minor

billow *verb*
1. *Smoke billowed from the mouth of the cave.* • pour, swirl, spiral
2. *The sheets on the washing line billowed in the wind.* • swell, bulge, puff, balloon

bird *noun*

WORD WEB
• A female bird is a **hen**. • A male bird is a **cock**. • A young bird is a **chick**, **fledgling** or **nestling**. • A family of chicks is a **brood**.
• A group of birds is a **colony** or **flock**.
• A group of flying birds is a **flight** or **skein**.
• A person who studies birds is an **ornithologist**.
SOME COMMON BRITISH BIRDS
• blackbird, bluetit, bullfinch, bunting, chaffinch, crow, cuckoo, dove, greenfinch, jackdaw, jay, linnet, magpie, martin, nightingale, pigeon, raven, robin, rook, skylark, sparrow, starling, swallow, swift, thrush, tit, wagtail, waxwing, woodpecker, wren, yellowhammer
BIRDS OF PREY
• buzzard, eagle, falcon, hawk, kestrel, kite, merlin, osprey, owl, sparrowhawk, vulture
FARM AND GAME BIRDS
• chicken, duck, goose, grouse, partridge, pheasant, quail, turkey • Birds kept by farmers are called **poultry**.

26

A dictionary tells you what a word means and a thesaurus gives you synonyms or words that have the same, or nearly the same, meaning. You use a thesaurus to find different words, more precise words or words that will make your writing more interesting.

For help with writing in different styles there is a quick reference supplement at the back of the book.

---

bit   blame

SEA AND WATER BIRDS
• albatross, auk, bittern, coot, cormorant, crane, curlew, duck, gannet, goose, guillemot, gull, heron, kingfisher, kittiwake, lapwing, mallard, moorhen, oystercatcher, peewit, pelican, penguin, puffin, seagull, snipe, stork, swan, teal

BIRDS FROM OTHER COUNTRIES
• bird of paradise, budgerigar, canary, cockatoo, flamingo, hummingbird, ibis, kookaburra, macaw, mynah bird, parakeet, parrot, toucan

BIRDS WHICH CANNOT FLY
• emu, kiwi, ostrich, peacock, penguin

PARTS OF A BIRD'S BODY
• beak, bill; claw, talon; breast, crown, throat; crest, feather, down, plumage, plume, wing

SOME TYPES OF BIRD HOME
• nest, nesting box; aviary, coop, roost

SOUNDS MADE BY BIRDS
• cackle, caw, cheep, chirp, chirrup, cluck, coo, crow, gabble, honk, peep, pipe, quack, screech, squawk, trill, tweet, twitter, warble • A turkey **gobbles**. • An owl **hoots**.

SPECIAL NAMES
• A female peacock is a **peahen**.
• A young duck is a **duckling**. • A young goose is a **gosling**. • A young swan is a **cygnet**. • An eagle's nest is an **eyrie**.
• A place where rooks nest is a **rookery**.

WRITING TIPS

You can use these words to describe a bird.

TO DESCRIBE HOW A BIRD MOVES
• circle, dart, flit, flutter, fly, glide, hop, hover, peck, perch, preen, skim, soar, swoop, waddle, wheel
A pair of swallows flitted among the rooftops.

TO DESCRIBE A BIRD'S FEATHERS
• bedraggled, downy, drab, fluffy, gleaming, iridescent, ruffled, smooth, speckled
The peacock displayed its iridescent tail.

bit noun
1. *Mum divided the cake into eight bits.* • piece, portion, part, section, segment, share, slice
2. *These jeans are a bit long for me.* • a little, slightly, rather, fairly, somewhat, quite

(!)   OVERUSED WORD

Try to vary the words you use for bit. Here are some other words you could use.

FOR A LARGE BIT OF SOMETHING
• chunk, lump, hunk, wedge, slab
Chunks of rock came tumbling down the mountain.

FOR A SMALL BIT OF SOMETHING
• fragment, scrap, chip, speck, pinch, touch, dab, particle, atom, (informal) smidgen
The map was drawn on a scrap of old paper.

FOR A BIT OF FOOD
• morsel, crumb, bite, nibble, taste, mouthful
Please try a mouthful of chocolate mousse.

FOR A BIT OF LIQUID
• drop, dash, drib, splash, spot
Add a splash of vinegar to the sauce.

bite verb biting, bit, bitten
1. *I bit a chunk out of my apple.* • munch, nibble, chew, crunch, gnaw, (informal) chomp
2. *Take care. These animals can bite.* • nip, pinch, pierce, wound • When an animal tries to bite you it **snaps** at you. • When an insect bites you it **stings** you. • A fierce animal **mauls** or **savages** its prey.

bitter adjective
1. *The medicine had a bitter taste.* • sour, sharp, acid, acrid, tart **opposite** sweet
2. *His brother was still bitter about the quarrel.* • resentful, embittered, disgruntled, aggrieved **opposite** contented
3. *The wind blowing in from the sea was bitter.* • biting, cold, freezing, icy, piercing, raw, wintry, (informal) perishing **opposite** mild

black adjective, noun
The pony had a shiny black coat. • coal-black, jet-black, pitch-black, ebony, inky, raven • You can also describe a black night as **pitch-dark**. • Someone in a bad mood is said to look **as black as thunder**. • Common similes are **as black as coal** and **as black as night**.

blame verb
Don't blame me if you miss the bus. • accuse, criticize, condemn, reproach, scold

27

---

alphabet
The alphabet runs down the side of the page and the letter that you are in is highlighted so you can find your way around the thesaurus quickly and easily.

example sentence
Examples show how the word is used, which helps you to see how and where you should use it.

word class
This tells you if the word is a *noun, adjective, verb, adverb, pronoun,* or *determiner;* sometimes a word may have more than one word class.

writing tips panel
Sentences and words, with examples, are here to inspire you to write creatively.

5

In this thesaurus,
you will find the following special panels.

WORD WEBS

aircraft	flower	pyramid
alien	food	red
animal	football	reptile
armour	fruit	room
artist	game	royalty
astronaut	ghost	ruler
bird	group	sea
boat	hair	seashore
body	horse	seaside
building	hospital	shoe
car	house	shop
cave	ice	sound
clothes	insect	space
colour	jewel	sport
cook	jungle	spy
criminal	kitchen	story
dance	knight	sweet
detective	magic	swim
dinosaur	moon	time
dragon	mountain	toy
explorer	music	transport
expression	myth	travel
eye	pirate	tree
face	planet	vehicle
fairy	plant	weather
family	poem	worried
farm	polar	writing
fish	punctuation	

OVERUSED WORDS

bad	hard	old
beautiful	like	sad
big	little	say
bit	look	small
eat	lovely	strong
good	move	walk
happy	nice	

WRITING TIPS

afraid	eye	sound
angry	face	surprised
animal	feel	teeth
ball	food	un-
bell	hair	voice
bird	light	water
body	nose	weather
clothes	river	writing
colour	smell	

6

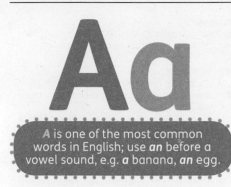

A is one of the most common words in English; use **an** before a vowel sound, e.g. **a** banana, **an** egg.

abandon *verb*
1. *The robbers abandoned the stolen car.*
• leave, desert, forsake, leave behind, strand, *(informal)* dump, ditch
2. *We abandoned our picnic because of the rain.* • cancel, give up, scrap, drop, abort, discard

ability *noun* **abilities**
Skin has a natural ability to heal itself.
• capability, competence, aptitude, talent, expertise, skill

able *adjective*
1. *Will you be able to come to my party?*
• allowed, permitted, free, willing
opposite unable
2. *Penguins are very able swimmers.*
• competent, capable, accomplished, expert, skilful, proficient, talented, gifted
opposite incompetent

abnormal *adjective*
It's abnormal to have snow in July. • unusual, exceptional, extraordinary, peculiar, odd, strange, unnatural, weird, bizarre, freakish
opposite normal

abolish *verb*
I wish someone would abolish homework!
• get rid of, do away with, put an end to, eliminate **opposite** create

about *preposition*
There are about two hundred children in the school. • approximately, roughly, close to, around
to be about something
The film is about a dog called Scruff. • concern, deal with, involve

abrupt *adjective*
1. *The book came to a very abrupt end.*
• sudden, hurried, hasty, quick, unexpected
opposite gradual

2. *The sales assistant had a very abrupt manner.* • blunt, curt, sharp, rude, gruff, impolite, tactless, unfriendly **opposite** polite

absent *adjective*
Why were you absent from school yesterday?
• away, missing • To be absent from school without a good reason is to **play truant**.
opposite present

absolute *adjective*
The hypnotist asked for absolute silence.
• complete, total, utter, perfect

absolutely *adverb*
This floor is absolutely filthy! • completely, thoroughly, totally, utterly, wholly, entirely

abundant *adjective*
Birds have an abundant supply of food in the summer. • ample, plentiful, generous, profuse, lavish, liberal **opposite** meagre, scarce

abuse *verb*
1. *The rescued dog had been abused by its owners.* • mistreat, maltreat, hurt, injure, damage, harm, misuse
2. *The referee was abused by players from both teams.* • be rude to, insult, swear at, *(informal)* call someone names

abuse *noun*
1. *They campaigned against the abuse of animals.* • mistreatment, misuse, damage, harm, injury
2. *A spectator yelled abuse at the referee.*
• insults, name-calling, swear words

accelerate *verb*
The bus accelerated when it reached the motorway. • go faster, speed up, pick up speed
opposite slow down

accent *noun*
1. *My mum speaks English with a Jamaican accent.* • pronunciation, intonation, tone
2. *Play the first note of each bar with a strong accent.* • beat, stress, emphasis, rhythm, pulse

accept *verb*
1. *I accepted the offer of a lift to the station.*
• take, receive, welcome **opposite** reject
2. *The club accepted my application for membership.* • approve, agree to, consent to
opposite reject
3. *Do you accept responsibility for the damage?*
• admit, acknowledge, recognize, face up to
opposite deny

4. *They had to* accept *the umpire's decision.*
• agree to, go along with, tolerate, put up with, resign yourself to

acceptable adjective
1. *Would a pound be* acceptable *as a tip?*
• welcome, agreeable, appreciated, pleasant, pleasing, worthwhile
2. *She said my handwriting was not* acceptable. • satisfactory, adequate, appropriate, permissible, suitable, tolerable, passable **opposite** unacceptable

accident noun
1. *There has been an* accident *at a fireworks display.* • misfortune, mishap, disaster, calamity, catastrophe • A person who is always having accidents is **accident-prone**.
2. *A motorway* accident *is causing traffic delays.* • collision, crash, smash • An accident involving a lot of vehicles is a **pile-up**. • A railway accident may involve a **derailment**.
3. *It was pure* accident *that led us to the secret passage.* • chance, luck, a fluke

accidental adjective
1. *The damage to the building was* accidental.
• unintentional, unfortunate, unlucky
2. *The professor made an* accidental *discovery.*
• unexpected, unforeseen, unplanned, fortunate, lucky, chance **opposite** deliberate

account noun
1. *I wrote an* account *of our camping trip in my diary.* • report, record, description, history, narrative, story, chronicle, log, (informal) write-up
2. *Money was of no* account *to him.*
• importance, significance, consequence, interest, value

accurate adjective
1. *The detective took* accurate *measurements of the room.* • careful, correct, exact, meticulous, minute, precise **opposite** inexact, rough
2. *Is this an* accurate *account of what happened?* • faithful, true, reliable, truthful, factual **opposite** inaccurate, false

accuse verb
accuse of
Miss Sharp accused *her opponent of cheating.*
• charge with, blame for, condemn for, denounce for **opposite** defend

ache noun
The ache *in my leg is getting worse.* • pain, soreness, throbbing, discomfort, pang, twinge

ache verb
My legs ached *from the long walk.* • hurt, be painful, be sore, throb, pound, smart

achieve verb
1. *He* achieved *his ambition to play rugby for Wales.* • accomplish, attain, succeed in, carry out, fulfil
2. *She* achieved *success with her first novel.*
• acquire, win, gain, earn, get, score

achievement noun
To climb Mount Everest would be an amazing achievement. • accomplishment, attainment, success, feat, triumph

acknowledge verb
1. *The queen did not* acknowledge *her cousin's claim to the throne.* • admit, accept, concede, grant, recognize **opposite** deny
2. *Please* acknowledge *my email.* • answer, reply to, respond to

acquire verb
Where can I acquire *a copy of this book?* • get, get hold of, obtain • To acquire something by paying for it is to **buy** or **purchase** it.

act noun
1. *Rescuing the boy from the river was a brave* act. • action, deed, feat, exploit, operation
2. *The clowns were the best* act *at the circus.*
• performance, sketch, item, turn

act verb
1. *We must* act *as soon as we hear the signal.*
• do something, take action
2. *Give the medicine time to* act. • work, take effect, have an effect, function
3. *Stop* acting *like a baby!* • behave, carry on
4. *I* acted *the part of a pirate in the play.*
• perform, play, portray, represent, appear as

action noun
1. *The driver's swift* action *prevented an accident.* • act, deed, effort, measure, feat
2. *The fruit ripens through the* action *of the sun.* • working, effect, mechanism
3. *The film was packed with* action. • drama, excitement, activity, liveliness, energy, vigour, vitality

active adjective
1. *Mr Aziz is very* active *for his age.* • energetic, lively, dynamic, vigorous, busy
2. *My uncle is an* active *member of the football club.* • enthusiastic, devoted, committed, dedicated, hard-working **opposite** inactive

activity noun **activities**
1. *The town centre was full of activity.*
• action, life, busyness, liveliness, excitement, movement, animation
2. *My mum's favourite activity is gardening.*
• hobby, interest, pastime, pursuit, job, occupation, task

actual adjective
Did you see the actual crime? • real, true, genuine, authentic **opposite** imaginary, supposed

actually adverb
What did the teacher actually say to you?
• really, truly, definitely, certainly, genuinely, in fact

acute adjective
1. *She felt an acute pain In her knee.* • Intense, severe, sharp, piercing, sudden, violent **opposite** mild, slight
2. *There is an acute shortage of food.*
• serious, urgent, crucial, important, vital **opposite** unimportant
3. *Clearly the aliens had an acute intelligence.*
• keen, quick, sharp, clever, intelligent, shrewd, smart, alert **opposite** stupid

adapt verb
1. *I'll adapt the goggles so that they fit you.*
• alter, change, modify, convert, reorganize, transform
2. *Our family adapted quickly to life in the country.* • become accustomed, adjust, acclimatize

add verb
The poet added an extra line in the last verse.
• join on, attach, append, insert
to add to
The herbs add to the flavour of the stew.
• improve, enhance, increase
to add up
1. *Can you add up these figures for me?*
• count up, find the sum of, find the total of, (informal) tot up
2. *(informal) Her story just doesn't add up.* • be convincing, make sense

additional adjective
There are additional toilets downstairs. • extra, further, more, supplementary

adequate adjective
1. *The wardrobe is more than adequate for my few clothes.* • enough, sufficient, ample
2. *Your work is adequate, but I'm sure you can do better.* • satisfactory, acceptable, tolerable, competent, passable, respectable

adjust verb
1. *You need to adjust the TV picture.* • correct, modify, put right, improve, tune
2. *She adjusted the central heating thermostat.* • alter, change, set, vary, regulate

admire verb
1. *I admire her skill with words.* • think highly of, look up to, value, have a high opinion of, respect, applaud, approve of, esteem **opposite** despise
2. *The tourists stopped to admire the view.*
• enjoy, appreciate, be delighted by

admit verb **admitting, admitted**
Did he admit that he told a lie? • acknowledge, agree, accept, confess, grant, own up **opposite** deny

adopt verb
1. *Our school has adopted a healthy eating policy.* • take up, accept, choose, follow, embrace
2. *We have adopted a stray kitten.* • foster, take in

adore verb
1. *Rosie adores her big sister.* • love, worship, idolize, dote on
2. *(informal) I adore chocolate milk shakes!*
• love, like, enjoy **opposite** hate, detest

adult adjective
An adult zebra can run at 80 kilometres an hour. • grown-up, mature, full-size, fully grown **opposite** young, immature

advance verb
1. *As the army advanced, the enemy fled.*
• move forward, go forward, proceed, approach, come near, press on, progress, forge ahead, gain ground, make headway, make progress **opposite** retreat
2. *Mobile phones have advanced in the last few years.* • develop, grow, improve, evolve, progress

advantage noun
We had the advantage of the wind behind us. • assistance, benefit, help, aid, asset **opposite** disadvantage, drawback

adventure noun
1. *He told us about his latest adventure.*
• enterprise, exploit, venture, escapade
2. *They travelled the world in search of adventure.* • excitement, danger, risk, thrills

A
B
C
D
E
F
G
H
I
J
K
L
M
N
O
P
Q
R
S
T
U
V
W
X
Y
Z

advertise verb
We made a poster to advertise the cake sale.
• publicize, promote, announce, make known, (informal) plug

advice noun
The website gives advice on building a bird table. • guidance, help, directions, recommendations, suggestions, tips, pointers

advise verb
1. *What did the doctor advise?* • recommend, suggest, advocate, prescribe
2. *He advised me to rest.* • encourage, urge

affair noun
The theft of the jewels was a mysterious affair.
• event, happening, incident, occurrence, occasion, thing

affect verb
1. *Global warming will affect our climate.*
• have an effect or impact on, influence, change, modify, alter
2. *The bad news affected us deeply.* • disturb, upset, concern, trouble, worry

afford verb
I can't afford a new bike just now. • have enough money for, pay for, manage, spare

afraid adjective
1. Deep in the woods *Rosie felt afraid and alone.* • frightened, scared, alarmed
2. *Don't be afraid to ask questions.* • hesitant, reluctant, shy

WRITING TIPS

You can use these words to describe someone who is feeling afraid:

Someone who is FEELING VERY AFRAID MIGHT BE
• terrified, petrified, panic-stricken

Someone who is FEELING AFRAID THAT SOMETHING BAD MIGHT HAPPEN MIGHT BE
• fearful, anxious, apprehensive **opposite** brave

SOMEONE WHO FEELS AFRAID MIGHT
• blanch, go or turn pale, have goosebumps, quake in their boots, shudder or shiver with fear, stand frozen or rooted to the spot, tremble like a leaf

SOMETHING WHICH MAKES YOU AFRAID MIGHT
• give you goosebumps, make your hair stand on end, make your knees tremble, strike fear into you or your heart

age noun
The book is set in the age of the Vikings.
• period, time, era, epoch, days

aggressive adjective
Bats are not aggressive creatures. • hostile, violent, provocative, quarrelsome, bullying, warlike **opposite** friendly

agile adjective
Mountain goats are extremely agile. • nimble, graceful, sure-footed, sprightly, acrobatic, supple, swift **opposite** clumsy, stiff

agony noun agonies
He screamed in agony when he broke his leg.
• pain, suffering, torture, torment, anguish, distress

agree verb
1. *I'm glad that we agree.* • be united, think the same, concur **opposite** disagree
2. *I agree that you are right.* • accept, acknowledge, admit, grant, allow **opposite** disagree
3. *I agree to pay my share.* • consent, promise, be willing, undertake **opposite** refuse

agreement noun
1. *There was agreement on the need for longer holidays.* • consensus, unanimity, unity, consent, harmony, sympathy, conformity **opposite** disagreement
2. *The two sides signed an agreement.*
• alliance, treaty • An agreement to end fighting is an **armistice** or **truce**. • A business agreement is a **bargain**, **contract** or **deal**.

aid noun
1. *We can climb out with the aid of this rope.* • help, support, assistance, backing, cooperation
2. *They agreed to send more aid to poorer countries.* • donations, subsidies, contributions

aid verb
The local people aided the police in their investigation. • help, assist, support, back, collaborate with, cooperate with, contribute to, lend a hand to, further, promote, subsidize

aim noun
What was the aim of the experiment?
• ambition, desire, dream, goal, hope, intention, objective, purpose, target, wish

aim verb
1. *She aims to be a professional dancer.*
• intend, mean, plan, propose, want, wish, seek

2. *He aimed his bow and arrow at the target.*
• point, direct, take aim with, line up, level, train, focus

air *noun*
1. *We shouldn't pollute the air we breathe.*
• atmosphere
2. *This room needs some air.* • fresh air, ventilation
3. *There was an air of mystery about the place.*
• feeling, mood, look, appearance, sense

air *verb*
1. *He opened the window to air the room.*
• freshen, refresh, ventilate
2. *I have a right to air my opinions.* • express, make known, make public, reveal, voice

aircraft *noun*

WORD WEB

SOME TYPES OF AIRCRAFT
• aeroplane, airliner, airship, biplane, bomber, fighter, glider, helicopter, hot-air balloon, jet, jumbo jet, seaplane

PARTS OF AIRCRAFT
• cabin, cargo hold, cockpit, engine, fin, flap, flight deck, fuselage, joystick, passenger cabin, propeller, rotor, rudder, tail, tailplane, undercarriage, wing

PLACES WHERE AIRCRAFT TAKE OFF AND LAND
• aerodrome, airfield, airport, airstrip, helipad, heliport, landing strip, runway

PEOPLE WHO FLY IN AIRCRAFT
• aviator, balloonist, pilot; cabin crew, co-pilot, flight attendant, passengers

alarm *verb*
The barking dog alarmed the sheep. • frighten, startle, scare, panic, agitate, distress, shock, surprise, upset, worry **opposite** reassure

alarm *noun*
1. *Did you hear the alarm?* • signal, alert, warning, siren
2. *The sudden noise filled me with alarm.*
• fright, fear, panic, anxiety, apprehension, distress, nervousness, terror, uneasiness

alien *adjective*
1. *The desert landscape looked alien to us.*
• strange, foreign, unfamiliar, different, exotic
opposite familiar
2. *They saw the lights of an alien spaceship.*
• extraterrestrial

alien *noun*

WORD WEB

I wrote a story about aliens from Mars.
• extraterrestrial, alien life-form, spaceman or spacewoman, starman or starwoman

AN ALIEN FROM ANOTHER PLANET MIGHT BE
• humanoid, insect-like, lizard-like, reptilian; intelligent, primitive, super-intelligent, telepathic

BODY PARTS AN ALIEN MIGHT HAVE
• antenna, blotches, scales, slime, sucker, tentacle, webbing

TRANSPORT AN ALIEN MIGHT USE
• alien vessel, flying saucer, mothership, pod, spacecraft, spaceship, starship, time-machine, transporter beam
• An alien might call someone from Earth an **Earthling**.

alive *adjective*
Fortunately, my goldfish was still alive.
• living, live, existing, in existence, surviving, breathing, flourishing **opposite** dead

alliance *noun*
The two countries formed an alliance.
• partnership, union, association, federation, league • An alliance between political parties is a **coalition**.

allow *verb*
1. *They don't allow skateboards in the playground.* • permit, let, authorize, approve of, agree to, consent to, give permission for, license, put up with, stand, support, tolerate
opposite forbid

a
b
c
d
e
f
g
h
i
j
k
l
m
n
o
p
q
r
s
t
u
v
w
x
y
z

2. *Have you allowed enough time for the journey?* • allocate, set aside, assign, grant, earmark

all right *adjective*
1. *'Is everyone all right?' she asked anxiously.*
• well, unhurt, unharmed, uninjured, safe
2. *The food in the hotel was all right.*
• satisfactory, acceptable, adequate, reasonable, passable
3. *Is it all right to play music in here?*
• acceptable, permissible

almost *adverb*
1. *I have almost finished the crossword.*
• nearly, practically, just about, virtually, all but, as good as, not quite
2. *Almost a hundred people came to the concert.* • about, approximately, around

alone *adjective, adverb*
1. *Did you go to the party alone?* • on your own, by yourself, unaccompanied
2. *Zoe had no friends and felt very alone.*
• lonely, friendless, isolated, solitary, lonesome, desolate

also *adverb*
We need some bread, and also more butter.
• in addition, besides, additionally, too, furthermore, moreover

alter *verb*
They have altered the route for the cycle race.
• change, adjust, adapt, modify, transform, amend, make different, revise, vary

altogether *adverb*
1. *I'm not altogether satisfied.* • completely, entirely, absolutely, quite, totally, utterly, wholly, fully, perfectly, thoroughly
2. *Our house has five rooms altogether.* • in all, in total, all told

always *adverb*
1. *The sea is always in motion.* • constantly, continuously, endlessly, eternally, for ever, perpetually, unceasingly
2. *This bus is always late.* • consistently, continually, invariably, persistently, regularly, repeatedly

amaze *verb*
It amazes me to think that the Earth is billions of years old. • astonish, astound, startle, surprise, stun, shock, stagger, dumbfound, *(informal)* flabbergast

amazed *adjective*
I was amazed by the number of replies I received. • astonished, astounded, stunned, surprised, dumbfounded, speechless, staggered, *(informal)* flabbergasted

amazement *noun*
They stared at each other in amazement.
• astonishment, surprise, shock, disbelief

amazing *adjective*
The Northern Lights are an amazing sight.
• astonishing, astounding, staggering, remarkable, surprising, extraordinary, incredible, breathtaking, phenomenal, sensational, stupendous, tremendous, wonderful, mind-boggling

ambition *noun*
1. *She had great ambition when she was young.* • drive, enthusiasm, enterprise, push, zeal
2. *My ambition is to play tennis at Wimbledon.*
• goal, aim, intention, objective, target, desire, dream, wish, hope, aspiration

ambitious *adjective*
1. *If you're ambitious, you will probably succeed.* • enterprising, enthusiastic, committed, go-ahead, keen
opposite unambitious
2. *I think your plan is too ambitious.* • grand, big, large-scale

amount *noun*
1. *Mum wrote a cheque for the correct amount.*
• sum, total, whole
2. *There's a large amount of paper in the cupboard.* • quantity, measure, supply, volume, mass, bulk

ample *adjective*
1. *The car has an ample boot.* • big, large, spacious, roomy **opposite** small
2. *We had an ample supply of food.*
• abundant, plentiful, generous, substantial, considerable, profuse, lavish, liberal
opposite meagre
3. *No more juice, thanks—that's ample.*
• plenty, sufficient, lots, more than enough, *(informal)* heaps, masses, loads, stacks
opposite insufficient

amuse *verb*
I think this joke will amuse you.
• make you laugh, entertain, cheer up, divert, *(informal)* tickle

amusing *adjective*
I didn't find his jokes very amusing. • funny, witty, humorous, comic, comical, hilarious, diverting, entertaining **opposite** unamusing, serious

ancestor *noun*
Our family's ancestors came from France.
• forebear, forefather, predecessor
opposite descendant

ancient *adjective*
1. *Does that ancient car still go?* • old, old-fashioned, antiquated, out-of-date, obsolete
2. *In ancient times, our ancestors were hunters.* • early, primitive, prehistoric, remote, long past, olden • The times before written records were kept are **prehistoric** times. • The ancient Greeks and Romans lived in **classical** times. **opposite** modern

anger *noun*
I was filled with anger when I read her letter.
• rage, fury, indignation, *(old use)* wrath, ire • An outburst of anger is a **tantrum** or a **temper**.

anger *verb*
His cruelty towards his dog angered me.
• enrage, infuriate, incense, madden, annoy, irritate, exasperate, antagonize, provoke, *(informal)* make your blood boil, make you see red **opposite** pacify

angry *adjective* angrier, angriest
Miss Potts turns purple when she gets angry.
• irritated, cross, annoyed, displeased, put out

✏️ WRITING TIPS

Someone who is FEELING VERY ANGRY MIGHT BE
• furious, enraged, infuriated, irate, livid, raging

Someone who is FEELING ANGRY BECAUSE OF UNFAIRNESS MIGHT BE
• incensed, indignant

Someone who is FEELING ANGRY AND FRUSTRATED MIGHT BE
• exasperated

SOMEONE WHO IS FEELING ANGRY BUT NOT SHOWING IT MUCH MIGHT BE
• fuming, seething, *(informal)* mad, hopping mad • To become angry is to **lose your temper. opposite** calm

---

SOMEONE WHO GETS ANGRY MIGHT
• blow a fuse, blow their top, fly off the handle, have a face like thunder, have steam coming out of their ears, hit the roof, see red

---

animal *noun*

🕸️ WORD WEB

Wild animals roam freely in the safari park. • creature, beast, brute • A word for wild animals in general is **wildlife**. • A scientific word for animals is **fauna**.

VARIOUS KINDS OF ANIMAL
• amphibian, arachnid, bird, fish, insect, invertebrate, mammal, marsupial, mollusc, reptile, rodent, vertebrate • An animal that eats meat is a **carnivore**. • An animal that eats plants is a **herbivore**. • An animal that eats many things is an **omnivore**. • Animals that sleep most of the winter are **hibernating animals**. • Animals that are active at night are **nocturnal animals**.

SOME ANIMALS THAT LIVE ON LAND
• aardvark, antelope, ape, armadillo, baboon, badger, bat, bear, beaver, bison, buffalo, camel, cheetah, chimpanzee, chinchilla, chipmunk, deer, dormouse, elephant, elk, fox, gazelle, gibbon, giraffe, gnu, gorilla, grizzly bear, hare, hedgehog, hippopotamus, hyena, jackal, jaguar, kangaroo, koala, lemming, lemur, leopard, lion, llama, lynx, mongoose, monkey, moose, mouse, ocelot, opossum, orang-utan, otter, panda, panther, platypus, polar bear, porcupine, rabbit, rat, reindeer, rhinoceros, skunk, squirrel, stoat, tapir, tiger, vole, wallaby, weasel, wildebeest, wolf, wolverine, wombat, yak, zebra

A
B
C
D
E
F
G
H
I
J
K
L
M
N
O
P
Q
R
S
T
U
V
W
X
Y
Z

SOME ANIMALS THAT LIVE IN THE SEA
• dolphin, porpoise, seal, sea lion, walrus, whale

SOME EXTINCT ANIMALS
• dinosaur, dodo, quagga

PARTS OF AN ANIMAL'S BODY
• antler, claw, fang, foreleg, hindleg, hoof, horn, jaws, mane, muzzle, paw, snout, tail, trotter, tusk, whisker, coat, fleece, fur, hide, pelt

MALE AND FEMALE ANIMALS
• A male elephant or whale is a **bull** and a female is a **cow**. • A male fox is a **dog** and a female is a **vixen**. • A male goat is a **billy goat** and a female is a **nanny goat**. • A male hare or rabbit is a **buck** and a female is a **doe**. • A male horse is a **stallion** and a female is a **mare**. • A female lion is a **lioness**. • A female pig is a **sow**. • A male sheep is a **ram** and a female is a **ewe**. • A female tiger is a **tigress**. • A male wolf is a **dog** and a female is a **bitch**.

YOUNG ANIMALS
• A young beaver is a **kit**. • A young fox or lion is a **cub**. • A young goat is a **kid**. • A young hare is a **leveret**. • A young horse is a **foal**, **colt** (male) or **filly** (female). • A young otter or seal is a **pup**. • A young pig is a **piglet**. • A young sheep is a **lamb**.

HOMES OF WILD ANIMALS
• den, lair • A badger lives in a **sett**. • A beaver or otter lives in a **lodge**. • A fox lives in an **earth**. • A rabbit lives in a **burrow** or **warren**. • A squirrel lives in a **drey**.

SOUNDS MADE BY ANIMALS
• bark, bay, bellow, buzz, gnash, growl, grunt, hiss, howl, jabber, purr, roar, snap, snarl, snort, snuffle, squeak, trumpet, whimper, whine, yap, yelp, yowl • A cat **mews** or **miaows**. • Cattle **low** or **moo**. • A donkey **brays**. • A frog **croaks**. • A horse **neighs** or **whinnies**. • A sheep **bleats**.

✏️ **WRITING TIPS**

You can use these words to describe an animal.

TO DESCRIBE HOW AN ANIMAL MOVES
• bound, creep, crouch, dart, gallop, gambol, leap, lumber, nuzzle, pad, paw, pounce, roam, scuttle, skip, slink, slither, spring, stamp, stampede, trot, waddle
The jaguar padded along silently.

TO DESCRIBE AN ANIMAL'S BODY
• agile, nimble, sinewy, wiry; lumbering, majestic, mighty, muscular, powerful
The cheetah stretched its long, sinewy body.

TO DESCRIBE AN ANIMAL'S SKIN OR COAT
• coarse, fluffy, furry, glistening, glossy, hairy, leathery, matted, prickly, scaly, shaggy, shiny, silky, sleek, slimy, slippery, smooth, spiky, thick, thorny, tough, wiry, woolly; mottled, piebald, spotted, striped
The otters' coats were smooth and silky.

announce *verb*
1. *The head announced that sports day was cancelled.* • declare, state, proclaim, report
2. *The guests were announced as they arrived at the ball.* • present, introduce

announcement *noun*
1. *The head reads the announcements in assembly.* • notice
2. *The prime minister issued an announcement.* • statement, declaration, proclamation, pronouncement
3. *I heard the announcement on TV.* • report, bulletin, news flash

annoy *verb*
1. *I was annoyed that I missed the bus.* • irritate, bother, displease, exasperate, anger, upset, vex, trouble, worry **opposite** please
2. *Please don't annoy me while I'm working.* • pester, bother, harass, badger, nag, plague, trouble, try, (informal) bug

annoyed *adjective*
She got quite annoyed with me when I told her to shut up. • irritated, cross, peeved, fed up, put out, displeased, vexed, (informal) miffed

annoying *adjective*
My brother has a lot of annoying habits. • irritating, exasperating, maddening, provoking, tiresome, trying, vexing, troublesome, infuriating

answer *noun*
1. *Did you get an answer to your letter?* • reply, response, acknowledgement, reaction
• A quick or angry answer is a **retort**
2. *The answers to the quiz are on the next page.* • solution, explanation

answer *verb*
1. *You haven't answered my question.* • give an answer to, reply to, respond to,

react to, acknowledge
2. *'I'm quite well,' I* answered. • reply, respond, return • To answer quickly or angrily is to **retort**.

anticipate *verb*
I anticipate *that the result will be a draw.*
• expect, predict, forecast, foretell

anxious *adjective*
1. *Are you* anxious *about your exams?*
• nervous, worried, apprehensive, concerned, uneasy, fearful, edgy, fraught, tense, troubled, *(informal)* uptight, jittery **opposite** calm
2. *I'm* anxious *to do my best.* • eager, keen, impatient, enthusiastic, willing

apologize *verb*
The ogre apologized *for being rude.* • make an apology, say sorry, express regret, repent, be penitent This word can also be spelled **apologise**.

appal *verb* **appalling, appalled**
They were appalled *by conditions in the prison.*
• disgust, revolt, shock, sicken, horrify, distress

apparent *adjective*
There was no apparent *reason for the crash.* • obvious, evident, clear, noticeable, detectable, perceptible, recognizable, conspicuous, visible **opposite** concealed

appeal *verb*
to appeal for
The prisoners appealed *for our help.* • request, beg for, plead for, cry out for, entreat, ask earnestly for, pray for
to appeal to
That kind of music doesn't appeal *to me.*
• attract, interest, fascinate, tempt, *(informal)* grab

appear *verb*
1. *Snowdrops* appear *in the spring.* • come out, emerge, become visible, come into view, develop, occur, show, crop up, spring up, surface
2. *Our visitors didn't* appear *until midnight.*
• arrive, come, turn up, *(informal)* show up
3. *It* appears *that the baby is asleep.* • seem, look
4. *I once* appeared *in a musical.* • act, perform, take part, feature

appearance *noun*
1. *They were startled by the* appearance *of the ghost.* • approach, arrival, entrance, entry
2. *Mr Hogweed had a grim* appearance. • air, aspect, bearing, look

appetite *noun*
1. *When I was ill, I completely lost my* appetite. • hunger
2. *Explorers have a great* appetite *for adventure.* • desire, eagerness, enthusiasm, passion, keenness, wish, urge, taste, thirst, longing, yearning, craving, lust, zest

apply *verb* applies, applying, applied
1. *The ointment should be* applied *to the affected area.* • administer, put on, lay on, spread
2. *My brother has* applied *for a new job.*
• make an application for, ask for, request
3. *The rules* apply *to all our members.*
• be relevant, relate, refer
4. *The vet* applied *all her skill to save the dog's life.* • use, employ, exercise, utilize

appreciate *verb*
1. *He* appreciates *good music.* • enjoy, like, love
2. *I* appreciate *her good qualities.* • admire, respect, regard highly, approve of, value, esteem **opposite** despise
3. *I* appreciate *that you can't afford much.*
• realize, recognize, understand, comprehend, know, see

approach *verb*
1. *We watched as the lioness* approached *her prey.* • draw near to, move towards, come near to, advance on
2. *I* approached *the head to ask if we could put on a show.* • speak to, contact, go to
3. *The volunteers* approached *their work cheerfully.* • begin, undertake, embark on, set about

approach *noun*
1. *We could hear the* approach *of heavy footsteps.* • arrival, advance, coming
2. *I like her positive* approach. • attitude, manner, style, way
3. *The easiest* approach *to the castle is from the west.* • access, entry, entrance, way in

appropriate *adjective*
It's not appropriate *to wear jeans to a wedding.* • suitable, proper, fitting, apt, right, tactful, tasteful, well-judged **opposite** inappropriate

approval *noun*
1. *We cheered to show our* approval.
• appreciation, admiration, praise, high regard, acclaim, respect, support **opposite** disapproval

2. *The head gave her approval to our plan.*
• agreement, consent, authorization, assent, go-ahead, permission, support, blessing
opposite refusal

approve *verb*
The head approved our request to put on a show. • agree to, consent to, authorize, allow, accept, pass, permit, support, back
opposite refuse

approximate *adjective*
What is the approximate length of the journey? • estimated, rough, inexact, near
opposite exact

approximately *adverb*
The film will finish at approximately five o'clock. • roughly, about, around, round about, close to, nearly, more or less

apt *adjective*
1. *He is apt to be careless with money.* • likely, liable, inclined, prone
2. *Your comments on my essay were very apt.*
• appropriate, suitable, proper, fitting, right, well-judged, pertinent, *(informal)* spot on
3. *She turned out to be a very apt pupil.*
• clever, quick, bright, sharp

area *noun*
1. *From the plane we saw a vast area of desert.*
• expanse, stretch, tract • A small area is a
patch. • An area of water or ice is a **sheet.**
2. *I live in an urban area.* • district, locality, neighbourhood, region, zone, vicinity

argue *verb*
1. *You two are always arguing over something.*
• quarrel, disagree, differ, fall out, fight, have an argument, squabble, wrangle, bicker
opposite agree
2. *We argued over the price of the cloth.*
• bargain, haggle
3. *He argued that it was my turn to walk the dog.* • claim, assert, try to prove, maintain, reason, suggest

argument *noun*
1. *There was an argument over who should pay for the meal.* • disagreement, quarrel, row, dispute, clash, controversy, debate, difference, fight, squabble, altercation
2. *I didn't quite follow his argument.* • line of reasoning, theme, outline, gist

arise *verb* **arising, arose, arisen**
1. *We can phone for help if the need arises.*
• occur, emerge, develop, ensue, appear, come into existence, come up, crop up, happen

2. *(old use) 'Arise, Sir Lancelot!' said the king.*
• stand up, get up

armour *noun*

⬥ **WORD WEB**

PARTS OF A MEDIEVAL KNIGHT'S ARMOUR
• breastplate, cuirass (breast and back plate), gauntlet, greave (shin guard), habergeon (sleeveless coat), helmet, visor • Armour made of linked rings is **chain mail.**
• An outfit of armour is a **suit of armour.**

arrange *verb*
1. *The books are arranged in alphabetical order.* • sort, order, put in order, group, organize, categorize, classify, collate, display, sort out, set out, lay out, line up
2. *Do you need any help arranging the party?*
• plan, organize, prepare, set up, see to

arrangement *noun*
1. *They have improved the arrangement of the garden.* • layout, organization, design, planning
2. *I've changed the arrangement of my CDs.*
• order, grouping, display, distribution, spacing
3. *We have an arrangement to use the swimming pool.* • agreement, deal, bargain, contract, scheme

arrive *verb*
When is the train due to arrive? • appear, come, turn up, show up, get in • When a plane arrives it **lands** or **touches down.**
to arrive at
We arrived at the castle before midnight.
• get to, reach

arrogant *adjective*
His arrogant manner annoys me. • boastful, conceited, proud, haughty, self-important, bumptious, pompous, snobbish, superior, vain, *(informal)* cocky, snooty, stuck-up
opposite modest

arrow *noun*
• The spine of an arrow is the **shaft.** • The point of an arrow is the **arrowhead.** • Arrows are shot using a **bow.** • A holder for several arrows is a **quiver.** • The sport of shooting arrows at a target is **archery.** • Someone who practises archery is an **archer.**

art, artist noun

SOME ARTISTS AND CRAFTSPEOPLE
• animator, blacksmith, carpenter, cartoonist, designer, draughtsman or draughtswoman, embroiderer, engraver, goldsmith, graphic designer, illustrator, knitter, mason, painter, photographer, potter, printer, quilter, sculptor, silversmith, weaver

article noun
1. *Have you any articles for the jumble sale?*
• item, object, thing
2. *Did you read my article in the magazine?*
• essay, report, piece of writing

artificial adjective
1. *Organic gardeners don't use artificial fertilizers.* • man-made, synthetic, unnatural, manufactured **opposite** natural
2. *She had an artificial flower in her buttonhole.* • fake, false, imitation, unreal, bogus, counterfeit **opposite** genuine, real

artistic adjective
Mum's flower arrangements are very artistic.
• creative, imaginative, aesthetic, attractive, beautiful, tasteful **opposite** ugly

ascend verb
1. *It took the rescuers a long time to ascend the mountain.* • climb, go up, mount, move up, scale
2. *The plane began to ascend.* • lift off, take off
3. *The eagle ascended into the air.* • fly up, rise, soar

ashamed adjective
He was ashamed because of what he had done. • sorry, remorseful, repentant, embarrassed, shamefaced, abashed, mortified apologetic, penitent, (informal) red-faced **opposite** unashamed, unrepentant

ask verb
1. *I asked them to be careful with the parcel.*
• request, beg, entreat, appeal to, implore, plead with
2. *'Are you ready?' I asked.* • demand, enquire, inquire, query, question
3. *I'm going to ask you to my party.* • invite, have round or over, (formal) request the pleasure of someone's company

asleep adjective
I didn't hear the phone because I was asleep.
• sleeping, dozing, having a nap, napping, (formal) slumbering • A patient asleep for an operation is **anaesthetized** or **under sedation**. • An animal asleep for the winter is **hibernating. opposite** awake
to fall asleep
We waited until the giant fell asleep. • drop off, doze, nod off • To fall asleep quickly is **to go out like a light**.

aspect noun
1. *The book describes some aspects of life in ancient Rome.* • part, feature, element, angle, detail, side, facet
2. *The ruined tower had an unfriendly aspect.*
• appearance, look, manner, air, expression, face, countenance
3. *The front room has a southern aspect.*
• outlook, view, prospect

assemble verb
1. *A crowd assembled to watch the rescue.*
• gather, come together, converge, accumulate, crowd together, flock together, meet, convene **opposite** disperse
2. *We assembled our luggage at the front door.*
• collect, gather, bring together, pile up, put together
3. *The general assembled his troops.* • round up, rally, muster

assembly noun
There was a large assembly of people in the market square. • gathering, meeting, crowd, throng • An assembly for worship is a **service**. • A large assembly to show support for something, often out of doors, is a **rally**.
• An assembly to discuss political matters is a **council** or **parliament**. • An assembly to discuss and learn about a particular topic is a **conference** or **congress**.

assess verb
The test will assess your knowledge of French.
• evaluate, determine, judge, estimate, measure, gauge, value, weigh up

asset *noun*
Good health is a great asset. • advantage, benefit, help, blessing

assist *verb*
We were asked to assist the gardener with the weeding. • help, aid, support, cooperate with, collaborate with **opposite** hinder

assistance *noun*
1. *Do you need assistance with your luggage?*
• help, aid, support, encouragement
2. *We bought new sports equipment with the assistance of a local firm.* • backing, collaboration, cooperation, sponsorship, subsidy, support

assistant *noun*
The magician was training a new assistant.
• helper, partner, colleague, associate, supporter

assorted *adjective*
I bought a bag of sweets with assorted flavours. • various, different, mixed, diverse, miscellaneous, several

assortment *noun*
There was an assortment of sandwiches to choose from. • variety, mixture, selection, array, choice, collection, diversity

assume *verb*
1. *I assume you'd like some chocolate.*
• suppose, presume, imagine, believe, guess, expect, gather, suspect, think
2. *The bandit assumed a disguise.* • put on, adopt, dress up in, wear

assure *verb*
I assure you that I will take care of your dog.
• promise, give your word to

astonish *verb*
It astonished us to learn that the house was haunted. • surprise, startle, amaze, astound, stagger, shock, dumbfound, stun • If you are surprised by something, you can also say that you were **taken aback** or **taken by surprise**.
• If something surprises you very much, you can say that it **takes your breath away** or **leaves you speechless**.

astonished *adjective*
We were astonished to see that the lake had disappeared. • surprised, taken aback, taken by surprise, startled, amazed, astounded, staggered, shocked, dumbfounded, thunderstruck, stunned, *(informal)* flabbergasted

astonishing *adjective*
The volcano was an astonishing sight.
• amazing, astounding, staggering, remarkable, surprising, extraordinary, incredible, breathtaking, phenomenal, sensational, stupendous, tremendous, wonderful

astonishment *noun*
Tom gasped in astonishment at the sight.
• amazement, surprise, shock, disbelief

astronaut *noun*

WORD WEB

The astronauts climbed aboard the space shuttle. • cosmonaut, spaceman or spacewoman

THINGS AN ASTRONAUT MIGHT USE OR WEAR
• jet pack, oxygen tank, spacesuit; gloves, helmet, moonboots or spaceboots, visor

PLACES AN ASTRONAUT MIGHT VISIT
• alien planet, moonbase, spacelab, space shuttle, space station, starbase

athletic *adjective*
You need to be athletic to run in a marathon.
• fit, active, energetic, strong, muscular, powerful, robust, sturdy, vigorous, well-built, *(informal)* sporty **opposite** feeble, puny

atrocious *adjective*
Everyone was shocked by the atrocious crime.
• wicked, terrible, dreadful, abominable, brutal, savage, barbaric, bloodthirsty, callous, cruel, diabolical, evil, fiendish, horrifying, merciless, outrageous, sadistic, terrible, vicious, villainous

attach *verb*
Attach this label to the parcel. • fasten, fix, join, tie, bind, secure, connect, link, couple, stick, affix, add, append **opposite** detach

attack noun
1. *The pirates' attack took us by surprise.*
• assault, strike, charge, rush, raid, ambush, invasion, onslaught • An attack with big guns or bombs is a **blitz** or **bombardment**. • An attack by planes is an **air raid**.
2. *The newspaper published an attack on his character.* • criticism, outburst, abuse, tirade
3. *I had an attack of hay fever in assembly.*
• bout, fit, spasm, (informal) turn

attack verb
1. *The travellers were attacked by highwaymen.* • assault, beat up, mug, set on, assail • To attack someone else's territory is to **invade** or **raid** it. • To attack someone from a hidden place is to **ambush** them. • To attack the enemy with bombs or heavy guns is to **bombard** them. • To attack by rushing at the enemy is to **charge**. • To attack a place suddenly is to **storm** it. • If an animal attacks you, it might **savage** you.
2. *He attacked her reputation.* • abuse, criticize, denounce, savage, tear to shreds, tear apart, (informal) go for **opposite** defend

attempt verb
They will attempt to reconstruct a Viking ship.
• try, endeavour, strive, seek, aim, make an effort

attend verb
Are you going to attend the end-of-term concert? • go to, appear at, be present at
to attend to
1. *Please attend carefully to my instructions.*
• listen to, pay attention to, follow carefully, heed, mark, mind, note, notice, observe, think about
2. *Mr Jackson promised to attend to the matter right away.* • deal with, see to
3. *The nurses attended to the wounded.* • take care of, care for, look after, help, mind, tend

attention noun
1. *Please give your full attention to the teacher.* • concentration, consideration, thought, observation, awareness, heed, concern
2. *The survivors need urgent medical attention.* • treatment, care

attitude noun
I'm trying to take a more positive attitude to life. • outlook, approach, behaviour, stance, frame of mind, disposition, view, position, manner, mood

attract verb
1. *The museum has changed its displays to attract young visitors.* • interest, appeal to, fascinate, tempt, entice
2. *Baby animals attract big crowds at the zoo.*
• draw, pull in

attractive adjective
1. *Miranda was a very attractive young woman.* • beautiful, pretty, good-looking, handsome, gorgeous, glamorous, striking, fetching, charming, lovely, delightful, pleasing, fascinating, captivating, enchanting • **Good-looking** and **handsome** are usually used to refer to boys and men. • **Pretty** and **beautiful** are usually used to refer to girls and women. **opposite** unattractive, repulsive
2. *There are some attractive bargains in the sale.* • appealing, agreeable, interesting, desirable, tempting, irresistible

authentic adjective
1. *That is an authentic painting by Picasso.*
• genuine, real, actual **opposite** counterfeit
2. *The book is an authentic account of life at sea.* • accurate, truthful, reliable, true, honest, dependable, factual **opposite** false

authority noun authorities
1. *We need the head's authority to stay after school.* • permission, consent, approval
2. *The king had the authority to execute the prisoners.* • power, right, influence
3. *My uncle is an authority on steam trains.*
• expert, specialist

automatic adjective
1. *We took our car through the automatic car wash.* • automated, mechanical, programmed, computerized
2. *My sneezing was an automatic response to the chilli.* • instinctive, involuntary, impulsive, spontaneous, reflex, natural, unconscious, unthinking

available adjective
1. *There are no more seats available.*
• obtainable, free
2. *A number of computers are available in the library.* • accessible, ready, usable, at hand, handy, within reach, convenient

average adjective
It was an average kind of day at school.
• everyday, ordinary, normal, typical, usual, regular, commonplace, familiar **opposite** unusual, extraordinary

avoid *verb*
1. *The driver tried hard to avoid the collision.*
• get out of the way of, avert, dodge, keep clear of, steer clear of, fend off, shun
2. *The outlaws avoided capture for months.*
• elude, evade, run away from, escape from
3. *How did you manage to avoid the washing-up?* • get out of, shirk

awake *adjective*
Hester lay awake all night worrying. • wide awake, restless, sleepless, conscious, wakeful
• Not being able to sleep is to be suffering from **insomnia**. • Sometimes when you cannot sleep you **toss and turn**. **opposite** asleep

award *noun*
Kirsty got a national award for gymnastics.
• prize, trophy, medal

aware *adjective*
aware of
The spy was aware of the dangers of the mission. • acquainted with, conscious of, familiar with, informed about
opposite ignorant of

awful *adjective*
1. *The weather was awful last weekend.* • bad, dreadful, terrible, appalling, dire, abysmal, *(informal)* rubbish, lousy
2. *The teacher complained about our*

awful behaviour. • disgraceful, shameful, disobedient, naughty
3. *Cinderella's stepmother was an awful woman.* • unpleasant, disagreeable, nasty, horrid, detestable, unkind, unfriendly
4. *The country was shocked by the awful crime.* • horrifying, shocking, atrocious, abominable, outrageous
5. *I feel awful about forgetting your birthday.* • sorry, ashamed, embarrassed, guilty, remorseful

awkward *adjective*
1. *The parcel was an awkward shape.* • bulky, inconvenient, unmanageable, unwieldy **opposite** convenient
2. *The giant was very awkward with his knife and fork.* • clumsy, ungainly, bungling, uncoordinated • When someone is awkward with their hands, you can say that they are **all fingers and thumbs. opposite** skilful
3. *We found ourselves in a very awkward situation.* • difficult, troublesome, trying, perplexing, tough **opposite** straightforward, easy
4. *Are you trying to be awkward?* • obstinate, stubborn, uncooperative, unhelpful, exasperating **opposite** cooperative
5. *I felt awkward as I didn't know anyone at the party.* • embarrassed, uncomfortable, uneasy, out of place **opposite** comfortable, at ease

Bad, beautiful, big and bit are all words that are used a lot. Have a look at the hundreds of other words you could use instead.

baby noun babies
• infant, child • A baby who has just been born is a **newborn**. • A baby just learning to walk is a **toddler**. • The time when someone is a baby is their **babyhood**.

babyish adjective
My brother says that dolls are babyish.
• childish, immature, infantile
opposite grown-up, mature

back noun
We always sit at the back of the bus. • end, rear, tail end • The back of a ship is the **stern**. • The back of an animal is the **hindquarters**, **rear** or **rump**. • The back of a piece of paper is the **reverse**. **opposite** front

back adjective
The back door of the cabin was locked. • end, rear, tail • The back legs of an animal are its **hind** legs. **opposite** front

back verb
1. A big lorry was backing into our driveway.
• go backwards, reverse
2. I'm backing the blue team to win the race.
• bet on, put money on
3. The council is backing the plan to build a skate park. • support, sponsor, endorse
to back away
When the dog growled, the robber backed away. • back off, retreat, give way, retire, recoil **opposite** approach
to back out of something
The injured player may have to back out of the final. • drop out of, withdraw from
to back someone up
Will you back me up if I need help? • support, second

background noun
1. I drew a mermaid with the sea in the background. **opposite** foreground

2. The first chapter deals with the background to the war. • circumstances (of), history (of), lead-up (to)
3. The children at the school come from many different backgrounds. • tradition, heritage, ancestry, beginnings

bad adjective worse, worst
This has been a bad week for all of us. • awful, horrible, terrible **opposite** good, fine, excellent

! OVERUSED WORD

Try to vary the words you use for bad. Here are some other words you could use.

FOR A BAD PERSON
• wicked, evil, cruel, malevolent, malicious, vicious, villainous, mean, nasty, beastly, monstrous, corrupt, deplorable, detestable, immoral, infamous, shameful, sinful
Gobo was a detestable king who was loathed by his subjects. • A bad person is a **scoundrel**, **rogue** or **rascal**. • A bad character in a story or film is a **villain** or (informal) **baddy**. **opposite** good, virtuous

FOR A BAD ACCIDENT OR BAD ILLNESS
• serious, severe, grave, distressing, acute
Ingrid has a severe case of chickenpox.
opposite minor

FOR BAD BEHAVIOUR
• naughty, mischievous, disobedient, disgraceful, wrong
That mischievous kitten drank my milk!
opposite exemplary, angelic

FOR A BAD EXPERIENCE OR BAD NEWS
• unpleasant, unwelcome, disagreeable, terrible, shocking, horrible, upsetting, awful, dreadful, horrific, appalling, hideous, disastrous, ghastly, devastating, abominable, diabolical
The letter contained some disagreeable news. • Another word for a bad experience is an **ordeal**. **opposite** good, excellent

FOR A BAD HABIT OR SOMETHING THAT IS BAD FOR YOU
• harmful, damaging, dangerous, undesirable, detrimental, injurious
Fizzy drinks can be harmful to your teeth.

FOR A BAD PERFORMANCE OR BAD WORK
• poor, inferior, weak, unsatisfactory, inadequate, incompetent, awful, hopeless, terrible, useless, worthless, abysmal, shoddy, (informal) rubbish
The worst thing about the film is the terrible acting.

FOR A BAD SMELL OR BAD TASTE
• disgusting, revolting, repulsive, sickening, nauseating, repugnant, foul, loathsome, offensive, vile
A nauseating smell wafted from the kitchen. **opposite** pleasant, appetizing

FOR BAD TIMING
• inconvenient, unsuitable, unfortunate, inappropriate
You've caught me at an inconvenient moment. **opposite** convenient, opportune

FOR BAD WEATHER
• harsh, hostile, unfavourable, adverse, miserable, *(informal)* lousy
Penguins face hostile conditions in the Antarctic. **opposite** fine, favourable

FOR FOOD THAT HAS GONE BAD
• mouldy, rotten, off, decayed, sour, spoiled, rancid
The strawberries have started to go mouldy. **opposite** fresh

TO FEEL BAD ABOUT SOMETHING
• guilty, ashamed, sorry, remorseful, repentant
Scrooge feels repentant by the end of the story. **opposite** unashamed, unrepentant
• guilty, ashamed, sorry, remorseful, repentant
Scrooge feels repentant by the end of the story. **opposite** unashamed, unrepentant

badly *adverb*
1. *He was badly injured in a car crash.*
• seriously, gravely, severely • Someone who is hurt so badly that they die is **fatally** or **mortally** injured.
2. *They played really badly today!* • terribly, awfully, dreadfully, appallingly, poorly
opposite well

bad-tempered *adjective*
Trolls are always bad-tempered before breakfast. • cross, grumpy, irritable, moody, quarrelsome, fractious, ill-tempered, short-tempered, cantankerous, crotchety, snappy, testy, sullen
opposite good-tempered, cheerful

bag *noun*
I put my wet clothes in a plastic bag. • sack, carrier, holdall, satchel, handbag, shoulder bag • A bag you carry on your back is a **backpack** or **rucksack**.

bald *adjective*
The ogre had a bald patch on the top of his head. • bare, hairless **opposite** hairy

ball *noun*
Wind the string into a ball. • sphere, globe, orb • A small ball of something is a **pellet** or **globule**.

WRITING TIPS
You can use these words to describe how a ball moves or how you hit or throw a ball:
• arc, bounce, bowl, dribble, drive, fling, head, hook, hurl, kick, lob, pitch, scoop, spin, strike, stroke, swerve, toss, volley; belt, blast, smash, sock, swipe, wham
The ball dribbled into the back of the net.
Murray smashed the ball across the court.

ban *verb* banning, banned
Rollerblades are banned from the playground.
• forbid, prohibit, bar, exclude, outlaw
opposite allow, permit

band *noun*
1. *The king was surrounded by a band of knights.* • company, group, gang, party, troop, crew
2. *I play clarinet in the junior jazz band.*
• group, ensemble, orchestra
3. *The team captain wears a red arm band.*
• strip, stripe, ring, line, belt, hoop

bandit *noun*
Bandits used to live in these mountains.
• robber, brigand, thief, outlaw, desperado, highwayman, pirate, buccaneer

bang *noun*
1. *There was a loud bang as the balloon burst.*
• blast, crash, pop, explosion, report, thud, thump, boom
2. *He got a bang on the head from the low ceiling.* • bump, blow, hit, knock, thump, punch, smack, whack, clout, *(informal)* wallop

bang *verb*
Miss Crabbit banged her fist on the desk and scowled. • hit, thump, strike, bash, slam, wham, pound, hammer

banish *verb*
The king's brother was banished forever.
• exile, expel, deport, send away, eject

bank *noun*
1. *The temple was built on the banks of the River Nile.* • edge, side, shore, margin, brink
2. *We rolled our Easter eggs down a grassy bank.* • slope, mound, ridge, embankment

banner *noun*
The turrets were decorated with colourful *banners*. • flag, standard, streamer, pennant

banquet *noun*
There was a *banquet* on the queen's birthday. • dinner, feast, (*informal*) spread

bar *noun*
1. Did you eat the whole *bar* of chocolate? • block, slab, chunk, wedge • A bar of gold or silver is an **ingot**. • A bar of soap is a **cake**.
2. The window had iron *bars* across it. • rod, pole, rail, stake, beam, girder

bar *verb* **barring, barred**
1. Two athletes were *barred* from competing in the race. • ban, prohibit, exclude, keep out
2. A fallen tree *barred* our way. • block, hinder, impede, obstruct, stop, check

bare *adjective*
1. I put suncream on my *bare* arms and legs. • naked, nude, exposed, uncovered, unclothed, undressed
2. The wolf had a *bare* patch on its back. • bald, hairless
3. Above the green slopes were *bare* hillsides crowned with snow. • barren, bleak, treeless, arid
4. Inside, the dungeon was cold and *bare*. • empty, unfurnished, vacant
5. There wasn't a *bare* patch of wall left. • blank, plain, clear, empty
6. There is only room to pack the *bare* essentials. • basic, minimum

barely *adverb*
We *barely* had time to get dressed. • hardly, scarcely, only just

bargain *noun*
1. We made a *bargain* with the captain to take us ashore. • deal, agreement, promise, pact
2. That camera you bought was a *bargain*. • good buy, special offer, (*informal*) snip, steal

bargain *verb*
He refused to *bargain* with the pirates for his life. • argue, do a deal, haggle, negotiate

bark *verb*
The guard dog began to *bark* fiercely. • woof, yap, yelp, growl

barrel *noun*
The smugglers carried *barrels* of gunpowder. • cask, drum, tub, keg, butt

barrier *noun*
1. Spectators were asked to stay behind the *barrier*. • wall, fence, railing, barricade • A barrier across a road is a **roadblock**.
2. His shyness was a *barrier* to making friends. • obstacle, hurdle, drawback, handicap, hindrance, stumbling block

base *noun*
1. The footprints stop at the *base* of the pyramid. • bottom, foot
2. The dolls' house comes with a wooden *base*. • foundation, support • A base under a statue is a **pedestal** or **plinth**.
3. The mountaineers returned to their *base*. • headquarters, camp, depot

basement *noun*
• cellar, vault • A room underneath a church is a **crypt**. • An underground cell in a castle is a **dungeon**.

basic *adjective*
1. These are the *basic* moves in ice skating. • main, chief, principal, key, central, essential, fundamental, crucial
2. My knowledge of French is very *basic*. • elementary, simple **opposite** advanced

basically *adverb*
Basically I think you're right. • essentially, in essence, at heart, fundamentally

basis *noun* **bases**
What is the *basis* of your argument? • base, core, foundation

batch *noun*
Mum made a fresh *batch* of pancakes. • lot, bunch, amount, quantity

bathe *verb*
1. It was too cold to *bathe* in the sea. • swim, go swimming, splash about, take a dip • To walk about in shallow water is to **paddle**. • To walk through deep water is to **wade**.
2. The nurse gently *bathed* the wound. • clean, cleanse, wash, rinse

battle *noun*
The *battle* raged for many hours. • fight, clash, conflict, action, engagement, hostilities, struggle

beach *noun*
We found these shells on the *beach*. • sands, seashore, seaside, shore

beam *noun*
1. *Wooden beams ran across the ceiling.* • bar, timber, joist, plank, post, rafter, boom, spar, strut, support
2. *A beam of sunlight entered the cave.*
• ray, shaft, stream, gleam • A strong narrow beam of light used in various devices is a **laser**.

bear *verb* **bore, born, borne**
1. *The rope won't bear my weight.* • carry, support, hold, take
2. *The messenger bore a letter from the king.*
• bring, carry, convey, transport, take, transfer
3. *The gravestone bears an old inscription.*
• display, show, have
4. *The stench in the cave was too much to bear.* • put up with, cope with, stand, suffer, tolerate, endure, abide
5. *Mammals bear live young.* • give birth to

beast *noun*
In the darkness, they heard a wild beast howl.
• animal, creature • You might call a large or frightening beast a **brute** or **monster**.

beat *verb* **beating, beat, beaten**
1. *It's cruel to beat an animal.* • hit, strike, thrash, batter, whip, lash, flog, (*informal*) whack, wallop, thump, clout
2. *I beat my brother at chess for the first time.*
• defeat, conquer, vanquish, win against, get the better of, overcome, overwhelm, rout, thrash, trounce, (*informal*) hammer
3. *Beat the eggs, milk and sugar together.*
• whisk, whip, blend, mix, stir
4. *Can you feel your heart beating?* • pound, thump, palpitate
to beat someone up
The bully threatened to beat me up. • assault, attack, knock around or about

beat *noun*
1. *Can you feel the beat of your heart?* • pulse, throb
2. *Reggae music has a strong beat.* • rhythm, accent, stress

beautiful *adjective*

(!) **OVERUSED WORD**

Try to vary the words you use for **beautiful**. Here are some other words you could use.

FOR A BEAUTIFUL PERSON
• attractive, good-looking, pretty, gorgeous, glamorous, radiant, elegant, enchanting, dazzling, stunning, magnificent, resplendent

The fairy queen looked radiant by moonlight. • A man who is pleasing to look at is **good-looking** or **handsome**.
opposite ugly, unattractive

FOR A BEAUTIFUL DAY OR BEAUTIFUL WEATHER
• fine, excellent, glorious, marvellous, sunny, superb, splendid, wonderful
It was a glorious day for a bicycle trip.
opposite dull, gloomy, drab

FOR A BEAUTIFUL SIGHT
• glorious, magnificent, picturesque, scenic, spectacular, splendid
The Northern Lights are a spectacular sight.

FOR A BEAUTIFUL SOUND
• harmonious, mellifluous, melodious, sweet-sounding
The nightingale has a sweet-sounding song.
opposite grating

beauty *noun* **beauties**
The film star was famous for her beauty.
• attractiveness, prettiness, loveliness, charm, allure, magnificence, radiance, splendour
opposite ugliness

beckon *verb*
The guard was beckoning me to approach.
• signal, gesture, motion, gesticulate

become *verb* **becoming, became, become**
1. *I soon became frustrated with the video game.* • begin to be, start to be, turn, get, grow
2. *Eventually, the tadpoles will become frogs.*
• grow into, change into, develop into, turn into

bed *noun*
1. *The children slept on hard wooden beds.*
• bunk, mattress • A bed for a baby is a **cot**, **cradle** or **crib**. • Two single beds one above the other are **bunk beds**. • A bed on a ship or train is a **berth**. • A bed made of net or cloth hung up above the ground is a **hammock**.
2. *We planted daffodils in the flower beds.*
• plot, patch, border
3. *These creatures feed on the bed of the ocean.* • bottom, floor **opposite** surface

before *adverb*
1. *Have you used a camera before?*
• previously, in the past, earlier, sooner
opposite later
2. *Those people were before us in the queue.* • in front of, ahead of, in advance of
opposite after

beg *verb* begging, begged
He begged me not to let go of the rope. • ask, plead with, entreat, implore, beseech

begin *verb* beginning, began, begun
1. *The hunters began their search at dawn.*
• start, commence, embark on, set about
opposite end, finish, conclude
2. *When did the trouble begin?* • start, commence, arise, emerge, appear, originate, spring up **opposite** end, stop, cease

beginning *noun*
The house was built at the beginning of the last century. • start, opening, commencement, introduction, establishment, foundation, initiation, launch, dawn • The beginning of the day is **dawn** or **daybreak**. • The beginning of a journey is the **starting point**. • The beginning of a stream or river is the **origin** or **source**. • A piece of writing at the beginning of a book is an **introduction**, **preface** or **prologue**. • A piece of music at the beginning of a musical or opera is a **prelude** or **overture**. **opposite** end, conclusion

behave *verb*
Our neighbour is behaving very strangely.
• act, react, perform
to behave yourself
We promised to behave ourselves in the car.
• be good, behave, be on your best behaviour

behaviour *noun*
I give my puppy treats for good behaviour.
• actions, conduct, manners, attitude

belief *noun*
1. *She was a woman of strong religious beliefs.*
• faith, principle, creed, doctrine
2. *It is my belief is that he stole the money.*
• opinion, view, conviction, feeling, notion, theory

believable *adjective*
None of the characters in the book are believable. • credible, plausible
opposite unbelievable, implausible

believe *verb*
1. *I don't believe anything he says.*
• accept, have faith in, rely on, trust
opposite disbelieve, doubt
2. *I believe they used to live in Canada.*
• assume, feel, know, presume, reckon, suppose, think

bell *noun*
Church bells were ringing in the distance.

✏️ **WRITING TIPS**

You can use these words to describe how a **bell** sounds:
• chime, clang, jangle, jingle, peal, ring, tinkle, toll

---

belong *verb*
1. *This ring belonged to my grandmother.*
• be owned by
2. *Do you belong to the sports club?*
• be a member of, be connected with

belongings *plural noun*
Don't leave any belongings on the bus.
• possessions, property, goods, things

bend *verb* bending, bent
This drinking straw bends in the middle.
• curve, turn, twist, curl, coil, loop, arch, warp, wind • A word for things which bend easily is **flexible** or (informal) **bendy**.
opposite straighten
to bend down
I bent down to tie my shoelaces. • stoop, bow, crouch, duck, kneel

bend *noun*
Watch out for the sharp bend in the road.
• curve, turn, angle, corner, twist, zigzag

benefit *noun*
What are the benefits of regular exercise?
• advantage, reward, gain, good point
opposite disadvantage, drawback

benefit *verb*
The rainy weather will benefit gardeners.
• help, aid, assist, be good for, profit
opposite hinder, harm

bent *adjective*
1. *After the crash, the car was a mass of bent metal.* • curved, twisted, coiled, looped, buckled, crooked, arched, folded, warped, (informal) wonky
2. *The witch had a bent back and walked with a stick.* • crooked, hunched, curved, arched, bowed

besides *adverb*
1. *No one knows the secret, besides you and me.* • as well as, in addition to, apart from, other than
2. *It's too cold to go out. Besides, it's dark now.* • also, in addition, additionally, furthermore, moreover

a b c d e f g h i j k l m n o p q r s t u v w x y z

best adjective
1. *She is our best goalkeeper.* • top, leading, finest, foremost, supreme, star, outstanding, unequalled, unrivalled **opposite** worst
2. *We did what we thought was best.* • most suitable, most appropriate, correct, right

betray verb
1. *He betrayed us by telling the enemy our plan.* • be disloyal to, be a traitor to, cheat, conspire against, double-cross • Someone who betrays you is a **traitor**. • To betray your country is to commit **treason**.
2. *The look in her eyes betrayed her true feelings.* • reveal, show, indicate, disclose, divulge, expose, tell

better adjective
1. *Which of these books do you think is better?* • superior, finer, preferable
2. *I had a cold, but I'm better now.* • recovered, cured, healed, improved, well

beware verb beware
Beware! There are thieves about. • be careful!, watch out!, look out!, take care!, be on your guard!
beware of
Beware of the bull. • watch out for, avoid, mind, heed, keep clear of

biased adjective
A referee should not make biased decisions. • prejudiced, partial, one-sided, partisan, unfair **opposite** impartial

bid noun
1. *There were several bids for the painting at the auction.* • offer, price, tender
2. *His bid to beat the world record failed.* • attempt, effort, try, go

big adjective bigger, biggest
The giant owned three pairs of big boots. • large, huge, great, massive, enormous, gigantic, colossal, mammoth, (informal) whopping, ginormous, humungous **opposite** small, little, tiny

(!) OVERUSED WORD

Try to vary the words you use for big. Here are some other words you could use.

FOR A BIG PERSON OR BIG CREATURE
• burly, giant, hefty, hulking, mighty, monstrous, towering
The mighty robot clanked as it moved.

FOR A BIG OBJECT
• bulky, heavy, hefty, weighty
What could be inside that bulky envelope?

FOR A BIG ROOM OR BIG CONTAINER
• roomy, sizeable, spacious
Inside, the spaceship was surprisingly roomy. **opposite** cramped

FOR A BIG DISTANCE
• immense, infinite, vast
A vast stretch of ocean lay before them.

FOR A BIG AMOUNT OR BIG HELPING
• ample, considerable, substantial, generous, abundant
We each got an ample helping of porridge. **opposite** meagre, paltry

FOR A BIG DECISION OR BIG MOMENT
• grave, important, serious, significant
Yesterday was the most significant day in my whole life. **opposite** unimportant, minor

billow verb
1. *Smoke billowed from the mouth of the cave.* • pour, swirl, spiral
2. *The sheets on the washing line billowed in the wind.* • swell, bulge, puff, balloon

bird noun

WORD WEB

• A female bird is a **hen**. • A male bird is a **cock**. • A young bird is a **chick**, **fledgling** or **nestling**. • A family of chicks is a **brood**.
• A group of birds is a **colony** or **flock**.
• A group of flying birds is a **flight** or **skein**.
• A person who studies birds is an **ornithologist**.

SOME COMMON BRITISH BIRDS
• blackbird, bluetit, bullfinch, bunting, chaffinch, crow, cuckoo, dove, greenfinch, jackdaw, jay, linnet, magpie, martin, nightingale, pigeon, raven, robin, rook, skylark, sparrow, starling, swallow, swift, thrush, tit, wagtail, waxwing, woodpecker, wren, yellowhammer

BIRDS OF PREY
• buzzard, eagle, falcon, hawk, kestrel, kite, merlin, osprey, owl, sparrowhawk, vulture

FARM AND GAME BIRDS
• chicken, duck, goose, grouse, partridge, pheasant, quail, turkey • Birds kept by farmers are called **poultry**.

SEA AND WATER BIRDS
• albatross, auk, bittern, coot, cormorant, crane, curlew, duck, gannet, goose, guillemot, gull, heron, kingfisher, kittiwake, lapwing, mallard, moorhen, oystercatcher, peewit, pelican, penguin, puffin, seagull, snipe, stork, swan, teal

BIRDS FROM OTHER COUNTRIES
• bird of paradise, budgerigar, canary, cockatoo, flamingo, hummingbird, ibis, kookaburra, macaw, mynah bird, parakeet, parrot, toucan

BIRDS WHICH CANNOT FLY
• emu, kiwi, ostrich, peacock, penguin

PARTS OF A BIRD'S BODY
• beak, bill; claw, talon; breast, crown, throat; crest, feather, down, plumage, plume, wing

SOME TYPES OF BIRD HOME
• nest, nesting box; aviary, coop, roost

SOUNDS MADE BY BIRDS
• cackle, caw, cheep, chirp, chirrup, cluck, coo, crow, gabble, honk, peep, pipe, quack, screech, squawk, trill, tweet, twitter, warble • A turkey **gobbles**. • An owl **hoots**.

SPECIAL NAMES
• A female peacock is a **peahen**.
• A young duck is a **duckling**. • A young goose is a **gosling**. • A young swan is a **cygnet**. • An eagle's nest is an **eyrie**.
• A place where rooks nest is a **rookery**.

✏️ **WRITING TIPS**

You can use these words to describe a **bird**.

TO DESCRIBE HOW A BIRD MOVES
• circle, dart, flit, flutter, fly, glide, hop, hover, peck, perch, preen, skim, soar, swoop, waddle, wheel
A pair of swallows flitted among the rooftops.

TO DESCRIBE A BIRD'S FEATHERS
• bedraggled, downy, drab, fluffy, gleaming, iridescent, ruffled, smooth, speckled
The peacock displayed its iridescent tail.

bit *noun*
1. *Mum divided the cake into eight bits.* • piece, portion, part, section, segment, share, slice
2. *These jeans are a bit long for me.* • a little, slightly, rather, fairly, somewhat, quite

⚠️ **OVERUSED WORD**

Try to vary the words you use for **bit**. Here are some other words you could use.

FOR A LARGE BIT OF SOMETHING
• chunk, lump, hunk, wedge, slab
Chunks of rock came tumbling down the mountain.

FOR A SMALL BIT OF SOMETHING
• fragment, scrap, chip, speck, pinch, touch, dab, particle, atom, (informal) smidgen
The map was drawn on a scrap of old paper.

FOR A BIT OF FOOD
• morsel, crumb, bite, nibble, taste, mouthful
Please try a mouthful of chocolate mousse.

FOR A BIT OF LIQUID
• drop, dash, drib, splash, spot
Add a splash of vinegar to the sauce.

bite *verb* **biting, bit, bitten**
1. *I bit a chunk out of my apple.* • munch, nibble, chew, crunch, gnaw, (informal) chomp
2. *Take care. These animals can bite.* • nip, pinch, pierce, wound • When an animal tries to bite you it **snaps** at you. • When an insect bites you it **stings** you. • A fierce animal **mauls** or **savages** its prey.

bitter *adjective*
1. *The medicine had a bitter taste.* • sour, sharp, acid, acrid, tart **opposite** sweet
2. *His brother was still bitter about the quarrel.* • resentful, embittered, disgruntled, aggrieved **opposite** contented
3. *The wind blowing in from the sea was bitter.* • biting, cold, freezing, icy, piercing, raw, wintry, (informal) perishing **opposite** mild

black *adjective, noun*
The pony had a shiny black coat. • coal-black, jet-black, pitch-black, ebony, inky, raven • You can also describe a black night as **pitch-dark**. • Someone in a bad mood is said to look **as black as thunder**. • Common similes are **as black as coal** and **as black as night**.

blame *verb*
Don't blame me if you miss the bus. • accuse, criticize, condemn, reproach, scold

blank *adjective*
1. *There are no blank pages left in my jotter.*
• empty, bare, clean, plain, unmarked, unused
2. *The old woman gave us a blank look.*
• expressionless, vacant, impassive

blanket *noun*
1. *The baby was wrapped in a woollen blanket.*
• cover, sheet, quilt, rug, throw
2. *A blanket of snow covered the lawn.*
• covering, layer, film, sheet, mantle

blast *noun*
1. *A blast of cold air came through the door.*
• gust, rush, draught, burst
2. *They heard the blast of a trumpet.* • blare, noise, roar
3. *Many people were injured in the blast.*
• explosion, shock

blaze *noun*
Firefighters fought the blaze for hours. • fire, flames, inferno

blaze *verb*
Within a few minutes the campfire was blazing. • burn brightly, flare up

bleak *adjective*
1. *The countryside was bleak and barren.*
• bare, barren, desolate, empty, exposed, stark
2. *The future looks bleak for the club.* • gloomy, hopeless, depressing, dismal, grim, miserable **opposite** promising

blend *verb*
1. *Blend the flour with a tablespoon of water.*
• beat together, mix, stir together, whip, whisk
2. *The paint colours blend well with each other.* • go together, match, fit, harmonize **opposite** clash

blind *adjective*
Polar bear cubs are born blind. • sightless, unsighted, unseeing • A common simile is **as blind as a bat**. **opposite** sighted, seeing
blind to
The captain was blind to his own faults.
• ignorant of, unaware of, oblivious to **opposite** aware of

bliss *noun*
Having a whole day off school was sheer bliss.
• joy, delight, pleasure, happiness, heaven, ecstasy **opposite** misery

blob *noun*
The alien left blobs of green slime on the carpet. • drop, lump, spot, dollop, daub, globule

block *noun*
1. *A block of ice fell from the glacier.* • chunk, hunk, lump, piece
2. *There must be a block in the drainpipe.*
• blockage, jam, obstacle, obstruction

block *verb*
1. *A tall hedge blocked our view of the house.*
• obstruct, hamper, hinder, interfere with
2. *A mass of leaves had blocked the drain.*
• clog, choke, jam, plug, stop up, congest, *(informal)* bung up

bloodcurdling *adjective*
We heard a bloodcurdling scream in the night.
• terrifying, frightening, horrifying, fearful, spine-chilling, hair-raising

bloodthirsty *adjective* **bloodthirstier, bloodthirstiest**
The bloodthirsty pirates rattled their swords.
• brutal, cruel, barbaric, murderous, inhuman, pitiless, ruthless, savage, vicious

bloom *noun*
The bush was covered in perfect white blooms.
• flower, blossom, bud

bloom *verb*
The roses bloomed early this year. • blossom, flower, open **opposite** fade

blot *noun*
The old map was covered with ink blots. • spot, blotch, mark, blob, splodge, smudge, smear, stain

blot *verb* **blotting, blotted**
to blot something out
The new tower block blots out the view.
• conceal, hide, mask, obliterate, obscure

blow *noun*
1. *He was knocked out by a blow on the head.*
• knock, bang, bash, hit, punch, clout, slap, smack, swipe, thump, *(informal)* wallop, whack
2. *Losing the championship was a terrible blow.* • shock, upset, setback, disappointment, misfortune, catastrophe, disaster, calamity

blow *verb* **blowing, blew, blown**
The wind was blowing from the east. • blast, gust, puff, rise, get up • To make a shrill sound by blowing is to **whistle**. • If the wind makes a shrill sound it **howls**.

blue adjective, noun

Bella had dark hair and bright blue eyes. Blue is my favourite colour. • azure, baby-blue, cobalt, indigo, navy blue, royal blue, sapphire, sky-blue, turquoise • Something which is rather blue is **bluish**. • A common simile is **as blue as the sky**.

blunder noun

Forgetting her birthday was a terrible blunder. • mistake, error, fault, slip, slip-up, gaffe, (*informal*) howler

blunt adjective

1. *This pencil is blunt.* • dull, worn, unsharpened **opposite** sharp, pointed
2. *Her reply to my question was very blunt.* • abrupt, curt, frank, direct, outspoken, plain, tactless **opposite** tactful

blurred adjective

The background of the photograph is all blurred. • indistinct, vague, blurry, fuzzy, hazy, out of focus **opposite** clear, distinct

blush verb

Emily blushed with embarrassment. • flush, go red or pink, turn red or pink, colour, redden

boast verb

The knight was always boasting about his fighting skills. • brag, show off, crow, gloat, swagger, (*informal*) blow your own trumpet

boastful adjective

Giants are boastful creatures and brag about everything. • arrogant, big-headed, conceited, vain, bumptious, (*informal*) cocky, swanky **opposite** modest, humble

boat noun

WORD WEB

Several fishing boats were moored in the harbour. • ship, craft, vessel

SOME TYPES OF BOAT OR SHIP
• barge, canoe, catamaran, cruise liner, dhow, dinghy, dugout, ferry, freighter, gondola, hovercraft, hydrofoil, junk, launch, lifeboat, motor boat, oil tanker, paper boat, punt, raft, rowing boat, schooner, skiff, speedboat, steamship, tanker, trawler, tug, yacht

MILITARY BOATS OR SHIPS
• aircraft carrier, battleship, destroyer, frigate, gunboat, minesweeper, submarine, warship

SOME BOATS USED IN THE PAST
• brigantine, clipper, coracle, cutter, galleon, galley, man-of-war, paddle steamer, schooner, trireme, windjammer

WORDS FOR PARTS OF A BOAT OR SHIP
• boom, bridge, bulwark, cabin, crow's nest, deck, engine room, fo'c's'le or forecastle, funnel, galley, helm, hull, keel, mast, poop, porthole, propeller, quarterdeck, rigging, rudder, sail, tiller

SPECIAL NAMES
• The front part of a boat is the **bow** or **prow**. • The back part of a boat is the **stern**. • The left-hand side of a boat is called **port**. • The right-hand side of a boat is called **starboard**. • A shed where boats are stored is a **boathouse**.

WRITING TIPS

You can use these words to describe how a boat moves:
• cut through the waves or water, drift, float, glide, lurch, pitch, roll, sail, steam, tack
The tiny raft pitched from side to side in the storm.

body *noun* bodies

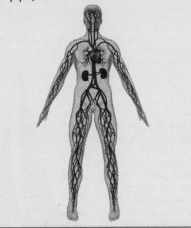

WORD WEB

• The study of the human body is **anatomy**.
• The main part of your body except your head, arms and legs is your **trunk** or **torso**.
• The shape of your body is your **build**, **figure** or **physique**. • A person's dead body is a **corpse**. • The dead body of an animal is a **carcass**.

OUTER PARTS OF THE HUMAN BODY
• abdomen, ankle, arm, armpit, breast, buttock, calf, cheek, chest, chin, ear, elbow, eye, finger, foot, forehead, genitals, groin, hand, head, heel, hip, instep, jaw, knee, kneecap, knuckle, leg, lip, mouth, navel, neck, nipple, nose, pores, shin, shoulder, skin, stomach, temple, thigh, throat, waist, wrist

INNER PARTS OF THE HUMAN BODY
• arteries, bladder, bowels, brain, eardrum, glands, gullet, gums, guts, heart, intestines, kidney, larynx, liver, lung, muscles, nerves, ovary, pancreas, sinews, stomach, tendons, tongue, tonsil, tooth, uterus, veins, windpipe, womb

WRITING TIPS

You can use these words to describe someone's **body**:
• athletic, beefy, brawny, burly, hefty, hulking, muscular, sinewy, squat, stocky; fat, chubby, flabby, obese, plump, rotund, stout, well-rounded; lean, slight, slender, svelte, thin, wiry; petite, short, tiny, puny; tall, lanky, gangly; bony, gaunt, scraggy, scrawny, spindly

bog *noun*
We felt our boots sinking into the **bog**.
• swamp, quagmire, quicksand, fen

boisterous *adjective*
Baby dragons can be loud and **boisterous**.
• lively, noisy, rowdy, unruly, wild, disorderly **opposite** restrained, calm

bold *adjective*
1. It was a **bold** move to attack the fortress.
• brave, courageous, daring, adventurous, audacious, confident, enterprising, fearless, heroic, valiant, intrepid, plucky **opposite** cowardly
2. The poster uses large letters in **bold** colours. • striking, strong, bright, loud, showy, conspicuous, eye-catching, noticeable, prominent **opposite** inconspicuous, subtle

bolt *verb*
1. Did you remember to **bolt** the door? • fasten, latch, lock, secure, bar
2. The horses **bolted** when they heard the thunder. • dash away, dart, flee, sprint, run away, rush off
3. Don't **bolt** your food. • gobble, gulp, guzzle, wolf down

bonus *noun*
I got a **bonus** on top of my pocket money last week. • extra, supplement, reward, tip, handout

book *verb*
1. Have you **booked** a seat on the train? • order, reserve
2. I've **booked** the disco for the party.
• arrange, engage, organize

boom *verb*
1. Miss Barker's voice **boomed** along the corridor. • shout, roar, bellow, blast, thunder, resound, reverberate
2. Business was **booming** in the Riverbank Cafe. • be successful, do well, expand, flourish, grow, prosper, thrive

boost *verb*
Winning the cup really **boosted** the team's morale. • raise, uplift, improve, increase, bolster, help, encourage, enhance **opposite** lower, dampen

border *noun*
1. The town is on the **border** between France and Germany. • boundary, frontier
2. I drew a thin line around the **border** of the picture. • edge, margin, perimeter
• A decorative border round the top of a wall is

a **frieze**. • A border round the bottom of a skirt is a **hem**. • A decorative border on fabric is a **frill**, **fringe** or **trimming**.

boring adjective
The film was so boring I fell asleep. • dull, dreary, tedious, tiresome, unexciting, uninteresting, dry, monotonous, uninspiring, insipid, unimaginative, uneventful, humdrum **opposite** interesting, exciting

boss noun
She needed to impress her boss if she wanted a pay rise. • chief, head, director, supervisor, manager, controller, foreman, superintendent, governor, proprietor, employer • An informal name for a boss is **gaffer**.

bossy adjective bossier, bossiest
Stop being so bossy towards your sister. • domineering, bullying, dictatorial, officious, tyrannical • An informal name for a bossy person is **bossy boots**.

bother verb
1. Would it bother you if I played some music? • disturb, trouble, upset, annoy, irritate, pester, worry, vex, exasperate, (informal) bug, hassle
2. Don't bother to phone tonight. • make an effort, take trouble, concern yourself, care, mind

bother noun
It's such a bother to remember the password. • nuisance, annoyance, irritation, inconvenience, pest, trouble, difficulty, problem, (informal) hassle

bottle noun
Bring a bottle of water with you. • flask, flagon, jar, pitcher • A bottle for serving water or wine is a **carafe** or **decanter**. • A small bottle for perfume or medicine is a **phial**.

bottom noun
1. We camped at the bottom of the mountain. • foot, base **opposite** top, peak
2. The wreck sank to the bottom of the sea. • bed, floor **opposite** surface
3. A wasp stung me on the bottom. • backside, behind, buttocks, rear, rump, seat, (informal) bum

bottom adjective
I got the bottom mark in the maths test. • least, lowest **opposite** top

bounce verb
The ball bounced twice before it reached the net. • rebound, ricochet, spring, leap

bound adjective
1. It's bound to rain at the weekend. • certain, sure
2. I felt bound to invite my cousin to the party. • obliged, duty-bound, committed, compelled, forced, required
3. The accident was bound to happen. • destined, doomed, fated
bound for
The space rocket was bound for Jupiter. • going to, heading for, making for, travelling towards, off to

bound verb
The puppies bounded across the lawn. • leap, bounce, jump, spring, skip, gambol, caper, frisk

boundary noun boundaries
The lamp post marks the boundary of Narnia. • border, frontier, edge, end, limit, perimeter, dividing line

bow verb
1. The prisoner bowed his head in shame. • lower, bend, duck
2. The knight knelt and bowed in front of the king. • The corresponding movement of a woman is to **curtsy**.

bowl verb
Can you bowl a faster ball next time? • throw, pitch, fling, hurl, toss

box noun
• case, chest, crate, carton, packet • A small box for jewellery or treasure is a **casket**. • A large box for luggage is a **trunk**.

boy noun
• lad, youngster, youth, (informal) kid

brag verb bragging, bragged
Flo is still bragging about her swimming medal. • show off, boast, gloat, crow, (informal) blow your own trumpet • A person who is always bragging is a **braggart**.

brain noun
You'll need to use your brain to solve this riddle. • intelligence, intellect, mind, reason, sense, wit

brainy adjective brainier, brainiest
Brian was the brainiest kid you could ever meet. • clever, smart, intelligent, bright, brilliant, intellectual, quick-witted

branch *noun*
1. *A robin perched on a branch of the tree.*
• bough, limb
2. *I've joined the local branch of the Scouts.*
• section, division, department, wing

branch *verb*
Follow the track until it branches into two.
• divide, fork

brand *noun*
Which brand of trainers do you like? • make, kind, sort, type, variety, label • The sign of a particular brand of goods is a **trademark**.

brandish *verb*
Captain Hook brandished his cutlass at the crew. • flourish, wield, flaunt, wave

brave *adjective*
It was brave of you to save the cat from drowning. • courageous, heroic, valiant, fearless, daring, gallant, intrepid, plucky
• A common simile is **as brave as a lion**.
opposite cowardly

bravely *adverb*
They fought bravely but were completely outnumbered. • courageously, fearlessly, daringly, heroically, boldly, valiantly

bravery *noun*
The police dog was awarded a medal for bravery. • courage, heroism, valour, fearlessness, daring, nerve, gallantry, grit, pluck, (*informal*) guts, bottle
opposite cowardice

brawl *noun*
We could hear a brawl on the street outside.
• fight, quarrel, scuffle, tussle, (*informal*) scrap

break *noun*
1. *Can you see any breaks in the chain?*
• breach, crack, hole, gap, opening, split, rift, puncture, rupture, fracture, fissure
2. *Let's take a break for lunch.* • interval, pause, rest, lull, time-out, (*informal*) breather

break *verb* breaking, broke, broken
1. *The vase fell off the shelf and broke.*
• smash, shatter, fracture, chip, crack, split, snap, splinter, (*informal*) bust
2. *He knew he was breaking the law by trespassing.* • disobey, disregard, defy, breach, violate, flout
3. *In her last race, she broke the world record.*
• beat, better, exceed, surpass, outdo

breakthrough *noun*
Scientists have made a breakthrough in medicine. • advance, leap forward, discovery, development, revolution, progress
opposite setback

breath *noun*
There wasn't a breath of wind in the air.
• breeze, puff, waft, whiff, whisper, sigh

breathe *verb*
• To breathe in is to **inhale**. • To breathe out is to **exhale**. • To breathe heavily when you have been running is to **pant** or **puff**. • The formal word for breathing is **respiration**.

breathtaking *adjective*
The view from the summit was breathtaking.
• spectacular, stunning, staggering, astonishing, overwhelming, awe-inspiring

breed *verb* breeding, bred
1. *Salmon swim upstream to breed every year.*
• reproduce, have young, multiply, procreate, spawn
2. *Bad hygiene breeds disease.* • cause, produce, generate, encourage, promote, cultivate, induce

breed *noun*
What breed of dog is that? • kind, sort, type, variety • The evidence of how a dog has been bred is its **pedigree**.

breezy *adjective* breezier, breeziest
This morning the weather was bright and breezy. • windy, blowy, blustery, gusty, fresh, draughty

bridge *noun*
• A bridge you can walk over is a **footbridge**.
• A bridge to carry water is an **aqueduct**.
• A long bridge carrying a road or railway is a **viaduct**.

brief *adjective*
1. *We paid a brief visit to our cousins on the way home.* • short, quick, hasty, fleeting, temporary
2. *Give me a brief account of what happened.*
• short, concise, abbreviated, condensed, compact, succint

bright *adjective*
1. *We saw the bright lights of the town in the distance.* • shining, brilliant, blazing, dazzling, glaring, gleaming **opposite** dull, dim, weak
2. *Bright colours will make the poster stand out.* • strong, intense, vivid • Colours that

shine in the dark are **luminous** colours.
opposite dull, faded, muted
3. *Her teachers thought she was very* bright.
• clever, intelligent, gifted, sharp, quick-witted, *(informal)* brainy • A common simile is
as bright as a button. opposite stupid, dull-witted
4. *Miranda gave me a* bright *smile.*
• cheerful, happy, lively, merry, jolly, radiant **opposite** sad, gloomy
5. *The day was cold, but* bright. • sunny, fine, fair, clear, cloudless **opposite** dull, cloudy, overcast

brighten verb
It was a cloudy morning, but it brightened *after lunch.* • become sunny, clear up, improve
to brighten up
A new coat of paint will brighten up *the room.*
• cheer up, light up, enliven

brilliant adjective
1. *The fireworks gave off a* brilliant *light.*
• bright, blazing, dazzling, glaring, gleaming, glittering, glorious, shining, splendid, vivid **opposite** dim, dull
2. *Brunel was a* brilliant *engineer.* • clever, exceptional, outstanding, gifted, talented **opposite** incompetent, talentless
3. *(informal) I saw a* brilliant *film last week.*
• excellent, marvellous, outstanding, wonderful, superb, *(informal)* fantastic, fabulous

brim noun
I filled my glass to the brim. • top, rim, edge, brink, lip

bring verb bringing, brought
1. *Can you* bring *the shopping in from the car?*
• carry, fetch, deliver, bear, transport
2. *You can* bring *a friend to the party.* • invite, conduct, escort, guide, lead
3. *The war has* brought *great sorrow to our people.* • cause, produce, lead to, result in, generate
to bring something about
The new coach brought about *some changes.*
• cause, effect, create, introduce, be responsible for
to bring someone up
In the story, Tarzan is brought up *by apes.*
• rear, raise, care for, foster, look after, nurture, educate, train
to bring something up
I wish you hadn't brought up *the subject of money.* • mention, talk about, raise, broach

brisk adjective
1. *Mr Hastie went for a* brisk *walk every evening.* • lively, fast-paced, energetic, invigorating, vigorous, refreshing, bracing **opposite** slow, leisurely
2. *The flower shop does a* brisk *trade around Easter.* • busy, lively, bustling, hectic **opposite** quiet, slack, slow

brittle adjective
The bones of the skeleton were dry and brittle. • breakable, fragile, delicate, frail **opposite** soft, flexible

broad adjective broader, broadest
1. *The streets in the city were* broad *and straight.* • wide, open, large, roomy, spacious, vast, extensive **opposite** narrow
2. *Just give me a* broad *outline of what happened.* • general, rough, vague, loose, indefinite, imprecise **opposite** specific, detailed

broken adjective
1. *Don't use that computer—it's* broken.
• faulty, defective, damaged, out of order **opposite** working
2. *After losing all his money, Forbes was a* broken *man.* • crushed, defeated, beaten, spiritless

brood verb
He was still brooding *over what I had said.*
• fret, mope, worry, dwell on

brown adjective, noun
He wore a long brown *coat with the collar turned up.* Brown *is my favourite colour.*
• beige, bronze, buff, chestnut, chocolate, fawn, hazel, khaki, nut-brown, russet, sepia, tawny • Something which is rather brown is **brownish** or **browny**.

browse verb
1. *I like* browsing *through toy catalogues.*
• flick through, leaf through, scan, skim
2. *The cattle were* browsing *in the meadow.*
• graze, feed

brush verb
1. *Jill spends ages every morning* brushing *her hair.* • groom, comb, tidy
2. *A bird* brushed *my cheek as it flew past.*
• touch, contact, graze, stroke, rub, scrape

brutal adjective
The bandits launched a brutal *attack.* • savage, vicious, cruel, barbaric, bloodthirsty, callous, ferocious, inhuman, merciless, pitiless, ruthless, sadistic **opposite** gentle, humane

bubble verb
A green liquid bubbled in the witch's cauldron.
• boil, seethe, gurgle, froth, foam

bubbly adjective bubblier, bubbliest
1. *Bubbly drinks get up my nose.* • fizzy, sparkling, effervescent
2. *Sophie has a bright and bubbly personality.* • cheerful, lively, vivacious, spirited, animated

buckle noun
The pirate wore a belt with a large silver buckle. • clasp, fastener, fastening, clip, catch

buckle verb
1. *Please buckle your seat belts.* • fasten, secure, clasp, clip, do up, hook up
2. *The bridge buckled under the force of the hurricane.* • bend, warp, twist, crumple, cave in, collapse

budding adjective
My sister is a budding actor. • promising, aspiring, potential, would-be, (informal) wannabe **opposite** experienced

budge verb
The window was stuck and wouldn't budge.
• give way, move, shift, stir

bug noun
1. *Birds help to control bugs in the garden.*
• insect, pest
2. *(informal) I can't seem to get rid of this stomach bug.* • infection, virus, germ, disease, illness
3. *They found some bugs in the computer program.* • fault, error, defect, flaw, (informal) gremlin

build verb building, built
Dad is going to build a shed in the garden.
• construct, erect, put together, put up, set up, assemble
to build up
1. *I'm building up a collection of football stickers.* • accumulate, assemble, collect, put together
2. *We felt the tension building up in the crowd.* • increase, intensify, rise, grow, mount up, escalate

build noun
Charlotte was a girl of slender build. • body, form, frame, figure, physique

building noun

WORD WEB

The new building will have seven storeys.
• construction, structure, dwelling
• A person who designs buildings is an **architect**.

BUILDINGS WHERE PEOPLE LIVE
• apartment, barracks, bungalow, castle, cottage, farmhouse, flat, fort, fortress, house, mansion, palace, skyscraper, tenement, terrace, tower, villa

BUILDINGS WHERE PEOPLE WORK
• factory, garage, lighthouse, mill, shop, store, warehouse

BUILDINGS WHERE PEOPLE WORSHIP
• abbey, cathedral, chapel, church, monastery, mosque, pagoda, shrine, synagogue, temple

OTHER TYPES OF BUILDING
• cabin, cafe, cinema, college, gallery, hotel, inn, library, museum, observatory, police station, post office, power station, prison, pub or public house, restaurant, school, shed, theatre

PARTS YOU MIGHT FIND INSIDE A BUILDING
• balcony, basement, cellar, conservatory, corridor, courtyard, crypt, dungeon, foyer, gallery, lobby, porch, quadrangle, room, staircase, veranda

PARTS YOU MIGHT FIND OUTSIDE A BUILDING
• arch, balustrade, bay window, bow window, buttress, chimney, colonnade, column, dome, dormer window, drainpipe, eaves, foundations, gable, gutter, masonry, parapet, pediment, pillar, pipes, roof, tower, turret, vault, wall, window, windowsill

CASTLES AND OTHER FORTIFIED BUILDINGS
• château, citadel, fort, fortress, motte and bailey, palace, stronghold, tower

PARTS OF A CASTLE
• bailey, barbican, battlement, buttress, courtyard, donjon, drawbridge, dungeon, gate, gateway, keep, magazine, moat, motte, parapet, portcullis, postern, rampart, tower, turret, wall, watchtower

bulge *noun*
There was a large bulge in the robber's sack.
• bump, hump, lump, swelling, protuberance

bulge *verb*
The creature had eyes which bulged out of its head. • stick out, swell, puff out, protrude

bulky *adjective* **bulkier, bulkiest**
The parcel is too bulky to go through the letterbox. • big, large, hefty, substantial, sizeable, cumbersome, unwieldy
opposite small, compact

bully *verb* **bullies, bullying, bullied**
Some of the children were afraid of being bullied. • persecute, torment, intimidate, terrorize, push around

bump *verb*
1. *The baby bumped his head on the table.*
• hit, strike, knock, bang
2. *My bicycle bumped up and down over the cobbles.* • bounce, shake, jerk, jolt
to bump into
1. *The taxi bumped into the car in front of it.*
• collide with, bang into, run into, crash into
2. *I bumped into one of my friends in the bookshop.* • meet, come across, run into

bump *noun*
1. *We felt a bump as the plane landed.* • thud, thump, bang, blow, knock
2. *How did you get that bump on your head?*
• lump, swelling, bulge

bumpy *adjective* **bumpier, bumpiest**
1. *The car jolted up and down on the bumpy road.* • rough, uneven, irregular, lumpy
opposite smooth, even
2. *We had a bumpy ride in a jeep over muddy tracks.* • bouncy, jerky, jolting, lurching, choppy

bunch *noun*
1. *The jailer jangled a bunch of keys.* • bundle, cluster, collection, set
2. *She picked a bunch of flowers.* • bouquet, posy, spray
3. *(informal) They're a friendly bunch of people.*
• group, set, circle, band, gang, crowd

bundle *noun*
I found a bundle of old newspapers. • bunch, batch, pile, stack, collection, pack, bale

burn *verb* **burning, burnt, burned**
1. *We could see the campfire burning in the distance.* • be alight, be on fire, blaze, flame, flare, flicker • To burn without flames is to **glow** or **smoulder**.

2. *The village had been burned to the ground.*
• set fire to, incinerate, reduce to ashes • To start something burning is to **ignite**, **kindle** or **light** it. • To burn something slightly is to **char**, **scorch** or **singe** it. • To hurt someone with boiling liquid or steam is to **scald** them. • To burn a dead body is to **cremate** it. • To burn a mark on an animal is to **brand** it.

burst *verb* **bursting, burst**
The balloon burst when my brother sat on it.
• puncture, rupture, break, give way, split, tear

bury *verb* **buries, burying, buried**
1. *The document was buried under a pile of old letters.* • cover, conceal, hide, secrete
2. *They say a pirate chief was buried in that graveyard.* • inter, entomb

bushy *adjective* **bushier, bushiest**
The troll had bushy green eyebrows. • hairy, thick, dense, shaggy, bristly

business *noun*
1. *My uncle runs his own business.* • company, firm, organization
2. *The new bookshop does a lot of business.*
• trade, trading, buying and selling, commerce
3. *He left early to attend to some urgent business.* • matter, issue, affair, problem, point, concern, question

bustle *verb*
Miss Flyte bustled about the kitchen making tea. • rush, dash, hurry, scurry, scuttle, fuss

busy *adjective* **busier, busiest**
1. *Mum is busy making a birthday cake just now.* • occupied, engaged, employed, working, slaving away, beavering away, (informal) hard at it, up to your eyes • A common simile is **as busy as a bee**. **opposite** idle
2. *Christmas is a very busy time for shops.*
• active, hectic, frantic, lively **opposite** quiet, restful
3. *Is the town always this busy on Saturdays?*
• crowded, bustling, hectic, lively, teeming
opposite quiet, peaceful

buy *verb* **buying, bought**
I'm saving up to buy a skateboard. • get, pay for, purchase, acquire **opposite** sell

cabin noun
The outlaws hid in a *cabin* in the woods. • hut, shack, shed, lodge, chalet, shelter

cable noun
1. *The tent was held down with strong cables.* • rope, cord, line, chain
2. *Don't trip over the computer cable.* • flex, lead, wire, cord

cafe noun
We had lunch in a *cafe* overlooking the river. • cafeteria, coffee shop, tearoom, snack bar, buffet, canteen, bistro

cage noun
• A large cage or enclosure for birds is an **aviary**. • A cage or enclosure for poultry is a **coop**. • A cage or enclosure for animals is a **pen**. • A cage or box for a pet rabbit is a **hutch**.

calculate verb
I calculated that it would take an hour to walk home. • work out, compute, figure out, reckon, add up, count, total • To calculate something roughly is to **estimate**.

call noun calls
1. *We heard a call for help from inside the cave.* • cry, exclamation, scream, shout, yell
2. *They decided to pay a call on Miss Jenkins.* • visit, stop, stay
3. *There's not much call for suncream in winter.* • demand, need

call verb
1. *'Stop that racket!' called the janitor.* • cry out, exclaim, shout, yell
2. *It was too late at night to call my friends.* • phone, ring, telephone
3. *The headteacher called me to her office.* • summon, invite, send for, order
4. *The doctor called to see if I was feeling better.* • visit, pay a visit, drop in, drop by
5. *They called the baby Jessica.* • name, baptize, christen, dub
6. *What is your new book going to be called?* • name, title, entitle

to call something off
The match was called off due to bad weather. • cancel, abandon, scrap, *(informal)* scrub, ditch, axe • To delay something until later is to **postpone** it or to **put it off**.

calm adjective
1. *The weather was too calm to fly our kites.* • still, quiet, peaceful, tranquil, serene, windless **opposite** stormy, windy
2. *The sea was calm, and we had a pleasant voyage.* • smooth, still, flat, motionless, tranquil **opposite** rough, choppy
3. *I tried to stay calm before my judo exam.* • cool, level-headed, patient, relaxed, sedate, unemotional, unexcitable, untroubled **opposite** anxious, nervous

campaign noun
1. *Will you join our campaign to save the whale?* • movement, crusade, drive, fight, effort, struggle
2. *The army launched a campaign to recapture the city.* • operation, offensive, action, war

cancel verb cancelling, cancelled
We had to cancel the race because of the weather. • abandon, call off, scrap, drop, *(informal)* scrub, ditch, axe • To cancel something after it has already begun is to **abort** it. • To put something off until later is to **postpone** it. • To cancel items on a list is to **cross out**, **delete** or **erase** them.

cape noun
The lady wore a cape of black velvet. • cloak, shawl, wrap, robe, *(old use)* mantle

capsize verb
The canoe capsized when it hit a rock. • overturn, tip over, turn over, keel over, *(informal)* turn turtle

capsule noun
1. *This capsule contains poison.* • pill, tablet, lozenge
2. *The space capsule is designed to orbit Mars.* • module, craft, pod

captain noun
The captain brought his ship safely into harbour. • commander, commanding officer, master, skipper

captive noun
The captives were thrown into the dungeon. • prisoner, convict • A person who is held

captive until some demand is met is a **hostage**.

capture verb
1. *The bank robbers were* capture *by police this morning.* • catch, arrest, apprehend, seize, take prisoner, *(informal)* nab, nick
2. *The castle has never been* captured *by enemy forces.* • occupy, seize, take, take over, win

car noun

Our car *is being repaired at the garage.*
• motor, *(American)* automobile, *(informal)* wheels • An informal name for an old, noisy car is a **banger**. • A very early car is a **veteran** or **vintage** car.

SOME TYPES OF CAR
• convertible, coupé, electric car, estate (car), four-wheel drive, hatchback, hybrid car, *(trademark)* Jeep, *(trademark)* Land Rover, *(informal)* limo, limousine, *(trademark)* Mini, patrol car or police car, people carrier, racing car, saloon, sports car, *(American)* station wagon, supermini, SUV

THE MAIN PARTS OF A CAR ARE
• body, bonnet, boot, bumper, chassis, doors, engine, exhaust pipe, fuel tank, gear box, headlights or headlamps, lights, mirrors, roof, tyres, undercarriage, wheels, windscreen, wings

THE MAIN CONTROLS IN A CAR ARE
• accelerator, brake, choke, clutch, gear lever, handbrake, ignition, indicators, steering wheel, windscreen wipers

care noun
1. *The old wizard's face was full of* care.
• worry, anxiety, trouble, concern, burden, responsibility, sorrow, stress
2. *I took great* care *with my handwriting.* • attention, concentration, thoroughness, thought, meticulousness **opposite** carelessness
3. *Jake left his pet hamster in my* care.
• charge, keeping, protection, safe keeping, supervision
to take care
Please take care *crossing the road.* • be careful, be on your guard, look out, watch out
to take care of someone or **something**
My granny takes care of *me after school.* • care for, look after, mind, watch over, attend to, tend

care verb
Do you care *which team wins the World Cup?*
• mind, bother, worry, be interested, be troubled, be bothered, be worried
to care for someone or **something**
1. *The veterinary hospital* cares for *sick animals.* • take care of, look after, attend to, tend, nurse
2. *I don't really* care for *sport.* • like, be fond of, be keen on, love

career noun
Max had a successful career *as a racing driver.*
• job, occupation, profession, trade, business, employment, calling

carefree adjective
We spent two carefree *weeks on holiday.*
• easygoing, relaxing, light-hearted, untroubled, stress-free, peaceful, restful, *(informal)* laid-back **opposite** tense, stressful, hectic

careful adjective
1. *You must be more* careful *with your spelling.* • accurate, conscientious, thorough, thoughtful, meticulous, painstaking, precise **opposite** careless, inaccurate
2. *Dad kept a* careful *watch on the bonfire.*
• attentive, cautious, watchful, alert, wary, vigilant **opposite** careless, inattentive
to be careful
Please be careful *with those scissors.* • take care, be on your guard, look out, watch out

carefully adverb
1. *Sam crept* carefully *down the stairs into the hall.* • cautiously, gently, deliberately, stealthily
2. *Please listen* carefully *to what I am about to say.* • closely, minutely, thoroughly, studiously, attentively

careless adjective
1. *This is a very* careless *piece of work.*
• messy, untidy, thoughtless, inaccurate, slapdash, shoddy, scrappy, sloppy, slovenly

A B C D E F G H I J K L M N O P Q R S T U V W X Y Z

opposite careful, accurate
2. *I was careless and cut my finger.*
• inattentive, thoughtless, absent-minded, heedless, irresponsible, negligent, reckless
opposite careful, attentive

cargo *noun* **cargoes**
Some planes carry cargo instead of passengers. • goods, freight, merchandise

carnival *noun*
The whole village comes out for the annual carnival. • fair, festival, fete, gala, parade, procession, show, celebration, pageant

carry *verb* **carries, carrying, carried**
1. *I helped Mum to carry the shopping to the car.* • take, transfer, lift, fetch, bring, lug
2. *Aircraft carry passengers and goods.*
• transport, convey
3. *The rear axle carries the greatest weight.*
• bear, support, hold up
to carry on
We carried on in spite of the rain. • continue, go on, persevere, persist, keep on, remain, stay, survive
to carry something out
The soldiers carried out the captain's orders.
• perform, do, execute, accomplish, achieve, complete, finish

carve *verb*
1. *The statue was carved out of stone.* • sculpt, chisel, hew
2. *Mum carved the chicken for Sunday dinner.*
• cut, slice

case *noun*
1. *I loaded my case into the boot of the car.*
• suitcase, trunk • A number of suitcases that you take on holiday is your **baggage** or **luggage**.
2. *What's in those cases in the attic?* • box, chest, crate, carton, casket
3. *This has been a clear case of mistaken identity.* • instance, occurrence, example, illustration
4. *It was one of Sherlock Holmes's most famous cases.* • inquiry, investigation
5. *She presented a good case for abolishing hunting.* • argument, line of reasoning

cash *noun*
How much cash do you have? • money, change, loose change, ready money, coins, notes, currency

casual *adjective*
1. *It was just a casual remark, so don't take it too seriously.* • accidental, chance,

unexpected, unintentional, unplanned
opposite deliberate
2. *The restaurant had a casual atmosphere.*
• easy-going, informal, relaxed
opposite formal
3. *The teacher complained about our casual attitude.* • apathetic, careless, slack, unenthusiastic **opposite** enthusiastic

cat *noun*
• A male cat is a **tom**. • A young cat is a **kitten**.
• An informal word for a cat is **puss** or **pussy**.
• A cat whose ancestors are all of the same breed is a **pedigree**. • A word meaning 'to do with cats' is **feline**.

catastrophe *noun*
The drought is a catastrophe for the farmers.
• disaster, calamity, misfortune, mishap, tragedy

catch *verb* **catches, catching, caught**
1. *My friends yelled at me to catch the ball.*
• clutch, grab, grasp, grip, hang on to, hold, seize, snatch, take
2. *One of the anglers caught a fish.* • hook, net, trap
3. *The police hoped to catch the thief red-handed.* • arrest, capture, corner, *(informal)* nab, collar
4. *I hope you don't catch my cold.* • become infected by, contract, get, *(informal)* go down with
5. *You must hurry if you want to catch the bus.*
• be in time for, get on

catch *noun* **catches**
1. *The fishermen were hauling in their catch.*
• haul
2. *The car is so cheap that there must be a catch.* • problem, obstacle, snag, difficulty, disadvantage, drawback, trap, trick
3. *All the windows are fitted with safety catches.* • fastening, latch, lock, bolt, hook

cattle *plural noun*
• Male cattle are **bulls**, **steers** or **oxen**.
• Female cattle are **cows**. • Young male cattle are **calves** or **bullocks**. • Young female cattle are **calves** or **heifers**. • A word meaning 'to do with cattle' is **bovine**. • Farm animals in general are **livestock**.

cause *noun*
1. *What was the cause of the trouble?* • origin, source, start • You can also talk about the **reasons** for the trouble.
2. *You've got no cause to complain.* • grounds, basis, motive, reason

3. *The sponsored walk is for a good cause.*
• purpose, object

cause *verb*
A single spark from the fire could cause an explosion. • bring about, create, generate, lead to, give rise to, result in, provoke, arouse

caution *noun*
1. *We decided to proceed with caution.* • care, attention, watchfulness, wariness, vigilance
2. *The traffic warden let him off with a caution.* • warning, reprimand, telling-off, (informal) ticking-off

cautious *adjective*
My grandad is a cautious driver. • careful, attentive, watchful, wary, vigilant, hesitant
opposite reckless

cave *noun*

WORD WEB

The cave walls were covered with prehistoric paintings. • cavern, pothole, underground chamber • A man-made cave with decorative walls is a **grotto**.

THINGS YOU MIGHT SEE IN A CAVE
• cave painting, stalactite, stalagmite • The entrance to a cave is the **mouth**. • The top of a cave is the **roof** and the bottom is the **floor**. • Prehistoric people who lived in caves were **cavemen** and **cavewomen** or **troglodytes**. • Someone who enjoys exploring caves is a **potholer**.

---

cease *verb*
The fighting ceased at midnight. • come to an end, end, finish, stop, halt **opposite** begin

celebrate *verb*
1. *Let's celebrate!* • enjoy yourself, have a good time, be happy, rejoice
2. *What shall we do to celebrate Granny's birthday?* • commemorate, observe, keep

celebration *noun*
We had a big celebration for my cousin's wedding. • festivity, party, feast, festival, banquet, jamboree

celebrity *noun* **celebrities**
The awards were handed out by a TV celebrity. • famous person, personality, public figure, VIP, star, idol

cemetery *noun* **cemeteries**
A famous author is buried in the local cemetery. • graveyard, burial ground,
churchyard • A place where dead people are cremated is a **crematorium**.

central *adjective*
1. *We are now in the central part of the building.* • middle, core, inner, interior
opposite outer
2. *Who are the central characters in the story?* • chief, crucial, essential, fundamental, important, main, major, principal, vital
opposite unimportant

centre *noun*
The library is in the centre of the town. The burial chamber is in the centre of the pyramid. • middle, heart, core, inside, interior • The centre of a planet or a piece of fruit is the **core**. • The centre of an atom or a living cell is the **nucleus**. • The centre of a wheel is the **hub**. • The point at the centre of a see-saw is the **pivot**. • The edible part in the centre of a nut is the **kernel**. **opposite** edge, outside, surface

ceremony *noun* **ceremonies**
1. *We watched the ceremony of the opening of parliament.* • rite, ritual, formalities
• A ceremony where someone is given a prize is a **presentation**. • A ceremony where someone is given a special honour is an **investiture**. • A ceremony to celebrate something new is an **inauguration** or **opening**. • A ceremony where someone becomes a member of a society is an **initiation**. • A ceremony to make a church or other building sacred is a **dedication**. • A ceremony to remember a dead person or a past event is a **commemoration**. • A ceremony held in a church is a **service**.
2. *They had a quiet wedding without a lot of ceremony.* • formality, pomp, pageantry, spectacle

certain *adjective*
1. *My mum was certain she would win the cookery competition.* • confident, convinced, positive, sure, determined **opposite** uncertain
2. *We have certain proof that the painting is a forgery.* • definite, clear, convincing, absolute, unquestionable, reliable, trustworthy, undeniable, infallible, genuine, valid
opposite unreliable
3. *The damaged plane faced certain disaster.* • inevitable, unavoidable **opposite** possible
4. *Her new book is certain to be a bestseller.* • bound, sure

certainly adverb
Baby dragons are certainly not timid.
• definitely, undoubtedly, unquestionably, assuredly, without a doubt

certificate noun
At the end of the course, you will receive a certificate. • diploma, document, licence

chain noun
1. *The anchor was attached to a chain.* • One ring in a chain is a **link**. • A chain used to link railway wagons together is a **coupling**.
2. *The police formed a chain to keep the crowd back.* • line, row, cordon
3. *Holmes described the chain of events that led to the murder.* • series, sequence, succession, string

champion noun
1. *She is the current world champion at ice-skating.* • title-holder, prizewinner, victor, winner, conqueror
2. *Martin Luther King was a champion of civil rights.* • supporter, advocate, defender, upholder, patron, backer

championship noun
Fifteen schools took part in the karate championship. • competition, contest, tournament

chance noun
1. *There's a chance of more rain later.*
• possibility, likelihood, probability, prospect
• A chance of something bad is a **danger** or a **risk**.
2. *I haven't had a chance to reply yet.*
• opportunity, time, occasion
3. *The director took a chance in hiring an unknown actor.* • gamble, risk
by chance
I found the house quite by chance.
• by accident, accidentally, by coincidence
• An unfortunate chance is **bad luck** or a **misfortune**. • A fortunate chance is **good luck** or a **fluke**.

change verb
1. *They've changed the programme for the concert.* • alter, modify, rearrange, reorganize, adjust, adapt, vary
2. *The town has changed a lot since Victorian times.* • alter, become different, develop, grow, move on
3. *Can I change these jeans for a bigger size, please?* • exchange, replace, switch, substitute, (informal) swap

to change into
Tadpoles change into frogs. • become, turn into, be transformed into

change noun
There has been a slight change of plan.
• alteration, modification, variation, difference, break • A change to something worse is a **deterioration**. • A change to something better is an **improvement** or a **reform**. • A very big change is a **revolution** or **transformation** or **U-turn**. • A change in which one person or thing is replaced by another is a **substitution**.

channel noun
1. *The rainwater runs along this channel.*
• ditch, duct, gully, gutter, furrow, trough
2. *How many TV channels do you get?* • station

chaos noun
After the earthquake, the city was in chaos.
• confusion, disorder, mayhem, uproar, tumult, pandemonium, anarchy, bedlam, muddle, shambles **opposite** order

chaotic adjective
Alice finds that life in Wonderland is chaotic.
• confused, disorderly, disorganized, muddled, topsy-turvy, untidy, unruly, riotous **opposite** orderly, organized

chapter noun
I read a chapter of my book last night. • part, section, division • One section of a play is an **act** or **scene**. • One part of a serial is an **episode** or **instalment**.

character noun
1. *Her character is quite different from her sister's.* • personality, temperament, nature, disposition, make-up, manner
2. *A mysterious character dressed in black was watching them closely.* • figure, personality, individual, person
3. *Which character would you like to play in 'Peter Pan'?* • part, role

charge noun
1. *The admission charge is five euros.* • price, rate • The charge made for a ride on public transport is the **fare**. • The charge made to post a letter or parcel is the **postage**.
• A charge made to join a club is a **fee** or **subscription**. • A charge made for certain things by the government is a **duty** or a **tax**.
• A charge made to use a private road, bridge or tunnel is a **toll**.
2. *The robbers face several criminal charges.*
• accusation, allegation

3. *Many soldiers were killed in the* charge.
• assault, attack, onslaught, raid
4. *My best friend left her hamster in my* charge.
• care, keeping, protection, custody, trust
to be in charge of something
An experienced sailor was in charge of *the crew.* • manage, lead, command, direct, supervise, run

charge *verb*
1. *The library* charges *ten pence for a photocopy.* • ask for, make you pay
2. *A man has been* charged *with attempted robbery* • accuse (of)
3. *The cavalry* charged *the enemy line.*
• attack, assault, storm, rush

charm *verb*
Winnie-the-Pooh has charmed *readers all over the world.* • bewitch, captivate, delight, enchant, entrance, fascinate, please

charming *adjective*
We stayed in a charming *little cottage in the country.* • delightful, attractive, pleasant, pleasing, likeable, appealing, captivating, enchanting

chart *noun*
1. *The explorer stopped to consult his* chart.
• map
2. *This* chart *shows the average rainfall for each month.* • diagram, graph, table

chase *verb*
The wolves chased *a deer through the forest.*
• pursue, run after, follow, track, trail, hunt

chatty *adjective*
Frank is usually shy, but today he's quite chatty. • talkative, communicative
opposite silent

cheap *adjective*
1. *We got a* cheap *flight to London.*
• inexpensive, affordable, bargain, cut-price, discount, reasonable
2. *These tyres are made from* cheap *rubber.* • inferior, shoddy, second-rate, worthless, trashy, (informal) tacky, tatty
opposite superior, good-quality

cheat *verb*
1. *She was* cheated *into buying a fake diamond ring.* • deceive, trick, swindle, double-cross, hoax, (informal) con, diddle, fleece, fool, rip off
2. *Anyone who* cheats *in the quiz will be disqualified.* • copy, crib

cheat *noun*
Don't trust him—he's a cheat. • cheater, deceiver, swindler, fraud, impostor, hoaxer

check *verb*
1. *Have you* checked *your work carefully?*
• examine, inspect, look over, scrutinize, go over or through, read through
2. *The heavy snow* checked *their progress towards the Pole.* • hamper, hinder, block, obstruct, delay, hold back, slow, slow down, halt, stop

check *noun*
I need to run some checks *on your computer.*
• test, examination, inspection, check-up

cheeky *adjective* cheekier, cheekiest
Don't be so cheeky! • disrespectful, facetious, flippant, impertinent, impolite, impudent, insolent, insulting, irreverent, mocking, rude, saucy, shameless **opposite** respectful

cheer *verb*
1. *We* cheered *when our team scored a goal.*
• clap, applaud, shout, yell **opposite** jeer
2. *Everyone was* cheered *by the news.*
• comfort, console, gladden, delight, please, encourage, uplift, hearten **opposite** sadden

cheerful *adjective*
The sun was shining, and we set out in a cheerful *mood.* • happy, good-humoured, light-hearted, merry, jolly, joyful, joyous, jaunty, glad, pleased, optimistic, lively, elated, animated, bright, buoyant, jovial, gleeful, chirpy, perky **opposite** sad

chemist *noun*
• pharmacist, (old use) apothecary, alchemist
• A chemist's shop is a **dispensary** or **pharmacy**. *He claimed he was a* chemist *with a miracle cure.*

chest *noun*
I found some old books in a chest *in the attic.*
• box, crate, case, trunk

chew *verb*
Are you still chewing *that toffee?* • eat, gnaw, munch

chicken *noun*
• A female chicken is a **hen**. • A male chicken is a **rooster**. • A young chicken is a **chick**.
• A group of chickens is a **brood**. • A farm which keeps chickens is a **poultry farm**.

chief *noun*
The pirates chose Redbeard as their chief.
• leader, ruler, head, commander, captain,

chieftain, master, governor, president, principal, (informal) boss

chief adjective
1. *The chief ingredients in a trifle are jelly, custard and cream.* • main, central, key, principal, crucial, basic, essential, important, vital, major, primary, foremost, fundamental, indispensable, necessary, significant, predominant, prominent **opposite** unimportant, minor, trivial
2. *Albert was Queen Victoria's chief adviser.* • head, senior

chiefly adverb
Kangaroos are found chiefly in Australia. • mainly, mostly, predominantly, primarily, principally, especially

child noun children
1. *The book festival is aimed especially at children.* • boy or girl, infant, juvenile, youngster, youth, lad or lass, (informal) kid, tot, nipper
2. *How many children do you have?* • son or daughter, offspring • A child who expects to inherit a title or fortune from parents is an **heir** or **heiress**. • A child whose parents are dead is an **orphan**. • A child looked after by a guardian is a **ward**. • A child who is related to someone who lived in the past is their **descendant**.

childish adjective
It's childish to make rude noises. • babyish, immature, juvenile, infantile **opposite** mature

chill verb
Chill the pudding before serving it. • freeze, cool, make cold, refrigerate **opposite** warm

chilly adjective chillier, chilliest
1. *It's a chilly evening, so wrap up well.* • cold, cool, frosty, icy, crisp, fresh, raw, wintry, (informal) nippy **opposite** warm
2. *The librarian gave me a very chilly look.* • unfriendly, hostile, unwelcoming, unsympathetic **opposite** friendly

chip noun
1. *There were chips of broken glass on the pavement.* • bit, piece, fragment, scrap, sliver, splinter, flake, shaving
2. *This mug's got a chip in it.* • crack, nick, notch, flaw

chip verb chipping, chipped
I chipped a cup while I was washing-up. • crack, nick, notch, damage

choice noun
1. *My bike had a flat tyre, so I had no choice but to walk.* • alternative, option
2. *She wouldn't be my choice as team captain.* • preference, selection, pick, vote
3. *The library has a good choice of games.* • range, selection, assortment, array, mixture, variety, diversity

choke verb
1. *This tie is so tight it's choking me.* • strangle, suffocate, stifle, throttle
2. *Thick fumes made the firefighters choke.* • cough, gasp

choose verb choosing, chose, chosen
1. *We had a show of hands to choose a winner.* • select, appoint, elect, vote for
2. *I chose the blue shoes to go with my dress.* • decide on, select, pick out, opt for, plump for, settle on, single out
3. *Lola chose to stay at home.* • decide, make a decision, determine, prefer, resolve

chop verb chopping, chopped
1. *Chop the celery into large chunks.* • cut, split
2. *They chopped down the undergrowth to make a path.* • hack, slash • To chop down a tree is to **fell** it. • To chop off an arm or leg is to **amputate** it. • To chop a branch off a tree is to **lop** it. • To chop food into small pieces is to **dice** or **mince** it.

chubby adjective chubbier, chubbiest
The baby chicks are fluffy and chubby. • plump, tubby, podgy, dumpy

chunk noun
I bit a chunk out of my apple. • piece, portion, lump, block, hunk, slab, wedge

circle noun
1. *We arranged the chairs in a circle.* • ring, round, hoop, loop, band • A flat, solid circle is a **disc**. • A three-dimensional round shape is a **sphere**. • An egg shape is an **oval** or **ellipse**. • The distance round a circle is the **circumference**. • The distance across a circle is the **diameter**. • The distance from the centre to the circumference is the **radius**. • A circular movement is a **revolution** or **rotation**. • A circular trip round the world is a **circumnavigation**. • A circular trip of a satellite round a planet is an **orbit**.
2. *She has a wide circle of friends.* • group, set, crowd

circular adjective
The flying saucer was circular in shape. • round, ring-shaped, disc-shaped

circumstances *plural noun*
He described the circumstances which led to the accident. • situation, conditions, background, causes, context, details, facts, particulars

citizen *noun*
The citizens of New York are proud of their city. • resident, inhabitant

city *noun* **cities**
• The chief city of a country or region is the **metropolis**. • An area of houses outside the central part of a city is the **suburbs**. • A word meaning 'to do with a town or city' is **urban**. • A word meaning 'to do with a city and its suburbs' is **metropolitan**.

civilization *noun*
We are studying the civilization of ancient Egypt. • culture, society, achievements, attainments This word can also be spelled **civilisation**.

claim *verb*
1. *You can claim your prize for the raffle here.* • ask for, request, collect, demand, insist on
2. *He claimed to be an expert on dinosaurs.* • declare, assert, allege, maintain, argue, insist

clap *verb* **clapping, clapped**
1. *The audience clapped loudly at the end of the concert.* • applaud, cheer
2. *Suddenly, a hand clapped me on the shoulder.* • slap, hit, pat, smack

clash *noun*
1. *The clash of cymbals made me jump.* • crash, bang, ringing
2. *There was a clash between rival supporters at the match.* • argument, confrontation, conflict, fight, scuffle, *(informal)* scrap

clash *verb*
1. *The cymbals clashed.* • crash, resound
2. *Two good films clash on TV tonight.* • coincide, happen at the same time
3. *Demonstrators clashed with the police.* • argue, fight, get into conflict, squabble

class *noun*
1. *There are 26 children in our class.* • form, set, stream • The other pupils in your class are your **classmates**.
2. *There are many different classes of plants.* • category, group, classification, division, set, sort, type, kind, species
3. *The ancient Romans divided people into social classes.* • level, rank, status

classic *adjective*

> Notice that **classic** means *excellent of its kind*, while **classical** means either 'to do with the ancient Greeks and Romans' or 'to do with serious music written in the past'.

That was a classic tennis final this year. • excellent, first-class, first-rate, top-notch, exceptional, fine, great, admirable, masterly, model, perfect **opposite** ordinary

classify *verb* **classifies, classifying, classified**
We classified the leaves according to their shape. • group, organize, put into sets, sort, class, grade

clean *adjective*
1. *Can you bring me a clean cup, please?* • spotless, washed, scrubbed, swept, tidy, immaculate, hygienic, sanitary • An informal word meaning 'very clean' is **squeaky-clean**. • A common simile is **as clean as a whistle**. **opposite** dirty
2. *I began my diary on a clean piece of paper.* • blank, unused, unmarked, empty, bare, fresh, new **opposite** used
3. *This plaster will keep the wound clean.* • sterile, sterilized, uninfected
4. *You can get clean water from this tap.* • pure, clear, fresh, unpolluted, uncontaminated
5. *The referee said he wanted a clean fight.* • fair, honest, honourable, sporting, sportsmanlike **opposite** dishonourable

clean *verb*
1. *We cleaned the house from top to bottom. I tried to clean the mud off my boots.* • wash, wipe, mop, scour, scrub, polish, dust, sweep, vacuum, rinse, wring out, hose down, sponge, shampoo, swill • To clean clothes is to **launder** them. **opposite** dirty, mess up
2. *The nurse cleaned the wound with an antiseptic wipe.* • cleanse, bathe, disinfect, sanitize, sterilize **opposite** infect, contaminate

clear *adjective*
1. *We saw fish swimming in the clear water.* • clean, pure, colourless, transparent • A common simile is **as clear as crystal**. • A simile which means the opposite is **as clear as mud**. **opposite** cloudy, opaque
2. *It was a beautiful clear day.* • bright, sunny, cloudless, unclouded • A clear night is a **moonlit** or **starlit** night. **opposite** cloudy
3. *The instructions on the map were quite clear.* • plain, understandable, intelligible, lucid, unambiguous **opposite** ambiguous, confusing

4. *A clear voice cut through the silence.*
• distinct, audible • A common simile is **as clear as a bell. opposite** muffled
5. *The signature on this letter is not clear.* • legible, recognizable, visible **opposite** illegible
6. *My camera takes nice clear pictures.* • sharp, well-defined, focused **opposite** unfocused
7. *Are you sure that your conscience is clear?* • innocent, untroubled, blameless **opposite** guilty
8. *There's a clear difference between a male blackbird and a female.* • obvious, definite, noticeable, conspicuous, perceptible, pronounced **opposite** imperceptible
9. *They made sure the road was clear for the ambulance.* • open, empty, free, passable, uncrowded, unobstructed **opposite** congested

clear *verb*
1. *I cleared the weeds from the flower bed.*
• get rid of, remove, eliminate, strip
2. *The plumber cleared the blocked drain.*
• unblock, unclog, clean out, open up • To clear a channel is to **dredge** it.
3. *The windscreen wipers cleared the misty windows.* • clean, wipe, polish
4. *If the fire alarm goes, clear the building.*
• empty, evacuate
5. *The fog cleared slowly.* • disappear, vanish, disperse, evaporate, melt away
6. *The forecast said that the weather will clear.*
• become clear, brighten up
7. *He was cleared of all the charges against him.* • acquit, absolve, find not guilty
8. *The runners cleared the first hurdle.* • go over, get over, jump over, pass over, vault
to clear up
Please clear up this mess before you go.
• clean up, tidy up, put right, put straight

clever *adjective*
1. *Dr Hafiz is very clever and can read hieroglyphics.* • intelligent, bright, gifted, able, knowledgeable, *(informal)* brainy, smart **opposite** unintelligent • An informal name for a clever person is a **brainbox**. • An uncomplimentary synonym is **clever clogs** or **smartypants**.
2. *The elves were very clever with their fingers.*
• accomplished, capable, gifted, skilful, talented, nimble • If you are clever at a lot of things, you are **versatile. opposite** unskilful
3. *They are clever enough to get away with it.* • quick, sharp, shrewd, smart
• Uncomplimentary synonyms are **artful, crafty, cunning, wily. opposite** stupid

cliff *noun*
The car rolled over the edge of a cliff. • crag, precipice, rock face

climax *noun*
The climax of the film is a stunning car chase. • high point, highlight, peak, crisis **opposite** anticlimax

climb *verb*
1. *It took us several hours to climb the mountain.* • ascend, clamber up, go up, scale
2. *The plane climbed into the clouds.* • lift off, soar, take off, rise
3. *The road climbs steeply up to the castle.*
• rise, slope
to climb down
1. *It's harder to climb down the rock than to get up it.* • descend, get down from
2. *We all told him he was wrong, so he had to climb down.* • admit defeat, give in, surrender

cling *verb* clinging, clung
to cling to someone or **something**
1. *The baby koala clung to its mother.* • clasp, grasp, clutch, embrace, hug
2. *Ivy clings to the wall.* • adhere to, fasten on to, stick to

clip *verb* clipping, clipped
1. *The sheets of paper were clipped together.*
• pin, staple
2. *Dad clipped the hedges in the back garden.*
• cut, trim • To cut unwanted twigs off a tree or bush is to **prune** it.

cloak *noun*
The girl wrapped her cloak tightly around herself. • cape, coat, wrap, *(old use)* mantle

clog *verb* clogging, clogged
The dead leaves are clogging the drain.
• block, choke, congest, obstruct, bung up, jam, stop up

close *adjective*
1. *Our house is close to the shops.* • near, nearby, not far • To be actually by the side of something is to be **adjacent. opposite** far, distant
2. *Anisha and I are close friends.* • intimate, dear, devoted, fond, affectionate
3. *The police made a close examination of the stolen car.* • careful, detailed, painstaking, minute, thorough **opposite** casual
4. *It was an exciting race because it was so close.* • equal, even, level, well-matched
5. *Open the window—it's very close in here.*
• humid, muggy, stuffy, clammy, airless, stifling, suffocating **opposite** airy

close *verb*
1. *Don't forget to close the lid.* • shut, fasten, seal, secure
2. *The road has been closed to traffic for the parade.* • barricade, block, obstruct, stop up
3. *The band closed the concert with my favourite song.* • finish, end, complete, conclude, stop, terminate, *(informal)* wind up

clothe *verb* clothing, clothed
to be clothed in
The bridesmaids were clothed in white.
• be dressed in, be wearing

clothes *plural noun*

⭐ WORD WEB

What clothes are you taking on holiday?
• clothing, garments, outfits, dress, attire, garb, finery, *(informal)* gear, togs, get-up
• A set of clothes to wear is a **costume**, **outfit** or **suit**. • An official set of clothes worn for school or work is a **uniform**.

SOME ITEMS OF CLOTHING
• blouse, caftan, camisole, chador or chuddar, dhoti, dress, dungarees, jeans, jersey, jodhpurs, jumper, kilt, kimono, leggings, miniskirt, pinafore dress, playsuit, polo shirt, pullover, robe, sari, sarong, shirt, shorts, skirt, slacks, smock, suit, sweater, sweatshirt, trousers, trunks, T-shirt, tunic, waistcoat

OUTER CLOTHES
• anorak, blazer, cagoule, cape, cardigan, cloak, coat, duffel coat, fleece, gilet, greatcoat, hoodie, jacket, mackintosh or *(informal)* mac, overcoat, parka, pashmina, poncho, raincoat, shawl, tracksuit, windcheater

UNDERWEAR
• boxer shorts or *(informal)* boxers, bra, briefs, crop top, drawers, knickers, pants, petticoat, slip, socks, stockings, tights, underpants, vest

CLOTHES FOR SLEEPING IN
• nightdress or *(informal)* nightie, nightshirt, onesie, pyjamas

CLOTHES FOR WORKING IN
• apron, boilersuit, oilskins, overalls

CLOTHES WORN IN THE PAST
• corset, crinoline, doublet, frock coat, gauntlet, gown, greatcoat, ruff, toga, tunic

ACCESSORIES WORN WITH CLOTHES
• belt, braces, cravat, earmuffs, gloves, sash, scarf, shawl, tie

PARTS OF A GARMENT
• bodice, button, buttonhole, collar, cuff, hem, lapel, pocket, seam, sleeve, waistband, zip

THINGS USED TO DECORATE CLOTHES
• beads, frills, fringes, lace, ruffles, sequins, tassels

SOME KINDS OF HAT
• balaclava, baseball cap, bearskin, beret, boater, bonnet, bowler, cap, deerstalker, fez, helmet, mitre, mortarboard, panama hat, skull cap, sombrero, sou'wester, stetson, sun-hat, tam-o'-shanter, top hat, trilby, turban

✏️ WRITING TIPS

You can use these words to describe clothes:
• baggy, loose, roomy, casual, sporty, chic, fashionable, fine, flashy, flattering, glamorous, luxurious, ornate, frilly, stylish, smart, trendy, tight-fitting, skimpy, dowdy, drab, frumpy, old-fashioned, ill-fitting, ragged, shabby, tattered or in tatters, threadbare, worn

cloud *noun*
A cloud of steam billowed from the kettle.
• billow, puff, haze, mist

cloudy *adjective* cloudier, cloudiest
1. *The day was cold and cloudy.* • dull, overcast, grey, dark, dismal, gloomy, sunless
opposite cloudless
2. *We couldn't see any fish in the cloudy water.* • muddy, murky, hazy, milky, opaque
opposite clear, transparent

club *noun*
1. *The warrior brandished a wooden club.*
• stick, baton, truncheon, cudgel
2. *Would you like to join our club?* • group, society, association, organization, circle, union

clue noun
1. *I don't know the answer. Can you give me a clue?* • hint, suggestion, indication, pointer, tip, idea
2. *'This footprint is an important clue,' said the detective.* • piece of evidence, lead

clump noun
The owl flew into a clump of trees on the hill. • group, thicket, cluster, collection • A clump of grass or hair is a **tuft**.

clumsy adjective clumsier, clumsiest
The clumsy gnome was always breaking things. • careless, awkward, ungainly, inept • An informal name for a clumsy person is **butterfingers**. • When someone is clumsy with their hands you can say that they are **all fingers and thumbs**. opposite graceful

cluster noun
A cluster of people waited outside the cinema. • crowd, bunch, collection, assembly, gathering, knot

clutch verb
The mountaineer clutched his rope. • catch, clasp, cling to, grab, grasp, grip, hang on to, hold on to, seize, snatch

clutter noun
We'll have to clear up all this clutter. • mess, muddle, junk, litter, rubbish, odds and ends

coach verb
He was coached by a former champion. • train, teach, instruct

coarse adjective
1. *The blanket was made of coarse woollen material.* • rough, harsh, scratchy, bristly, hairy **opposite** soft
2. *We were shocked by their coarse table manners.* • rude, offensive, impolite, improper, indecent, crude, vulgar **opposite** polite, refined

coat noun
1. *The detective was wearing a thick winter coat.*
2. *The fox had a reddish brown coat.* • hide, pelt, skin, fur, hair • A sheep's coat is a **fleece**.
3. *The front door needs a coat of paint.* • layer, coating, covering

coat verb
We ate marshmallows coated with chocolate. • cover, spread, smear, glaze

coax verb
Sam coaxed the hamster back into its cage. • persuade, tempt, entice

code noun
1. *There is a strict code of conduct for using the pool.* • rules, regulations, laws
2. *The message was written in a secret code.* • To put a message in code is to **encode** or **encrypt** it. • To understand a message in code is to **decode**, **decipher** or *(informal)* **crack** it.

coil noun
The snake twisted itself into a coil. • spiral, twist, curl, twirl, screw, corkscrew, whirl, whorl, roll, scroll • A coil of wool or thread is a **skein**.

coil verb
The snake coiled itself round a branch. • curl, loop, roll, spiral, turn, twist, twirl, wind, writhe

coin verb
We coined a new name for our group. • invent, make up, think up, create, devise, produce

coincide verb
My birthday coincides with the school holidays. • clash, fall together, happen together

cold adjective
1. *Wrap up warm in this cold weather.* • freezing, chilly, frosty, icy, raw, arctic, bitter, cool, crisp, snowy, wintry, *(informal)* perishing • A common simile is **as cold as ice**. opposite hot, warm
2. *I tried to shelter from the cold wind.* • biting, bitter, keen, penetrating, piercing
3. *I was cold in spite of my woolly hat.* • freezing, frozen, chilly, chilled, shivering, shivery • To be so cold that you become ill is to suffer from **hypothermia**. opposite hot, warm
4. *The Cyclops gave us a cold stare from his one eye.* • unfriendly, unkind, unfeeling, distant, cool, heartless, indifferent, reserved, stony, uncaring, unemotional, unsympathetic **opposite** warm, friendly

collapse verb
1. *Many buildings collapsed in the earthquake.* • fall down, fall in, cave in, give way, crumple, buckle, disintegrate, tumble down
2. *Some of the runners collapsed in the heat.* • faint, pass out, fall over, keel over

colleague noun
The police officer discussed the plan with her colleagues. • associate, partner, team-mate, co-worker, workmate

collect verb
1. *Squirrels collect nuts for the winter.* • gather, accumulate, hoard, heap, pile up, store up, stockpile, amass
2. *A crowd collected to watch the fire.*
• assemble, gather, come together, converge **opposite** scatter, disperse
3. *We collected a large sum for charity.* • raise, take in
4. *She collected the car from the garage.* • pick up, fetch, get, obtain, bring **opposite** drop off, hand in

collection noun
Would you like to see my fossil collection?
• assortment, set, accumulation, array, hoard, pile • A collection of books is a **library**.
• A collection of poems or short stories is an **anthology**.

collide verb
to collide with
The runaway trolley collided with a wall.
• bump into, crash into, run into, smash into, hit, strike

collision noun
The collision dented the front wheel of my bike. • bump, crash, smash, knock, accident
• A collision involving a lot of vehicles is a **pile-up**.

colossal adjective
A colossal statue towered above us. • huge, enormous, gigantic, immense, massive, giant, mammoth, monumental, towering, vast **opposite** small, tiny

colour noun

WORD WEB

What do you call that colour? • hue, shade, tinge, tint, tone

NAMES OF VARIOUS COLOURS
• black, blue, brown, cream, gold, golden, green, grey, lavender, orange, pink, purple, red, silver, turquoise, violet, white, yellow
• The colours red, yellow and blue are known as **primary colours**.

WRITING TIPS

You can use these words to describe a colour.

TO DESCRIBE A PALE COLOUR
• clear, delicate, light, neutral, pale, pastel, faded, muted, washed-out, wishy-washy

TO DESCRIBE A STRONG COLOUR
• bright, deep, glowing, intense

TO DESCRIBE A VERY BRIGHT COLOUR
• fluorescent, garish, harsh, loud, neon, vibrant, zingy

colourful adjective
1. *The rose garden is very colourful in the summer.* • multicoloured, showy, vibrant, bright, brilliant, gaudy **opposite** colourless
2. *The book gives a colourful account of life on the island.* • exciting, interesting, lively, vivid, striking, rich, picturesque **opposite** dull

colourless adjective
1. *The flask contained a colourless liquid.*
• clear, transparent, translucent, pale
2. *All the characters in the book are rather colourless.* • dull, uninteresting, boring, drab, dreary, unexciting, lacklustre **opposite** colourful

column noun
1. *The roof of the temple was supported by stone columns.* • pillar, post, support, shaft
2. *A column of soldiers wound its way across the desert.* • line, file, procession, row, string
3. *I sometimes read the sports column in the newspaper.* • article, piece, report, feature

combat verb
There's a new campaign to combat crime in the city. • fight, oppose, resist, stand up to, tackle, battle against, grapple with

combine verb
1. *We combined our pocket money to buy a kite.* • put together, add together, join, merge, unite, amalgamate **opposite** divide
2. *Combine the mixture with water to make a paste.* • mix, stir together, blend, mingle, bind **opposite** separate

come verb coming, came, come
1. *We expect our guests to come in the afternoon.* • arrive, appear, visit **opposite** go
2. *When you hear a cuckoo, you know that summer is coming.* • advance, draw near

to come about
Can you tell me how the accident came about?

• happen, occur, take place, result
to come across
I came across an old friend of mine. • find, discover, chance upon, meet, bump into
to come to
1. *Tell me when you come to the last chapter.*
• reach, get to, arrive at
2. *What did the repair bill come to?* • add up to, amount to, total

comfort *noun*
1. *My teddy bear was a comfort to me when I was ill.* • reassurance, consolation, encouragement, support, relief
2. *If I had a million pounds, I could live in comfort.* • ease, luxury, contentment, well-being, prosperity, luxury

comfort *verb*
They tried to comfort me but it was no use.
• cheer up, console, reassure, encourage, hearten, sympathize with, soothe

comfortable *adjective*
1. *The bed was so comfortable that Goldilocks fell fast asleep.* • cosy, snug, relaxing, easy, soft, warm, roomy, padded, plush, (informal) comfy **opposite** uncomfortable
2. *We'll need comfortable clothes for travelling.* • casual, informal, loose-fitting
3. *Our cat leads a comfortable life.*
• contented, happy, pleasant, agreeable, well-off, prosperous, luxurious, affluent

comic, comical *adjective*
We laughed at his comic remarks. • amusing, humorous, funny, hilarious, witty, diverting, (informal) hysterical • To be comical in a cheeky way is to be **facetious**. • To be comical in a silly way is to be **absurd**, **farcical**, **ludicrous** or **ridiculous**. • To be comical in a hurtful way is to be **sarcastic**.

command *noun*
1. *The general gave the command to attack.*
• order, instruction, commandment, edict
2. *Captain Nemo has command of the whole crew.* • charge, control, authority (over), power (over), management, supervision
3. *My sister has a good command of Spanish.*
• knowledge, mastery, grasp, understanding, ability (in), skill (in)

command *verb*
1. *The officer commanded his troops to fire.*
• order, instruct, direct, tell, bid
2. *The captain commands the ship.* • control, direct, be in charge of, govern, head, lead, manage, administer, supervise

commence *verb*
The flag is a signal for the race to commence.
• begin, start, embark on

comment *noun*
He made some nasty comments about his boss. • remark, statement, observation, opinion, mention, reference • A hostile comment is a **criticism**.

commit *verb* **committing, committed**
The thieves were planning to commit another robbery. • carry out, do, perform, execute

common *adjective*
1. *Colds are a common complaint in winter.*
• commonplace, everyday, frequent, normal, ordinary, familiar, well known, widespread **opposite** rare
2. *'Good morning' is a common way to greet people.* • typical, usual, regular, routine, standard, customary, conventional, habitual, traditional **opposite** uncommon
3. *My friends and I have a common interest in music.* • shared, mutual, joint

commotion *noun*
Football supporters were causing a commotion outside. • disturbance, row, fuss, trouble, disorder, unrest, agitation, turmoil, uproar, racket, rumpus, upheaval, riot, fracas, furore, hullabaloo, brouhaha, pandemonium, bedlam

communicate *verb*
1. *Steve communicated his boredom with a yawn.* • express, make known, indicate, convey, disclose, announce, pass on, proclaim, publish, report
2. *Nowadays, we communicate by text.*
• contact each other, correspond, be in touch

communication *noun*
1. *Dolphins use sound for communication.*
• communicating, contact, understanding each other
2. *I've received an urgent communication.*
• message, dispatch, letter, text, email, statement, announcement

compact *adjective*
This camera is light and compact. • small, portable, petite **opposite** large

companion *noun*
Zak's pony was his favourite companion.
• friend, partner, comrade, (informal) mate, buddy, pal, chum

company *noun* **companies**
1. *My cousin works for a computer company.*
• business, firm, corporation, organization, establishment
2. *Shrek shunned the company of other ogres.*
• fellowship, companionship, friendship, society

compare *verb*
Can you compare these sets of figures?
• contrast, juxtapose, relate, set side by side
to compare with
This copy can't compare with the original painting. • compete with, rival, emulate, equal, match

compartment *noun*
The sewing box has compartments for needles and pins. • section, division, area, space

compel *verb* **compelling, compelled**
You can't compel me to come with you. • force, make

compete *verb*
Five schools will be competing in the hockey tournament. • participate, perform, take part, enter
to compete against
We are competing against a strong team this week. • oppose, play against, contend with

competent *adjective*
You have to be a competent swimmer to join the club. • able, capable, skilful, skilled, accomplished, proficient, experienced, expert, qualified, trained **opposite** incompetent

competitor *noun*
The competitors lined up for the start of the race. • contestant, contender, challenger, participant, opponent, rival • People who take part in an exam are **candidates** or **entrants**.

complain *verb*
Miss Grouch spent most of her life complaining.
• moan, protest, grumble, grouse, gripe, whinge, make a fuss
to complain about
I wrote a letter complaining about the noise.
• protest about, object to, criticize, find fault with **opposite** praise

complaint *noun*
1. *They received hundreds of complaints about the film.* • criticism, objection, protest, moan, grumble
2. *You have a nasty stomach complaint.*
• disease, illness, ailment, sickness, infection, (informal) upset

complete *adjective*
1. *Your training as a witch is not yet complete.*
• completed, ended, finished, accomplished, concluded **opposite** unfinished
2. *Have you got a complete set of cards?*
• whole, entire, full, intact
opposite incomplete
3. *My birthday party was a complete disaster.*
• total, utter, sheer, absolute, thorough, downright, perfect, pure

complete *verb*
We have completed all the tasks on the sheet.
• finish, end, conclude, carry out, perform

completely *adverb*
I completely understand why you're upset.
• totally, utterly, entirely, fully, thoroughly, absolutely

complex *adjective*
Defusing a bomb is a complex task.
• complicated, difficult, elaborate, detailed, intricate, involved, (informal) fiddly
opposite simple

complicated *adjective*
The plot of the film is very complicated.
• complex, intricate, involved, difficult, elaborate, convoluted **opposite** simple, straightforward

compliment *noun*
It was nice to get so many compliments about my cooking. • praise, appreciation, approval, congratulations, tribute • Compliments which you don't deserve are **flattery**. • To praise someone by saying something nice is to **pay them a compliment.** **opposite** insult

complimentary *adjective*
1. *My teacher made complimentary remarks on my playing.* • appreciative, approving, admiring, positive, favourable, flattering **opposite** critical, insulting, negative
2. *We were given complimentary tickets for the game.* • free, gratis

compose *verb*
Beethoven composed nine symphonies.
• create, devise, produce, make up, think up, write

to be composed of
The quilt is *composed of* hundreds of pieces of cloth. • be made of, consist of, comprise

comprehend *verb*
The crowd couldn't *comprehend* what was happening. • understand, realize, appreciate, figure out, grasp, perceive, follow

comprehensive *adjective*
She gave us a *comprehensive* account of her travels. • complete, full, thorough, detailed, extensive, inclusive, exhaustive, wide-ranging, encyclopedic **opposite** selective

compress *verb*
I tried to *compress* all my clothes into one bag. • press, squeeze, cram, crush, jam, squash, stuff, flatten

comprise *verb*
The team *comprised* athletes from several countries. • be composed of, consist of, include, contain

compulsory *adjective*
The wearing of seat belts is *compulsory*. • required, obligatory, necessary **opposite** optional

conceal *verb*
1. The dog tried to *conceal* its bone. • hide, cover up, bury
2. We tried to *conceal* our hiding place. • disguise, mask, screen, camouflage, make invisible
3. Don't *conceal* the truth. • keep quiet about, keep secret, hush up, suppress

conceited *adjective*
He was so *conceited* when he won first prize! • boastful, arrogant, proud, vain, self-satisfied, (informal) big-headed, cocky **opposite** modest

conceive *verb*
1. Who *conceived* this silly plan? • think up, devise, invent, make up, originate, plan, produce, work out, (informal) dream up
2. I could not *conceive* how the plan would work. • imagine, see

concentrate *verb*
I had to *concentrate* to hear what she was saying. • be attentive, think hard, focus

concept *noun*
I find the *concept* of time travel fascinating. • idea, thought, notion

concern *verb*
1. This conversation doesn't *concern* you. • affect, involve, be important to, matter to, be relevant to, relate to
2. It *concerns* me greatly that we are destroying the rainforests. • bother, distress, trouble, upset, worry

concern *noun*
1. My private life is no *concern* of theirs. • affair, business
2. Global warming is a great *concern* to us all. • worry, anxiety, fear

concerned *adjective*
1. After waiting an hour, Julia began to feel *concerned*. • worried, bothered, troubled, anxious, upset, distressed
2. We're writing a letter to all those *concerned*. • involved, connected, related, affected

concerning *preposition*
The head spoke to me *concerning* my future. • about, regarding, relating to, with reference to, relevant to

concise *adjective*
He gave the police a *concise* account of what happened. • brief, short, condensed, succinct • A concise account of something is a **précis** or **summary**. **opposite** long

conclude *verb*
1. We *concluded* the Christmas concert with carols. • end, finish, complete, round off, wind up
2. The concert *concluded* with some carols. • close, terminate, culminate
3. They *concluded* that he was guilty. • decide, deduce, infer, suppose, assume, gather

conclusion *noun*
1. The *conclusion* of the film was a bit puzzling. • close, end, finale, finish, completion, culmination
2. 'What is your *conclusion*, Inspector?' • decision, judgement, opinion, verdict, deduction

condemn *verb*
1. The manager *condemned* the behaviour of the players. • criticize, disapprove of, denounce, deplore, reproach **opposite** praise
2. The judge *condemned* the men to death. • sentence **opposite** acquit

condense *verb*
I *condensed* my poem so that it fitted on one page. • reduce, shorten, compress, summarize **opposite** expand

condition noun
1. *Is your bike in good condition?* • state, order, repair
2. *A dog needs exercise to stay in good condition.* • fitness, health, shape
3. *It's a condition of membership that you pay a subscription.* • requirement, obligation, term

conduct verb
1. *A guide conducted us round the museum.* • guide, lead, take, accompany, escort
2. *We asked the eldest girl to conduct our meeting.* • lead, manage, control, run, administer, supervise, preside over, organize, handle

conduct noun
Our teacher congratulated us on our good conduct. • behaviour, manners, attitude

conference noun
All the witches were invited to a grand conference. • meeting, consultation, discussion

confess verb
The goblin confessed that he had stolen the gold. • admit, own up to, acknowledge, reveal

confidence noun
1. *We can face the future with confidence.* • hope, optimism, faith **opposite** doubt
2. *I wish I had her confidence.* • self-confidence, assurance, boldness, conviction

confident adjective
1. *I am confident that we will win.* • certain, sure, positive, optimistic **opposite** doubtful
2. *She is a confident sort of person.* • self-confident, assertive, bold, fearless, unafraid

confine verb
1. *They confined their discussion to the weather.* • limit, restrict
2. *Our farm animals are not confined indoors.* • enclose, surround, fence in, shut in, coop up, hem in

confirm verb
1. *The strange events confirmed his belief in ghosts.* • prove, justify, support, back up, reinforce **opposite** disprove
2. *I phoned to confirm my appointment at the dentist.* • verify, make official **opposite** cancel

conflict noun
There's a lot of conflict in their family. • disagreement, quarrelling, fighting, hostility, friction, antagonism, opposition, strife, unrest

conflict verb
to conflict with
Her account of what happened conflicts with mine. • disagree with, differ from, contradict, contrast with, clash with

conform verb
to conform to or with
The club expels anyone who doesn't conform with the rules. • follow, keep to, obey, abide by, agree with, fit in with, submit to **opposite** disobey

confront verb
I decided to confront her and demand an apology. • challenge, stand up to, face up to **opposite** avoid

confuse verb
1. *I was confused by the directions on the map.* • puzzle, bewilder, mystify, baffle, perplex
2. *You must be confusing me with someone else.* • mix up, muddle

confusion noun
1. *There was great confusion when the lights went out.* • chaos, commotion, fuss, uproar, turmoil, pandemonium, bedlam, hullabaloo
2. *There was a look of confusion on her face.* • bewilderment, puzzlement, perplexity

congested adjective
The roads are congested during the rush hour. • crowded, full, jammed, clogged, blocked, obstructed, *(informal)* snarled up **opposite** clear

congratulate verb
We congratulated the winners. • praise, applaud, compliment **opposite** criticize

congregate verb
The party guests congregated in the hall. • gather, assemble, collect, come together **opposite** disperse

connect verb
1. *What's the best way to connect these wires?* • join, attach, fasten, link, couple, fix together, tie together **opposite** separate
2. *The fingerprints connected him with the crime.* • make a connection between, associate, relate

connection *noun*
There is a close connection between our two families. • association, relationship, link

conquer *verb*
1. *Extra troops were sent to conquer the invading army.* • beat, defeat, overcome, vanquish, get the better of, overwhelm, crush, rout, thrash
2. *Gaul was conquered by Julius Caesar.* • seize, capture, take, win, occupy, possess

conscientious *adjective*
Elves are very conscientious workers. • hard working, careful, dependable, reliable, responsible, dutiful, meticulous, painstaking, thorough, diligent **opposite** careless

conscious *adjective*
1. *The patient was conscious throughout the operation.* • awake, alert, aware **opposite** unconscious
2. *She made a conscious effort to improve her work.* • deliberate, intentional, planned **opposite** accidental

consent *verb*
to consent to
The head has consented to our request. • agree to, grant, approve of, authorize **opposite** refuse

consequence *noun*
1. *He drank the potion without thinking of the consequences.* • effect, result, outcome, sequel, upshot
2. *The loss of a few pence is of no consequence.* • importance, significance

conservation *noun*
Our group supports the conservation of wildlife. • preservation, protection, maintenance, upkeep **opposite** destruction

consider *verb*
1. *The detective considered the problem carefully.* • think about, examine, contemplate, ponder on, reflect on, study, weigh up, meditate about
2. *I consider this to be my best work.* • believe, judge, reckon

considerable *adjective*
$1000 is a considerable sum of money. • big, large, significant, substantial, sizeable **opposite** negligible, insignificant

considerate *adjective*
It was considerate of you to lend me your umbrella. • kind, kind-hearted, helpful, obliging, sympathetic, thoughtful, unselfish, caring, charitable, neighbourly **opposite** selfish

consist *verb*
to consist of
1. *The planet consists largely of gas.* • be made of, be composed of, comprise, contain, include, incorporate
2. *His job consists mostly of answering the phone.* • involve

consistent *adjective*
1. *These plants need to be kept at a consistent temperature.* • steady, constant, regular, stable, unchanging
2. *Fortunately, our goalkeeper is a consistent player.* • predictable, dependable, reliable

console *verb*
He did his best to console me when my dog died. • comfort, soothe, sympathize with, support

conspicuous *adjective*
1. *The clock tower is a conspicuous landmark.* • prominent, notable, obvious, eye-catching, unmistakable, visible
2. *I had made some conspicuous mistakes.* • clear, noticeable, obvious, evident, glaring

constant *adjective*
1. *There is a constant noise of traffic on the motorway.* • continual, continuous, never-ending, non-stop, ceaseless, incessant, interminable, endless, everlasting, permanent, perpetual, unending, persistent, relentless **opposite** changeable
2. *My dog has been my constant friend for many years.* • faithful, loyal, dependable, reliable, firm, true, trustworthy, devoted **opposite** unreliable

construct *verb*
We constructed a tree house in the back garden. • build, erect, assemble, make, put together, put up, set up **opposite** demolish

construction *noun*
1. *The construction of the tree house took all afternoon.* • building, erecting, erection, assembly, setting-up
2. *The hut was a flimsy construction.* • building, structure

consult *verb*
1. *You should consult the dentist about your sore tooth.* • ask, get advice from, speak to
2. *If you don't know how to spell a word, consult your dictionary.* • refer to

contact *verb*
I'll contact you when I have some news. • call, call on, get in touch with, communicate with, notify, speak to, talk to, correspond with, email, phone, ring, text, message, write to

contain *verb*
1. *This box contains various odds and ends.* • hold
2. *A dictionary contains words and definitions.* • include, incorporate, comprise, consist of

container *noun*
Put the left-over sauce in a container. • vessel, receptacle, holder, box, case, canister, carton, pot, tub, tin

contemplate *verb*
1. *The princess contemplated herself in the mirror.* • look at, view, observe, survey, watch, stare at, gaze at
2. *The robbers contemplated what to do next.* • think about, consider, ponder, study, reflect on, weigh up, meditate about

contempt *noun*
The knight stared at his enemy with a look of contempt. • hatred, scorn, loathing, disgust, dislike, distaste **opposite** admiration

contend *verb*
I contend that I was right. • declare, claim, argue, assert, maintain
to contend with
1. *The team had to contend with strong opposition.* • compete with, fight against, oppose, grapple with, struggle against, strive against
2. *We had to contend with bad weather and midges!* • cope with, deal with, face, put up with

content *adjective*
Fergus was perfectly content to sit reading a book. • happy, contented, satisfied, pleased, willing **opposite** unwilling

contented *adjective*
After her meal, the cat looked very contented. • happy, pleased, content, satisfied, fulfilled, serene, peaceful, relaxed, comfortable, tranquil, untroubled **opposite** discontented

contest *noun*
The tennis final was an exciting contest. • competition, challenge, fight, bout, encounter, struggle, game, match, tournament

contestant *noun*
There are twenty contestants in the spelling bee. • competitor, participant, player, contender

continual *adjective*
I get sick of their continual arguing. • constant, persistent, perpetual, repeated, frequent, recurrent, eternal, unending
opposite occasional

continue *verb*
1. *We continued our search until it got dark.* • keep up, prolong, sustain, persevere with, pursue, (informal) stick at
2. *This rain can't continue for much longer.* • carry on, last, persist, endure, keep on, go on, linger
3. *We'll continue the game after lunch.* • resume, proceed with, pick up, carry on with

continuous *adjective*
We had continuous rain all through our holiday. • never-ending, non-stop, ceaseless, everlasting, incessant, unbroken, unceasing, uninterrupted • An illness which continues for a long time is a **chronic** illness.
opposite intermittent

contract *noun*
The actress has signed a contract for a new film. • agreement, deal, undertaking • A contract between two countries is an **alliance** or **treaty**. • A contract to end a dispute about money is a **settlement**.

contract *verb*
1. *Metal contracts when it gets colder.* • reduce, lessen, shrink, tighten
opposite expand
2. *The crew contracted a mysterious illness.* • catch, develop, get

contraption *noun*
The inventor's house was full of weird contraptions. • machine, device, gadget, invention, apparatus, contrivance, mechanism, gizmo

contrast *verb*
1. *We were asked to contrast two of our favourite poems.* • compare, juxtapose, distinguish between
2. *She had rose red lips which contrasted with her pale skin.* • clash (with), stand out (against)

contrast *noun*
There is a sharp contrast between the two paintings. • difference, distinction, opposition
opposite similarity

contribute verb
Will you contribute something to our charity collection? • donate, give, provide, (informal) chip in
to contribute to
The sunny weather contributed to our enjoyment. • add to, help, aid, encourage, enhance

control noun
The captain had complete control over the crew. • authority, power, command, government, management, direction, leadership, guidance

control verb controlling, controlled
1. The government controls the country's affairs. • be in control of, be in charge of, manage, run, command, direct, lead, guide, govern, administer, regulate, rule, superintend, supervise
2. Can't you control that dog? • manage, handle, restrain
3. They built a dam to control the floods. • check, curb, hold back, contain

controversy noun controversies
There is much controversy about the election results. • disagreement, debate, argument, dispute, quarrelling

convenient adjective
1. Is there a convenient place to put my umbrella? • suitable, appropriate, available, nearby, accessible **opposite** inconvenient
2. Mum has a convenient tool for opening jars. • handy, helpful, useful, labour-saving, neat

conventional adjective
The conventional way to greet someone is to shake hands. • customary, traditional, usual, accepted, common, normal, ordinary, everyday, routine, standard, regular, habitual, orthodox **opposite** unconventional

converge verb
The two rivers converge at this point. • come together, join, meet, merge, combine, coincide **opposite** divide

conversation noun
• An informal conversation is a **chat** or **gossip**.
• A more formal conversation is a **discussion**.
• A very formal conversation is a **conference**.
• Conversation in a play or novel is **dialogue**.

convert verb
1. We have converted our attic into a games room. • change, adapt, alter, transform

2. I never used to like football, but my cousin converted me. • change someone's mind, persuade, convince, win over

convey verb
1. The breakdown truck conveyed our car to a garage. • bring, carry, deliver, take, move, bear, transfer, transport • To convey something by sea is to **ferry** or **ship** it.
2. What does his message convey to you? • communicate, tell, reveal, indicate, signify, mean

convince verb
The prisoner convinced them that he was innocent. • persuade, assure, satisfy, make believe, win round

convincing adjective
I tried to think of a convincing excuse. • persuasive, believable, credible, plausible

cook verb

WORD WEB

• To cook food for guests or customers is to **cater** for them. • Cooking as a business is **catering**. • The art or skill of cooking is **cookery**.

SOME WAYS TO COOK FOOD
• bake, barbecue, boil, braise, brew, broil, casserole, deep-fry, fry, grill, poach, roast, sauté, simmer, steam, stew, toast

OTHER WAYS TO PREPARE FOOD
• baste, blend, chop, dice, grate, grind, infuse, knead, liquidize, marinade, mince, mix, peel, purée, sieve, sift, stir, whisk

SOME ITEMS THAT ARE USED FOR COOKING
• baking tin or tray, barbecue, blender, bowl, carving knife, casserole, cauldron, chopping board, colander, cooker, dish, food processor, frying pan, grill, ladle, liquidizer, microwave, mincer, oven, pan, pot, rolling pin, saucepan, skewer, spatula, spit, strainer, toaster, whisk, wok, wooden spoon

cool *adjective*
1. *The weather is cool for the time of year.*
• chilly, coldish **opposite** hot, warm
2. *Would you like a cool glass of lemonade?*
• chilled, iced, refreshing **opposite** hot
3. *Clifford remained cool when everyone else panicked.* • calm, level-headed, relaxed, unexcitable, unflustered, *(informal)* laid-back
• A common simile is **as cool as a cucumber**. **opposite** frantic
4. *(informal) Those roller skates are really cool!*
• chic, fashionable, smart, *(informal)* trendy

cooperate *verb*
to cooperate with
The scouts cooperated with each other to build a fire. • work with or together with, collaborate with, aid, assist, support

cope *verb*
Shall I help you or can you cope on your own?
• manage, carry on, get by, make do, survive
to cope with
I can't cope with all this homework! • deal with, handle, manage, get through

copy *noun* copies
That isn't the original painting—it's a copy.
• replica, reproduction, duplicate, imitation, likeness • A copy made to deceive someone is a **fake** or a **forgery**. • A living organism which is identical to another is a **clone**.

copy *verb* copies, copying, copied
1. *I copied the poem into my exercise book.*
• duplicate, reproduce, write out • To copy something in order to deceive is to **fake** or **forge** it.
2. *My parrot can copy my voice.* • imitate, impersonate, mimic

core *noun*
It is very hot at the earth's core. • centre, middle, inside, heart, nucleus

corner *noun*
1. *I'll meet you at the corner of the road.* • turn, turning, junction, crossroads, intersection
• The place where two lines meet is an **angle**.
2. *I sat in a quiet corner and read her letter.*
• alcove, recess, nook

correct *adjective*
1. *Your answers are all correct.* • right, accurate, exact, faultless
2. *I hope he has given us correct information.*
• true, genuine, authentic, precise, reliable, factual

3. *What is the correct way to address this letter?* • proper, acceptable, regular, appropriate, suitable **opposite** wrong

correct *verb*
1. *I have to correct my spelling mistakes.*
• alter, put right, make better, improve
2. *Miss Nicol spent the day correcting exam papers.* • mark

correspond *verb*
to correspond with
1. *Her version of the story doesn't correspond with mine.* • agree with, match, be similar to, be consistent with, tally with
2. *Carol corresponds with a friend in Paris.*
• write to, communicate with, send letters to

corrupt *adjective*
Corrupt officials had accepted millions of pounds in bribes. • dishonest, criminal, untrustworthy, *(informal)* bent, crooked **opposite** honest

cost *noun*
The bill shows the total cost. • price, charge, amount, payment, fee, figure, expense, expenditure, tariff • The cost of travelling on public transport is the **fare**.

costume *noun*
The Irish dancers were wearing national costumes. • outfit, dress, clothing, suit, attire, garment, garb, *(informal)* get-up • A costume you dress up in for a party is **fancy dress**.
• A set of clothes worn by soldiers or members of an organization is a **uniform**.

cosy *adjective* cosier, cosiest
It's good to feel cosy in bed when it's cold outside. • comfortable, snug, soft, warm, secure **opposite** uncomfortable

count *verb*
1. *I'm counting the days until my birthday.*
• add up, calculate, compute, estimate, reckon, figure out, work out, total
2. *It's playing well that counts, not winning.*
• be important, be significant, matter
to count on
You can count on me to support you. • depend on, rely on, trust, bank on

country *noun* countries
1. *England and Wales are separate countries.*
• nation, state, land, territory • A country ruled by a king or queen is a **kingdom**, **monarchy** or **realm**. • A country governed by leaders elected by the people is a **democracy**. • A democratic country with a

president is a **republic**.
2. *We went for a picnic in the country.*
• countryside, landscape, outdoors, scenery • A word meaning 'to do with the country' is **rural** and its opposite is **urban**.
opposite town, city

courage *noun*
The rescue dogs showed great courage.
• bravery, boldness, daring, fearlessness, nerve, pluck, valour, heroism, grit, (*informal*) guts **opposite** cowardice

courageous *adjective*
The warriors were always courageous in battle.
• brave, bold, daring, fearless, heroic, intrepid, plucky, gallant, valiant **opposite** cowardly

course *noun*
1. *The hot-air balloon was drifting off its course.* • direction, path, route, way, progress, passage
2. *The war changed the course of history.*
• development, progression, sequence, succession

cover *verb*
1. *A coat of paint will cover the graffiti.*
• conceal, disguise, hide, obscure, mask, blot out
2. *She covered her face with her hands.*
• shield, screen, protect, shade, veil
3. *An encyclopedia covers many subjects.*
• deal with, include, contain, incorporate

cover *noun*
1. *The cover of the book was torn.* • wrapper
• A cover for a letter is an **envelope**. • A cover for a book is a **jacket**. • A cover to keep papers in is a **file** or **folder**.
2. *On the bare hillside, there was no cover from the storm.* • shelter, protection, defence, shield, refuge, sanctuary

covering *noun*
There was a light covering of snow on the hills.
• coating, coat, layer, blanket, carpet, film, sheet, skin, veil

cowardly *adjective*
It was cowardly of him to run away.
• timid, faint-hearted, spineless, gutless, (*informal*) yellow, chicken, lily-livered
opposite brave

cower *verb*
A frightened creature was cowering in the corner. • cringe, shrink, crouch, flinch, quail

crack *noun*
1. *There's a crack in this cup.* • break, chip, fracture, flaw, chink, split
2. *The outlaw hid in a crack between two rocks.*
• gap, opening, crevice, rift, cranny
3. *The detective heard the crack of a pistol shot.* • bang, fire, explosion, snap, pop
4. *She gave the robber a crack on the head.*
• blow, bang, knock, smack, whack
5. *I had a crack at writing a poem.* • try, attempt, shot, go

crack *verb*
A brick fell down and cracked the pavement.
• break, fracture, chip, split, shatter, splinter

craft *noun*
1. *I'd like to learn the craft of weaving.* • art, skill, technique, expertise, handicraft
2. *All sorts of craft were in the harbour.*
• boats, ships, vessels

crafty *adjective* **craftier, craftiest**
The evil sorceress had a crafty plan. • cunning, clever, shrewd, scheming, sneaky, sly, tricky, wily, artful

cram *verb* **cramming, crammed**
1. *We can't cram any more people in—the bus is full.* • pack, squeeze, crush, force, jam, compress
2. *My sister is cramming for her maths exam.*
• revise, study, (*informal*) swot

cramped *adjective*
The seating on the train was a bit cramped.
• confined, narrow, restricted, tight, uncomfortable, crowded, (*informal*) poky
opposite roomy

crash *noun*
1. *I heard a loud crash from the kitchen.*
• bang, smash
2. *We saw a nasty crash on the motorway.*
• accident, collision, smash, bump • A crash involving a lot of vehicles is a **pile-up**. • A train crash may involve a **derailment**.

crash *verb*
The car crashed into a lamp post. • bump, smash, collide, knock

crawl *verb*
I saw a caterpillar crawling along a leaf.
• creep, edge, inch, slither, clamber

craze *noun*
This game is the latest craze in the playground.
• fad, trend, vogue, fashion, enthusiasm, obsession, passion

crazy adjective crazier, craziest
1. *The dog went crazy when it was stung by a wasp.* • mad, insane, frenzied, hysterical, frantic, berserk, delirious, wild, (informal) loopy, nuts
2. *It was a crazy idea to try to build a space rocket!* • absurd, ridiculous, ludicrous, daft, idiotic, senseless, silly, stupid, foolhardy, preposterous, (informal) bonkers, barmy, wacky **opposite** sensible

create verb
1. *The cats were creating a racket outside.* • make, cause, produce
2. *We have created a website for our running club.* • set up, start up, bring about, bring into existence, originate • You **write** a poem or story. • You **compose** music. • You **draw** or **paint** a picture. • You **carve** a statue. • You **invent** or **think up** a new idea. • You **design** a new product. • You **devise** a plan. • You **found** a new club or organization. • You **manufacture** goods. • You **generate** electricity. • You **build** or **construct** a model or a building.

creative adjective
My aunt is a very creative person. • artistic, imaginative, inventive, original, inspired **opposite** unimaginative

creator noun
Walt Disney was the creator of Mickey Mouse. • inventor, maker, originator, producer, deviser • The creator of a design is an **architect** or **designer**. • The creator of goods for sale is a **manufacturer**.

creature noun
A wild-looking creature emerged from the swamp. • animal, beast, being

creep verb creeping, crept
1. *I watched the lizard creep back into its hiding place.* • crawl, edge, inch, slither, wriggle
2. *I crept out of bed without waking the others.* • move quietly, sneak, tiptoe, slip, slink, steal

creepy adjective creepier, creepiest
There were creepy noises coming from the cellar. • scary, frightening, eerie, ghostly, weird, sinister, uncanny, unearthly, (informal) spooky

crest noun
1. *The bird had a large red crest on its head.* • comb, plume, tuft
2. *There was a wonderful view from the crest of the hill.* • top, peak, summit, crown, head, brow

crevice noun
Moss was growing in the crevices in the rock. • crack, cranny, gap, opening, rift, split • A deep crack in a glacier is a **crevasse**.

criminal noun
These men are dangerous criminals. • offender, lawbreaker, rogue, villain, wrongdoer, (informal) crook

criminal adjective
The gang were involved in many criminal schemes. • illegal, unlawful, corrupt, dishonest, wrong, (informal) crooked, bent

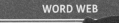

WORD WEB

SOME TYPES OF CRIMINAL
• burglar, cat burglar, pickpocket, robber, shoplifter, thief; assassin, murderer; bandit, brigand, highwayman, outlaw, pirate, poacher, smuggler; blackmailer, con man, gangster, mugger, thug, vandal; hijacker, kidnapper, terrorist

cripple verb
1. *The fall may have crippled the horse.* • disable, handicap, maim, lame
2. *The country was nearly crippled by the war.* • ruin, destroy, crush, wreck, damage, weaken

crisis noun crises
The election result caused a crisis in the country. • emergency, problem, difficulty, predicament

crisp adjective
1. *Fry the bacon until it's crisp.* • crispy, crunchy, brittle **opposite** soft, soggy, limp
2. *It was a crisp winter morning.* • cold, fresh, frosty

critical adjective
1. *Aunt Lily started making critical remarks about our house.* • negative, disapproving,

derogatory, uncomplimentary, unfavourable **opposite** complimentary
2. *This match is critical for our team's chances of success.* • crucial, important, vital, serious, decisive **opposite** unimportant

criticism noun
I think his criticism of my singing was unfair. • attack, disapproval, reprimand, reproach

criticize verb
She criticized us for being so careless. • blame, condemn, disapprove of, find fault with, reprimand, reproach, scold, berate **opposite** praise This word can also be spelled **criticise**.

crooked adjective
1. *The wizard carried a long crooked stick in his right hand.* • bent, twisted, warped, gnarled **opposite** straight
2. *(informal) The crooked salesman was selling fake DVDs.* • criminal, dishonest, corrupt, illegal, unlawful, *(informal)* bent **opposite** honest

crop verb cropping, cropped
Miss Marshall was cropping her garden hedge. • cut, trim, clip, snip, shear
to crop up
Several problems have cropped up. • arise, appear, occur, emerge, come up, turn up

cross verb
1. *There is a bus stop where the two roads cross.* • criss-cross, intersect
2. *You can cross the river at the footbridge.* • go across, pass over, traverse, ford, span

cross adjective
My mum will be cross if we're late. • angry, annoyed, upset, vexed, bad-tempered, ill-tempered, irritable, grumpy, testy, irate **opposite** pleased

crouch verb
The outlaws crouched silently in the bushes. • squat, kneel, stoop, bend, duck, bob down, hunch, huddle

crowd noun
1. *A crowd of people waited outside the theatre.* • gathering, group, assembly, bunch, cluster, throng, mob, multitude, crush, horde, swarm
2. *There was a huge crowd for the tennis final.* • audience, spectators, attendance • The total number of people who attend a sporting event is called the **gate**.

crowd verb
1. *People crowded on the pavement to watch the parade.* • gather, collect, assemble, congregate, mass, flock, muster
2. *Hundreds of people crowded into the hall.* • push, pile, squeeze, pack, cram, crush, jam, bundle, herd

crowded adjective
The shops are always crowded at Christmas time. • full, packed, teeming, swarming, overflowing, jammed, congested **opposite** empty

crude adjective
1. *The refinery processes crude oil.* • raw, natural, unprocessed, unrefined **opposite** refined
2. *We made a crude shelter out of branches.* • rough, clumsy, makeshift, primitive **opposite** skilful
3. *The teacher told them to stop using crude language.* • rude, obscene, coarse, dirty, foul, impolite, indecent, vulgar **opposite** polite

cruel adjective crueller, cruellest
I think hunting is a cruel way to kill animals. • brutal, savage, vicious, fierce, barbaric, bloodthirsty, barbarous, heartless, ruthless, merciless, inhuman, sadistic, uncivilized, beastly **opposite** kind, humane, gentle

crumb noun
We put out some crumbs of bread for the birds. • bit, fragment, scrap, morsel

crumble verb
1. *The walls of the castle were beginning to crumble.* • disintegrate, break up, collapse, fall apart, decay, decompose
2. *The farmer crumbled some bread into his soup.* • crush, grind, pound, pulverize

crumpled adjective
Your shirt is crumpled. • creased, wrinkled, crinkled, crushed

crunch verb
1. *The dog was crunching on a bone.* • chew, munch, chomp, grind
2. *I heard heavy footsteps crunching up the path.* • crush, grind, pound, smash

crush verb
1. *He crushed his anorak into his schoolbag.* • squash, squeeze, mangle, pound, press, bruise, crunch, scrunch • To crush something into a soft mess is to **mash** or **pulp** it. • To crush something into a powder is to **grind**

or **pulverize** it. • To crush something out of shape is to **crumple** or **smash** it.
2. *Our soldiers crushed the attacking army.* • defeat, conquer, vanquish, overcome, overwhelm, quash, trounce, rout

crush noun
There was a crush of people at the front gates. • crowd, press, mob, throng, jam, horde

cry verb cries, crying, cried
1. *Someone was crying for help from inside the burning house.* • call, shout, yell, exclaim, roar, bawl, bellow, scream, screech, shriek
2. *The baby started to cry when she dropped her rattle.* • sob, weep, bawl, blubber, wail, shed tears, snivel • When someone starts to cry, their eyes **well up with tears**.

cry noun cries
The wounded man let out a cry of pain. • call, shout, yell, roar, howl, exclamation, bellow, scream, screech, shriek, yelp

cuddle verb
My baby brother cuddles a teddy bear in bed. • hug, hold closely, clasp, embrace, caress, nestle against, snuggle against

culprit noun
Police are searching for the culprits. • criminal, offender, wrongdoer

culture noun
The exhibition is about the culture of ancient Greece. • civilization, society, traditions, customs, learning, arts

cunning adjective
The pirates had a cunning plan to seize the ship. • clever, crafty, devious, wily, ingenious, shrewd, artful, scheming, sly, tricky

cup noun
• A tall cup with straight sides is a **mug**. • A tall cup without a handle is a **beaker** or **tumbler**. • A decorative drinking cup is a **goblet**.

cure verb
1. *These pills will cure your headache.* • ease, heal, help, improve, make better, relieve **opposite** aggravate
2. *No one can cure the problem with my computer.* • correct, mend, sort, repair, fix, put an end to, put right

cure noun
I wish they could find a cure for colds. • remedy, treatment, antidote, medicine, therapy

curious adjective
1. *We were all very curious about the secret chamber.* • inquisitive, inquiring, interested (in) intrigued, agog • An uncomplimentary word is **nosy**. **opposite** uninterested, indifferent
2. *What is that curious smell?* • odd, strange, peculiar, abnormal, unusual, extraordinary, funny, mysterious, puzzling, weird

curl verb
1. *The snake curled itself around a branch.* • wind, twist, loop, coil, wrap, curve, turn, twine
2. *Steam curled upwards from the cauldron.* • coil, spiral, twirl, swirl, furl, snake, writhe, ripple

curl noun
1. *The girl's hair was a mass of golden curls.* • wave, ringlet, coil, loop, twist, roll
2. *Curls of smoke rose up from the campfire.* • coil, spiral, twist, scroll

curly adjective curlier, curliest
My new doll has curly black hair. • curled, curling, wavy, frizzy, crinkly, ringleted **opposite** straight

current noun
The wooden raft drifted along with the current. • flow, tide, stream • A current of air is a **draught**.

current adjective
1. *The shop sells all the current teenage fashions.* • modern, contemporary, present-day, up to date, topical, prevailing, prevalent **opposite** past, old-fashioned
2. *Have you got a current passport?* • valid, usable, up-to-date **opposite** out-of-date
3. *Who is the current prime minister?* • present, existing **opposite** past, former

curse noun
1. *Long ago, a wizard put a curse on the family.* • jinx, hex
2. *When the gardener hit his finger, he let out a curse.* • swearword, oath

curve noun
Try to draw a straight line without any curves. • bend, curl, loop, turn, twist, arch, arc, bow, bulge, wave • A curve in the shape of a new moon is a **crescent**. • A curve on a road surface is a **camber**.

curve verb
The road ahead curves round to the right. • bend, wind, turn, twist, curl, loop, swerve, veer, snake, meander

curved *adjective*
The wall was painted with a series of **curved** *lines.* • curving, curvy, curled, looped, coiled, rounded, bulging, bent, arched, bowed, twisted, crooked, spiral, winding, meandering, serpentine, snaking, undulating • A surface which is curved like the inside of a circle is **concave**. • A surface which is curved like the outside of a circle is **convex**.

custom *noun*
1. *It's our* **custom** *to give presents at Christmas.* • tradition, practice, habit, convention, fashion, routine, way
2. *The shop is having a sale to attract more* **custom**. • customers, buyers, trade, business

customer *noun*
There was a queue of **customers** *at the checkout.* • buyer, shopper, client

cut *verb* **cutting, cut**
1. *The woodcutter* **cut** *the tree trunk to make logs.* • chop, slit, split, chip, notch, axe, hack, hew, cleave • To cut off a limb is to **amputate** or **sever** it. • To cut down a tree is to **fell** it. • To cut branches off a tree is to **lop** them. • To cut twigs off a growing plant is to **prune** it. • To cut something up to examine it is to **dissect** it. • To cut stone to make a statue is to **carve** it. • To cut an inscription in stone is to **engrave** it.
2. *The cook* **cut** *the apples into small pieces.* • chop, slice, dice, grate, mince, shred
3. *I'm going to get my hair* **cut** *in the holidays.* • trim, clip, crop, snip, shave • To cut wool off a sheep is to **shear** it. • To cut grass is to **mow** it. • To cut corn is to **harvest** or **reap** it.
4. *Josh* **cut** *his foot on a sharp stone.* • gash, slash, nick, stab, pierce, wound
5. *This letter is too long—I'll need to* **cut** *it.* • shorten, condense, edit
6. *The shop has* **cut** *its prices by 10%.* • lower, reduce, decrease • If you cut something by half, you **halve** it.

cut *noun*
I got a nasty **cut** *when I was slicing bread.* • gash, wound, injury, nick, slash, scratch, slit, snip

Dd

Discover how to describe *detectives*, *dinosaurs* and *dragons* using this thesaurus.

damage verb
Many books were damaged in the fire.
• harm, spoil, mar, break, impair, weaken, disfigure, deface, mutilate, scar
• To damage something beyond repair is to **destroy**, **ruin** or **wreck** it. • To damage something deliberately is to **sabotage** or **vandalize** it.

damp adjective
1. *Don't wear those clothes if they are damp.*
• moist, soggy, clammy, dank
2. *I don't like this damp weather.* • drizzly, foggy, misty, rainy, wet • Weather which is both damp and warm is **humid** or **muggy** weather. **opposite** dry

dance noun

WORD WEB

SOME KINDS OF DANCE OR DANCING
• ballet, ballroom dancing, barn dance, belly-dancing, bolero, break-dancing, cancan, disco, flamenco, folk dance, Highland dancing, hornpipe, jazz dance, jig, jive dancing, limbo dancing, line-dancing, mazurka, morris dance, quadrille, reel, rumba, samba, Scottish country dancing, square dance, step dancing, street dance, tap dancing, tarantella
• A person who writes the steps for a dance is a **choreographer**.

SOME BALLROOM DANCES
• foxtrot, minuet, polka, quickstep, tango, waltz

GATHERINGS WHERE PEOPLE DANCE
• ball, ceilidh, club, disco

dance verb
I could have danced for joy. • caper, cavort, frisk, frolic, gambol, hop about, jig about, jump about, leap, prance, skip, whirl

danger noun
1. *Who knows what dangers lie ahead?* • peril, jeopardy, trouble, crisis, hazard, menace, pitfall, threat, trap **opposite** safety
2. *The forecast says there's a danger of frost.*
• chance, possibility, risk

dangerous adjective
1. *We were in a dangerous situation.*
• hazardous, perilous, risky, precarious, treacherous, unsafe, alarming, menacing, (informal) hairy
2. *The police arrested him for dangerous driving.* • careless, reckless
3. *A dangerous criminal had escaped from prison.* • violent, desperate, ruthless, treacherous
4. *The factory had emptied dangerous chemicals into the river.* • harmful, poisonous, deadly, toxic **opposite** harmless, safe

dangle verb
There was a bunch of keys dangling from the chain. • hang, swing, sway, droop, wave about, flap, trail

dare verb
1. *I wouldn't dare to make a parachute jump.*
• have the courage, take the risk
2. *They dared me to climb the tree.*
• challenge, defy

daring adjective
It was a very daring plan. • bold, brave, adventurous, courageous, fearless, intrepid, plucky, valiant • A daring person is a **daredevil**. **opposite** timid

dark adjective
1. *It was a very dark night.* • black, dim, murky, shadowy, gloomy, dingy **opposite** bright
2. *She wore a dark green coat.* **opposite** pale, light

dash verb
1. *We dashed home because it was raining.*
• hurry, run, rush, race, hasten, sprint, speed, tear, zoom

2. *She dashed her cup against the wall.*
• throw, hurl, knock, smash

data *plural noun*
I entered all the data into the computer.
• information, details, facts • Data can be in the form of **figures**, **numbers** or **statistics**.

dawn *noun*
1. *I was woken at dawn by the birds singing outside.* • daybreak, sunrise, first light
opposite dusk, sunset
2. *It was the dawn of the modern age.*
• beginning, start, birth, origin

day *noun*
1. *Badgers sleep during the day.* • daytime
opposite night
2. *Things were different in my grandfather's day.* • age, time, era, epoch, period

dazed *adjective*
He had a dazed expression on his face.
• confused, bewildered, muddled, perplexed

dazzle *verb*
1. *My eyes were dazzled by the bright lights.*
• daze, blind
2. *The acrobats dazzled the audience with their skill.* • amaze, astonish, impress, fascinate, awe

dead *adjective*
1. *Dead fish were floating in the river.*
• deceased, lifeless • Instead of 'the king who has just died', you can say 'the **late** king'.
• A dead body is a **corpse**. • The dead body of an animal is a **carcass**. • A common simile is **as dead as a doornail. opposite** alive
2. *This battery is dead.* • flat, not working, worn out
3. *The seaside resort is dead in winter.* • dull, boring, uninteresting, lifeless, tedious, flat, dreary **opposite** lively

deaden *verb*
1. *The dentist gave me an injection to deaden the pain.* • anaesthetize, lessen, reduce, suppress **opposite** increase
2. *Double glazing deadens the noise of the traffic.* • dampen, muffle, quieten
opposite amplify

deadly *adjective* **deadlier, deadliest**
The witch gave her a deadly dose of poison.
• lethal, fatal, harmful, dangerous, destructive
opposite harmless

deafening *adjective*
We complained about the deafening noise.
• loud, blaring, booming, thunderous, penetrating

deal *verb* **dealing, dealt**
1. *Who is going to deal the cards?* • give out, distribute, share out
2. *My uncle used to deal in second-hand cars.*
• do business, trade
to deal with something
1. *I can deal with this problem.* • cope with, sort out, attend to, see to, handle, manage, control, grapple with, look after, solve
2. *The book deals with the history of Rome.*
• be concerned with, cover, explain about

deal *noun*
She made a deal with the garage for her new car. • arrangement, agreement, contract, bargain

dear *adjective*
1. *She is a very dear friend.* • close, loved, valued, beloved **opposite** distant
2. *I didn't buy the watch because it was too dear.* • expensive, costly, *(informal)* pricey
opposite cheap

debate *noun*
We had a debate about animal rights.
• discussion, argument, dispute • Something which people argue about a lot is a **controversy**.

debate *verb*
1. *We debated whether it is right to kill animals for food.* • discuss, argue
2. *I debated what to do next.* • consider, ponder, deliberate, weigh up, reflect on

decay *verb*
Dead leaves fall to the ground and decay.
• decompose, rot, disintegrate, break down

deceit *noun*
I saw through his deceit. • deception, trickery, dishonesty, fraud, duplicity, double-dealing, pretence, bluff, cheating, deceitfulness, lying
opposite honesty

deceitful *adjective*
Don't trust him—he's a deceitful person.
• dishonest, underhand, insincere, duplicitous, false, cheating, hypocritical, lying, treacherous, two-faced, sneaky
opposite honest

deceive *verb*
The spy had been deceiving them for years.
• fool, trick, delude, dupe, hoodwink, cheat,

double-cross, mislead, swindle, take in, (informal) con, diddle

decent *adjective*
1. *I did the decent thing and owned up.*
• honest, honourable
2. *The coat was the only decent thing I had to wear.* • polite, proper, respectable, acceptable, appropriate, suitable, fitting **opposite** indecent
3. *I haven't had a decent meal for ages!*
• satisfactory, agreeable, good, nice **opposite** bad

deceptive *adjective*
Appearances can be deceptive. • misleading, unreliable, false

decide *verb*
1. *We decided to finish our work instead of going out to play.* • choose, make a decision, make up your mind, opt, elect, resolve
2. *The referee decided that the player was offside.* • conclude, judge, rule
3. *The last lap decided the result of the race.*
• determine, settle

decision *noun*
1. *Can you tell me what your decision is?*
• choice, preference
2. *The judge announced his decision.*
• conclusion, judgement, verdict, findings

decisive *adjective*
1. *A decisive piece of evidence proved that he was innocent.* • crucial, convincing, definite **opposite** uncertain
2. *A referee needs to be decisive.* • firm, forceful, strong-minded, resolute, quick-thinking **opposite** hesitant

declare *verb*
He declared that he was innocent. • announce, state, assert, make known, pronounce, proclaim, swear

decline *verb*
1. *Our enthusiasm declined as the day went on.* • become less, decrease, diminish, lessen, weaken, dwindle, flag, wane, tail off **opposite** increase
2. *I offered to help, but he declined the offer.*
• refuse, reject, turn down **opposite** accept

decorate *verb*
1. *We decorated the Christmas tree with tinsel.*
• ornament, adorn, beautify, prettify, deck, festoon • To decorate a dish of food is to **garnish** it. • To decorate clothes with lace or ribbon is to **trim** them.

2. *Dad is going to decorate my bedroom next weekend.* • paint, paper, wallpaper, (informal) do up, make over
3. *The firefighters were decorated for their bravery.* • award or give a medal to, honour, reward

decrease *verb*
1. *The jet decreased its speed as it came in to land.* • reduce, cut, lower, slacken
2. *Our enthusiasm decreased as the day went on.* • become less, decline, decrease, diminish, lessen, weaken, dwindle, flag, wane, tail off, shrink, subside **opposite** increase

dedicate *verb*
He dedicates himself entirely to his art.
• commit, devote

deduce *verb*
The detective deduced that the footprints were fresh. • conclude, work out, infer, reason, gather

deed *noun*
They thanked the rescue team for their heroic deed. • act, action, feat, exploit, effort, achievement

deep *adjective*
1. *The pond is quite deep in the middle.* **opposite** shallow
2. *The letter expressed his deep regret.*
• intense, earnest, genuine, sincere **opposite** insincere
3. *Veronica fell into a deep sleep.* • heavy, sound **opposite** light
4. *The actor spoke in a deep and sombre voice.*
• low, bass **opposite** high

deer *noun* deer
• A male deer is a **buck**, **hart**, **roebuck** or **stag**.
• A female deer is a **doe** or **hind**. • A young deer is a **fawn**. • Deer's flesh used as food is **venison**.

defeat *verb*
The Greeks attacked and defeated the Trojans.
• beat, conquer, vanquish, triumph over, win a victory over, overcome, overpower, crush, rout, trounce • To defeat someone in chess is to **checkmate** them. • To be defeated is to **lose**.

defeat *noun*
The team suffered a humiliating defeat.
• failure, humiliation, rout, trouncing **opposite** victory

a b c d e f g h i j k l m n o p q r s t u v w x y z

defect noun
Cars are tested for defects before they leave the factory. • fault, flaw, imperfection, shortcoming, failure, weakness • A defect in a computer program is a **bug**.

defective adjective
If the goods are defective, take them back to the shop. • faulty, damaged, imperfect, out of order **opposite** perfect

defence noun
1. *What was the accused woman's defence?* • justification, excuse, explanation, argument, case
2. *The castle was built as a defence against enemy attack.* • protection, guard, safeguard, fortification, barricade, shield

defend verb
1. *They tried to defend themselves against the enemy.* • protect, guard, keep safe **opposite** attack
2. *He gave a speech defending his actions.* • justify, support, stand up for, make a case for **opposite** accuse

defiant adjective
The prisoner cursed with a defiant look in his eye. • rebellious, insolent, aggressive, challenging, disobedient, obstinate, quarrelsome, uncooperative, stubborn, mutinous **opposite** submissive, compliant

definite adjective
1. *Is it definite that we're going to move?* • certain, sure, fixed, settled, decided
2. *The doctor saw definite signs of improvement.* • clear, distinct, noticeable, obvious, marked, positive, pronounced, unmistakable **opposite** indefinite

definitely adverb
I'll definitely phone you tomorrow. • certainly, for certain, positively, surely, unquestionably, without doubt, without fail **opposite** perhaps

deflect verb
The goalkeeper was able to deflect the shot. • divert, turn aside, intercept, avert, fend off, ward off

defy verb **defies, defying, defied**
1. *The rebel army decided to defy the king.* • disobey, refuse to obey, resist, stand up to, confront **opposite** obey
2. *I defy you to come up with a better idea.* • challenge, dare
3. *The jammed door defied our efforts to open it.* • resist, withstand, defeat, frustrate, beat

degree noun
The young gymnast showed a high degree of skill. • standard, level, grade, measure, extent

delay verb
1. *Don't let me delay you.* • detain, hold up, keep waiting, make late, hinder, slow down
2. *They delayed the race because of bad weather.* • postpone, put off, defer
3. *You'll miss the bus if you delay.* • hesitate, linger, pause, wait, dawdle, loiter, (informal) hang about or around, drag your feet

delay noun
There has been a delay with the building work. • hold-up, wait, pause

deliberate adjective
1. *That remark was a deliberate insult.* • intentional, planned, calculated, conscious, premeditated **opposite** accidental, unintentional
2. *He walked with deliberate steps across the room.* • careful, steady, cautious, slow, unhurried **opposite** hasty, careless

deliberately adverb
Did you say that deliberately to hurt my feelings? • on purpose, intentionally, wilfully **opposite** accidentally, unintentionally

delicate adjective
1. *The blouse has delicate embroidery on the cuffs.* • dainty, exquisite, intricate, neat
2. *Take care not to damage the delicate material.* • fragile, fine, flimsy, thin
3. *Delicate plants should be protected from frost.* • sensitive, tender **opposite** tough, hardy
4. *The child was born with a delicate constitution.* • frail, weak, feeble, sickly, unhealthy **opposite** strong
5. *The pianist's fingers had a delicate touch.* • gentle, light, soft

delicious adjective
The food at the banquet was delicious. • tasty, appetizing, mouth-watering, delectable, (informal) scrumptious, yummy **opposite** horrible, disgusting

delight noun
Imagine my delight when I saw my friend again! • happiness, joy, pleasure, enjoyment, bliss, ecstasy

delight verb
The puppet show delighted the children. • please, charm, entertain, amuse, divert, enchant, entrance, fascinate, thrill **opposite** dismay

delighted *adjective*
The delighted crowd cheered the winners.
• pleased, happy, joyful, thrilled, ecstatic, elated, exultant

deliver *verb*
1. *Does anyone deliver mail to the island?*
• convey, bring, hand over, distribute, present, supply, take round
2. *The head delivered a lecture on good behaviour.* • give, make, read out

delude *verb*
He deluded us into thinking he was very rich.
• deceive, fool, trick, mislead, hoax, bluff, (informal) con

demand *verb*
1. *I demanded a refund for my train fare.*
• insist on, claim, call for, require, want
2. *'What do you want?' demanded a voice inside.* • ask, enquire, inquire

demand *noun*
1. *The king refused the demands of his people.*
• request, claim, requirement
2. *There is not much demand for ice lollies in winter.* • need, call

demolish *verb*
They demolished a building to make way for the road. • destroy, flatten, knock down, level, pull down, tear down, bulldoze
opposite build, construct

demonstrate *verb*
1. *The teacher demonstrated how warm air rises.* • show, exhibit, illustrate
2. *Animal rights campaigners were demonstrating in the street.* • protest, march, parade

demonstration *noun*
1. *I watched a demonstration of the new computer game.* • show, display, presentation
2. *Everyone joined the demonstration against world poverty.* • protest, rally, march, parade (informal) demo

den *noun*
We built a den in the garden. • hideout, shelter, hiding place, secret place • The den of a wild animal is its **lair**.

dense *adjective*
1. *The accident happened in dense fog.* • thick, heavy
2. *A dense crowd waited in the square.*
• compact, packed, solid
3. *I'm being rather dense today!* • stupid, slow

dent *noun*
There was a large dent in the car door.
• indentation, depression, hollow, dip, dimple

deny *verb* denies, denying, denied
1. *The boy denied that he had stolen the money.* • reject, dispute, disagree with, contradict, dismiss, oppose
opposite admit, accept
2. *Her parents don't deny her anything.*
• refuse, deprive of, withhold **opposite** give

depart *verb*
1. *What time is the train due to depart?*
• leave, set off, get going, set out, start, begin a journey **opposite** arrive, get in
2. *It looks as if the robbers departed in a hurry.*
• leave, exit, go away, retreat, withdraw, make off, (informal) clear off, scram, scarper
opposite arrive

depend *verb*
to depend on someone
I depend on you to help me. • rely on, count on, bank on, trust
to depend on something
My success will depend on good luck. • be decided by, rest on, hinge on

dependable *adjective*
Are these friends of yours dependable?
• reliable, trustworthy, loyal, faithful, trusty, honest, sound, steady **opposite** unreliable

depict *verb*
1. *She depicted the landscape in watercolours.*
• draw, paint, sketch
2. *The film depicts the horror of war.* • show, represent, portray, describe, illustrate, outline

deplore *verb*
We all deplore cruelty to animals. • condemn, disapprove of, hate

depress *verb*
The miserable weather was depressing us.
• sadden, discourage, dishearten, dispirit
opposite cheer

depressed *adjective*
After his friends left, he began to feel depressed. • disheartened, dejected, discouraged, downcast, downhearted, unhappy, sad, low, gloomy, glum, melancholy, miserable, despondent, desolate, in despair, (informal) down **opposite** cheerful

deputy *noun* **deputies**
The sheriff appointed a new deputy.
• second-in-command, assistant, stand-in, substitute

> Words with the prefix *vice* often mean 'the deputy for a particular person', e.g. *vice-captain, vice-president.*

derelict *adjective*
They plan to pull down those derelict buildings.
• dilapidated, crumbling, decrepit, neglected, deserted, abandoned, ruined

derive *verb*
1. *Bill derives a lot of pleasure from his garden.*
• get, obtain, receive, gain
2. *She derived many of her ideas from books.*
• borrow, draw, pick up, take, *(informal)* lift

descend *verb*
1. *After admiring the view, we began to descend the mountain.* • climb down, come down, go down, move down • To descend through the air is to **drop** or **fall**. • To descend through water is to **sink**.
2. *The road descends gradually into the valley.*
• drop, fall, slope, dip, incline **opposite** ascend
to be descended from someone
She's descended from a French family. • come from, originate from

descent *noun*
The path makes a steep descent into the valley. • drop, fall, dip, incline **opposite** ascent

describe *verb*
1. *An eyewitness described how the accident happened.* • report, tell about, depict, explain, outline
2. *Friends described him as a quiet, shy man.*
• portray, characterize, represent, present

description *noun*
1. *I wrote a description of our day at the seaside.* • report, account, story
2. *Write a description of your favourite character in the play.* • portrait, representation, sketch

descriptive *adjective*
The author writes in a very descriptive style.
• expressive, colourful, detailed, graphic, vivid

desert *verb*
He deserted his friends when they needed him most. • abandon, leave, forsake, betray, *(informal)* walk out on • To desert someone in a place they can't get away from is to **maroon** or **strand** them.

deserted *adjective*
By midnight, the streets of the town were deserted. • empty, unoccupied, uninhabited, vacant **opposite** crowded

deserve *verb*
You deserve a break after all your hard work.
• be worthy of, be entitled to, have earned, merit, warrant

design *noun*
1. *This is the winning design for the new art gallery.* • plan, drawing, outline, blueprint, sketch • A first example of something, used as a model for making others, is a **prototype**.
2. *Do you like the design of this wallpaper?*
• style, pattern, arrangement, composition

design *verb*
She designs all her own clothes. • create, develop, invent, devise, conceive, think up

desire *verb*
The magic mirror will show you what you most desire. • wish for, long for, want, crave, fancy, hanker after, yearn for, pine for, set your heart on, have a yen for

desire *noun*
My greatest desire is to swim with dolphins.
• wish, want, longing, ambition, craving, fancy, hankering, urge, yearning • A desire for food is **appetite** or **hunger**. • A desire for drink is **thirst**. • Excessive desire for money or other things is **greed**.

desolate *adjective*
1. *Jamie felt desolate when his dog died.*
• depressed, dejected, miserable, sad, melancholy, hopeless, wretched, forlorn **opposite** cheerful
2. *No one wants to live in that desolate place.* • bleak, depressing, dreary, gloomy, dismal, cheerless, inhospitable, deserted, uninhabited, abandoned, godforsaken **opposite** pleasant

despair *noun*
The defeated knight was overcome by despair. • depression, desperation, gloom, hopelessness, misery, anguish, dejection, melancholy, pessimism, wretchedness **opposite** hope

desperate *adjective*
1. *The shipwrecked crew were in a desperate situation.* • difficult, critical, grave, serious, severe, drastic, dire, urgent, extreme

2. *The hills were home to a band of desp, desperate outlaws.* • dangerous, violent, reckless

despise *verb*
I despise people who cheat at cards. • hate, loathe, feel contempt for, deride, have a low opinion of, look down on, scorn, sneer at **opposite** admire

destined *adjective*
1. *It was destined that he would become a famous actor.* • fated, doomed, intended, meant, certain, inevitable, unavoidable, inescapable
2. *This parcel is destined for Japan.* • bound, directed, intended, headed

destiny *noun* **destinies**
Was it destiny that brought us together? • fate, fortune

destroy *verb*
1. *An avalanche destroyed the village.* • demolish, devastate, crush, flatten, knock down, level, pull down, shatter, smash, sweep away
2. *He tried to destroy the good work we had done.* • ruin, wreck, sabotage, undo

destruction *noun*
1. *The hurricane caused destruction all along the coast.* • devastation, damage, demolition, ruin, wrecking **opposite** creation
2. *Global warming may cause the destruction of many animal species.* • elimination, annihilation, obliteration, extermination, extinction **opposite** conservation

detach *verb*
The camera lens can be detached for cleaning. • remove, separate, disconnect, take off, release, undo, unfasten, part • To detach a caravan from a vehicle is to **unhitch** it. • To detach railway wagons from a locomotive is to **uncouple** them. • To detach something by cutting it off is to **sever** it. **opposite** attach

detail *noun*
Her account of what happened was accurate in every detail. • fact, feature, particular, aspect, item, point, respect

detect *verb*
I could detect the smell of burning in the air. • identify, recognize, spot, find, discover, reveal, diagnose, track down

detective *noun*

WORD WEB

Detective Dewar solved the case of the stolen tiara. • investigator, sleuth, (informal) private eye

THINGS A DETECTIVE MIGHT LOOK FOR
• clues, evidence, eyewitness, fingerprints, footprints, murder weapon, tracks; criminal, crook, culprit, felon, suspect, mastermind

THINGS A DETECTIVE MIGHT DO
• analyse, comb (an area), deduce, detect, dig up, ferret out, follow a hunch, follow a lead or a tip-off, interrogate or question (a witness), investigate, pursue, shadow, solve (a case) stake out (a hiding place), tail or track down (a suspect) • An informal name for a story in which a detective solves a crime is a **whodunnit**.

deter *verb* **deterring, deterred**
How can we deter birds from eating the pears? • discourage, put off, dissuade, prevent, stop **opposite** encourage

deteriorate *verb*
1. *The queen's health had begun to deteriorate.* • worsen, decline, degenerate, get worse, go downhill
2. *The walls will deteriorate if we don't maintain them.* • decay, disintegrate, crumble **opposite** improve

determination *noun*
Marathon runners show great determination.
• resolve, commitment, will power, courage, dedication, drive, grit, perseverance, persistence, spirit, *(informal)* guts

determined *adjective*
1. *Boudicca must have been a very determined woman.* • resolute, decisive, firm, strong-minded, assertive, persistent, tough **opposite** weak-minded
2. *I was determined to finish the race.*
• committed, resolved

detest *verb*
I detest the smell of boiled cabbage. • dislike, hate, loathe • Informal expressions are **can't bear** and **can't stand. opposite** love

develop *verb*
1. *The zoo is developing its education programme.* • expand, extend, enlarge, build up, diversify
2. *Her piano playing has developed this year.*
• improve, progress, evolve, advance, get better
3. *Plants need light and water to develop properly.* • grow, flourish
4. *Bruno had developed the habit of ignoring most of his sister's questions.* • get, acquire, pick up, cultivate

device *noun*
The TV comes with a remote control device. • tool, implement, instrument, appliance, apparatus, gadget, contraption, *(informal)* gizmo

devious *adjective*
1. *The mad professor had a devious plan to take over the world.* • cunning, deceitful, dishonest, furtive, scheming, sly, sneaky, treacherous, wily
2. *Because of the roadworks, we took a devious route home.* • indirect, roundabout, winding, meandering **opposite** direct

devise *verb*
We need to devise a strategy for Saturday's game. • conceive, form, invent, contrive, formulate, come up with, make up, plan, prepare, map out, think out, think up

devoted *adjective*
She's a devoted supporter of our team. • loyal, faithful, dedicated, enthusiastic, committed **opposite** apathetic

devour *verb*
He devoured a whole plateful of sandwiches.
• eat, consume, guzzle, gobble up, gulp down, swallow, *(informal)* scoff, wolf down

diagram *noun*
We drew a diagram of the life cycle of a frog.
• chart, plan, sketch, outline

diary *noun* diaries
I wrote all about my birthday party in my diary.
• journal, daily record • A diary describing a voyage or mission is a **log** or **logbook**.
• A diary in which you insert pictures and souvenirs is a **scrapbook**. • A diary published on a website is a **blog**.

die *verb* dying, died
1. *My sister's hamster died last week.*
• expire, pass away, perish, lose your life, *(informal)* snuff it, drop dead, kick the bucket, croak • To die of hunger is to **starve**. • To die in water is to **drown**.
2. *The flowers will die if they don't have water.*
• wither, wilt, droop, fade
to die out
When did the dinosaurs die out? • become extinct, cease to exist, come to an end, disappear, vanish

differ *verb*
The two men differed in their beliefs.
• disagree, conflict, argue, clash, contradict each other, oppose each other, quarrel **opposite** agree
to differ from
My style of painting differs from hers. • be different from, contrast with

difference *noun*
1. *Can you see any difference between these two colours?* • contrast, distinction **opposite** similarity
2. *This money will make a great difference to their lives.* • change, alteration, modification, variation

different *adjective*
1. *We have different views about global warming.* • differing, contradictory, opposite, clashing, conflicting,
2. *It's important that the teams wear different colours.* • contrasting, dissimilar, distinguishable
3. *The packet contains sweets of different flavours.* • various, assorted, mixed, several, diverse, numerous, miscellaneous
4. *Let's go somewhere different on holiday this year.* • new, original, fresh

5. *Everyone's handwriting is different.*
• distinct, distinctive, individual, special, unique

difficult *adjective*
1. *This crossword is really difficult. We were faced with a difficult problem.* • hard, complicated, complex, involved, intricate, baffling, perplexing, puzzling, *(informal)* tricky, thorny, knotty **opposite** simple
2. *It is a difficult climb to the top of the hill.* • challenging, arduous, demanding, taxing, exhausting, formidable, gruelling, laborious, strenuous, tough **opposite** easy
3. *Mum says I was a difficult child when I was little.* • troublesome, awkward, trying, tiresome, annoying, disruptive, obstinate, stubborn, uncooperative, unhelpful **opposite** cooperative

difficulty *noun* **difficulties**
1. *The explorers were used to facing difficulty.* • trouble, adversity, challenges, hardship
2. *We are experiencing some difficulties with the spaceship.* • problem, complication, hitch, obstacle, snag

dig *verb* **digging, dug**
1. *We spent the afternoon digging the garden.* • cultivate, fork over, turn over
2. *Rabbits dig holes in the ground.* • burrow, excavate, tunnel, gouge, hollow out, scoop out
3. *Did you dig me in the back?* • poke, prod, jab

dignified *adjective*
Lady Snodgrass was a very dignified old lady. • refined, stately, distinguished, noble, sedate, solemn, proper, grave, grand, august **opposite** undignified

dignity *noun*
1. *Their laughter spoilt the dignity of the occasion.* • formality, seriousness, solemnity
2. *She handled the problem with dignity.* • calmness, poise, self-control

dim *adjective* **dimmer, dimmest**
1. *I could see the dim outline of a figure in the mist.* • indistinct, faint, blurred, fuzzy, hazy, shadowy, vague **opposite** clear
2. *The light in the cave was rather dim.* • dark, dull, dingy, murky, gloomy **opposite** bright

din *noun*
I can't hear you because of that awful din! • noise, racket, row, clatter, hullabaloo

dingy *adjective* **dingier, dingiest**
How can we brighten up this dingy room? • dull, drab, dreary, dowdy, colourless, dismal, gloomy, murky **opposite** bright

dinosaur *noun*

WORD WEB

SOME TYPES OF DINOSAUR
• apatosaurus, archaeopteryx, brachiosaurus, diplodocus, gallimimus, iguanodon, megalosaurus, pterodactylus, stegosaurus, triceratops, tyrannosaurus rex, velociraptor

BODY PARTS WHICH A DINOSAUR MAY HAVE
• bony frill, crest, dorsal plates, fleshy fin, horn, wings • A person who studies dinosaurs and other fossils is a **palaeontologist**.

dip *verb* **dipping, dipped**
I dipped my hand in the water. • immerse, lower, plunge, submerge, dunk

dip *noun*
1. *There was a dip in the road ahead.* • hollow, hole, depression, slope
2. *It was so hot we decided to have a dip in the sea.* • swim, bathe

dire *adjective*
1. *The survivors were in a* **dire** *situation.*
• dreadful, terrible, awful, appalling, severe, grave, drastic, extreme
2. *After weeks of drought, the garden is in* **dire** *need of rain.* • urgent, desperate, pressing, sore

direct *adjective*
1. *It would be quicker to take the* **direct** *route.*
• straight, shortest **opposite** indirect
2. *Please give me a* **direct** *answer.*
• straightforward, frank, honest, sincere, blunt, plain, outspoken, candid, unambiguous **opposite** evasive

direct *verb*
1. *Can you* **direct** *me to the station?* • guide, point, show the way, give directions to
2. *A new manager has been apppointed to* **direct** *the company.* • manage, run, be in charge of, control, administer, superintend, supervise, take charge of • To direct an orchestra is to **conduct** it.
3. *The conductor* **directed** *us to begin playing.*
• instruct, command, order, tell

dirt *noun*
1. *The floor was covered in* **dirt**. • filth, grime, mess, muck, mud, dust
2. *Chickens scratched about in the* **dirt**. • earth, soil, clay, loam, mud

dirty *adjective* **dirtier, dirtiest**
1. *Those* **dirty** *clothes need to be washed.*
• unclean, filthy, grimy, grubby, soiled, stained, messy, mucky, muddy, sooty, foul, *(informal)* manky, grotty **opposite** clean
2. *We refused to drink the* **dirty** *water.*
• impure, polluted, murky, cloudy **opposite** pure
3. *The other team used* **dirty** *tactics.* • unfair, dishonest, illegal, mean, unsporting **opposite** honest
4. *The comedian used a lot of* **dirty** *words.*
• rude, offensive, coarse, crude, improper, indecent, obscene **opposite** decent

disadvantage *noun*
It's a **disadvantage** *to be small if you play basketball.* • drawback, handicap, hindrance, inconvenience, downside, snag

disagree *verb*
My sister and I often **disagree** *about music.*
• argue, differ, clash, quarrel, squabble, bicker, fall out **opposite** agree
to disagree with
He **disagrees with** *everything I say.* • argue with, contradict, oppose, object to

disagreement *noun*
We had a **disagreement** *over who should pay for the meal.* • argument, dispute, difference of opinion, quarrel, row, clash, squabble, conflict **opposite** agreement

disappear *verb*
1. *The markings will* **disappear** *as the chicks grow older.* • become invisible, vanish, fade, clear, disperse, dissolve
2. *The thief* **disappeared** *around the corner.*
• run away, escape, flee, go away, withdraw **opposite** appear

disappoint *verb*
She didn't want to **disappoint** *her fans by cancelling the show.* • let down, fail, dissatisfy, displease, upset **opposite** please, satisfy

disappointed *adjective*
I'm **disappointed** *that you can't come to my party.* • saddened, unhappy, upset, let down, unsatisfied, displeased **opposite** pleased, satisfied

disapprove *verb*
to disapprove of
My aunt **disapproves of** *watching television.*
• object to, take exception to, dislike, deplore, condemn, criticize, denounce, frown on, *(informal)* take a dim view of **opposite** approve of

disaster *noun*
The trip turned into a complete **disaster**.
• calamity, catastrophe, tragedy, misfortune, mishap, blow

discard *verb*
I **discarded** *some of my old toys.* • get rid of, throw away, throw out, reject, cast off, dispose of, dump, scrap

discipline *noun*
Discipline *is important in the army.* • order, control

disclose *verb*
He never **disclosed** *the truth.* • reveal, tell, make known, confess, make public **opposite** conceal

discontented *adjective*
She felt very **discontented** *with her job.*
• dissatisfied, miserable, unhappy, upset, *(informal)* fed up **opposite** happy, satisfied

discourage *verb*
1. *Don't let her criticism* **discourage** *you.*
• demoralize, depress, *(informal)* put you off

2. *The burglar alarm will discourage thieves.*
• deter, dissuade, prevent, restrain, stop, hinder

discover verb
I discovered some old toys in the attic. • find, come across, spot, stumble across, uncover
• To discover something that has been buried is to **unearth** it. • To discover something that has been under water is to **dredge it up**.
• To discover something you have been pursuing is to **track it down**. **opposite** hide

discovery noun discoveries
Scientists have made an exciting new discovery. • find, breakthrough

discriminate verb
It's sometimes hard to discriminate between poisonous mushrooms and edible ones.
• distinguish, tell the difference
to discriminate against
It's wrong to discriminate against people because of their age. • be biased against, be intolerant of, be prejudiced against

discrimination noun
The school has policies against any kind of discrimination. • prejudice, bias, intolerance, unfairness • Discrimination against people because of their sex is **sexism**.
• Discrimination against people because of their race is **racism**. • Discrimination against people because of their age is **ageism**.

discuss verb
I discussed the idea with my parents. • talk about, confer about, debate

discussion noun
We had a lively discussion about pocket money. • conversation, argument, exchange of views • A formal discussion is a **conference** or **debate**.

disease noun
He was suffering from a serious disease.
• illness, ailment, sickness, complaint, affliction, (informal) bug

disgrace noun
1. *He never got over the disgrace of being caught cheating.* • humiliation, shame, embarrassment, dishonour
2. *The way he treats them is a disgrace!*
• outrage, scandal

disgraceful adjective
We were shocked by her disgraceful behaviour.
• shameful, shocking, appalling, outrageous, scandalous **opposite** honourable

disguise verb
I tried to disguise my feelings. • conceal, hide, cover up, camouflage, mask
to disguise yourself as
The spy disguised himself as a hotel porter.
• dress up as, pretend to be

disguise noun
I didn't recognize him in that disguise.
• costume, camouflage, make-up, mask

disgust noun
The sight of the carcass filled me with disgust.
• repulsion, repugnance, distaste, dislike, horror, loathing, detestation **opposite** liking

disgust verb
The smell of rotten eggs disgusts me. • repel, revolt, sicken, appal, offend, distress, shock, horrify, (informal) put you off, turn your stomach **opposite** please

disgusting adjective
The brew in the cauldron looked disgusting. • repulsive, revolting, horrible, nasty, loathsome, repellent, repugnant, offensive, appalling, sickening, nauseating, (informal) yucky, icky, gross **opposite** delightful, pleasing

dishonest adjective
1. *They were taken in by a dishonest salesman.*
• deceitful, cheating, corrupt, disreputable, untrustworthy, immoral, lying, swindling, thieving, (informal) bent, crooked, dodgy, shady
2. *The author makes some dishonest claims.*
• false, misleading, untruthful, fraudulent, devious

dishonesty noun
The politician was accused of dishonesty.
• deceit, cheating, corruption, insincerity, lying, deviousness, (informal) crookedness **opposite** honesty

disintegrate verb
The cloth is so old that it's starting to disintegrate. • break up, fall apart, break into pieces, crumble, decay, decompose

dislike noun
His colleagues regarded him with intense dislike. • hatred, loathing, detestation, disapproval, disgust, revulsion **opposite** liking

dislike verb
I dislike people who hunt wild animals. • hate, loathe, detest, disapprove of **opposite** like

disloyal adjective
The rebels were accused of being disloyal to the king. • unfaithful, treacherous, faithless, false, unreliable, untrustworthy **opposite** loyal

dismal adjective
1. How can we brighten up this dismal room? • dull, drab, dreary, dingy, colourless, cheerless, gloomy, murky
opposite bright, cheerful
2. (informal) It was a dismal performance by the home team. • dreadful, awful, terrible, feeble, useless, hopeless, (informal) pathetic

dismay noun
The girls uttered a cry of dismay. • distress, alarm, shock, concern, anxiety, gloom

dismayed adjective
I was dismayed by the failure of our plan. • distressed, discouraged, depressed, devastated, shocked, appalled
opposite encouraged

dismiss verb
1. The teacher dismissed the class. • send away, discharge, free, let go, release
2. The firm has dismissed half its workers. • sack, give the sack, give notice to, make redundant, (informal) fire
3. The weather was so bad that we dismissed the idea of having a picnic. • discard, drop, reject

disobedient adjective
She said she had never known such a disobedient child. • naughty, badly behaved, undisciplined, uncontrollable, unmanageable, unruly, ungovernable, troublesome, defiant, disruptive, mutinous, rebellious, contrary
opposite obedient

disobey verb
1. You will be penalized if you disobey the rules. • break, ignore, disregard, defy, violate
2. Soldiers are trained never to disobey. • be disobedient, rebel, revolt, mutiny
opposite obey

disorder noun
1. The public meeting broke up in disorder. • disturbance, uproar, commotion, quarrelling, rioting, brawling, fighting, lawlessness, anarchy

2. It's time I tidied up the disorder in my room. • mess, muddle, untidiness, chaos, confusion, clutter, jumble **opposite** order

dispatch noun
The messenger brought a dispatch from headquarters. • message, communication, report, letter, bulletin

dispatch verb
The parcel has already been dispatched. • post, send, transmit

disperse verb
1. The police dispersed the crowd. • break up, send away, drive away, separate, send in different directions
2. The crowd dispersed quickly after the match. • scatter, spread out, disappear, dissolve, melt away, vanish **opposite** gather

display verb
We planned the best way to display our work. • demonstrate, exhibit, present, put on show, set out, show, show off • To display something boastfully is to **flaunt** it.

display noun
We set out a display of our art work. • exhibition, show, presentation, demonstration

dispose verb
to dispose of something
Let's dispose of this old carpet. • get rid of, discard, throw away, give away, scrap, (informal) dump

dispute noun
We settled the dispute about who should wash the dishes. • argument, disagreement, quarrel, debate, controversy, difference of opinion

disregard verb
I disregarded the doctor's advice. • ignore, pay no attention to, take no notice of, reject
opposite heed

disrespectful adjective
She was very disrespectful towards her parents. • rude, bad-mannered, insulting, impolite, insolent, cheeky **opposite** respectful

disrupt verb
Bad weather has disrupted the tennis tournament. • interrupt, upset, interfere with, throw into confusion or disorder

dissatisfied *adjective*
I was dissatisfied with my piano playing.
• displeased, disappointed, discontented, frustrated, annoyed **opposite** satisfied

distance *noun*
What is the distance from Earth to the Sun? • measurement, space, extent, reach, mileage • The distance across something is the **breadth** or **width**. • The distance along something is the **length**. • The distance between two points is a **gap** or **interval**.

distant *adjective*
1. *I'd love to travel to distant countries.*
• faraway, remote, out-of-the-way, inaccessible, exotic **opposite** close
2. *His distant manner puts me off.* • unfriendly, unapproachable, formal, reserved, withdrawn, cool, haughty, aloof **opposite** friendly

distinct *adjective*
1. *There is a distinct improvement in your handwriting.* • definite, evident, noticeable, obvious, perceptible **opposite** imperceptible
2. *It was a small photo, but the details were quite distinct.* • clear, distinguishable, plain, recognizable, sharp, unmistakable, visible, well-defined **opposite** indistinct
3. *Organize your essay into distinct sections.*
• individual, separate

distinctive *adjective*
We spotted the distinctive footprints of a yeti in the snow. • characteristic, recognizable, unmistakable, special, unique

distinguish *verb*
1. *It was impossible to distinguish one twin from the other.* • tell apart, pick out, discriminate, differentiate, make a distinction, decide
2. *In the dark we couldn't distinguish who was walking past.* • identify, tell, make out, determine, perceive, recognize, single out

distinguished *adjective*
1. *The school has a distinguished academic record.* • excellent, first-rate, outstanding, exceptional **opposite** ordinary
2. *He is a very distinguished actor.* • famous, celebrated, well-known, eminent, notable, prominent, renowned **opposite** unknown, obscure

distort *verb*
1. *When my bike hit the kerb, it distorted the wheel.* • bend, buckle, twist, warp, contort
2. *The newspaper distorted the facts of the story.* • twist, slant, misrepresent

distract *verb*
Don't distract the bus driver. • divert the attention of, disturb, put off

distress *verb*
We could see that the news had distressed her. • upset, disturb, trouble, worry, alarm, dismay, torment **opposite** comfort

distribute *verb*
1. *The coach distributed water to the players at half-time.* • give out, hand round, circulate, dispense, issue, share out, take round, (informal) dish out, doll out
2. *Distribute the seeds evenly.* • scatter, spread, disperse

district *noun*
Granny lives in a quiet district. • area, neighbourhood, locality, region, vicinity

distrust *verb*
I distrusted the professor from the moment I met him. • doubt, mistrust, question, suspect, be suspicious or wary of, be sceptical about, feel uncertain or uneasy or unsure about **opposite** trust

disturb *verb*
1. *Don't disturb the baby when she's asleep.*
• bother, interrupt, annoy, pester
2. *They were greatly disturbed by what they had heard.* • distress, trouble, upset, worry, alarm, frighten
3. *Please don't disturb the papers on my desk.*
• muddle, mix up, move around, mess about with

ditch *noun*
We dug a ditch to drain away the water.
• trench, channel, drain, gully

dive *verb*
1. *The mermaid dived into the water.* • plunge, jump, leap • A dive in which you land flat on your front is a **bellyflop**.
2. *The eagle dived towards its prey.* • pounce, swoop

diverse *adjective*
People from many diverse cultures live in the area. • different, differing, varied, various, contrasting

divide *verb*
1. *We divided the class into two groups.*
• separate, split, break up, move apart, part **opposite** combine
2. *I divided the cake between my friends.*
• distribute, share out, give out, allot, deal out, dispense

3. *Which way do we go? The path divides here.*
• branch, fork **opposite** converge

division noun
1. *The map shows the division of Europe after the war.* • dividing, splitting, separation, partition
2. *There was a division in the government.* • disagreement, split, feud
3. *There is a movable division between the two classrooms.* • partition, divider, dividing wall, screen
4. *They work in different divisions of the same company.* • branch, department, section, unit

dizzy adjective **dizzier, dizziest**
Going on a roundabout makes me feel dizzy. • dazed, giddy, faint, reeling, unsteady

do verb **does, doing, did, done**
1. *My friend always knows what to do in a crisis.* • act, behave, conduct yourself
2. *The vet has a lot of work to do this morning.* • attend to, cope with, deal with, handle, look after, perform, undertake
3. *It took me half an hour to do the washing-up.* • accomplish, achieve, carry out, complete, execute, finish
4. *I need to do all of these sums.* • answer, puzzle out, solve, work out
5. *Staring at the sun can do damage to your eyes.* • bring about, cause, produce, result in
6. *If you don't have lemonade, water will do.* • be acceptable, be enough, be satisfactory, be sufficient, serve

docile adjective
Don't be afraid of the dog—he's quite docile. • tame, gentle, meek, obedient, manageable, safe, submissive **opposite** fierce

dock noun
A boat was waiting for us at the end of the dock. • harbour, quay, jetty, wharf, landing stage, dockyard, pier, port, marina

document noun
The library contains many old documents. • paper, record, file, certificate, deed

dodge verb
I just managed to dodge the snowball. • avoid, evade, side-step

dog noun
• A female dog is a **bitch**. • A young dog is a **puppy** or a **pup**. • An uncomplimentary word for a dog is **cur**. • A dog whose ancestors are

all of the same breed is a **pedigree**. • A dog whose ancestors are of different breeds is a **mongrel**. • A dog used for hunting is a **hound**. • A word meaning 'to do with dogs' is **canine**.

dominant adjective
1. *The captain plays a dominant role in the team.* • leading, main, chief, major, powerful, principal, important, influential **opposite** minor
2. *The castle is a dominant feature in the landscape.* • conspicuous, prominent, obvious, large, imposing, eye-catching **opposite** insignificant

dominate verb
The visiting team dominated the game. • control, direct, monopolize, govern, take control of, take over

donation noun
The museum relies on donations from the public. • contribution, gift, offering

done adjective
1. *All my thank-you letters are done now.* • finished, complete, over
2. *The cake will be brown on top when it's done.* • cooked, ready

doomed adjective
The expedition was doomed from the start. • ill-fated, condemned, fated, cursed, jinxed, damned

door noun
• A door in a floor or ceiling is a **hatch** or **trapdoor**. • The plank or stone underneath a door is the **threshold**. • The beam or stone above a door is the **lintel**. • The device on which most doors swing is the **hinge**.

dot noun
She was furious when she saw dots of paint on the carpet. • spot, speck, fleck, point, mark
• The dot you always put at the end of a sentence is a **full stop**.
on the dot (informal)
We left the house at nine o'clock on the dot. • exactly, precisely

double adjective
You enter the room through a double set of doors. • dual, paired, twin, matching, duplicate, twofold

double *noun*
She's so like you—she's almost your double.
• twin, *(informal)* lookalike, spitting image, dead ringer • A living organism created as an exact copy of another living organism is a **clone**.

doubt *noun*
1. *Have you any doubt about his honesty?*
• distrust, suspicion, mistrust, hesitation, reservation, scepticism **opposite** confidence
2. *There is no doubt that you will pass your exam.* • question, uncertainty, ambiguity, confusion **opposite** certainty

doubt *verb*
There is no reason to doubt her story.
• distrust, feel uncertain or uneasy or unsure about, question, mistrust, suspect, be sceptical about, be suspicious or wary of **opposite** trust

doubtful *adjective*
He looked doubtful, but agreed to let us go. • unsure, uncertain, unconvinced, hesitant, distrustful, sceptical, suspicious **opposite** certain

downfall *noun*
After the government's downfall, there was a general election. • collapse, fall, ruin

doze *verb*
Dad often dozes off in the evening.
• rest, sleep, nod off, have or take a nap, *(informal)* drop off, snooze, have forty winks

drab *adjective*
That dress is too drab to wear to the party.
• dull, dingy, dreary, cheerless, colourless, dismal, gloomy, grey **opposite** bright, cheerful

draft *noun*
I jotted down a draft of my story. • outline, plan, sketch, rough version

draft *verb*
I began to draft my story. • outline, plan, prepare, sketch, work out

drag *verb* **dragging, dragged**
The tractor dragged the car out of the ditch. • pull, tow, tug, draw, haul, lug **opposite** push

dragon *noun*

WORD WEB

A fearsome dragon once lived in these hills.

SOME WAYS TO DESCRIBE A DRAGON
• ancient, fearsome, fiery, fire-breathing, mighty, monstrous, scaly

BODY PARTS A DRAGON MIGHT HAVE
• bat-like wings, claws, crest, forked tail or tongue, scales, spikes or spines

A DRAGON'S SCALES MIGHT BE
• dazzling, iridescent, patterned, shimmering

A DRAGON'S BREATH MIGHT BE
• fiery, flaming, scorching, searing

THINGS A DRAGON MIGHT DO
• breathe fire, puff smoke, roar, snort; change shape, fly, soar, swoop

PLACES WHERE A DRAGON MIGHT LIVE
• cave, den, lair

drain *verb*
1. *If they drain the marsh, lots of waterbirds will die.* • dry out, remove water from
2. *She drained the oil from the engine.*
• draw off, empty
3. *The water slowly drained away.* • trickle, ooze, seep
4. *The tough climb drained my energy.*
• use up, consume, exhaust

dramatic *adjective*
We watched the dramatic rescue on TV.
• exciting, eventful, thrilling, sensational, spectacular, gripping

drastic *adjective*
After being without food for three days, the explorers needed to take drastic action.
• desperate, extreme, radical, harsh, severe **opposite** moderate

draw *verb* **drawing, drew, drawn**
1. *I drew some pictures of the flowers in our garden.* • sketch, trace, doodle
2. *I'm not very good at drawing faces.* • depict, portray, represent
3. *The horse was drawing a cart.* • pull, tow, drag, haul, tug, lug

4. We expect tomorrow's match to draw a big crowd. • attract, bring in, pull in
5. The two teams drew 1–1. • finish equal, tie
to draw near
As the spaceship drew near, I began to get nervous. • approach, advance, come near

drawback *noun*
It's a drawback to be small if you play basketball. • disadvantage, difficulty, handicap, obstacle, inconvenience, hindrance, downside, snag

dread *noun*
Our teacher has a dread of spiders. • fear, horror, terror, phobia (about), anxiety (about)

dreadful *adjective*
1. There has been a dreadful accident at sea. • horrible, terrible, appalling, horrendous, distressing, shocking, upsetting, tragic, grim
2. The weather at the weekend was dreadful. • bad, awful, terrible, abysmal, abominable, dire, foul, nasty **opposite** good, pleasant

dream *noun*
• A bad dream is a **nightmare**. • A dreamlike experience you have while awake is a **daydream**, **fantasy** or **reverie**. • Something you see in a dream or daydream is a **vision**. • The dreamlike state when you are hypnotized is a **trance**. • Something you think you see that is not real is a **hallucination** or **illusion**.

dreary *adjective* **drearier, dreariest**
1. The newsreader had a very dreary voice. • dull, boring, flat, tedious, unexciting, uninteresting **opposite** lively
2. When will this dreary weather end? • depressing, dismal, dull, gloomy, cheerless, murky, overcast **opposite** bright, sunny

dress *noun*
1. What kind of dress are you wearing to the party? • frock • A long dress worn on special occasions is a **gown**.
2. The invitation said to wear casual dress. • clothes, clothing, outfit, costume, garments

dress *verb*
1. I helped to dress my little brother. • get dressed, put clothes on, clothe • You can also use these expressions to talk about putting on clothes: **get into**, **pull on**, **slip on**, **slip into**, **try on**. **opposite** undress
2. A nurse dressed my wound. • bandage, put a dressing on, bind up

dribble *verb*
1. Careful, the baby's dribbling on your jumper. • drool
2. Water dribbled out of the hole in the tank. • drip, trickle, leak, ooze, seep

drift *verb*
1. The boat drifted downstream. • float, be carried, move slowly
2. The crowd lost interest and drifted away. • stray, wander, meander, ramble, walk aimlessly
3. The snow will drift in this wind. • pile up, accumulate, make drifts

drift *noun*
1. The car was stuck in a snow drift. • bank, heap, mound, pile, ridge
2. I just about got the drift of the speech. • gist, main idea, point

drill *verb*
It took a long time to drill through the wall. • bore, penetrate, pierce

drink *verb* **drinking, drank, drunk**
• To drink greedily is to **gulp**, **guzzle** or **swig**.
• To drink noisily is to **slurp**. • To drink a small amount at a time is to **sip**. • To drink with the tongue as a cat does is to **lap**.

drip *noun*
Dad was worried by the drips of oil underneath the car. • spot, dribble, splash, trickle

drip *verb* **dripping, dripped**
The oil dripped onto the garage floor. • drop, leak, dribble, splash, trickle

drive *verb* **driving, drove, driven**
1. The dog drove the sheep through the gate. • direct, guide, herd
2. I couldn't drive the spade into the hard ground. • push, thrust, hammer, plunge, ram
3. When can I learn to drive a car? • control, handle, manage
4. Lack of money drove him to steal. • force, compel, oblige
to drive someone or **something out**
The invading army drove the government out. • eject, expel, throw out • To drive people out of their homes is to **evict** them. • To drive people out of their country is to **banish** or **exile** them.

drive *noun*
1. We went for a drive in the country. • ride, trip, journey, outing, excursion, jaunt
2. Have you got the drive to succeed? • ambition, determination, keenness, motivation, energy, zeal

driver noun
Many **drivers** go too fast. • motorist
• A person who drives someone's car as a job is a **chauffeur**.

droop verb
Plants tend to **droop** in dry weather. • sag, wilt, bend, flop, be limp

drop noun
1. Large **drops** of rain began to fall. • drip, droplet, spot, bead, blob
2. Could I have another **drop** of milk in my tea? • dash, small quantity
3. We expect a **drop** in the price of fruit in the summer. • decrease, reduction, cut
4. There's a **drop** of two metres on the other side of the wall. • fall, descent, plunge

drop verb dropping, dropped
1. The hawk **dropped** onto its prey.
• descend, dive, plunge, swoop
2. I **dropped** to the ground exhausted.
• collapse, fall, sink, subside, slump, tumble
3. Why did you **drop** me from the team?
• omit, eliminate, exclude, leave out
4. They **dropped** the plan for a new bypass.
• abandon, discard, reject, give up, scrap

drown verb
The music from upstairs **drowned** our conversation. • overwhelm, overpower, drown out

drowsy adjective drowsier, drowsiest
If you feel **drowsy**, why not go to bed?
• sleepy, tired, weary

drug noun
A new **drug** has been discovered for back pain.
• medicine, remedy, treatment • A drug which relieves pain is an **analgesic** or **painkiller**.
• A drug which calms you down is a **sedative** or **tranquillizer**. • Drugs which make you more active are **stimulants**.

dry adjective drier, driest
1. Nothing will grow in this **dry** soil. • arid, parched, moistureless, waterless, dehydrated, desiccated, barren • A common simile is **as dry as a bone. opposite** wet
2. He gave rather a **dry** speech. • dull, boring, dreary, tedious, uninteresting **opposite** interesting
3. A lot of people don't understand his **dry** sense of humour. • ironic, wry, witty, subtle

dual adjective
The building has a **dual** purpose: it can be either a cinema or a theatre. • double, twofold, twin, combined

dubious adjective
I'm a bit **dubious** about getting a snake for a pet. • doubtful, uncertain, unsure, hesitant **opposite** certain, sure

duck verb
Oliver **ducked** to avoid the snowball. • bend down, bob down, crouch, stoop

due adjective
1. The train is **due** in five minutes. • expected, anticipated
2. Subscriptions are now **due**. • owed, owing, payable
3. I give her **due** credit for what she did.
• fitting, proper, appropriate, suitable, deserved, well-earned

dull adjective
1. I don't like the **dull** colours in this room.
• dim, dingy, drab, dreary, dismal, faded, gloomy, sombre, subdued **opposite** bright, colourful
2. The sky was **dull** that day. • cloudy, overcast, grey, sunless, murky **opposite** clear
3. I heard a **dull** thud from upstairs.
• indistinct, muffled, muted **opposite** distinct
4. He's rather a **dull** student. • stupid, slow, unintelligent, dim, unimaginative, dense, obtuse, (informal) thick **opposite** clever
5. The play was so **dull** that I fell asleep.
• boring, dry, monotonous, tedious, uninteresting, unexciting, lacklustre
• A common simile is **as dull as ditchwater. opposite** interesting

dumb adjective
1. The spectators were struck **dumb** with amazement. • If you do not speak, you are **mute** or **silent**. • If you cannot speak because you are surprised, confused or embarrassed, you are **speechless** or **tongue-tied**. • If you find it hard to express yourself, you are **inarticulate**.
2. (informal) He's too **dumb** to understand.
• stupid, unintelligent, dim, slow, dense, obtuse, (informal) thick

dumbfounded adjective
I was **dumbfounded** when I heard the news.
• amazed, astonished, astounded, stunned, staggered, thunderstruck, speechless, struck dumb, (informal) flabbergasted, gobsmacked

dump *verb*
1. *I decided to dump some of my old toys.* • get rid of, throw away, throw out, discard, dispose of, scrap
2. *Just dump your things in the bedroom.* • put down, set down, deposit, place, drop, throw down, tip

duplicate *noun*
We made a duplicate of the original document. • copy, photocopy, reproduction, replica
• An exact copy of a historic document or manuscript is a **facsimile**. • A person who looks like you is your **double** or **twin**. • A living organism which is a duplicate of another living organism is a **clone**.

dusk *noun*
Bats begin to emerge at dusk. • twilight, nightfall, sunset, sundown **opposite** dawn

duty *noun* **duties**
1. *I have a duty to help my parents.* • responsibility, obligation
2. *I carried out my duties conscientiously.* • job, task, assignment, chore
3. *The government has increased the duty on petrol.* • charge, tax

dwell *verb* **dwelling, dwelt**
to dwell in
It is said that bandits dwell in these caves. • live in, inhabit, occupy, reside in
to dwell on
Try not to dwell on things that happened in the past. • keep thinking about, worry about, brood over

dwindle *verb*
Our enthusiasm dwindled as the day went on. • become less, diminish, decline, decrease, lessen, subside, wane, weaken **opposite** increase

dynamic *adjective*
The team has a new, dynamic captain. • energetic, lively, enthusiastic, vigorous, active, forceful, powerful **opposite** apathetic

Ee

Did you know, there are more than 15 different types of **edge** in this thesaurus? Look it up!

eager adjective
He is always eager to help. • keen, enthusiastic, desperate, anxious
opposite unenthusiastic

early adjective **earlier, earliest**
1. *The bus was early today.* • ahead of time, ahead of schedule **opposite** late
2. *The early computers were huge machines.* • first, old, primitive, ancient **opposite** recent, new

earth noun
The earth was so dry that many plants died. • ground, land, soil • Rich, fertile earth is **loam**. • The top layer of fertile earth is **topsoil**. • Rich earth consisting of decayed plants is **humus**. • A heavy, sticky kind of earth is **clay**.

ease noun
1. *She swam ten lengths of the pool with ease.* • facility, skill, speed **opposite** difficulty
2. *Lady Deadwood leads a life of ease.* • comfort, contentment, leisure, peace, quiet, relaxation, rest, tranquillity **opposite** stress

ease verb
1. *The doctor gave her some pills to ease her pain.* • relieve, lessen, soothe, moderate **opposite** aggravate
2. *After taking the pills, the pain began to ease.* • decrease, reduce, slacken **opposite** increase
3. *We eased the piano into position.* • edge, guide, manoeuvre, inch, slide, slip

easy adjective **easier, easiest**
1. *Tonight's homework is really easy.* • undemanding, effortless, light • An informal word for an easy task is a **doddle**.
2. *The instructions were easy to understand.* • simple, straightforward, clear, plain, elementary • A common simile is **as easy as ABC**.

3. *Our cat has an easy life.* • carefree, comfortable, peaceful, relaxed, leisurely, restful, tranquil, untroubled **opposite** difficult

eat verb **eating, ate, eaten**
Hannah was eating a cheese sandwich. • consume, devour, (informal) scoff • When sheep or cattle eat grass they are **grazing**. • A person who eats a large amount is said to **eat like a horse**.

> **(!) OVERUSED WORD**
>
> Try to vary the words you use for **eat**. Here are some other words you could use.
>
> **TO EAT GREEDILY OR QUICKLY**
> • bolt down, demolish, gobble, gulp, guzzle, gorge (on), polish off, wolf down
> *I was so hungry, I wolfed down a whole pizza.*
>
> **TO EAT NOISILY**
> • chomp, crunch, gnaw, munch, slurp
> *Rabbits like to chomp raw carrots.*
>
> **TO EAT IN SMALL AMOUNTS**
> • nibble, peck, pick at or pick away at, taste
> *Do you have any biscuits we could nibble?*
>
> **TO EAT WITH ENJOYMENT**
> • relish, savour, tuck into
> *Mr Hogg was savouring a sausage roll.*
>
> **TO EAT A FORMAL MEAL**
> • banquet, dine, feast
> *The guests will be dining in the great hall.*

eccentric adjective
We never discovered the reason for his eccentric behaviour. • odd, peculiar, strange, weird, abnormal, unusual, curious, unconventional, unorthodox, quirky, zany, (informal) way-out, dotty **opposite** conventional, orthodox

echo verb **echoes, echoing, echoed**
1. *The sound echoed across the valley.* • resound, reverberate
2. *'He's gone home.' 'Gone home?' she echoed.* • repeat, imitate, mimic

economical adjective
1. *My uncle is very economical with his money.* • careful, prudent, thrifty, frugal • If you are economical with money in a selfish way, you are **mean** or **miserly**. **opposite** wasteful
2. *Our new car is very economical to run.* • cheap, inexpensive, reasonable **opposite** expensive

a b c d e f g h i j k l m n o p q r s t u v w x y z

ecstatic adjective
I was absolutely ecstatic about going to Disneyland. • elated, delighted, overjoyed, gleeful, joyful, blissful, rapturous, euphoric, exultant, delirious, fervent, frenzied

edge noun
• The edge of a cliff or other steep place is the **brink**. • The edge of a cup or other container is the **brim** or **rim**. • The line round the edge of a circle is the **circumference**. • The line round the edge of any other shape is its **outline**. • The distance round the edge of an area is the **perimeter**. • The stones along the edge of a road are the **kerb**. • Grass along the edge of a road is the **verge**. • The space down the edge of a page is the **margin**. • The space round the edge of a picture is a **border**. • Something that fits round the edge of a picture is a **frame**. • The edge of a garment is the **hem**. • An edge with threads or hair hanging loosely down is a **fringe**. • The edge of a crowd also is the **fringe** of the crowd. • The area round the edge of a city is the **outskirts** or **suburbs**. • The edge of a cricket field is the **boundary**. • The edge of a football pitch is the **touchline**.

edge verb
1. *We edged away from the lion's den.* • creep, inch, move stealthily, steal, slink
2. *Her bonnet was edged with black lace.* • trim, hem

edgy adjective **edgier**, **edgiest**
Horses become edgy during thunderstorms. • nervous, restless, anxious, agitated, excitable, tense, jumpy, fidgety, (informal) uptight, jittery **opposite** calm

educate verb
The job of a school is to educate young people. • teach, train, inform, instruct, tutor

eerie adjective
They heard nothing, just an eerie silence. • strange, weird, uncanny, mysterious, frightening, creepy, ghostly, sinister, unearthly, unnatural, (informal) scary, spooky

effect noun
1. *The effect of eating too much is that you get fat!* • result, consequence, outcome, sequel, upshot
2. *Does this music have any effect on you?* • impact, influence
3. *The lighting gives an effect of warmth.* • feeling, impression, sense, illusion

effective adjective
1. *I wish they could find an effective cure for colds.* • successful
2. *Our team needs an effective goalkeeper.* • competent, able, capable, proficient, skilled
3. *He presented an effective argument against hunting.* • convincing, persuasive, compelling, impressive, telling **opposite** useless

efficient adjective
1. *An efficient worker can do the job in an hour.* • effective, competent, able, capable, proficient
2. *Dad tried to work out an efficient way of heating our house.* • economic, productive

effort noun
1. *A lot of effort went into making the film.* • work, trouble, exertion, industry, labour, toil
2. *She congratulated us on a good effort.* • attempt, try, endeavour, go, shot

elaborate adjective
The plot of the book is so elaborate that I got lost halfway through. • complicated, complex, detailed, intricate, involved, convoluted **opposite** simple

elect verb
We elected a new captain. • vote for, appoint

election noun
We had an election to choose a new captain. • vote, ballot, poll

elegant adjective
She always looks so elegant. • graceful, stylish, fashionable, chic, smart, tasteful, sophisticated **opposite** inelegant

elementary adjective
Anyone can solve such an elementary problem. • basic, simple, easy, fundamental, straightforward, uncomplicated **opposite** advanced, complex

eliminate verb
We need to eliminate the threat of hunger. • get rid of, put an end to, root out • To be eliminated from a competition is to be **knocked out**.

embarrass verb
I can't believe you embarrassed me in front of my friends! • humiliate, shame, distress, mortify, make you blush

embarrassed adjective
Don't feel embarrassed—it happens to everyone! • awkward, uncomfortable,

self-conscious, flustered, bashful, ashamed, distressed, humiliated, mortified

emblem noun
The dove is an emblem of peace. • sign, symbol

embrace verb
1. *The mother gorilla embraced her baby.*
• hug, clasp, cuddle, hold
2. *She's always ready to embrace new ideas.*
• welcome, accept, adopt, take on

emerge verb
He didn't emerge from his bedroom until ten o'clock. • appear, come out

emergency noun emergencies
Try to keep calm in an emergency. • crisis, serious situation, danger, difficulty

emit verb emitting, emitted
1. *The exhaust pipe emitted clouds of smoke.*
• discharge, expel, belch, blow out, give off
2. *The satellite was emitting radio signals.*
• transmit, give out, send out

emotion noun
His voice was full of emotion. • feeling, passion, sentiment, fervour

emotional adjective
1. *He made an emotional farewell speech.*
• moving, touching
2. *The music for the love scenes was very emotional.* • romantic, sentimental
3. *She's a very emotional woman.*
• passionate, intense

emphasize verb
She emphasized the important points.
• highlight, stress, focus on, dwell on, underline This word can also be spelled **emphasise**.

employ verb
1. *The new factory plans to employ 100 workers.* • hire, engage, give work to, take on
2. *The factory will employ the latest methods.*
• use, utilize

empty adjective emptier, emptiest
1. *Please put the empty milk bottles outside the door.* **opposite** full
2. *The house next to ours has been empty for weeks.* • unoccupied, uninhabited, vacant, deserted **opposite** occupied
3. *After we put up our display, there was still some empty space on the wall.* • blank, bare, clear, unused

empty verb empties, emptying, emptied
1. *Empty the dirty water into the sink.* • drain, pour out **opposite** fill
2. *The building emptied when the fire alarm went off.* • clear, evacuate, vacate
3. *Did you empty all the shopping out of the trolley?* • remove, unload

enchanting adjective
The ballet dancers were enchanting.
• delightful, charming, appealing, attractive, bewitching, spellbinding

enchantment noun
1. *The forest was filled with enchantment.*
• magic, wonder, delight, pleasure
2. *The castle was under an enchantment.*
• spell, incantation

enclose verb
1. *The documents were enclosed in a brown paper envelope.* • contain, insert, wrap, bind, sheathe
2. *The animals were enclosed within a wire fence.* • confine, restrict, fence in, shut in, imprison

enclosure noun
• An animal's enclosure with bars is a **cage**.
• An enclosure for chickens is a **coop** or **run**.
• An enclosure for cattle and other animals is a **pen** or **corral**. • An enclosure for horses is a **paddock**. • An enclosure for sheep is a **fold**.

encounter verb
1. *He encountered her outside the station.*
• meet, come across, run into, bump into, come face to face with
2. *We encountered some problems.*
• experience, come upon, confront, be faced with

encourage verb
1. *We sang and chanted to encourage our team.* • inspire, support, motivate, cheer, spur on, egg on
2. *The poster campaign encourages people to eat healthily.* • persuade, urge

encouragement noun
Our team needs some encouragement.
• reassurance, inspiration, incitement, stimulation, urging, incentive, stimulus, support

encouraging adjective
The results of the tests were encouraging.
• hopeful, positive, promising, reassuring, optimistic, cheering, favourable

a b c d e f g h i j k l m n o p q r s t u v w x y z

end *noun*
1. *The fence marks the end of the garden.*
• boundary, limit, bottom
2. *The end of the film was the most exciting part.* • ending, finish, close, conclusion, culmination, climax, termination • The last part of a show or piece of music is the **finale**. • A section added at the end of a letter is a **postscript**. • A section added at the end of a story is an **epilogue**.
3. *I was tired by the time we got to the end of the journey.* • The end of your journey is your **destination**.
4. *We arrived late and found ourselves at the end of the queue.* • back, rear, tail
5. *What end did you have in view when you started?* • aim, purpose, intention, objective, plan, outcome, result

end *verb*
1. *The meeting should end in time for lunch.*
• finish, complete, conclude, break off, halt, *(informal)* wind up
2. *When did they end corporal punishment in schools?* • abolish, do away with, get rid of, put an end to, discontinue, eliminate
3. *The festival ended with a show of fireworks.*
• close, come to an end, stop, cease, terminate, culminate, wind up, round off

endanger *verb*
Bad driving endangers other people. • put at risk, threaten **opposite** protect

ending *noun*
The ending of the film was the most exciting part. • end, finish, close, conclusion, culmination, last part • The ending of a show or piece of music is the **finale**.

endless *adjective*
1. *Teachers need endless patience.* • unending, limitless, infinite, inexhaustible, unlimited
2. *There's an endless procession of cars along the main road.* • continual, continuous, constant, incessant, interminable, perpetual, unbroken, uninterrupted, everlasting, ceaseless

endurance *noun*
The climb was a test of their endurance.
• perseverance, persistence, determination, resolution, stamina

endure *verb*
1. *She had to endure a lot of pain.* • bear, stand, suffer, cope with, experience, go through, put up with, tolerate, undergo

2. *These traditions have endured for centuries.*
• survive, continue, last, persist, carry on, keep going

enemy *noun* enemies
They used to be friends but now they are bitter enemies. • opponent, adversary, foe, rival **opposite** friend, ally

energetic *adjective*
1. *She's a very energetic person.* • dynamic, spirited, enthusiastic, animated, active, zestful **opposite** inactive, lethargic
2. *It was a very energetic exercise routine.*
• lively, vigorous, brisk, fast, quick-moving, strenuous **opposite** slow-paced, sluggish

energy *noun* energies
1. *The dancers had tremendous energy.*
• liveliness, spirit, vitality, vigour, life, drive, zest, verve, enthusiasm, dynamism, *(informal)* get-up-and-go, zip **opposite** lethargy
2. *Wind power is a renewable source of energy.*
• power, fuel

engage *verb*
1. *The builder engaged extra workers in order to complete the job on time.* • employ, hire, take on
2. *The general decided to engage the enemy at dawn.* • attack, start fighting

enjoy *verb*
I really enjoyed the film. • like, love, get pleasure from, be pleased by, admire, appreciate

enjoyable *adjective*
It was an enjoyable party. • pleasant, agreeable, delightful, entertaining, amusing **opposite** unpleasant

enjoyment *noun*
Tom refused to let this disappointment spoil his enjoyment of the garden. • pleasure, delight, thrill, anticipation

enlarge *verb*
The zoo is going to enlarge the lion enclosure.
• expand, extend, develop, make bigger • To make something wider is to **broaden** or **widen** it. • To make something longer is to **extend**, **lengthen** or **stretch** it. • To make something seem larger is to **magnify** it. **opposite** reduce

enormous *adjective*
Enormous waves battered the ship.
• huge, gigantic, immense, colossal, massive, monstrous, monumental,

mountainous, towering, tremendous, vast, *(informal)* ginormous, humungous
opposite small

enough *adjective*
Is there enough food for ten people?
• sufficient, adequate, ample

enquire *verb*
to enquire about
I enquired about train times to Bristol.
• ask for, get information about, request, investigate

enquiry *noun*
The librarian helped me with my enquiry.
• question, query, request, investigation, research

enter *verb*
1. *Silence fell as I entered the room.* • come in, walk in • To enter a place without permission is to **invade** it. **opposite** leave
2. *The arrow entered his shoulder.* • go into, penetrate, pierce
3. *Can I enter my name on the list?* • insert, record, register, put down, set down, sign, write, inscribe **opposite** cancel
4. *Our class decided to enter the competition.* • take part in, enrol in, sign up for, go in for, join in, participate in, volunteer for **opposite** withdraw from

entertain *verb*
1. *The storyteller entertained us with scary ghost stories.* • amuse, divert, keep amused, make you laugh, please, cheer up **opposite** bore
2. *You can entertain friends in the private dining room.* • receive, welcome, cater for, give hospitality to

entertainment *noun*
Our hosts had arranged some entertainment for us. • amusements, recreation, diversions, enjoyment, fun, pastimes

enthusiasm *noun*
1. *The young athletes showed plenty of enthusiasm.* • keenness, ambition, commitment, drive, zeal, zest **opposite** apathy
2. *His latest enthusiasm is collecting fossils.* • interest, passion, pastime, hobby, craze, diversion, fad

enthusiast *noun*
My brother is a football enthusiast. • fan, fanatic, devotee, lover, supporter, addict, *(informal)* freak, nut

enthusiastic *adjective*
1. *He's an enthusiastic supporter of our local team.* • keen, passionate, avid, devoted, energetic, fervent, zealous
2. *The audience burst into enthusiastic applause.* • eager, excited, lively, vigorous, exuberant, hearty

entire *adjective*
Donald spent the entire evening watching television. • complete, whole, total, full

entirely *adverb*
I'm not entirely sure that I agree with you.
• completely, absolutely, wholly, totally, utterly, fully, perfectly, quite

entrance *noun*
1. *Please pay at the entrance.* • entry, way in, access, door, gate • When you go through the entrance to a building, you cross the **threshold**.
2. *I'll meet you in the entrance.* • entrance hall, foyer, lobby, porch
3. *Her sudden entrance took everyone by surprise.* • entry, arrival, appearance

entrance *verb*
The crowd were entranced by the fireworks display. • charm, delight, please, enchant

entry *noun* **entries**
1. *A van was blocking the entry to the school.*
• way in, entrance, access, door, gate
2. *Every evening I write an entry in my diary.*
• item, note

envious *adjective*
He was envious of his brother's success.
• jealous, resentful

environment *noun*
Animals should live in their natural environment, not in cages. • habitat, surroundings, setting, conditions, situation
the environment
We must do all we can to protect the environment. • the natural world, nature, the Earth, the world

envy *noun*
I was full of envy when I saw how rich she was.
• jealousy, resentment, bitterness

envy *verb* **envies, envying, envied**
The evil queen envied Snow White's beauty.
• be jealous of, begrudge, grudge, resent

episode *noun*
1. *I paid for the broken window, and now I want to forget the whole episode.* • event, incident, experience

2. *I missed last night's episode of 'Dr Who'.*
• instalment, part

equal *adjective*
1. *Give everyone an equal amount.*
• equivalent, identical, matching, similar, corresponding, fair
2. *The scores were equal at half-time.*
• even, level, the same, square • To make the scores equal is to **equalize**.

equip *verb* **equipping, equipped**
All the bedrooms are equipped with a colour television. • provide, supply • To equip soldiers with weapons is to **arm** them. • To equip a room with furniture is to **furnish** it.

equipment *noun*
The shed is full of gardening equipment.
• apparatus, gear, kit, tackle, tools, implements, instruments, materials, machinery, paraphernalia, things • Computing equipment is **hardware**.

era *noun*
Shakespeare lived in the Elizabethan era.
• age, period, time, epoch

erase *verb*
I erased the writing on the blackboard.
• delete, remove, rub out, wipe out, get rid of

erode *verb* **erodes, eroding, eroded**
The flood water eroded the river bank.
• wear away, eat away, destroy

errand *noun*
I went on an errand to the corner shop.
• job, task, assignment, trip

error *noun*
1. *The accident was the result of an error by the driver.* • mistake, fault, lapse, blunder
2. *I think there is an error in your argument.*
• flaw, inaccuracy, misunderstanding, inconsistency • The error of leaving something out is an **omission** or **oversight**.

erupt *verb*
Smoke began to erupt from the volcano. • be discharged, be emitted, pour out, issue, spout, gush, spurt, belch

escape *verb*
1. *Why did you let him escape?* • get away, get out, run away, break free, break out, (informal) give you the slip • A performer who escapes from chains, etc., is an **escape artist** or **escapologist**.

2. *She always escapes the nasty jobs.*
• avoid, get out of, evade, dodge, shirk

escape *noun*
1. *The prisoner's escape was filmed by security cameras.* • getaway, breakout, flight
2. *The explosion was caused by an escape of gas.* • leak, leakage, seepage

escort *verb*
The queen was escorted by a number of attendants. • accompany, guard, protect, look after

especially *adverb*
I like apple pie, especially with ice cream.
• above all, chiefly, most of all

essential *adjective*
Fruit and vegetables are an essential part of our diet. • important, necessary, basic, vital, principal, fundamental, chief, crucial, indispensable

establish *verb*
1. *He plans to establish a new business.*
• set up, start, begin, create, found, initiate, institute, introduce, launch, originate
2. *The police have not managed to establish his guilt.* • prove, show to be true, confirm, verify

estimate *verb*
The builders estimate that the work will take four months. • calculate, assess, work out, compute, count up, evaluate, judge, reckon, think out

eternal *adjective*
1. *The magic fountain was said to give eternal youth.* • everlasting, infinite, lasting, unending, timeless • Beings with eternal life are said to be **immortal**.
2. *I'm sick of your eternal quarrelling!*
• constant, continual, never-ending, non-stop, persistent, perpetual, endless, ceaseless, incessant, unceasing

evacuate *verb*
1. *The firefighters evacuated everyone from the building.* • remove, clear, send away, move out
2. *We were told to evacuate the building.*
• leave, quit, abandon, withdraw from, empty, vacate

evade *verb*
Don't try to evade your responsibilities.
• avoid, dodge, shirk, escape from, steer clear of, fend off **opposite** confront

even adjective
1. *You need an even surface for ice-skating.*
• level, flat, smooth, straight **opposite** uneven
2. *The runners kept up an even pace.* • regular, steady, unvarying, rhythmical, monotonous **opposite** irregular
3. *Mr Humphreys has an even temper.* • calm, cool, placid, unexcitable **opposite** excitable
4. *The scores were even at half-time.* • equal, level, matching, identical, the same, square **opposite** different
5. *The numbers 2, 4 and 6 are even numbers.* **opposite** odd

evening noun
Towards evening it clouded over and began to rain. • dusk, nightfall, sundown, sunset, twilight

event noun
1. *Her autobiography describes the main events of her life.* • happening, incident, occurrence
2. *There was an event to mark the launch of the new film.* • function, occasion, ceremony, entertainment, party, reception
3. *The World Cup is an important event for football fans.* • competition, contest, fixture, engagement, meeting, game, match, tournament

eventually adverb
The journey took ages, but eventually we arrived safely. • finally, at last, in the end, ultimately

everlasting adjective
I'm sick of their everlasting chatter! • constant, continual, persistent, incessant, never-ending, non-stop, endless, ceaseless, perpetual, unending, eternal, recurrent, repeated, unceasing • Everlasting life is **immortality**. **opposite** occasional, transient

everyday adjective
Don't dress up—just wear your everyday clothes. • normal, ordinary, usual, regular, customary

evict verb
The landlord threatened to evict the tenants. • expel, eject, remove, throw out, turn out, put out

evidence noun
This piece of paper is evidence that he is lying. • proof, confirmation • Evidence that someone accused of a crime was not there when the crime was committed is an **alibi**. • Evidence given in a law court is a **testimony**. • To give evidence in court is to **testify**.

evil adjective
1. *The charm was used to keep away evil spirits.* • malevolent, fiendish, diabolical, devilish
2. *Who would do such an evil deed?* • wicked, immoral, cruel, sinful, villainous, malicious, foul, hateful, vile **opposite** good

evil noun
1. *The book is about the struggle between good and evil.* • wickedness, badness, wrongdoing, sin, immorality, villainy, malevolence, malice
2. *They had to endure the evils of famine and drought.* • disaster, misfortune, suffering, pain, affliction, curse

exact adjective
1. *I gave the police an exact account of what happened.* • accurate, precise, correct, true, faithful, detailed, meticulous, strict
2. *Is this an exact copy of the original document?* • identical, perfect, indistinguishable **opposite** inaccurate

exactly adverb
At what time exactly did you leave the house? • precisely, specifically, accurately, correctly, strictly • A phrase meaning 'exactly on time' is to be **on the dot**. **opposite** roughly, inaccurately

exaggerate verb
He tends to exaggerate his problems. • magnify, inflate, overdo, make too much of **opposite** minimize

examination noun
1. *The results of the examinations will be announced next month.* • test, assessment, (informal) exam
2. *The judge made a thorough examination of the facts.* • investigation, inspection, study, analysis, survey, review, appraisal
3. *He was sent to hospital for an examination.* • check-up • A medical examination of a dead person is a **post-mortem**.

examine verb
1. *The judge examined the evidence.* • inspect, study, investigate, analyse, look closely at, pore over, scrutinize, probe, survey, review, weigh up, sift
2. *They were examined on their knowledge of history.* • question, interrogate, quiz • To examine someone rigorously is to **grill** them.

a
b
c
d
e
f
g
h
i
j
k
l
m
n
o
p
q
r
s
t
u
v
w
x
y
z

example *noun*
1. *Give me an example of what you mean.*
• instance, illustration, sample, specimen, case
2. *She's an example to us all.* • model, ideal

exceed *verb*
She exceeded the previous race record by two seconds. • beat, better, outdo, pass, surpass, go over

excel *verb* **excelling, excelled**
She's a good all-round athlete, but she excels at sprinting. • do best, stand out, shine

excellent *adjective*
That's an excellent idea! • first-class, first-rate, outstanding, exceptional, remarkable, tremendous, wonderful, superb, great, fine, marvellous, superior, superlative, top-notch, *(informal)* brilliant, fantastic, terrific, fabulous, sensational, super **opposite** bad, awful, second-rate

except *preposition*
Everyone got a prize except me. • apart from, but, with the exception of, excluding

exceptional *adjective*
1. *Beth is an exceptional swimmer for her age.* • outstanding, excellent, extraordinary, superb, wonderful, amazing **opposite** average
2. *It is exceptional to have such cold weather in June.* • unusual, extraordinary, uncommon, unexpected, amazing, rare, odd, peculiar, strange, surprising, special, abnormal, phenomenal, unheard-of, bizarre **opposite** normal, usual

excessive *adjective*
1. *I think his enthusiasm for football is excessive.* • extreme, exaggerated, fanatical, overdone
2. *Mum prepared excessive amounts of food for the party.* • unnecessary, needless, superfluous, extravagant, wasteful, unreasonable

exchange *verb*
The shop will exchange faulty goods. • change, replace • To exchange goods for other goods without using money is to **barter**. • To exchange an old thing for part of the cost of a new one is to **trade it in**. • To exchange things with your friends is to **swap** or **swop** them. • To exchange players for other players in football, etc., is to **substitute** them.

excite *verb*
The prospect of going to Italy excited Miss MacKillop. • thrill, enthuse, stimulate, arouse, electrify, rouse, stir up **opposite** calm

excited *adjective*
On Christmas Eve, my little brother was too excited to sleep. • agitated, lively, enthusiastic, exuberant, thrilled, elated, eager, animated **opposite** calm

excitement *noun*
I could hardly bear the excitement! • suspense, tension, drama, thrill

exciting *adjective*
The last minutes of the match were the most exciting of all! • dramatic, eventful, thrilling, gripping, sensational, stirring, rousing, stimulating, electrifying **opposite** dull, boring

exclaim *verb*
'Get out of my house!' she exclaimed. • call, shout, cry out, yell

exclamation *noun*
Dr Doyle gave an exclamation of surprise. • cry, shout, yell • An impolite exclamation is an **oath** or **swear word**.

exclude *verb*
1. *They excluded me from all their activities.* • ban, bar, prohibit, keep out, banish, reject
2. *She had to exclude dairy products from her diet.* • leave out, omit

excuse *noun*
What is your excuse for being so late? • reason, explanation, defence, justification

excuse *verb*
I can't excuse his bad behaviour. • forgive, overlook, pardon **opposite** punish
to be excused something
May I be excused swimming? • be exempt from, be let off, be released from

exercise *noun*
1. *Exercise helps to keep you fit.* • physical activity, working out, keep fit, training
2. *Doing exercises will improve your guitar playing.* • practice, training, drill

exercise *verb*
1. *If you exercise regularly, you will keep fit.* • keep fit, train, exert yourself
2. *I sometimes exercise our neighbour's dog.* • take for a walk, take out, walk
3. *We must exercise patience.* • show, use, apply, display, employ

exhausted *adjective*
After a hard race, we lay exhausted on the grass. • tired, weary, worn out, fatigued, breathless, gasping, panting, *(informal)* all in, done in, bushed, zonked

exhausting *adjective*
Digging the garden is exhausting work. • tiring, demanding, hard, laborious, strenuous, difficult, gruelling, wearisome **opposite** easy

exhaustion *noun*
He was overcome by sheer exhaustion.
• tiredness, fatigue, weariness, weakness

exhibit *verb*
1. *Her paintings were exhibited in galleries all over Europe and America.* • display, show, present, put up, set up, arrange
2. *He was exhibiting signs of anxiety.* • show, demonstrate, reveal **opposite** hide

exhibition *noun*
We went to see an exhibition of paintings by Picasso. • display, show

exile *verb*
As a result of the war, many people were exiled from their own country. • banish, expel, drive out, deport, eject, send away

exile *noun*
He returned to his country after 24 years of exile. • banishment, expulsion, deportation
• A person who has been exiled is a **refugee**.

exist *verb*
1. *Some people claim that ghosts actually exist.* • be real, occur
2. *We can't exist without food.* • live, remain alive, survive, keep going, last, continue, endure

existing *adjective*
1. *There are only two existing species of elephants.* • surviving, living, remaining
2. *Next year, the existing rules will be replaced by new ones.* • present, current

exit *noun*
1. *I'll wait for you by the exit.* • door, way out, doorway, gate, barrier **opposite** entrance
2. *The robbers made a hurried exit.* • departure **opposite** entrance

exit *verb*
The actors exited from the left of the stage. • go out, leave, depart, withdraw **opposite** enter

expand *verb*
Their computer business is expanding rapidly. • increase, enlarge, extend, build up, develop, make bigger • To become larger is to **grow** or **swell**. • To become wider is to **broaden**, **thicken** or **widen**. • To become longer is to **extend**, **lengthen** or **stretch**. **opposite** contract, reduce

expect *verb*
1. *I expect it will rain today.* • anticipate, imagine, forecast, predict, foresee, prophesy
2. *She expects me to do everything for her!* • require, want, count on, insist on, demand
3. *I expect they missed the bus.* • believe, imagine, guess, suppose, presume, assume, think

expedition *noun*
• An expedition into unknown territory is an **exploration**. • An expedition to carry out a special task is a **mission**. • An expedition to find something is a **quest**. • An expedition to worship at a holy place is a **pilgrimage**. • An expedition to see or hunt wild animals is a **safari**.

expel *verb* expelling, expelled
1. *A fan expels the stale air and fumes.* • send out, force out
2. *He was expelled from school.* • dismiss, ban, remove, throw out, send away • To expel someone from their home is to **eject** or **evict** them. • To expel someone from their country is to **banish** or **exile** them. • To expel evil spirits is to **exorcise** them.

experience *noun*
1. *Have you had any experience of singing in a choir?* • practice, involvement, participation
2. *I had an unusual experience today.*
• happening, event, occurrence, incident
• An exciting experience is an **adventure**.
• An unpleasant experience is an **ordeal**.

expert *noun*
We became experts at building tree houses.
• specialist, authority, genius, wizard, *(informal)* dab hand, whizz

expert *adjective*
Only an expert sailor could cross the ocean alone. • brilliant, capable, clever, competent, experienced, knowledgeable, professional, proficient, qualified, skilful, skilled, specialized, trained **opposite** amateur, unskilful

explain *verb*
1. *The doctor* **explained** *the procedure carefully.* • make clear, give an explanation of, clarify, describe
2. *Can you* **explain** *your strange behaviour?* • give reasons for, account for, excuse, make excuses for, justify

explode *verb*
1. *The firework* **exploded** *with a bang.* • blow up, make an explosion, go off, burst, shatter
2. *The slightest movement might* **explode** *the bomb.* • detonate, set off

explore *verb*
1. *The spacecraft will* **explore** *the solar system.* • search, survey, travel through, probe
2. *We must* **explore** *all the possibilities.* • examine, inspect, investigate, look into, research, analyse, scrutinize

explorer *noun*

WORD WEB

The **explorers** *were looking for the legendary Lost City.* • discoverer, traveller, voyager, wanderer

THINGS AN EXPLORER MIGHT FIND
• catacombs, cave, cavern, chest, hieroglyphics, inscription, labyrinth, maze, mummy, parchment, pyramid, riddle, sarcophagus, seal, secret passage, skeleton, stone tablet, temple, tomb, treasure, tunnel, underground chamber

THINGS AN EXPLORER MIGHT USE OR CARRY
• binoculars, chart, compass, machete, map, penknife, rope, rucksack, telescope, tent, torch, water bottle

explosion *noun*
The **explosion** *rattled the windows.* • blast, bang • An explosion from a volcano is an **eruption**. • An explosion of laughter is an **outburst**. • The sound of a gun going off is a **report**.

expression *noun*
1. *'Tickled pink' is a colloquial* **expression**. • phrase, saying, term, wording • An expression that people use too much is a **cliché**.
2. *Did you see her* **expression** *when I told her the news?* • look, appearance, countenance, face

expression *noun*

WORD WEB

EXPRESSIONS YOU MIGHT SEE ON A FACE
• beam, frown, glare, glower, grimace, grin, laugh, leer, long face, poker-face, pout, scowl, smile, smirk, sneer, wide-eyed look, wince, yawn

extent *noun*
1. *The map shows the* **extent** *of the island.* • area, dimensions, expanse, spread, breadth, length, limits, measurement
2. *After the storm we went out to see the* **extent** *of the damage.* • amount, degree, level, size, scope, magnitude, range

exterior *noun*
He painted the **exterior** *of his house.* • outside
opposite interior

external *adjective*
In **external** *appearance, the house was rather gloomy.* • exterior, outside, outer
opposite internal

extra *adjective*
1. *There is an* **extra** *charge for taking your bike on the train.* • additional, further, added, supplementary, excess
2. *There is* **extra** *food in the kitchen if you need it.* • more, spare, surplus, reserve

extraordinary *adjective*
The astronauts saw many extraordinary sights. • amazing, astonishing, remarkable, outstanding, exceptional, incredible, fantastic, marvellous, miraculous, phenomenal, rare, special, strange, surprising, unheard of, unusual, weird, wonderful, abnormal, curious
opposite ordinary

extreme *adjective*
1. *Polar bears can withstand extreme cold.*
• great, intense, severe, acute, excessive
2. *She lives on the extreme edge of the forest.*
• farthest, furthest

extremely *adverb*
Michael looked extremely uncomfortable with the turn the conversation had taken.
• incredibly, extraordinarily, unusually, distinctly, enormously

eye *noun*

WORD WEB

PARTS OF YOUR EYE
• eyeball, eyebrow, eyelash, eyelid; cornea, iris, lens, pupil, retina • A person who tests your eyesight is an **optician**. • A word meaning 'to do with eyes' is **optical**.
• A person with good eyesight is said to have **eyes like a hawk**.

WRITING TIPS

You can use these words to describe **eyes**:
• beady, bulbous, bulging, deep-set, glassy, heavy-lidded, hooded, protuberant, saucer-like, sunken; cloudy, misty, moist, piercing, steely, tearful, watery
The monster had a single bulging red eye.

a
b
c
d
e
f
g
h
i
j
k
l
m
n
o
p
q
r
s
t
u
v
w
x
y
z

Ff

Look at the *food* panel for words to do with food: from *soggy* to *scrummy*, *kippers* to *custard*, and *pancakes* to *samosas*.

fabric *noun*
This *fabric* will make a lovely dress for my doll. • cloth, material, stuff • A plural word is **textiles**.

fabulous *adjective*
1. *(informal) We had a fabulous time at the party.* • excellent, first-class, marvellous, outstanding, superb, tremendous, wonderful, *(informal)* brilliant, fantastic, smashing
2. *Dragons are fabulous creatures.* • fictitious, imaginary, legendary, mythical

face *noun*
1. *The witch's face was dark with anger.* • expression, features, look, countenance
2. *The face of the clock had been smashed.* • front
3. *A cube has six faces.* • side, surface

✏ WRITING TIPS

You can use these words to describe a **face**.

TO DESCRIBE ITS SHAPE
• flat, heart-shaped, long, oval, round, rounded; lantern-jawed, square-jawed

TO DESCRIBE ITS FEATURES
• chiselled, chubby, craggy, delicate, fine, gaunt, haggard, hollow, pinched, prominent, puffy, skeletal, sunken
Their faces were gaunt and pinched from hunger.

TO DESCRIBE ITS SKIN OR COLOUR
• clear, dark, fair, flushed, freckled, fresh, glowing, healthy, rosy, ruddy, tanned; ashen, grey, leaden, pale, pallid, pasty, sallow, sickly, unhealthy, wan; flabby, saggy, shrivelled, weather-beaten, wizened, wrinkled, wrinkly; disfigured, pimply, pock-marked, scarred, spotty
The old lady's face was wizened like a prune.

TO DESCRIBE THE LOOK ON A FACE
• cheeky, cheerful, radiant, sunny; grave, grim, serious; sulky, sullen, surly; blank, deadpan, impassive, unmoving, vacant
The guard stared ahead, his face unmoving.

🕸 WORD WEB

EXPRESSIONS YOU MIGHT SEE ON A FACE
• beam, grin, smile, smirk, frown, glare, glower, grimace, leer, long face, poker-face, pout, scowl, sneer, wide-eyed look, wince, yawn

face *verb*
1. *Stand and face your partner.* • be opposite to, look towards
2. *The astronauts had to face many dangers.* • cope with, deal with, face up to, stand up to, tackle, meet, encounter, confront **opposite** avoid

fact *noun*
It is a *fact* that dodos are now extinct. • reality, truth, certainty **opposite** fiction
the facts
The detective considered the facts in the case. • details, particulars, information, data • Facts which are useful in trying to prove something are **evidence**. • Facts expressed as numbers are **statistics**.

factual *adjective*
She said I should read *factual* books instead of fairy tales. • real, true, truthful, accurate, authentic, faithful, genuine, objective, reliable • A film or story based on a person's life is **biographical**. • A film or story based on history is **historical**. • A film telling you about real events is a **documentary**. **opposite** made-up, fictional

fade *verb*
1. *Sunlight has* faded *the curtains.*
• make paler, bleach, blanch, whiten, dim
opposite brighten
2. *Those flowers will* fade *in a few days.* • wither, wilt, droop, flag, shrivel
opposite flourish
3. *Gradually, the light began to* fade.
• weaken, decline, diminish, dwindle, fail, wane, disappear, melt away, vanish
opposite increase

fail *verb*
1. *Their plan to steal the crown jewels* failed *miserably.* • be unsuccessful, go wrong, fall through, founder, come to grief, miscarry, *(informal)* flop, bomb
opposite succeed
2. *The rocket's engines* failed *just before take-off.* • break down, cut out, shut down, give up, stop working
3. *By late afternoon, the light had begun to* fail. • weaken, decline, diminish, dwindle, fade, gel worse, deteriorate
opposite improve
4. *The professor* failed *to warn us of the danger.* • neglect, forget, omit
opposite remember
5. *I hope I don't* fail *my violin exam.*
opposite pass

failure *noun*
1. *The storm caused a power* failure.
• breakdown, fault, malfunction, crash, loss, collapse, stoppage
2. *Their attempt to reach the North Pole was a* failure. • defeat, disappointment, disaster, fiasco, *(informal)* flop, wash-out
opposite success

faint *adjective*
1. *The details in the photograph are very* faint. • faded, dim, unclear, indistinct, vague, blurred, hazy, pale, shadowy, misty
opposite clear, distinct
2. *There was a* faint *smell of burning in the air.* • delicate, slight **opposite** strong
3. *We heard a* faint *cry for help.* • weak, low, muffled, distant, hushed, muted, soft, thin
opposite loud
4. *Gordon was so hungry that he felt* faint. • dizzy, giddy, light-headed, unsteady, weak, exhausted, feeble, *(informal)* woozy

faint *verb*
The explorers nearly fainted *from exhaustion.*
• become unconscious, collapse, pass out, black out, *(old use)* swoon

fair *adjective*
1. *I think the referee made a* fair *decision.*
• just, proper, right, fair-minded, honest, honourable, impartial, unbiased, unprejudiced, disinterested
opposite unfair
2. *The twins both have* fair *hair.* • blond or blonde, light, golden, yellow **opposite** dark
3. *Our team has a* fair *chance of winning the cup.* • reasonable, moderate, average, acceptable, adequate, satisfactory, passable, respectable, tolerable
4. *The weather should be* fair *today.*
• dry, fine, sunny, bright, clear, cloudless, pleasant, favourable

fair *noun*
1. *My sister won a teddy bear at the* fair.
• fairground, funfair, carnival, fete, gala
2. *Our school is holding a book* fair *next week.* • show, exhibition, display, market, bazaar

fairly *adverb*
1. *The competition will be judged* fairly.
• honestly, properly, justly, impartially
2. *The ground is still* fairly *wet. I'm* fairly *certain that we are heading north.*
• quite, rather, somewhat, slightly, moderately, up to a point, reasonably, tolerably, *(informal)* pretty

fairy *noun* fairies

WORD WEB

THINGS A FAIRY MIGHT HAVE OR USE
• fairy dust, lantern, wand, wings

A FAIRY'S WINGS OR CLOTHES MIGHT BE
• diaphanous, feathery, glittering, glowing, gossamer, lustrous, sheer, sparkling, translucent, transparent

PLACES WHERE A FAIRY MIGHT LIVE
• dell, glade, glen, magic forest or tree, mound, toadstool

SOME CREATURES LIKE FAIRIES
• brownie, elf, imp, leprechaun, nymph, pixie, sprite

faith noun
1. *The acrobat had complete* faith *in his assistant.* • belief, trust, confidence **opposite** doubt
2. *In our school, we have pupils of many different* faiths. • religion, creed, doctrine, belief

faithful adjective
My dog Scruffy is my most faithful *friend.* • loyal, devoted, reliable, trustworthy, dependable, firm, constant, close **opposite** unfaithful

fake noun
That's not a real Roman coin—it's a fake. • copy, imitation, reproduction, replica, forgery, *(informal)* phoney • An event which fakes a real event is a **hoax** or a **sham**. • An event which a practice for a real event is a **simulation**. • A person who pretends to be another person is an **impostor**.

fake verb
The spy tried to fake *a foreign accent.* • imitate, copy, pretend, put on, reproduce, simulate • To fake someone's signature is to **forge** it.

fall verb **falling, fell, fallen**
1. *The acrobat* fell *off a ladder and broke his leg.* • tumble, topple, crash down, pitch, plunge
2. *Snow was beginning to* fall *quite thickly.* • drop, come down, descend, rain down, plummet
3. *The level of the river had* fallen *since March.* • go down, subside, recede, sink, ebb
4. *The temperature in the cave* fell *to below freezing.* • go down, become lower, decrease, decline, lessen, diminish, dwindle
to fall in
The roof of the cabin fell in *during the storm.* • cave in, collapse, give way
to fall out
The twins are always falling out *with each other.* • argue, disagree, quarrel, squabble, bicker

fall noun
1. *Ellen had a* fall *and cut her knee.* • tumble
2. *We noticed a sharp* fall *in the temperature.* • drop, lowering **opposite** rise
3. *There has been a* fall *in the price of games consoles.* • decrease, reduction, decline **opposite** increase
4. *This is a story about the* fall *of Troy.* • defeat, surrender

false adjective
1. *They gave us* false *information about*

the treasure. • wrong, incorrect, untrue, inaccurate, mistaken, erroneous, faulty, invalid, misleading, deceptive **opposite** correct
2. *The spy was travelling with a* false *passport.* • fake, bogus, sham, counterfeit, forged **opposite** genuine, authentic
3. *Mrs Gummidge put in her* false *teeth.* • artificial, imitation **opposite** real, natural
4. *The Black Knight turned out to be a* false *ally.* • unfaithful, disloyal, unreliable, untrustworthy, deceitful, dishonest, treacherous **opposite** faithful, loyal

fame noun
Her Olympic medal brought her international fame. • celebrity, stardom, renown, glory, reputation, name, standing, stature, prominence • Fame that you get for doing something bad is **notoriety**.

familiar adjective
1. *Seagulls are a* familiar *sight at the seaside.* • common, everyday, normal, ordinary, usual, regular, customary, frequent, mundane, routine **opposite** rare
2. *It seems a bit* familiar *to call her by her first name.* • informal, friendly, intimate, relaxed, close **opposite** formal, unfriendly
to be familiar with something
Are you familiar with *the rules of chess?* • be acquainted with, be aware of, know

family noun **families**

```
   WORD WEB
```

Some members of my family *live in New Zealand.* • relations, relatives • An old-fashioned term for your family is your **kin**. • The official term for your closest relative is **next of kin**. • A group of related Scottish families is a **clan**. • A succession of people from the same powerful family is a **dynasty**. • In certain societies, a group of families living together is a **tribe**. • A single stage in a family is a **generation**. • The people in your family in previous generations are your **ancestors**. • The people in your family in later generations are your **descendants**. • The line of ancestors from which a family is descended is its **ancestry**. • A diagram showing how people in your family are related is a **family tree**. • The study of family history is **genealogy**. • A family of young birds is a **brood**. • A family of kittens or puppies is a **litter**.

MEMBERS OF A FAMILY MAY INCLUDE
• adopted child, aunt, brother, child, cousin, daughter, father, foster-child, foster-parent, grandchild, grandparent, great aunt, great uncle, husband, mother, nephew, niece, parent, sister, son, spouse, step-child, step-parent, uncle, wife • A person who looks after a child whose parents have died is a **guardian**. • A child who is looked after by a guardian is their **ward**.

famous *adjective*
Messi is a very *famous* *football player.*
• well-known, celebrated, renowned, acclaimed, notable, prominent, distinguished, eminent • To be famous for doing something bad is to be **notorious**. **opposite** unknown, obscure

fan *noun*
I used to be a big *fan* *of baseball.* • enthusiast, admirer, devotee • A fan of a sport or team is a **follower** or **supporter**.

fanatic *noun*
My brother is a rugby *fanatic.* • enthusiast, addict, devotee, *(informal)* freak, nut

fancy *adjective* **fancier, fanciest**
Mum bought a *fancy* *hat for her friend's wedding.* • elaborate, decorative, ornamental, ornate **opposite** plain

fancy *verb* **fancies, fancying, fancied**
1. *What do you* *fancy* *to eat?* • feel like, want, wish for, desire, prefer
2. *She* *fancied* *she heard a noise downstairs.*
• imagine, think, believe, suppose

fantastic *adjective*
1. *The story is full of* *fantastic* *creatures.*
• fanciful, extraordinary, strange, odd, weird, outlandish, far-fetched, incredible, imaginative **opposite** realistic

2. *(informal) We had a* *fantastic* *time at camp.* • excellent, first-class, outstanding, superb, wonderful, tremendous, marvellous, *(informal)* brilliant, fabulous, smashing

fantasy *noun* **fantasies**
Rosie had a *fantasy* *about being a mermaid.*
• dream, daydream, delusion, fancy

far *adjective* **farther, farthest**
1. *The castle stood in the* *far* *north of the country.* • distant, faraway, remote
2. *The ferry took us to the* *far* *side of the river.*
• opposite, other

farm *noun*

WORD WEB

• The formal word for farming is **agriculture**. • A farm which uses no artificial fertilizers or chemicals is an **organic farm**. • A very small farm is a **smallholding**. • A small farm growing fruit and vegetables is a **market garden**.
• A small farm in Scotland is a **croft**.
• A large cattle farm in America is a **ranch**.

FARM BUILDINGS
• barn, byre or cowshed, dairy, farmhouse, granary, milking parlour, outhouse, pigsty, stable

OTHER PARTS OF A FARM
• barnyard or farmyard, cattle pen, field, haystack, meadow, paddock, pasture, rick, sheepfold, silo
ITEMS OF FARM EQUIPMENT
• baler, combine harvester, cultivator, drill, harrow, harvester, mower, planter, plough, tractor, trailer
PEOPLE WHO WORK ON A FARM
• agricultural worker, *(old use)* dairymaid or

milkmaid, farmer, farm labourer, ploughman, shepherd, stockbreeder, tractor driver

SOME FARM ANIMALS
• bull, bullock, chicken or hen, cow, duck, goat, goose, horse, pig, sheep, turkey
• Birds kept on a farm are **poultry**.
• Cows and bulls kept for milk or beef are **cattle**. • Farm animals in general are **livestock**.

fascinate *verb*
Machines have always fascinated him.
• interest, intrigue, engross, captivate, enthrall, absorb, beguile, entrance, attract, charm, enchant, delight **opposite** bore

fascinated *adjective*
We were fascinated by the inventor's workshop. • interested, engrossed, captivated, enthralled, absorbed, beguiled, entranced, attracted, charmed, enchanted, delighted **opposite** bored

fashion *noun*
1. *The aliens were behaving in a very peculiar fashion.* • way, manner
2. *Zoe was always dressed in the latest fashion.* • trend, vogue, craze, fad, style, look

fashionable *adjective*
Megan has a fashionable new coat.
• stylish, chic, up-to-date, popular, elegant, smart, (informal) trendy, hip, in **opposite** unfashionable, out-of-date

fast *adjective*
The robber made a fast exit when he heard us coming. • quick, rapid, speedy, swift, brisk, hurried, hasty, high-speed, headlong, breakneck, (informal) nippy • Something which goes faster than sound is **supersonic**.
• A common simile is **as fast as lightning**.
opposite slow, unhurried

fast *adverb*
1. *Mr Toad was driving too fast in his motor car.* • quickly, speedily, swiftly, rapidly, briskly
2. *The boat was stuck fast on the rocks.*
• firmly, securely, tightly
3. *Be quiet! The baby is fast asleep.* • deeply, sound, completely

fasten *verb*
1. *They fastened their ropes to the rock face.* • tie, fix, attach, connect, join, link, bind, hitch, clamp, pin, clip, tack, stick • To fasten a boat is to **anchor** or **moor** it. • To fasten an animal is to **tether** it.

2. *They fastened the gate with a heavy chain.*
• secure, seal, lock, bolt, make fast

fat *adjective* **fatter, fattest**
1. *You'll get fat if you eat too many crisps!*
• overweight, big, chubby, tubby, plump, podgy, dumpy, flabby, portly, stout, round, rotund, obese
2. *The witch opened a big, fat book of spells.*
• thick, bulky, chunky, weighty, substantial **opposite** thin

fatal *adjective*
1. *The knight delivered a fatal wound to his enemy.* • deadly, lethal, mortal • A fatal illness is an **incurable** or **terminal** illness.
2. *Leaving the door unlocked was a fatal mistake.* • disastrous, catastrophic, dreadful, calamitous

fate *noun*
1. *The shipwrecked crew were in the hands of fate.* • fortune, destiny, providence, chance, luck
2. *The prisoner met with a terrible fate.*
• death, end

fault *noun*
1. *Danny has many faults, but meanness isn't one of them.* • defect, flaw, failing, imperfection, deficiency, weakness, shortcoming, inadequacy
2. *This laptop has a fault in it.* • defect, flaw, malfunction, snag, problem
3. *It was my fault that we missed our bus.*
• responsibility, liability

faulty *adjective* **faultier, faultiest**
The TV was faulty, so we took it back to the shop. • broken, not working, defective, out of order, unusable, damaged **opposite** perfect

favour *noun*
1. *I asked my friend to do me a favour.* • good deed, good turn, kindness, service, courtesy
2. *The captain's plan found favour with most of the crew.* • approval, support, liking, goodwill
to be in favour of something
We're all in favour of longer holidays. • agree to, approve of, support, like the idea of

favourite *adjective*
What is your favourite book? • best-loved, preferred, treasured, dearest, special, top

fear *noun*
When Garth heard the monster, he trembled with fear. • fright, terror, horror, alarm, panic, dread, anxiety, apprehension, trepidation • A formal word for a special

type of fear is **phobia**. • A fear of open spaces is **agoraphobia**. • A fear of spiders is **arachnophobia**. • A fear of enclosed spaces is **claustrophobia**. • A fear of heights is **acrophobia**.

fear *verb*
1. *My sister fears snakes and spiders.* • be frightened of, be afraid of, be scared of, dread
2. *I fear we may be too late.* • suspect, expect, anticipate

fearful *adjective*
1. *The young warrior had a fearful look in his eyes.* • frightened, scared, terrified, afraid, panicky, nervous, anxious, timid **opposite** brave
2. *The erupting volcano was a fearful sight.* • frightening, terrifying, shocking, fearsome, ghastly, dreadful, appalling, terrible

fearless *adjective*
The fearless explorers entered the dark cave. • brave, courageous, daring, heroic, valiant, intrepid, plucky **opposite** cowardly

feast *noun*
The king held a great feast to celebrate his birthday. • banquet, dinner, *(informal)* spread

feat *noun*
The trapeze artists performed many daring feats. • act, action, deed, exploit, achievement, performance

feather *noun*
• A large feather is a **plume**. • All the feathers on a bird are its **plumage**. • Soft, fluffy feathers are **down**. • A feather used as a pen is a **quill**.

feature *noun*
1. *The castle has several unusual features.* • characteristic, detail, point, aspect, quality, peculiarity, trait, facet • A person's features are their **face**.
2. *There was a feature about our school in the newspaper.* • article, report, story, item, piece

feeble *adjective*
1. *The elderly knight looked tired and feeble.* • weak, frail, infirm, delicate, poorly, sickly, puny, weary, weedy **opposite** strong, powerful
2. *I made a feeble attempt to stop the ball. Do you expect me to believe that feeble excuse?* • weak, poor, ineffective, inadequate, unconvincing, tame, flimsy, lame

feed *verb* **feeding, fed**
We have enough sandwiches to feed six people. • provide for, cater for, give food to, nourish
to feed on
The leopard was feeding on its prey. • eat, consume, devour

feel *verb* **feeling, felt**
1. *I felt the llama's soft, woolly fur.* • touch, caress, stroke, fondle
2. *It feels colder today.* • appear, seem, strike you as
3. *Older people tend to feel the cold more.* • notice, be aware of, be conscious of, experience, suffer from
4. *I feel that it's time we made a start.* • think, believe, consider
to feel like
Do you feel like going for a walk? • fancy, want, desire, wish for, long for, yearn for

---

✏️ WRITING TIPS

You can use these words to describe how something **feels**.

TO DESCRIBE SOMETHING HARD OR ROUGH
• bristly, coarse, crinkly, crunchy, dry, fibrous, grainy, hairy, knobbly, lumpy, rough, stiff, stringy
The sail was made of strips of coarse woollen cloth.

TO DESCRIBE SOMETHING SOFT OR SMOOTH
• creamy, feathery, fine, fluffy, papery, rubbery, silky, smooth, soft, spongy, springy, squashy, velvety, woolly
She slid in between the soft, smooth sheets and fell asleep immediately.

TO DESCRIBE SOMETHING WET OR DAMP
• boggy, creamy, gooey, moist, runny, slimy, sticky, watery
Mrs Campbell poured a glass of gooey, sticky liquid into two glasses.

---

feel *noun*
I love the feel of warm sand between my toes. • feeling, sensation, touch

feeling *noun*
1. *The cat had lost all feeling in its paw.* • sense of touch, sensation, sensitivity
2. *I didn't mean to hurt your feelings.* • emotion, passion, sentiment
3. *I have a feeling that something is wrong.* • suspicion, notion, inkling, hunch, idea, impression, fancy, intuition

fence noun
The house was surrounded by a tall fence.
• railing, barrier, wall, hedge, paling, stockade

fend verb
to fend for yourself
The lion cubs will soon have to fend for themselves. • look after, take care of, care for
to fend someone or **something off**
The knight raised his shield to fend off the blow. • repel, resist, ward off, fight off, hold off, thwart

ferocious adjective
The mansion was guarded by a ferocious dog. • fierce, fearsome, savage, wild, vicious, violent, bloodthirsty, brutal **opposite** tame

fertile adjective
The surrounding countryside was green and fertile. • fruitful, productive, rich, fecund **opposite** barren, sterile

festival noun
The town holds a festival every summer.
• carnival, fiesta, fete, gala, fair, celebration, jamboree • A celebration of a special anniversary is a **jubilee**.

festive adjective
Chinese New Year is a festive occasion.
• cheerful, happy, merry, jolly, cheery, joyful, joyous, jovial, light-hearted, celebratory **opposite** gloomy, sombre

fetch verb
1. *I fetched the shopping from the car.* • get, bring, carry, collect, transfer, transport, convey, pick up, retrieve, obtain
2. *If we sell my bike, how much will it fetch?*
• make, raise, sell for, go for, bring in, earn

feud noun
There has been a feud between their families for years. • quarrel, dispute, conflict, hostility, enmity, rivalry, strife, antagonism • A feud that lasts a long time is a **vendetta**.

feverish adjective
1. *The cold made me feel feverish.* • When you are feverish you are **hot** and **shivery**. • With a bad fever you may become **delirious**.
2. *There was feverish activity in the kitchen.*
• frenzied, frantic, frenetic, excited, agitated, hectic, busy, hurried, impatient, restless

fictional adjective
Harry Potter is a fictional character.
• imaginary, made-up, invented, fanciful **opposite** factual, real

fictitious adjective
The spy was using a fictitious name. • false, fake, fabricated, fraudulent, bogus, assumed, spurious, unreal **opposite** genuine, real

fiddle verb
1. *Who's been fiddling with the laptop?*
• tinker, meddle, tamper, play about, mess about, twiddle
2. *(informal) Mr Filch had been fiddling the accounts for years.* • falsify, alter, rig, *(informal)* cook the books

fiddly adjective
Icing a cake can be a fiddly job. • intricate, complicated, awkward, involved **opposite** simple

fidget verb
I begin to fidget when I'm bored. • be restless, fiddle about, play about, mess about

field noun
1. *Cattle were grazing in the field.* • meadow, pasture • A small field for horses is a **paddock**.
• An area of grass in a village is a **green**.
2. *The field is too wet to play football.* • ground, pitch, playing field
3. *Electronics is not really his field.* • special interest, speciality, area of study

fierce adjective
1. *The travellers were killed in a fierce attack by armed bandits.* • vicious, ferocious, savage, brutal, violent, wild, cruel, merciless, ruthless, pitiless
2. *Our team will face fierce opposition in the final.* • strong, keen, eager, aggressive, competitive, passionate, relentless
3. *The explorers braved the fierce heat of the desert sun.* • blazing, intense, raging

fiery adjective fierier, fieriest
1. *It's best to avoid the fiery heat of the midday sun.* • blazing, burning, hot, intense, fierce, raging, flaming, red-hot, glowing
2. *My great aunt has always had a fiery temper.* • violent, passionate, excitable, angry, furious

fight noun
1. *The warriors faced each other for a fight to the death.* • Fighting is **combat** or **hostilities**.
• A fight between armies is a **battle**. • A minor unplanned battle is a **skirmish**. • A series of battles is a **campaign** or **war**. • A minor fight is a **brawl**, **scrap**, **scuffle** or **tussle**. • A fight arranged between two people is a **duel**.
2. *We support the fight to save the rainforest.*
• campaign, crusade, struggle

fight *verb* **fighting, fought**
1. *Two seagulls were* **fighting** *over a scrap of bread.* • have a fight, scrap, scuffle, exchange blows, come to blows
2. *The two countries* **fought** *each other in the war.* • do battle with, wage war with, attack • Fighting with swords is **fencing**. • Fighting with fists is **boxing**. • Fighting in which you try to throw your opponent to the ground is **wrestling**. • Fighting sports such as karate and judo are **martial arts**.
3. *We will* **fight** *the decision to close our local library.* • protest against, oppose, resist, make a stand against, campaign against

figure *noun*
1. *Please write the* **figure** *'8' on the board.* • number, numeral, digit, integer
2. *I made out a group of shadowy* **figures** *in the gloom.* • body, build, form, shape
3. *Inside the temple were several clay* **figures**. • statue, carving, sculpture

figure *verb*
Donald Duck **figures** *in many cartoons.* • appear, feature, take part
to figure out
We couldn't **figure out** *what the riddle meant.* • work out, make out, understand, see

file *noun*
1. *I keep all my award certificates in a* **file**. • folder, binder, cover • A file containing information, especially secret information, is a **dossier**.
2. *Please walk in a single* **file**. • line, row, column, rank, queue, procession

fill *verb*
1. *Dad* **filled** *the trolley with shopping.* • load, pack, stuff, cram, top up • To fill a tyre or ball with air is to **inflate** it. **opposite** empty
2. *What can I use to* **fill** *this hole?* • close up, plug, seal, block up, stop up
3. *Sightseers* **filled** *the streets.* • crowd, jam, block, obstruct, (*informal*) bung up

film *noun*
1. *There is a good* **film** *on TV tonight.* • movie, picture, video, DVD • A long film is a **feature film**. • A short excerpt from a film is a **clip**. • A script for a film is a **screenplay** and a writer of screenplays is a **screenwriter**. • A well-known film actor is a **film star**. • A place where films are shown is a **cinema** or (*American*) **movie theater**. • An old-fashioned word for a place where films are shown is a **picture house**.
2. *There was a* **film** *of oil on the water.* • coat, coating, layer, covering, sheet, skin • A large patch of oil floating on water is a **slick**.

filthy *adjective*
Those trainers are **filthy**! • dirty, mucky, messy, grimy, grubby, muddy, soiled, stained **opposite** clean

final *adjective*
1. *The* **final** *moments of the match were very tense.* • last, closing, concluding **opposite** opening
2. *What was the* **final** *result?* • eventual, ultimate

finally *adverb*
I've **finally** *managed to finish my book.* • eventually, at last, in the end

find *verb* **finding, found**
1. *Did you* **find** *any fossils on the beach?* • come across, discover, see, spot, locate, encounter, stumble across, unearth
2. *The children never* **found** *the secret door again.* • trace, track down, recover, retrieve **opposite** lose
3. *Did the doctor* **find** *what was wrong?* • detect, identify, diagnose, ascertain
4. *You will* **find** *that building a tree house is hard work.* • become aware, realize, learn, recognize, notice, observe

fine *adjective*
1. *The young musicians gave a* **fine** *performance.* • excellent, first-class, superb, splendid, outstanding, admirable, commendable **opposite** poor, weak
2. *As the weather was* **fine**, *we took a picnic.* • sunny, fair, bright, clear, cloudless, pleasant, good **opposite** bad, dull
3. *Spiders spin very* **fine** *thread for their webs.* • delicate, fragile, thin, flimsy, slender, slim **opposite** thick
4. *The desert dunes were made of* **fine** *sand.* • dusty, powdery **opposite** coarse
5. *There is a* **fine** *line between teasing and bullying.* • delicate, precise, subtle

finish *verb*
1. *When are you likely to* **finish** *your homework?* • complete, reach the end of, cease, round off
2. *The film should* **finish** *around nine o'clock.* • end, stop, conclude, terminate, (*informal*) wind up

3. *I've already finished my bag of crisps.*
• consume, use up, get through, exhaust, *(informal)* polish off **opposite** start

finish *noun*
We stayed to watch the parade until the finish. • end, close, conclusion, completion, result, termination **opposite** start

fire *noun*
The campers toasted marshmallows in the fire. • blaze, flames, conflagration • A very big hot fire is an **inferno**. • An open fire out of doors is a **bonfire**. • An enclosed fire which produces great heat is a **furnace**. • An enclosed fire for cooking food is an **oven**. • An enclosed fire for making pottery is a **kiln**. • The process by which a fire starts is **combustion**. • A team of people whose job is to put out fires is a **fire brigade**. • A member of a fire brigade is a **firefighter**.

fire *verb*
1. *The soldier aimed his rifle and fired two shots.* • shoot, discharge, let off, set off • To fire a missile is to **launch** it.
2. *(informal) Miss Stark fired her assistant for being late for work.* • dismiss, sack, lay off

firm *noun*
Mr Perkins owns a firm that makes biscuits. • company, business, organization, enterprise

firm *adjective*
1. *The surface of the planet was dry and firm.* • hard, solid, dense, compact, rigid, set **opposite** soft
2. *Make sure the knots in the rope are firm.* • secure, tight, strong, stable, fixed, sturdy, steady
3. *Zelda had a firm belief in the power of magic.* • definite, certain, sure, decided, determined, resolute, unshakeable, unwavering **opposite** unsure
4. *The two girls have become firm friends.* • close, devoted, faithful, loyal, constant, dependable, reliable

first *adjective*
1. *The first inhabitants of the area were Picts.* • earliest, original
2. *The first thing to do in an emergency is to keep calm.* • principal, key, main, fundamental, basic, chief

fish *noun*

WORD WEB

SOME TYPES OF FISH
• brill, carp, catfish, chub, cod, conger, cuttlefish, dace, eel, flounder, goldfish, grayling, gudgeon, haddock, hake, halibut, herring, lamprey, ling, mackerel, minnow, mullet, perch, pike, pilchard, piranha, plaice, roach, salmon, sardine, sawfish, shark, skate, sole, sprat, squid, stickleback, sturgeon, swordfish, trout, tuna, turbot, whitebait, whiting

fishing *noun*
The cottage was full of fishing gear and boating equipment. • angling • A person who fishes is a **fisherman**, a **fisher** or an **angler**. • A long pole used for catching fish is a **fishing rod**. • To catch a fish is to **land** it. • Food that is used to catch fish is **bait**.

fit *adjective* **fitter, fittest**
1. *Cinderella's gown was fit for a princess.* • suitable, appropriate, fitting, right, good enough, worthy (of) **opposite** unsuitable
2. *I walk to school every day to keep fit.* • healthy, well, strong, robust, in shape, *(old use)* hale and hearty • A common simile is **as fit as a fiddle**. **opposite** unhealthy
3. *After a long ride, the horses were fit to collapse.* • ready, liable, likely, about

fit *verb* **fitting, fitted**
1. *We need to fit a new lock on the door.* • install, put in place, position
2. *This key doesn't fit the lock. He fits the description of the wanted criminal.* • match, correspond to, go together with, tally with
3. *Her speech fitted the occasion perfectly.* • be suitable for, be appropriate to, suit

fix *verb*
1. *The soldier fixed a bayonet to the end of his rifle.* • fasten, attach, connect, join, link
2. *We fixed the tent poles firmly in place.* • set, secure, make firm, stabilize
3. *Let's fix a time for the party.* • decide on,

agree on, set, arrange, settle, determine, specify, finalize
4. *Dad says he can* fix *my bike.* • repair, mend, sort, put right

fix *noun*
(informal) Can you help me? I'm in a fix.
• difficulty, mess, predicament, plight, *(informal)* jam, hole

fizzy *adjective*
Could I have a bottle of fizzy *water, please?*
• sparkling, bubbly, effervescent, gassy, foaming **opposite** still

flag *noun*
The street was decorated with flags *for the carnival.* • banner, pennant, streamer
• The flag of a regiment is its **colours** or **standard**. • A flag flown on a ship is an **ensign**.
• Decorative strips of small flags are **bunting**.

flap *verb* flapping, flapped
The sail flapped *in the wind.* • flutter, sway, swing, wave about, thrash about

flash *verb*
We saw a light flash *from an upstairs window.*
• shine, beam, blaze, flare, glare, gleam, glint, flicker, glimmer, sparkle

flash *noun*
There were flashes *of lightning in the sky.*
• blaze, flare, beam, ray, shaft, burst, gleam, glint, flicker, glimmer, sparkle

flat *adjective* flatter, flattest
1. *You need a* flat *surface to write on.* • even, level, smooth, plane • A common simile is **as flat as a pancake**. **opposite** uneven
2. *I lay* flat *on the ground.* • horizontal, outstretched, spread out • To be lying face downwards is to be **prone**. • To be lying face upwards is to be **supine**. **opposite** upright
3. *The robot spoke in a* flat, *electronic voice.* • dull, boring, lifeless, uninteresting, monotonous, tedious **opposite** lively
4. *The front tyre of my bike was* flat. • deflated, punctured **opposite** inflated
5. *Our request met with a* flat *refusal.*
• outright, straight, positive, absolute, total, utter, point-blank

flatten *verb*
1. *We* flattened *out the crumpled map on the desk.* • smooth, press, roll out, iron out
2. *The earthquake* flattened *several buildings.*
• demolish, destroy, knock down, pull down, level
3. *The young plants were* flattened *by the rain.*
• squash, crush, trample

flavour *noun*
1. *I don't like the* flavour *of raw onions.* • taste, tang
2. *Which* flavour *of ice cream do you like best?*
• kind, sort, variety

flaw *noun*
1. *Pride was the only* flaw *in his character.*
• weakness, fault, shortcoming, failing, lapse
2. *I can see a* flaw *in your argument.* • error, inaccuracy, mistake, slip

flee *verb* fleeing, fled
When they heard the alarm, the robbers fled.
• run away, bolt, fly, escape, get away, take off, hurry off, *(informal)* clear off, make off, scarper

fleet *noun*
• A fleet of boats or small ships is a **flotilla**.
• A fleet of warships is an **armada**. • A military fleet belonging to a country is its **navy**.

flexible *adjective*
1. *I need a pair of trainers with* flexible *soles.*
• bendable, supple, pliable, bendy, elastic, springy **opposite** rigid, inflexible
2. *My working hours are very* flexible.
• adjustable, adaptable, variable, open **opposite** fixed

flicker *verb*
The candles flickered *in the draught.* • twinkle, glimmer, waver, flutter, blink, shimmer

flimsy *adjective* flimsier, flimsiest
1. *The kite was so* flimsy *that it broke apart.*
• fragile, delicate, frail, brittle, weak, wobbly, shaky, rickety, **opposite** sturdy, robust
2. *The fairy wore a dress of the* flimsiest *silk.*
• thin, fine, light, lightweight, floaty

flinch *verb*
He flinched *as an arrow flew past his head.*
• back off, draw back, falter, recoil, shrink back, start, wince

fling *verb* flinging, flung
I flung *a stone into the pond.* • throw, cast, sling, toss, hurl, pitch, *(informal)* chuck, bung

float *verb*
We watched the twigs float *gently down the river.* • sail, drift, glide, slip, slide, waft

flood *noun*
1. *The* flood *of water swept away the bridge.*
• deluge, rush, torrent, spate, inundation

2. *The restaurant has received a flood of complaints.* • succession, barrage, storm, volley, avalanche, torrent

flood verb
1. *The river burst its banks and flooded the valley.* • drown, swamp, inundate, submerge, immerse, engulf
2. *We have been flooded with entries for our competition.* • overwhelm, swamp, besiege, deluge

flop verb flopping, flopped
1. *I was so tired that I just flopped onto my bed.* • collapse, drop, fall, slump
2. *The plants will flop if you don't water them.* • dangle, droop, hang down, sag, wilt
3. *(informal) The first film flopped, but the sequel was a big hit.* • be unsuccessful, fail, founder, fall flat, be a bust

floppy adjective floppier, floppiest
The dog had long, floppy ears. • droopy, limp, saggy, soft **opposite** stiff, rigid

flow verb
The rain water flowed along the gutter. • run, stream, pour, glide • To flow slowly is to **dribble**, **drip**, **ooze**, **seep** or **trickle**. • To flow fast is to **cascade**, **gush** or **sweep**. • To flow with sudden force is to **spurt** or **squirt**. • To flow over the edge of something is to **overflow** or **spill**. • When blood flows from a wound, it **bleeds**. • When the tide flows out, it **ebbs**.

flow noun
1. *It's hard work rowing against the flow of the river.* • current, tide, drift
2. *There was a steady flow of water into the pond.* • stream, flood, cascade, gush, rush, spate

flower noun

> ### WORD WEB
>
> • A single flower is a **bloom**. • A mass of small flowers growing together on a tree is **blossom**. • Flowers in a vase are an **arrangement**. • A bunch of flowers arranged for a special occasion is a **bouquet, posy** or **spray**. • Flowers arranged in a circle are a **garland** or **wreath**. • A person who sells and arranges flowers is a **florist**.
>
> **SOME WILD FLOWERS**
> • bluebell, buttercup, catkin, cornflower, cowslip, daisy, dandelion, foxglove, poppy, primrose, violet

SOME GARDEN FLOWERS
• carnation, chrysanthemum, crocus, daffodil, dahlia, forget-me-not, geranium, hollyhock, hyacinth, iris, lily, marigold, pansy, petunia, rose, snowdrop, sunflower, tulip

fluffy adjective
Four fluffy ducklings were swimming in the pond. • feathery, downy, furry, fuzzy, hairy, woolly, shaggy, soft

flush verb
Rory flushed with embarrassment. • blush, go red, colour, redden, burn

flustered adjective
I get flustered when I have to read in assembly. • confused, upset, bothered, agitated, unsettled, ruffled, *(informal)* rattled **opposite** calm

flutter verb
A butterfly fluttered about the garden. • flap, beat, flicker, quiver, tremble, vibrate

foam noun
The bath water was covered with pinkish foam. • bubbles, froth, suds, lather • Foam made by sea water is **surf** or **spume**.

foam verb
The mixture in the cauldron foamed and gurgled. • froth, bubble, fizz, boil, seethe, ferment, lather

fog noun
The top of the mountain was covered with fog. • Thin fog is **haze** or **mist**. • A thick mixture of fog and smoke is **smog**.

fold verb
Fold the paper along the dotted line. • bend, double over, crease, pleat

fold noun
She smoothed the soft folds of her dress. • crease, furrow, layer • A fold which is pressed into a garment is a **pleat**.

folder *noun*
I keep all my art work in a folder. • file, binder, wallet, portfolio

follow *verb*
1. *Why does thunder always follow lightning?* • come after, succeed, replace
opposite precede
2. *I think that car is following us!* • go after, chase, pursue, track, trail, tail, stalk, hunt, shadow
3. *Follow this path until you reach the river.* • go along, keep to, stick to
4. *I followed the instructions on the packet.* • carry out, comply with, heed, obey, observe
5. *Which football team do you follow?* • be a fan of, support
6. *We found it hard to follow what the creature was saying.* • understand, comprehend, grasp, take in, catch

fond *adjective*
1. *Mrs Walker gave her pet poodle a fond kiss.* • loving, tender, affectionate
2. *Anna had fond hopes of becoming a film star.* • foolish, silly, unrealistic, fanciful
to be fond of
I'm very fond of chocolate cake. • be keen on, be partial to, like, love

food *noun*

WORD WEB

In the banqueting hall were tables laden with rich food. • eatables, foodstuffs, (informal) grub, nosh, refreshments, nourishment, nutrition, provisions, rations
• The food that you normally eat or choose to eat is your **diet**. • A diet which includes no meat is a **vegetarian** diet.
• A diet which includes no animal products is a **vegan** diet. • Food which includes fish or shellfish is **seafood**. • Foods made from milk, butter, cheese or eggs are **dairy foods**. • Food for farm animals is **fodder**.

SOME TYPES OF SEAFOOD
• bloater, bream, caviar, cod, crab, eel, haddock, halibut, herring, kipper, lobster, mackerel, monkfish, mussels, oysters, pilchard, plaice, prawn, salmon, sardine, scampi, sea bass, shrimp, sole, sprat, trout, tuna, whelks, whitebait, whiting

SOME DAIRY FOODS
• butter, cheese, cream, custard, eggs, ice cream, milk, yoghurt

FOODS MADE FROM FLOUR OR CEREALS
• batter, biscuit, bread, bun, cornflakes, cracker, crispbread, muesli, noodles, oatcake, pancake, pastry, popcorn, porridge, rice cake, roll, scone

SOME PREPARED DISHES OF FOOD
• balti, bhaji, broth, casserole, chilli, chips, chop suey, chow mein, curry, dhal, fritters, goulash, hotpot, hummus, omelette, pakora, panini, pasta, pie, pizza, quiche, samosa, sandwich, soufflé, soup, stew, stir-fry, sushi

SOME PUDDINGS AND OTHER SWEET FOODS
• brownie, cake, chocolate, flan, gateau, honey, jam, jelly, marmalade, marzipan, meringue, mousse, muffin, sponge, steamed pudding, sugar, tart, treacle, trifle

SOME FLAVOURINGS AND SAUCES FOR FOOD
• chilli, chutney, French dressing, garlic, gravy, herbs, ketchup, mayonnaise, mustard, pepper, pickle, salsa, salt, spice, vinegar • Things like salt and pepper which you add to food are **condiments** or **seasoning**.

a b c d e f g h i j k l m n o p q r s t u v w x y z

WRITING TIPS

You can use these words to describe **food**.

TO DESCRIBE HOW IT LOOKS OR FEELS
• chewy, creamy, crisp, crumbly, crunchy, dry, flaky, greasy, juicy, leathery, lumpy, milky, mushy, rubbery, runny, slimy, sloppy, smooth, soggy, soupy, spongy, sticky, stodgy, stringy, velvety, watery
The pudding was a sloppy, watery mess.

TO DESCRIBE HOW IT TASTES
• bitter, fiery, flavoursome, fresh, fruity, hot, mild, peppery, piquant, pungent, refreshing, salty, savoury, sharp, sour, spicy, strong, sugary, sweet, syrupy, tangy, tart, vinegary
The sauce was hot but not too spicy.

TO DESCRIBE FOOD YOU LIKE
• appetizing, delicious, divine, mouth-watering, tasty, tempting, well-cooked *(informal)* scrummy, scrumptious, yummy
These chocolate brownies taste divine!
• Something especially tasty to eat is a **delicacy**.

TO DESCRIBE FOOD YOU DO NOT LIKE
• bland, disgusting, flavourless, indigestible, inedible, nauseating, stomach-turning, tasteless, unappetizing; charred, mouldy, overcooked, slimy, sloppy, soggy, stale, undercooked, watery *(informal)* yukky
She placed a tray with sloppy porridge in front of me.

fool *noun*
Only a fool would believe that ridiculous story.
• idiot, dope, ass, clown, halfwit, dimwit, dunce, simpleton, blockhead, buffoon, clot, dunderhead, imbecile, moron, *(informal)* twit, chump, nitwit, nincompoop

fool *verb*
The spy fooled everyone with his disguises.
• deceive, trick, mislead, hoax, dupe, hoodwink, *(informal)* con, kid, have you on, take you in, pull the wool over your eyes
to fool about or **around**
We were told not to fool about in the swimming pool. • play about, mess about or around, muck about or around, misbehave

foolish *adjective*
It would be foolish to stand too close to the lions. • stupid, silly, idiotic, senseless, ridiculous, nonsensical, unwise, ill-advised, half-witted, unintelligent, absurd, crazy, mad, hare-brained, *(informal)* daft
opposite sensible

foot *noun* **feet**
1. *Rhona walked on the sand in her bare feet.*
• The foot of an animal that has claws is a **paw**.
• The foot of a cow, deer or horse is a **hoof**.
• A pig's foot is a **trotter**. • A bird's feet are its **claws**. • The feet of a bird of prey are its **talons**.
2. *We set up camp at the foot of the mountain.*
• base, bottom

football *noun* **footballs**

WORD WEB

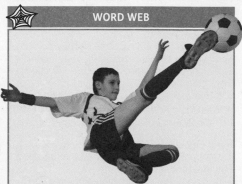

• Football is also known as **soccer**.
• Someone who plays football is a **footballer**. • Football is played on a **field** or **pitch** in a **ground**, **park** or **stadium**.

MEMBERS OF A FOOTBALL TEAM
• captain, defender, fullback, forward, goalkeeper or *(informal)* goalie, midfielder, striker, substitute, sweeper, winger

OTHER PEOPLE INVOLVED IN FOOTBALL
• ballboy or ballgirl, coach, linesman, manager, referee

SOME MOVES A FOOTBALLER MIGHT MAKE
• chip, dribble, dummy, header, kick, miss, pass, score, shot, tackle, volley

SOME OTHER TERMS USED IN FOOTBALL
• corner, crossbar, deflection, dugout, equalizer, extra time, final whistle, foul, free kick, goal, goalposts, half-time, kick-off, net, offside, penalty, penalty shootout, red or yellow card, sending off, throw-in

forbidden *adjective*
Skateboarding is forbidden in the playground.
• banned, barred, prohibited, disallowed, outlawed **opposite** allowed

force *noun*
1. *The firefighters had to use force to open the door.* • strength, power, might, muscle, vigour, effort, energy
2. *The force of the explosion broke all the windows.* • impact, effect, shock, intensity

3. *The soldiers are part of a peace-keeping force.* • group, unit, team, corps, army, troops

force *verb*
1. *The slaves were forced to work in the mines.* • compel, make, order, require, oblige, pressurize, coerce
2. *The king forced a new law upon the country.* • impose, inflict
3. *The firefighters had to force the door.* • break open, burst open, prise open, smash, wrench, (informal) yank

forecast *verb* forecasting, forecast, forecasted
Snow has been forecast for Tuesday. • foresee, foretell, predict

foreign *adjective*
1. *Lots of foreign tourists visit Edinburgh in the summer.* • overseas, international **opposite** native, domestic
2. *I like travelling to foreign countries.* • overseas, distant, faraway, exotic, remote, far-flung

forever *adverb*
Timmy is forever complaining about something. • constantly, continually, always, perpetually

forgery *noun* forgeries
One of these paintings is a forgery. • fake, copy, imitation, reproduction, replica, (informal) phoney

forget *verb* forgetting, forgot, forgotten
1. *I forgot my toothbrush when I packed my suitcase.* • leave out, leave behind, overlook
2. *I forgot to switch off the computer.* • omit, neglect, fail

forgive *verb* forgiving, forgave, forgiven
Please forgive me for being so rude. • excuse, pardon, let off, overlook, spare

form *noun*
1. *I made out the form of a man through the mist.* • shape, figure, outline, silhouette
2. *Ice is a form of water.* • kind, sort, type, variety
3. *Sally and I are in the same form at school.* • class, year, grade, set

form *verb*
1. *The sculptor formed the clay into the shape of a bird.* • shape, mould, model, fashion, work, cast
2. *My friends and I have formed a chess club.* • set up, establish, found, create, start

3. *Icicles had formed on the roof of the cave.* • appear, develop, grow, emerge, take shape

formal *adjective*
1. *I was invited to the formal opening of the museum.* • official, ceremonial
2. *The letter was written in a very formal style.* • correct, proper, conventional, dignified, solemn **opposite** informal, casual

former *adjective*
In former times, the castle was surrounded by a moat. • earlier, previous, past, bygone

fort *noun*
A few soldiers were left to defend the fort. • fortress, fortification, stronghold, castle, citadel, tower

fortunate *adjective*
We were fortunate to be alive. • lucky, in luck **opposite** unfortunate, unlucky

fortunately *adverb*
Fortunately we just caught the last train. • luckily, by good luck, by good fortune **opposite** unfortunately, unluckily

fortune *noun*
1. *By good fortune, I stumbled across a secret doorway.* • chance, luck, accident, fate
2. *The millionairess left her fortune to charity.* • wealth, riches, possessions, property, assets, estate, (informal) millions

forward *adjective*
1. *We need to do some forward planning for the camping trip.* • advance, early, future
2. *Would it be too forward to send him an email?* • bold, cheeky, brash, familiar, impudent, presumptuous

forwards *adverb*
1. *The queue moved forwards very slowly.* • on, onwards, along
2. *Will you all face forwards, please.* • to or toward the front, ahead

foul *adjective*
1. *The knight fainted at the foul smell of the dragon's breath.* • disgusting, revolting, repulsive, rotten, stinking, offensive, unpleasant, loathsome, nasty, horrible, vile **opposite** pleasant
2. *The walls and floor of the dungeon were foul.* • dirty, unclean, filthy, mucky, messy **opposite** clean, pure
3. *The player was sent off for using foul language.* • rude, offensive, insulting, abusive, improper, indecent, obscene

fragile adjective
Fossil dinosaur bones are very fragile.
• breakable, delicate, frail, brittle, easily damaged, weak **opposite** strong

fragment noun
I dug up a fragment of broken pottery.
• bit, piece, chip, sliver, shard

frail adjective
1. *My grandad felt frail after his illness.* • weak, infirm, feeble
2. *That step-ladder looks a bit frail.*
• flimsy, fragile, delicate, rickety, unsound **opposite** strong, robust

frame noun
1. *The frame of the house is made of timber.*
• framework, structure, shell, skeleton
2. *I put the photo of my friend in a frame.*
• mount, mounting, surround, border, setting, edging

frantic adjective
1. *I was frantic with worry when our kitten got lost.* • beside yourself, fraught, desperate, distraught, hysterical, worked up, berserk
2. *There was frantic activity on the day of the wedding.* • excited, hectic, frenzied, feverish, wild, mad

fraud noun
1. *The bank manager was found guilty of fraud.* • deceit, deception, dishonesty, swindling, cheating
2. *The prize draw was just a fraud—no one won anything.* • swindle, trick, hoax, pretence, sham, scam, (informal) con, scam • Someone who commits fraud is a **fraudster**. • Informal words are **con man**, **con artist** and **scammer**.

freaky adjective
The children said they heard freaky noises in the night. • scary, spooky, weird, creepy, strange, bizarre, peculiar

free adjective
1. *You are free to wander anywhere in the building.* • able, allowed, permitted, at liberty **opposite** restricted
2. *After ten years in jail, the prisoners were free at last.* • freed, liberated, released, emancipated, at large, on the loose • A common simile is **as free as a bird**. **opposite** imprisoned, enslaved
3. *I got a free drink with my sandwich.*
• complimentary, free of charge, gratis, on the house
4. *Are you free this weekend?* • available, unoccupied **opposite** busy, occupied

5. *The bathroom is free now.* • available, unoccupied, vacant, empty **opposite** engaged

free verb
1. *The soldiers freed the prisoners of war.*
• release, liberate, set free, deliver • To free slaves is to **emancipate** them. • To free prisoners by paying money to the captors is to **ransom** them. **opposite** imprison
2. *We freed the dogs and let them run about.*
• loose, turn loose, let go, untie, unchain **opposite** confine

freedom noun
The animals have a lot of freedom in the safari park. • liberty, independence

freeze verb freezing, froze, frozen
1. *Water begins to freeze at 0°C.* • become ice, ice over, harden, solidify
2. *If you freeze food, you can store it for a long time.* • deep-freeze, chill, refrigerate

freezing adjective
It's freezing cold outside. • chilly, frosty, icy, wintry, raw, bitter

frequent adjective
1. *I send frequent video messages to my friends.* • numerous, constant, continual, recurring, recurrent, repeated, countless **opposite** infrequent
2. *Badgers are frequent visitors to the garden.*
• regular, habitual, common, familiar, persistent **opposite** rare

frequently adverb
Pollyanna went very frequently to the great house on Pendleton Hill. • often, regularly, repeatedly, all the time **opposite** infrequently

fresh adjective
1. *This pudding is made with fresh fruit.*
• natural, raw, unprocessed
2. *The shop bakes fresh bread every day.* • new **opposite** old, stale
3. *Sally went outside to get some fresh air.*
• clean, cool, crisp, refreshing **opposite** stuffy
4. *Have you put fresh sheets on the bed?* • new, clean, laundered, washed **opposite** dirty
5. *Having a shower makes me feel nice and fresh.* • refreshed, revived, restored, invigorated
6. *We need some fresh ideas for our magazine.*
• new, original, different, novel, innovative **opposite** old

friend noun
I am inviting four friends to my birthday party.
• companion, comrade, (informal) mate,

pal, buddy, chum • A friend you play games with is a **playmate**. • A friend you work with is your **partner**. • A friend you write to but don't normally meet is a **penfriend**. • A friend you know only slightly is an **acquaintance**.
opposite enemy

friendly adjective friendlier, friendliest
1. *Our neighbour's pet dog is very friendly.* • affectionate, loving, good-natured, likeable, amiable, approachable, kind-hearted, kindly, amicable, genial, sociable, outgoing, sympathetic
2. *Those two are very friendly with each other.* • close, familiar, intimate, *(informal)* pally, chummy
3. *I like this cafe—it has a very friendly atmosphere.* • warm, welcoming, hospitable, cordial, neighbourly

friendship noun
Their friendship has lasted for many years. • closeness, affection, fondness, familiarity, intimacy, attachment, comradeship, fellowship • A formal friendship between countries or parties is an **alliance**.
opposite hostility

fright noun
1. *The girl jumped to her feet in fright and began to scream.* • fear, terror, alarm, horror, panic, dread
2. *The explosion gave us an awful fright!* • scare, shock, surprise, start, turn, jolt

frighten verb
Sorry—I didn't mean to frighten you. • scare, terrify, startle, alarm, shock, panic, petrify

frightened adjective
Mia was frightened of the dark. • afraid, scared, terrified, alarmed, fearful, panicky, petrified

frightening adjective
The ghost story she told was quite frightening. • terrifying, horrifying, scary, alarming, nightmarish, chilling, spine-chilling, hair-raising, bloodcurdling, chilling, eerie, sinister, fearsome, *(informal)* creepy, spooky

frisky adjective friskier, friskiest
The new lion cubs in the zoo are very frisky. • playful, lively, high-spirited, sprightly

frivolous adjective
Don't waste my time asking frivolous questions. • foolish, silly, ridiculous, shallow, superficial, pointless, unimportant, trivial, petty

front noun
1. *We stood at the front of the queue.* • head, start, beginning, lead, top
2. *The front of the house was painted white.* • face, frontage, facade • The front of a ship is the **bow** or **prow**. • The front of a picture is the **foreground**.

front adjective
1. *The front runners came into sight round the corner.* • first, leading, most advanced
opposite back
2. *The horse had injured one of its front legs.* • fore **opposite** back, rear, hind

frosty adjective
1. *It was a clear, frosty night.* • cold, crisp, icy, freezing, wintry
2. *The shopkeeper gave us a frosty stare.* • unfriendly, unwelcoming, cold, cool, stony

frown noun
On Christmas Eve, Scrooge had a frown on his face. • scowl, glare, grimace, glower, black look

frown verb
The witch frowned when her spell didn't work. • scowl, glare, grimace, glower, knit your brow(s) look sullen

fruit noun fruit, fruits

WORD WEB

SOME COMMON VARIETIES OF FRUIT
• apple, apricot, avocado, banana, bilberry, blackberry or bramble, blackcurrant, blueberry, cherry, coconut, cranberry, damson, date, fig, gooseberry, grape, guava, kiwi fruit, loganberry, lychee, mango, melon, nectarine, pawpaw or papaya, peach, pear, pineapple, plum, pomegranate, quince, raspberry, redcurrant, rosehip, sloe, strawberrry

a b c d e f g h i j k l m n o p q r s t u v w x y z

CITRUS FRUITS
• clementine, grapefruit, kumquat, lemon, lime, mandarin, orange, satsuma, tangerine

DRIED FRUITS
• currant, prune, raisin, sultana • **Rhubarb** is not a fruit, although it is often eaten like one. • **Avocados** and **tomatoes** are fruits, although they are eaten as vegetables.
• A person who sells fruit and vegetables is a **greengrocer**.

frustrate verb
Our plan for the day was *frustrated* by the weather. • block, foil, thwart, defeat, check, hinder, prevent

frustrating adjective
It was *frustrating* to have to wait in the long queues for the rides. • exasperating, discouraging, dispiriting, irritating

full adjective
1. My suitcase is *full* to the brim. • filled, loaded, topped up **opposite** empty
2. The shopping centre was *full* on Saturday. • busy, crowded, jammed, packed, crammed, congested **opposite** empty
3. The detective gave a *full* account of his findings. • complete, detailed, comprehensive, thorough, exhaustive **opposite** incomplete
4. The horses were galloping at *full* speed. • top, maximum, greatest, highest **opposite** minimum

fun noun
We had great *fun* on our holiday. • amusement, diversion, enjoyment, entertainment, games, jokes, laughter, merriment, play, pleasure, recreation, sport
to make fun of someone
It was unkind to *make fun of* her when she fell over. • jeer at, laugh at, mock, ridicule, taunt, tease, take the mickey out of

funny adjective **funnier, funniest**
1. There are some very *funny* jokes in the film. • amusing, humorous, comic, comical, hilarious, witty, entertaining, diverting, (informal) hysterical, priceless **opposite** serious
2. There's a *funny* smell in here. • strange, odd, peculiar, curious, puzzling, weird, queer, bizarre

furious adjective
The manager was *furious* when his team lost. • angry, mad, enraged, infuriated, incensed, livid, fuming, raging, seething

furry adjective **furrier, furriest**
A small, *furry* creature was curled inside the box. • hairy, fleecy, woolly, fuzzy, downy, feathery

fury noun **furies**
1. The *fury* of the creature showed in its eyes. • anger, rage, wrath, indignation
2. There was no shelter from the *fury* of the storm. • ferocity, fierceness, intensity, severity, violence, turbulence, savagery

fuss noun
There was a lot of *fuss* when the queen arrived. • bother, commotion, excitement, trouble, hullabaloo

fuss verb
Please don't *fuss*! • worry, fret, bother, get worked up

fussy adjective **fussier, fussiest**
1. Our cat is *fussy* about her food. • finicky, hard to please, particular, (informal) choosy, picky • An informal name for a fussy person is a **fusspot**.
2. I don't like clothes with *fussy* designs. • fancy, elaborate, ornate, florid

future noun
She has a bright *future* as a tennis player. • outlook, prospects **opposite** past

fuzzy adjective **fuzzier, fuzziest**
1. The TV picture has gone *fuzzy*. • blurred, bleary, unfocused, unclear, indistinct, hazy, cloudy **opposite** clear
2. Mia was wearing a *fuzzy* pink cardigan. • fluffy, furry, woolly, fleecy

A B C D E F G H I J K L M N O P Q R S T U V W X Y Z

Gg

There are lots of different words for **good** – try **wonderful**, **marvellous**, **excellent**, **exciting**, **interesting**, **beautiful** or **delicious**.

gadget *noun*
This torch and pen is a handy little gadget.
• tool, instrument, implement, device, contraption, *(informal)* gizmo

game *noun*
1. *My favourite game is hide-and-seek.*
• amusement, pastime, sport, activity, recreation
2. *The big game is on this Saturday.* • match, contest, competition, tournament

WORD WEB

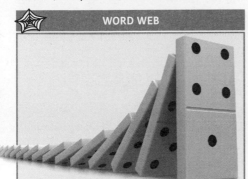

SOME BOARD AND TABLE GAMES
• backgammon, bagatelle, battleships, billiards, bingo, cards, chess, Chinese checkers, cribbage, dice, dominoes, draughts, go, hangman, lotto, ludo, ping-pong, pool, snakes and ladders, snooker, solitaire, table tennis, tiddlywinks

PARTY GAMES
• charades, hide-and-seek, I-spy, musical chairs, pass the parcel

PLAYGROUND AND OTHER OUTDOOR GAMES
• conkers, hopscotch, leapfrog, marbles, skittles, tag

gang *noun*
1. *The sea was swarming with gangs of pirates.*
• group, band, crowd, pack, set, mob
2. *A gang of workmen dug a hole in the road.*
• team, unit, crew, squad, party

gap *noun*
1. *The animals escaped through a gap in the fence.* • opening, space, hole, breach, break, crack, rift
2. *She returned to work after a gap of two years.* • break, interval, interruption, pause, lull

gate *noun*
People waited at the gate to be let in.
• gateway, doorway, entrance, portal

gather *verb*
1. *A crowd gathered to watch the street performers.* • assemble, collect, come together, congregate **opposite** disperse
2. *The captain gathered her team to give them a talk.* • bring together, round up, muster
3. *We gathered daisies to make into chains.*
• pick, pluck, collect, harvest
4. *I gather that you've been on holiday.*
• understand, hear, learn, believe, be told

general *adjective*
1. *There was a general air of gloom about the abbey.* • widespread, extensive, broad, sweeping, overall, prevalent
2. *I've only got a very general idea of where we are.* • rough, approximate, indefinite, vague, loose

generous *adjective*
1. *It was generous of you to give me your seat.* • unselfish, charitable, kind-hearted **opposite** selfish
2. *We each got a generous helping of ice cream.* • ample, large, lavish, plentiful **opposite** meagre

genius *noun*
Nila is a genius at maths. • expert, master, mastermind, wizard, ace, star, *(informal)* whizz

gentle *adjective*
1. *The vet is very gentle with sick animals.*
• kind, tender, good-tempered, humane
2. *Grasses swayed in the gentle breeze.* • light, slight, mild, soft, faint **opposite** strong
3. *There is a gentle slope to the top of the hill.*
• slight, gradual, easy **opposite** steep

genuine *adjective*
1. *Is that a genuine diamond?* • real, actual, true, authentic **opposite** fake
2. *Your friend seems like a very genuine person.* • honest, sincere, frank, earnest **opposite** false

gesture *noun*
She opened her arms in a gesture of welcome. • sign, signal, motion, movement

get *verb* **getting, got**
1. *We're getting a hamster for our classroom.* • acquire, obtain, buy, purchase
2. *Can you get me another blanket, please?* • bring, fetch, collect, pick up, retrieve
3. *Cara got a medal for swimming.* • receive, gain, earn, win, achieve
4. *What time did you get home?* • arrive at, reach, come to **opposite** leave
5. *It was starting to get dark outside.* • become, grow, turn
6. *I got a stomach bug on holiday last year.* • catch, develop, pick up, come down with
7. *You'll never get Oscar to eat celery.* • persuade, urge, influence, coax
8. *I didn't get the point of the film.* • understand, follow, comprehend, grasp
to get out of
My brother always gets out of doing the washing-up. • avoid, evade, shirk
to get over
He hasn't got over the accident yet. • get better from, recover from, shake off

ghastly *adjective* **ghastlier, ghastliest**
The boy's face turned a ghastly shade of green. • appalling, awful, dreadful, frightful, grim, grisly, horrible, horrifying, shocking, monstrous, terrible

ghost *noun*

WORD WEB

Meldrop House was haunted by several ghosts. • apparition, ghoul, phantom, shade, spectre, spirit, *(informal)* spook, wraith
• A ghost that makes a lot of noise is a **poltergeist**.

A GHOST OR GHOSTLY EXPERIENCE MIGHT BE
• bloodcurdling, chilling, grisly, gruesome, hair-raising, macabre, nightmarish, spine-chilling, spine-tingling

THINGS A GHOST MIGHT DO
• flit, float, glide, glow, haunt a person or place, hover, lurk, materialize, pass through walls, rattle chains, shimmer, vanish, waft

NOISES A GHOST MIGHT MAKE
• cackle, clang, clank, creak, groan, hoot, howl, moan, screech, sigh, sob, wail

PLACES A GHOST MIGHT BE FOUND
• catacombs, crypt, graveyard, haunted house or mansion, sepulchre, tomb, vault

OTHER THINGS THAT MIGHT BE IN A HAUNTED HOUSE
• bats, candles, cellar, cobwebs, dungeon, gargoyle, mummy, owl, secret door or passage, skeleton, skull, trap door, turret

ghostly *adjective*
The candlelight cast ghostly shadows on the wall. • spectral, phantom, ghoulish, unearthly, eerie, sinister, uncanny, *(informal)* spooky, creepy

giant *adjective*
A giant tree towered above us. • gigantic, huge, enormous, massive, immense, mammoth, colossal, monstrous **opposite** tiny

giddy *adjective* **giddier, giddiest**
I felt giddy when I stood at the edge of the cliff. • dizzy, faint, unsteady

gift *noun*
1. *I received some lovely gifts on my birthday.* • present
2. *Elsa has a gift for singing.* • talent, ability, flair, genius, knack

gigantic *adjective*
The dragon reared its gigantic head. • huge, giant, enormous, massive, colossal, immense, mammoth, monstrous, *(informal)* whopping, humungous **opposite** tiny

giggle *verb*
Ailsa and I couldn't stop giggling. • snigger, titter, chuckle, laugh, chortle

girl *noun*
• A synonym used in some parts of Britain is **lass**. • Old-fashioned words are **damsel**, **maid** and **maiden**.

give verb giving, gave, given
1. *Santa Claus gave each child a present.* • deal out, distribute, issue, supply, offer, present, hand over, pass, award
2. *Will you give something to our collection for charity?* • contribute, donate
3. *The giant gave a loud sneeze.* • utter, emit, let out
4. *We are giving a concert at the end of term.* • present, put on, lay on, organize, arrange
5. *Will this branch give if I sit on it?* • collapse, give way, bend, break, buckle
to give in
The boxer gave in after a long fight. • surrender, yield, submit, quit
to give up
He gave up trying to start the car. • abandon, stop, cease, quit

glad adjective gladder, gladdest
I'm glad to hear that you're feeling better. • pleased, happy, delighted, thrilled
opposite sad

gladly adverb
The travellers gladly agreed to the plan. • willingly, readily, happily, freely
opposite reluctantly

glance verb
The bus driver glanced quickly at his watch. • look quickly, peek, peep, glimpse

glare verb
The troll glared at us from under his bushy eyebrows. • stare, frown, scowl, glower
glare noun
1. *The glare of the lights dazzled me.* • dazzle, blaze, brightness, brilliance
2. *Miss Frump silenced the children with an angry glare.* • stare, scowl, glower, frown, nasty look

gleam noun
I saw a gleam of moonlight between the clouds. • glimmer, glint, flash, ray, shaft
gleam verb
The lights gleamed on the water. • glimmer, glint, glisten, shimmer, shine

gleaming adjective
The bear yawned, revealing its array of gleaming white teeth. • shiny, glossy, sparkling, glittering, brilliant, bright, glittery
opposite dull

glide verb
The boat glided gently across the lake. • move smoothly, slide, slip, drift, float, coast

glimmer verb
The city lights glimmered in the distance. • gleam, glint, glow, glisten, shimmer, flicker, blink
glimmer noun
I saw a glimmer of silver in the water. • glint, gleam, flash, sparkle, flicker

glimpse verb
I glimpsed a deer running through the forest. • catch sight of, spot, spy, sight
glimpse noun
We caught a glimpse of a whale in the sea. • peek, peep, glance, sighting, view

glint verb
Sunlight glinted on the windows. • flash, gleam, glitter, sparkle, twinkle
glint noun
A glint of gold caught my eye. • glimmer, gleam, flash, ray, shaft

glisten verb
The pavement glistened with frost. • gleam, shine, glint, shimmer, glimmer

glitter verb
The jewels glittered under the bright lights. • sparkle, twinkle, shimmer, glimmer, glint, glisten, flash, shine

gloat verb
He was gloating about winning the poetry prize. • boast, brag, crow, show off

global adjective
The Internet is a global network of computers. • worldwide, international, universal

gloom noun
1. *We could hardly see in the gloom of the cave.* • darkness, dimness, shade, shadow, murk • The gloomy light late in the evening is **dusk** or **twilight**.
2. *There was an air of gloom in the abandoned tower.* • depression, sadness, unhappiness, melancholy, misery, despair

gloomy adjective gloomier, gloomiest
1. *It was cold and gloomy in the cellar.* • dark, dingy, dim, dismal, dreary, sombre, cheerless, murky, shadowy **opposite** bright
2. *Eeyore was feeling gloomy again.* • depressed, sad, unhappy, glum, miserable, melancholy, low, downcast, dejected, disheartened, downhearted, (informal) down (in the dumps) **opposite** cheerful

glorious *adjective*
Look at that glorious sunset! • magnificent, splendid, stunning, spectacular, superb, wonderful, marvellous

glossy *adjective* **glossier, glossiest**
The bear had a thick, glossy coat of black fur. • shiny, sleek, silky, shining, gleaming, lustrous **opposite** dull

glow *noun*
The soft glow of burning candles lit the room. • brightness, shine, gleam, radiance

glow *verb*
The embers of the bonfire were still glowing. • shine, gleam, burn • Something that glows in the dark is **luminous** or **phosphorescent**.

glum *adjective* **glummer, glummest**
Why are you looking so glum? • depressed, sad, unhappy, gloomy, miserable, melancholy, low, downcast, dejected, *(informal)* down (in the dumps) **opposite** cheerful

gnarled *adjective*
The branches of the tree were gnarled with age. • bent, twisted, crooked, distorted, knobbly, knotty

gnaw *verb*
The wolves gnawed at a pile of bones. • chew, bite, munch, crunch, nibble

go *verb* **goes, going, went, gone**
1. *A carriage was going slowly along the road.* • move, progress, proceed
2. *My granny has always wanted to go to China.* • travel, journey
3. *Some of the guests had already gone.* • leave, depart, get away, withdraw
4. *By morning, the ice had all gone.* • disappear, vanish
5. *The canal goes all the way from Inverness to Fort William.* • extend, lead, reach, stretch, run
6. *The mountaineer's face went blue with cold.* • become, turn, grow
7. *Is that old grandfather clock still going?* • function, operate, work, run 8. *Cups and saucers go on the bottom shelf.* • belong, be kept, be placed
9. *Time goes slowly when you're stuck indoors.* • pass, go by, elapse
to go back
Sarah has gone back to the house. • return, retreat, retrace your steps
to go off
1. *A bomb went off nearby.* • explode, blow up, detonate

2. *The milk will go off if it's not in the fridge.* • turn sour, go bad, rot
to go on
1. *What's going on over there?* • happen, occur, take place
2. *Please go on with your story.* • carry on, continue, keep going, proceed

go *noun* **goes**
Would you like to have a go on my skateboard? • try, turn, chance, opportunity, *(informal)* shot, bash, stab

goal *noun*
The goal of the society is to protect wildlife. • aim, ambition, intention, object, objective, purpose, target

gobble *verb*
Ladybirds love to gobble greenfly. • guzzle, gulp, bolt, devour

good *adjective* **better, best**
That is a really good idea! • excellent, fine, lovely, nice, wonderful, *(informal)* fantastic, great, super, cool **opposite** bad

---

(!) OVERUSED WORD

Try to vary the words you use for **good**. Here are some other words you could use.

FOR A GOOD PERSON
• honest, worthy, honourable, moral, decent, virtuous, noble, kind, humane, charitable, merciful
The virtuous knight defeated the evil queen. **opposite** evil, wicked • A good character in a story or film is a **hero** or **heroine** or *(informal)* **goody**.

FOR GOOD BEHAVIOUR
• well-behaved, obedient, angelic, exemplary
The twins are surprisingly well-behaved. • A common simile is **as good as gold**. **opposite** naughty, disobedient

FOR A GOOD FRIEND
• true, loyal, loving, reliable, trusty, trustworthy
My dog Rusty is a loyal companion.

FOR A GOOD FEELING OR GOOD MOOD
• happy, cheerful, light-hearted, positive, contented
Mr Fox was in a cheerful mood after his tea.

FOR A GOOD EXPERIENCE OR GOOD NEWS
• pleasant, enjoyable, delightful, agreeable, pleasing, great, fantastic, wonderful, excellent, amazing, brilliant

---

opposite unpleasant, disagreeable
The girls had an enjoyable time at the party.
The letter contained some excellent news.

FOR A GOOD PERFORMER OR GOOD WORK
• capable, skilful, clever, able, talented, competent, commendable, sound
My friend Chris is a talented dancer.
opposite poor, awful

FOR GOOD FOOD OR A GOOD MEAL
• delicious, healthy, nourishing, nutritious, tasty, well-cooked, wholesome, substantial, hearty
The crew ate a hearty breakfast together.

FOR A GOOD EXCUSE OR GOOD REASON
• acceptable, valid, proper, satisfactory, legitimate
I hope you have a valid excuse for being late. **opposite** poor, unacceptable

FOR GOOD TIMING
• convenient, suitable, fortunate, appropriate, opportune
Is this a convenient time for a chat?
opposite inconvenient, unsuitable

FOR GOOD WEATHER
• fine, favourable, fair, bright, sunny
We are hoping for fine weather tomorrow.
opposite bad, adverse

gorgeous *adjective*
The gardens look gorgeous in the summer. • beautiful, glorious, dazzling, stunning, splendid, superb, glamorous, handsome

gossip *verb*
Two neighbours were gossiping over the fence. • chatter, tell tales, (informal) natter

gossip *noun*
1. *Don't believe all the gossip you hear.*
• chatter, rumour, hearsay, scandal, (informal) tittle-tattle
2. *Our next-door neighbour is a dreadful gossip.* • busybody, chatterbox, telltale, scandalmonger

govern *verb*
The ancient Romans governed a vast empire.
• rule, run, administer, direct, command, manage, be in charge of

gown *noun*
The mermaid wore a gown made of seaweed and pearls. • dress, robe, frock

grab *verb* **grabbing, grabbed**
The cowboy grabbed the reins of the runaway horse. • seize, grasp, catch, clutch, grip, get hold of, snatch

graceful *adjective*
The gymnast made a graceful landing.
• elegant, beautiful, stylish, smooth, flowing, agile, nimble **opposite** clumsy, graceless

grade *noun*
My sister has reached the top grade in judo.
• class, standard, level, stage, rank, degree

gradual *adjective*
There's been a gradual change in the weather.
• steady, slow, gentle, moderate, regular, even
opposite sudden

grand *adjective*
1. *The wedding was a grand occasion.*
• magnificent, splendid, stately, impressive, big, great, important, imposing
2. *(informal) Keep going—you're doing a grand job!* • excellent, fine, good, first-class

grapple *verb*
The guard grappled with the thief, but he got away. • struggle, wrestle, fight, tussle

grasp *verb*
1. *The climber grasped the end of the rope.*
• clutch, grab, grip, seize, catch, snatch, take hold of, hang on to
2. *The ideas were quite difficult to grasp.*
• understand, comprehend, follow, take in

grateful *adjective*
I'm grateful for your help. • thankful, appreciative, obliged, indebted
opposite ungrateful

grave *adjective*
1. *They looked grave when they heard the news.* • grim, sad, serious, thoughtful
opposite cheerful
2. *She made a grave mistake.* • crucial, important, serious, vital **opposite** trivial

graze *verb*
I grazed my knee when I fell off my bike.
• scrape, cut, scratch, scuff

great *adjective*
1. *The inventor had made a great discovery.*
• important, significant, major, leading, noteworthy **opposite** insignificant, minor
2. *Mozart was a great composer.* • famous, notable, celebrated, eminent, distinguished, outstanding, brilliant

a
b
c
d
e
f
g
h
i
j
k
l
m
n
o
p
q
r
s
t
u
v
w
x
y
z

3. *Their voices echoed round the **great** hall.*
• big, huge, large, enormous, vast, immense, gigantic, extensive, cavernous **opposite** small
4. *Beth took **great** care over her knitting.*
• considerable, extreme, exact **opposite** little
5. *(informal) That is a **great** idea!* • very good, excellent, marvellous, outstanding, superb, tremendous, wonderful, *(informal)* brilliant, fantastic, super, smashing, terrific
opposite bad, awful

greed noun
*The king wanted more gold to satisfy his **greed**.* • avarice, selfishness, hunger, craving, gluttony

greedy adjective **greedier, greediest**
1. *The boys were so **greedy** that they ate all the cakes.* • gluttonous, *(informal)* piggish
• A common simile is **as greedy as a pig**.
2. *Mr Skimp is very **greedy** about money.*
• grasping, selfish, ungenerous

green adjective, noun
*They lay down on the lush **green** grass. **Green** is my favourite colour.* • avocado, bottle-green, emerald, jade, khaki, lime, olive, pea-green
• Something which is rather green is **greenish** or **greeny**. • A common simile is **as green as grass**.

greet verb
*My aunt **greeted** us with a friendly wave.*
• welcome, hail, receive, salute

grey adjective
1. *The old wizard had a bushy **grey** beard. **Grey** is my favourite colour.* • silver, silvery, steel-grey, steely, grizzly, hoary, whitish
2. *The mother's face was **grey** with worry.*
• ashen, pale, leaden, wan
3. *The day began cold and **grey**.* • dull, cloudy, overcast

grief noun
*He couldn't hide his **grief** at his friend's death.*
• sorrow, sadness, mourning, unhappiness, distress, anguish, heartache **opposite** joy

grieve verb
*The family is still **grieving** over her death.* • mourn, lament, sorrow, weep
opposite rejoice

grim adjective **grimmer, grimmest**
1. *The judge wore a **grim** expression on his face.* • stern, severe, harsh, bad-tempered, sullen **opposite** cheerful
2. *The detective made the **grim** discovery of the body.* • unpleasant, horrible, dreadful,
terrible, hideous, shocking, gruesome, grisly
opposite pleasant

grimy adjective
*Don't wipe those **grimy** feet on the carpet!*
• dirty, filthy, grubby, mucky, soiled
opposite clean

grin noun
*Mark arrived with a silly **grin** on his face.*
• smile, beam, smirk • A large grin is a **broad**, **wide** or **cheesy** grin.

grind verb **grinding, ground**
1. ***Grind** the spices into a fine powder.*
• crush, pound, powder, pulverize, mill
2. *This tool is used for **grinding** knives.*
• sharpen, file, hone, whet

grip verb **gripping, gripped**
1. ***Grip** the handle tightly.* • grasp, seize, clutch, clasp, hold
2. *The audience was **gripped** by the film.*
• fascinate, engross, absorb, enthrall

grisly adjective **grislier, grisliest**
*We found the **grisly** remains of a dead sheep.*
• gruesome, gory, ghastly, hideous, nasty, revolting, sickening

groan verb
*The wounded soldier **groaned** with pain.*
• cry out, moan, sigh, wail

grope verb
*I **groped** in the dark for the light switch.*
• fumble, feel about, flounder

gross adjective
1. *That is a **gross** exaggeration!* • extreme, glaring, obvious, sheer, blatant, outright
2. *Ogres have **gross** table manners.* • offensive, rude, coarse, vulgar, disgusting, revolting

ground noun **grounds**
1. *I planted some seeds in the **ground**.*
• earth, soil, land
2. *The **ground** was too wet to play on.*
• field, pitch, park, stadium, arena

group noun
1. *Japan consists of a **group** of islands.*
• collection, set, batch, cluster, clump
2. *A **group** of children was waiting at the bus stop.* • crowd, bunch, gathering, band, body, gang
3. *The book **group** meets once a month.*
• club, society, association, circle

4. *We sorted the fossils into different groups.*
• category, class, type, kind, sort

WORD WEB

WORDS FOR GROUPS OF PEOPLE
• a **band** of musicians • a **class** of pupils
• a **company** or **troupe** of actors
• a **congregation** of worshippers in church
• a **coven** of witches • a **crew** of sailors
• a **gang** of workers • a **horde** of invaders
• a **team** of players

WORDS FOR GROUPS OF ANIMALS
• an **army** or **colony** of ants • a **band** of
gorillas • a **brood** of chicks • a **covey** of
partridges • a **flock** of sheep or birds
• a **gaggle** of geese • a **herd** of cattle or
elephants • a **litter** of pigs or puppies
• a **pack** of wolves • a **pride** of lions
• a **school** or **pod** of dolphins or whales
• a **shoal** of fish • a **swarm** of insects
• a **troop** of monkeys

WORDS FOR GROUPS OF THINGS
• a **battery** of guns • a **bunch** of flowers
• a **clump** of trees • a **clutch** of eggs in a
nest • a **constellation** or **galaxy** of stars
• a **convoy** or **fleet** of ships

grow *verb* growing, grew, grown
1. *I've grown an inch taller since last summer.*
• get bigger, put on growth, spring up, sprout,
shoot up
2. *The number of children in the school has
grown.* • increase, develop, enlarge, expand,
build up **opposite** decrease
3. *Our neighbour grows orchids in her
greenhouse.* • cultivate, produce, raise, farm
4. *It is growing dark outside.* • become, get,
turn

growth *noun*
*There's been a rapid growth of the country's
population.* • increase, rise, spread, expansion,
development, enlargement

grubby *adjective* grubbier, grubbiest
*My hands were grubby from working in the
garden.* • dirty, filthy, grimy, messy, mucky,
soiled **opposite** clean

gruesome *adjective*
The battlefield was a gruesome sight. • grisly,
gory, ghastly, hideous, monstrous, revolting,
sickening, appalling, dreadful, frightful,
shocking, abominable

gruff *adjective*
The ogre spoke in a gruff voice. • harsh, rough,
hoarse, husky, throaty

grumble *verb*
You're always grumbling about the weather!
• complain, moan, groan, protest, whine, gripe

grumpy *adjective* grumpier, grumpiest
*Marge was grumpy because she had a
headache.* • bad-tempered, cross, irritable,
testy, tetchy, cantankerous, *(informal)* grouchy
opposite good-humoured

guard *verb*
The cave was guarded by a one-eyed giant.
• protect, defend, stand guard over, patrol,
safeguard, shield, watch over

guard *noun*
A guard was on duty at the gate. • sentry,
sentinel, warder, lookout, watchman

guess *verb*
1. *There was a prize for guessing the weight of
the cake.* • estimate, judge, work out, gauge,
predict, reckon
2. *I guess you must be tired after your journey.*
• suppose, imagine, expect, assume, think

guest *noun*
We are having guests for tea on Sunday.
• visitor, caller, company

guide *noun*
1. *Our guide showed us around the zoo.*
• courier, escort, leader, chaperon
2. *We bought a useful guide to the city.*
• guidebook, handbook, manual

guide *verb*
*The explorers used the stars to guide them at
night.* • direct, lead, steer, conduct, escort,
show the way

guilty *adjective* guiltier, guiltiest
1. *The prisoner was found guilty of the crime.*
• responsible, to blame, at fault, in the wrong,
liable **opposite** innocent
2. *You have a guilty look on your face!*

• ashamed, guilt-ridden, remorseful, sorry, conscience-stricken, repentant, shamefaced, sheepish **opposite** unrepentant

gulp *verb*
Peter gulped down the cake in one go.
• swallow, bolt, gobble, guzzle, devour

gush *noun*
There was a gush of water from the pipe.
• rush, stream, torrent, rush, cascade, flood, jet, spout, spurt

gush *verb*
Water gushed from the broken pipe. • rush, stream, flow, pour, flood, spout, spurt, squirt

guzzle *verb*
The seagulls guzzled all the bread. • gobble, gulp, bolt, devour

Hh

Horrify your readers with *alarming*, *shocking*, *terrifying*, *sickening* and *disgusting* vocabulary!

habit *noun*
1. *It's her habit to go for a walk each morning.*
• custom, practice, routine, rule
2. *My dog has a habit of scratching its ear.*
• mannerism, way, tendency, inclination, quirk

hack *verb*
The explorers hacked their way through the jungle. • chop, cut, hew, slash, lop

haggard *adjective*
The warriors looked haggard after the battle.
• drawn, gaunt, thin, pinched, wasted, shrunken, wan **opposite** healthy

haggle *verb*
The men haggled over the price of the gems.
• bargain, negotiate, argue, wrangle

hair *noun*

WORD WEB

Rapunzel's hair reached down to the ground.
• locks, tresses, *(informal)* mop • A single piece of hair is a **strand**. • A bunch of hair is a **hank**, **lock** or **tress**. • False hair is a **hairpiece**, **toupee** or **wig**. • An area without hair is a **bald patch**. • The way hair is cut is

a **hairstyle** or *(informal)* **hairdo** or *(formal)* **coiffure**. • Hair is cut or styled by a **hairdresser** or **hairstylist**. • Men's hair is also cut by a **barber**.

SOME HAIRSTYLES
• Afro, bob, braids, bun, bunches, chignon, corn rows, crew-cut, curls, dreadlocks, fishtail, French braid or plait, fringe, Mohican, perm, pigtail, plaits, ponytail, quiff, ringlets, short back and sides, sideburns, skinhead, topknot

HAIR ON AN ANIMAL
• bristles, coat, down, fleece, fur, mane, whiskers

WRITING TIPS

You can use these words to describe **hair**.

TO DESCRIBE ITS COLOUR
• auburn, blond (male) or blonde (female), brunette, carroty, dark, fair, flaxen, ginger, golden, grey, grizzled, hoary, mousy, platinum blonde, raven, red, silver

TO DESCRIBE HOW IT LOOKS OR FEELS
• bushy, coarse, curly, dishevelled, fine, frizzy, glossy, greasy, lank, limp, ringleted, shaggy, shiny, silky, spiky, straggly, straight, stringy, tangled, thick, tousled, unkempt, wavy, windswept, wispy
The elderly knight had a long grizzled, straggly beard.

hairy *adjective* **hairier, hairiest**
Mammoths were like elephants with thick hairy coats. • shaggy, bushy, bristly, woolly, fleecy, furry, fuzzy, long-haired, hirsute

hall *noun*
1. *The hall was full for the concert.* • assembly hall, auditorium, concert hall, theatre
2. *You can use the coat stand in the hall.*
• entrance hall, hallway, lobby, foyer

halt *verb*
1. *The car halted at the red light.* • stop, come to a halt, draw up, pull up, wait
2. *The traffic was halted by a flock of sheep.*
• stop, check, obstruct
3. *Work halted when the whistle went.* • end, cease, terminate, break off **opposite** start, go

hand *verb*
The postman handed me several letters. • give, pass, present, offer, deliver

handle *verb*
1. *Please don't handle the exhibits.* • touch,

feel, hold, stroke, fondle, finger, grasp
2. *The referee handled the game well.*
• manage, control, conduct, deal with, cope with, tackle

handsome *adjective*
1. *Prince Charming was very handsome.*
• attractive, good-looking, nice-looking, gorgeous, *(informal)* dishy **opposite** ugly, unattractive
2. *They sold their house for a handsome profit.* • big, large, substantial, sizeable **opposite** slight

handy *adjective* handier, handiest
1. *This handy gadget is for peeling potatoes.*
• useful, helpful, convenient, practical **opposite** awkward
2. *I always keep my umbrella handy.*
• accessible, available, close at hand, nearby, ready **opposite** inaccessible

hang *verb*
1. *A monkey was hanging from the tree branch.* • dangle, be suspended, swing, sway
2. *The dog had hair hanging down over its eyes.* • droop, drape, flop, trail, cascade
3. *I hung the picture on the wall.* • fix, attach, fasten, stick, peg
4. *Smoke hung in the air.* • float, hover, drift, linger, cling

to hang about or **around**
Don't hang about, we'll miss the bus. • delay, dawdle, linger, loiter
to hang on *(informal)*
Try to hang on a bit longer. • carry on, continue, stay, remain, persist, keep going, persevere
to hang on to something
1. *Hang on to the rope.* • hold, grip, grasp, keep hold of
2. *Hang on to your bus ticket.* • keep, retain, save, hold on to

happily *adverb*
1. *Jess's parents happily agreed to the camping trip.* • willingly, readily, gladly, freely **opposite** reluctantly, unwillingly
2. *The baby smiled happily at her.*
• gladly, contentedly, cheerfully, joyfully **opposite** sadly

happiness *noun*
The bride's face glowed with happiness. • joy, joyfulness, delight, jubilation, pleasure, contentment, gladness, cheerfulness, merriment, ecstasy, bliss **opposite** sorrow

happy *adjective* happier, happiest

> ! **OVERUSED WORD**
>
> Try to vary the words you use for happy. Here are some other words you could use.
>
> **FOR A HAPPY MOOD OR HAPPY PERSON**
> • cheerful, joyful, jolly, light-hearted, contented, gleeful, delighted
> *The girls look really cheerful in the photograph.* • A common simile is **as happy as a lark. opposite** unhappy, sad
>
> **FOR A VERY HAPPY MOOD**
> • thrilled, ecstatic, elated, overjoyed, *(informal)* over the moon, thrilled to bits, tickled pink
> *Sandy was ecstatic when she won first prize.*
>
> **FOR A HAPPY TIME OR HAPPY EXPERIENCE**
> • enjoyable, joyous, glorious, blissful, heavenly, idyllic
> *They spent a glorious summer on the island.*
>
> **FOR A HAPPY COINCIDENCE**
> • lucky, fortunate, favourable
> *By a lucky coincidence, we took the same train.* **opposite** unfortunate
>
> **TO BE HAPPY TO DO SOMETHING**
> • pleased, glad, willing, delighted
> *I would be glad to help organize the party.* **opposite** unwilling

harbour *noun*
Several yachts were tied up in the harbour.
• port, dock, mooring, quay, pier, wharf

hard *adjective*

> ! **OVERUSED WORD**
>
> Try to vary the words you use for hard. Here are some other words you could use.
>
> **FOR HARD GROUND OR A HARD SURFACE**
> • solid, firm, dense, compact, rigid, stiff
> *The ground was solid and covered with frost.*
> • Common similes are **as hard as nails** and **as hard as a rock. opposite** soft
>
> **FOR A HARD PULL OR HARD PUSH**
> • strong, forceful, heavy, powerful, violent, sharp
> *The climber gave a sharp tug on the rope.* **opposite** light
>
> **FOR HARD WORK**
> • tough, gruelling, strenuous, tiring, exhausting, laborious, back-breaking
> *Digging the tunnel was back-breaking work.* **opposite** easy

A B C D E F G H I J K L M N O P Q R S T U V W X Y Z

FOR A HARD WORKER
• energetic, keen, diligent
The elves are very diligent workers.
opposite lazy

FOR A HARD PERSON OR HARD TREATMENT
• strict, stern, harsh, severe, cruel,
hard-hearted, heartless, unfeeling, unkind
*Cinderella's sisters were heartless and
selfish.* **opposite** mild

FOR A HARD PROBLEM OR HARD QUESTION
• difficult, complicated, complex, intricate,
perplexing, puzzling, baffling, knotty, thorny
None of us could solve the complex problem.
opposite simple

---

hard *adverb*
1. *Ros is working hard at learning French.*
• strenuously, energetically, diligently, keenly,
intently
2. *It has been raining hard all afternoon.*
• heavily, steadily, *(informal)* cats and dogs

hardly *adverb*
I could hardly see in the fog. • barely, scarcely,
only just, with difficulty

harm *verb*
1. *His captors didn't harm him.* • hurt, injure,
ill-treat, wound
2. *Too much direct sunlight may harm this
plant.* • damage, spoil, ruin

harm *noun*
I didn't mean to cause him any harm.
• damage, hurt, injury, pain **opposite** benefit

harmful *adjective*
Junk food can be harmful to your health.
• damaging, dangerous, destructive, injurious,
unhealthy **opposite** harmless, beneficial

harmless *adjective*
1. *You can drink the potion—it is quite
harmless.* • safe, non-toxic, innocuous
opposite harmful, dangerous
2. *It was just a bit of harmless fun.* • innocent,
inoffensive

harsh *adjective*
1. *The trumpet sounded loud and harsh.*
• rough, rasping, grating, jarring, shrill,
raucous **opposite** soft, gentle
2. *We blinked in the harsh light.* • bright,
brilliant, dazzling, glaring **opposite** soft,
subdued
3. *The rescue team braved the harsh weather.*
• severe, strict, cruel, hard, tough, bleak
opposite mild

4. *The coach had some harsh words to say.*
• strong, sharp, unkind, unfriendly

hasty *adjective* **hastier, hastiest**
1. *The robbers made a hasty exit.* • fast,
hurried, quick, sudden, swift, rapid, speedy
opposite slow
2. *The king regretted his hasty decision.* • rash,
reckless, impatient, foolhardy, thoughtless
opposite careful

hate *verb*
1. *Eddie hates broccoli and peas.* • dislike,
detest, despise, loathe
2. *I hate to bother you.* • be sorry, be reluctant,
regret

have *verb* **has, having, had**
1. *I have my own laptop.* • own, possess
2. *Our house has three bedrooms.* • consist of,
comprise, include, incorporate
3. *We are having a barbecue at the weekend.*
• hold, organize, provide, host, throw
4. *Dad had trouble finding a place to park.*
• experience, go through, meet with, run into,
face, suffer
5. *The girls had a great time at the party.*
• experience, enjoy
6. *The BBC has had thousands of tweets about
the programme.* • receive, get, be given, be
sent
7. *Sharon had the last toffee.* • take, consume,
eat
8. *One of the giraffes has had a baby.* • give
birth to, bear, produce
9. *I have to be home by six o'clock.* • must,
need to, ought to, should

hazard *noun*
*The road through the mountains is full of
hazards.* • danger, risk, threat, trap, pitfall,
snag

hazardous *adjective*
*They made the hazardous journey to the South
Pole.* • dangerous, risky, unsafe, perilous,
precarious **opposite** safe

hazy *adjective* **hazier, haziest**
1. *The buildings in the distance were rather
hazy.* • blurred, misty, unclear, dim, faint
2. *He's only got a hazy knowledge of history.*
• uncertain, vague

head *noun*
1. *My dad hit his head on the attic ceiling.*
• skull, crown, *(informal)* nut
2. *Can you add up these figures in your head?*
• brain, mind, intellect, intelligence

3. *There is a new head of the music department.* • chief, leader, manager, director, controller, *(informal)* boss
4. *The girls waited at the head of the queue.*
• front, lead, top **opposite** back, rear

head verb
The professor was chosen to head the expedition. • lead, be in charge of, direct, command, manage, oversee, supervise
to head for
At the end of the day we headed for home.
• go towards, make for, aim for

heal verb
1. *It took two months for my leg to heal properly.* • get better, mend, recover
2. *Part of a vet's job is to heal sick animals.*
• cure, make better, treat, restore

health noun
The puppies are in excellent health.
• condition, fitness, shape, strength, vigour, well-being

healthy adjective healthier, healthiest
1. *Neil has always been a healthy child.*
• well, fit, strong, sturdy, vigorous, robust, *(informal)* in good shape **opposite** ill
2. *Porridge makes a very healthy breakfast.*
• health-giving, wholesome, nutritious
opposite unhealthy

heap noun
There was an untidy heap of clothes on the floor. • mound, pile, stack, mountain, collection, mass

heap verb
We heaped up all the rubbish in the corner.
• pile, stack, collect, bank, mass

hear verb hearing, heard
1. *Did you hear what she said?* • catch, listen to, make out, pick up, overhear, pay attention to • A sound that you can hear is **audible**.
• A sound that you cannot hear is **inaudible**.
2. *Have you heard the news?* • be told, discover, find out, learn, gather

heart noun
1. *Have you no heart?* • compassion, feeling, sympathy, tenderness, affection, humanity, kindness, love
2. *The hotel is located right in the heart of the city.* • centre, middle, hub
3. *They tried to get to the heart of the problem.*
• core, essence

heat noun
1. *The cat basked in the heat of the fire.*
• warmth, hotness, glow
2. *Last summer, the heat made me feel ill.*
• hot weather, high temperatures, closeness
• A long period of hot weather is a **heatwave**.

heave verb
The men heaved the sacks onto a lorry.
• haul, drag, pull, draw, tow, tug, hoist, lug, lift, raise, throw

heavy adjective heavier, heaviest
1. *The box was too heavy for me to lift.*
• weighty, massive, dense, bulky
2. *Digging the garden is heavy work.*
• hard, tough, gruelling, back-breaking, strenuous
3. *This book makes heavy reading.*
• serious, intense, demanding
4. *The rain has caused heavy flooding.* • severe, extreme, torrential
5. *Both sides suffered heavy losses in the battle.* • large, substantial, considerable
6. *A heavy mist hung over the landscape.*
• dense, thick

hectic adjective
The days before the wedding were hectic.
• busy, frantic, feverish, frenzied, chaotic, *(informal)* manic **opposite** quiet, leisurely

help noun
1. *Thank you for your help.* • aid, assistance, support, guidance, cooperation, advice
opposite hindrance
2. *Would a torch be of any help to you?* • use, benefit

help verb
1. *Could you please help me with my luggage?*
• aid, assist, cooperate with, *(informal)* give a hand to
2. *The Red Cross is an organization that helps people in need.* • be helpful to, support, serve, stand by
3. *This medicine will help your cough.*
• make better, cure, ease, relieve, improve
opposite aggravate, worsen
4. *I can't help coughing.* • stop, avoid, prevent, refrain from

helpful adjective
1. *The staff were friendly and helpful.*
• obliging, cooperative, kind, considerate, thoughtful, sympathetic **opposite** unhelpful
2. *The shop assistant gave us some helpful advice.* • useful, valuable, worthwhile, beneficial, profitable **opposite** worthless

helpless *adjective*
Kittens are born blind and helpless.
• powerless, weak, feeble, dependent, defenceless, vulnerable
opposite independent, strong

heroic *adjective*
The firefighters made a heroic effort to put out the blaze. • bold, brave, courageous, daring, fearless, noble, selfless, valiant
opposite cowardly

hesitate *verb*
I hesitated for a moment before ringing the doorbell. • pause, delay, wait, hold back, dither, falter, waver, (informal) think twice

hidden *adjective*
1. *The giant kept his gold hidden in a wooden chest.* • concealed, out of sight, unseen, invisible, covered, disguised **opposite** visible
2. *There's a hidden message in the riddle.*
• secret, mysterious, obscure, coded, cryptic **opposite** obvious

hide *verb* hiding, hidden, hid, hidden
1. *Quick! Someone's coming—we'd better hide.*
• go into hiding, take cover, take refuge, keep out of sight, lie low, go to ground
2. *They hid the jewels in a secret drawer.*
• conceal, secrete, bury, (informal) stash **opposite** expose
3. *The clouds hid the sun.* • blot out, cover, screen, shroud, veil, mask **opposite** uncover
4. *I tried to hide my feelings.* • disguise, keep secret, suppress, camouflage, cloak **opposite** show

hideous *adjective*
The troll had a hideous grin on his face.
• repulsive, revolting, ugly, grotesque, monstrous, ghastly, gruesome, horrible, appalling, dreadful, frightful
opposite beautiful

high *adjective*
1. *The castle was surrounded by a high wall.*
• tall, towering, elevated, lofty **opposite** low
2. *Sir Grinalot was a knight of high rank and status.* • senior, top, leading, important, prominent, powerful **opposite** low, junior
3. *House prices are very high at the moment.* • expensive, dear, costly, excessive **opposite** low
4. *A high wind was blowing.* • strong, powerful, forceful, extreme **opposite** gentle
5. *The pixie spoke in a high squeaky voice.*
• high-pitched, sharp, shrill, piercing

• A high singing voice is **soprano** or **treble**.
opposite deep

hilarious *adjective*
The boys thought the cartoon was hilarious. • funny, amusing, comical, (informal) hysterical

hill *noun*
1. *From the top of this hill you can see for miles.* • mount, peak, ridge • A small hill is a **hillock** or **mound**. • The top of a hill is the **summit**.
2. *Jenny pushed her bike up the steep hill.*
• slope, rise, incline, ascent, gradient

hinder *verb*
The snowstorm hindered the rescue attempt.
• hamper, hold up, obstruct, impede, slow down, stand in the way of, restrict, handicap
opposite help

hint *noun*
1. *I don't know the answer—can you give me a hint?* • clue, indication, sign, suggestion, inkling
2. *The magazine offers handy hints for decorating.* • tip, pointer

hint *verb*
Mum hinted that we might be getting a puppy.
• give a hint, suggest, imply, indicate

historic *adjective*

> Take care not to confuse **historic**, which means famous or important in history, with **historical**, which simply refers to anything that happened in the past.

The first landing on the Moon was a historic event. • famous, notable, celebrated, important, renowned, momentous, significant, major **opposite** unimportant

historical *adjective*

> See note at **historic**.

Robin Hood may have been a historical character. • real, real-life, true, actual, authentic **opposite** fictitious

hit *noun*
1. *Matt got a nasty hit on the head.* • bump, blow, bang, knock, whack • A hit with your fist is a **punch**. • A hit with your open hand is a **slap** or **smack**. • A hit with a bat or club is a **drive**, **stroke** or **swipe**.
2. *Their new CD was an instant hit.* • success, triumph, (informal) winner

hit *verb* **hitting, hit**
1. *Auntie Flo hit the burglar on the head with her umbrella.* • strike, knock, bang, bash, thump, bump, crack, rap, slam, swipe, slog, cuff, *(informal)* whack, wham, wallop, sock, clout, clobber, belt, biff, *(old use)* smite • To hit with your fist is to **punch**. • To hit with the palm of your hand is to **slap** or **smack**. • To punish someone by hitting them is to **beat** them. • To hit someone with a stick is to **club** them. • To hit your toe on something is to **stub** it. • To kill an insect by hitting it is to **swat** it. • To hit something repeatedly is to **batter**, **buffet** or **pound** it. • To hit something gently is to **tap** it.
2. *The drought has hit many farms in the area.* • affect, damage, harm, hurt

hoard *noun*
Hamish keeps a hoard of sweets in his desk. • cache, store, stock, supply, pile, stockpile • A hoard of treasure is a **treasure trove**.

hoard *verb*
Squirrels hoard nuts for the winter. • store, collect, gather, save, put by, pile up, stockpile, *(informal)* stash away

hoarse *adjective*
Mr Barker's voice was hoarse from shouting. • rough, harsh, husky, croaky, throaty, gruff, rasping, gravelly

hobby *noun* **hobbies**
My favourite hobby is snorkelling. • pastime, pursuit, interest, activity, recreation

hold *verb* **holding, held**
1. *Please hold the dog's lead.* • clasp, grasp, grip, cling to, hang on to, clutch, seize
2. *Can I hold the baby?* • embrace, hug, cradle
3. *They held the suspect until the police arrived.* • confine, detain, keep
4. *Will the ladder hold my weight?* • bear, support, carry, take
5. *If our luck holds, we could reach the final.* • continue, last, carry on, persist, stay
6. *She holds strong opinions.* • believe in, maintain, stick to
to hold out
1. *The robot held out one of his arms.* • extend, reach out, stick out, stretch out
2. *Our supplies won't hold out much longer.* • keep going, last, carry on, continue, endure
to hold something up
1. *Please hold up your hand.* • lift, put up, raise
2. *The accident held up the traffic.* • delay, hinder, slow down

hole *noun*
1. *The meteor created a massive hole in the ground.* • pit, hollow, crater, dent, depression, cavity, chasm, abyss

2. *The rabbits escaped through a hole in the fence.* • gap, opening, breach, break, cut, slit, gash, split, tear, vent

hollow *adjective*
Tennis balls are hollow. • empty, unfilled
opposite solid

hollow *noun*
The ball rolled into a hollow in the ground. • dip, dent, depression, hole, pit, crater • A hollow between two hills is a **valley**.

holy *adjective* **holier, holiest**
1. *The pilgrims knelt to pray in the holy shrine.* • sacred, blessed, revered
2. *The pilgrims were holy people.* • religious, spiritual, devout, pious, godly, saintly

home *noun*
The hurricane forced people to flee their homes. • house, residence, dwelling, abode, lodging • A home for the sick is a **convalescent home** or **nursing home**. • A place where a bird or animal lives is its **habitat**.

honest *adjective*
1. *He's an honest boy, so he gave the money back.* • good, honourable, law-abiding, moral, trustworthy, upright, virtuous
opposite dishonest
2. *Please give me your honest opinion.* • sincere, genuine, truthful, direct, frank, candid, plain, straightforward, unbiased
opposite insincere

honour *noun*
1. *Her success brought honour to the school.* • credit, good reputation, good name, respect, praise, acclaim
2. *It's an honour to meet you.* • privilege, distinction

honour *verb*
The winners were honoured at a special ceremony. • praise, celebrate, salute, give credit to, pay tribute to, glorify

honourable *adjective*
1. *The knight was an honourable man.* • good, honest, sincere, noble, principled, moral, righteous, trustworthy, upright, virtuous, worthy, decent, fair, trusty
2. *It was an honourable thing to do.* • noble, admirable, praiseworthy, decent

hop *verb* hopping, hopped
The goblins hopped about in excitement.
• jump, leap, skip, spring, prance, caper, bound, dance

hope *verb*
I hope to see you again soon. • wish, trust, expect, look forward

hope *noun*
1. *Her dearest hope was to see her family again.* • ambition, dream, desire, wish
2. *There's hope of better weather tomorrow.*
• prospect, expectation, likelihood

hopeful *adjective*
1. *I am feeling hopeful about tomorrow's match.* • optimistic, confident, positive, expectant **opposite** pessimistic
2. *The future is beginning to look more hopeful.* • promising, encouraging, favourable, reassuring **opposite** discouraging

hopeless *adjective*
1. *The shipwrecked crew were in a hopeless situation.* • desperate, wretched, beyond hope **opposite** hopeful
2. *I'm hopeless at ice skating.* • bad, poor, incompetent, *(informal)* useless, rubbish **opposite** good, competent

hopelessly *adverb*
We soon realized we were hopelessly lost.
• completely, utterly

horde *noun*
Hordes of people were queuing for tickets.
• crowd, throng, mob, swarm, gang, group

horrible *adjective*
What a horrible smell! • awful, terrible, dreadful, appalling, unpleasant, disagreeable, offensive, objectionable, disgusting, repulsive, revolting, horrendous, horrid, nasty, hateful, odious, loathsome, beastly, ghastly **opposite** pleasant

horrific *adjective*
The film has some horrific scenes of battle.
• horrifying, terrifying, shocking, gruesome, dreadful, appalling, ghastly, hideous, atrocious, grisly, sickening

horrify *verb* horrifies, horrifying, horrified
We were horrified by the sight of the monster.
• appal, shock, terrify, frighten, alarm, scare, sicken, disgust

horror *noun*
1. *Ingrid screamed in horror when she saw the snake.* • terror, fear, fright, alarm, dread
2. *The film depicts the full horror of war.*
• awfulness, hideousness, gruesomeness, ghastliness, frightfulness

horse *noun*

WORD WEB

• A male horse is a **stallion** and a female is a **mare.** • A young horse is a **foal.** • A young male horse is a **colt** and a young female horse is a **filly.** • An uncomplimentary word for a horse is **nag.** • A poetic word for a horse is **steed.** • A word meaning 'to do with horses' is **equine.** • A cross between a horse and a donkey is a **mule.**

SOME TYPES OF HORSE
• bronco, carthorse, Clydesdale, mustang, piebald, pony, racehorse, Shetland pony, shire horse, warhorse

NOISES MADE BY A HORSE
• neigh, snicker, snort, whinny

WAYS A HORSE CAN MOVE
• canter, gallop, trot, walk

PARTS OF A HORSE'S HARNESS
• bit, blinker, bridle, girth, noseband, pommel, rein, saddle, stirrups

SPORTS AND ACTIVITIES INVOLVING HORSES
• gymkhana, horse-racing, jousting, rodeo, polo, showjumping, steeplechase
• A person who rides a horse in a race is a **jockey.** • A word meaning 'to do with horse riding' is **equestrian.** • Soldiers who fight on horseback are **cavalry.** • An old word for a cavalry horse was a **charger.**

hospital *noun*

WORD WEB

PLACES WHERE PEOPLE GO FOR MEDICAL TREATMENT
clinic, convalescent home, hospice, infirmary, nursing home, sanatorium

PARTS OF A HOSPITAL
accident and emergency, dispensary, intensive care unit, operating theatre, outpatients, pharmacy, X-ray department, ward

hostile *adjective*
The warriors shook their weapons in a hostile manner. • aggressive, antagonistic,

unfriendly, unwelcoming, warlike, malevolent **opposite** friendly

hot *adjective* **hotter, hottest**
1. *The weather has been* **hot** *this summer.*
• warm, balmy, blazing, roasting, scorching, blistering, sweltering, stifling
opposite cold, cool
2. *Careful—the soup's really* **hot***.* • burning, boiling, baking hot, piping hot, scalding, searing, sizzling, steaming **opposite** cold, cool
3. *I like curry, but only if it's not too* **hot***.* • spicy, peppery, fiery **opposite** mild
4. *My sister, Diana, has a* **hot** *temper.* • fierce, fiery, violent, passionate, raging, angry, intense **opposite** calm, mild

house *noun*

WORD WEB

WORDS FOR THE PLACE YOU LIVE IN
• abode, dwelling, home, lodging, quarters, residence

BUILDINGS WHERE PEOPLE LIVE
• apartment, bungalow, chalet, cottage, council house, croft, detached house, farmhouse, flat, hovel, hut, igloo, lodge, manor, manse, mansion, rectory, semi-detached house, shack, shanty, tenement, terraced house, thatched house, vicarage, villa

hover *verb*
1. *A flock of seagulls* **hovered** *overhead.*
• fly, flutter, float, hang, drift
2. *He* **hovered** *outside the room, afraid to knock.* • linger, pause, wait about, hesitate, dally, loiter, dither, *(informal)* hang about

however *adverb*
1. *Spider's silk is very thin;* **however** *it is also very strong.* • nevertheless, nonetheless, yet, still, even so
2. *I couldn't lift the stone,* **however** *hard I tried.* • no matter how

howl *verb*
1. *The injured boy* **howled** *in pain.* • cry, yell, scream, yelp, shriek, wail
2. *They heard wolves* **howling** *in the night.*
• bay, yowl

huddle *verb*
The penguins **huddled** *together to get warm.*
• crowd, gather, flock, cluster, squeeze, pack, nestle, cuddle, snuggle **opposite** scatter

hug *verb* **hugging, hugged**
Ellie was **hugging** *her favourite teddy bear.*
• cuddle, clasp, embrace, cling to, hold close, squeeze

huge *adjective*
Elephants are **huge** *animals.* • enormous, gigantic, massive, colossal, giant, immense, vast, mighty, mammoth, monumental, hulking, great, big, large, *(informal)* whopping, ginormous, humungous **opposite** small, little, tiny

hum *verb* **humming, hummed**
We heard insects **humming** *in the air.*
• buzz, drone, murmur, purr, whirr

humble *adjective*
1. *The gentle giant was both* **humble** *and kind.* • modest, meek, unassuming, polite, respectful, submissive **opposite** proud
2. *Hansel and Gretel lived a* **humble** *cottage.* • simple, modest, plain, ordinary, commonplace, lowly **opposite** grand

humid *adjective*
I don't like this **humid** *weather.* • muggy, clammy, close, sticky, steamy, sweaty **opposite** fresh

humiliate *verb*
He **humiliated** *her in front of her friends.*
• embarrass, disgrace, shame, make ashamed, humble, crush, degrade, *(informal)* put you in your place, take you down a peg

humour *noun*
1. *I liked the* **humour** *in the film.* • comedy, wit, amusement, jokes
2. *The ogre was in a very bad* **humour***.* • mood, temper, disposition, frame of mind, spirits

hunger *noun*
After a week without food, the crew were faint with **hunger***.* • lack of food, starvation, famine
• Bad health caused by not having enough food is **malnutrition**.

hungry *adjective* hungrier, hungriest
Our dog always seems to be hungry. • starving, famished, ravenous, *(informal)* peckish

hunt *noun*
Police have begun the hunt for clues. • search, quest, chase, pursuit (of)

hunt *verb*
1. *Some Native American tribes used to hunt buffalo.* • chase, pursue, track, trail, hound, stalk • An animal which hunts other animals for food is a **predator**.
2. *I hunted in the attic for our old photos.*
• search, seek, look, rummage, ferret, root around

hurdle *noun*
The biggest hurdle facing the team is lack of experience. • difficulty, problem, handicap, hindrance, snag, stumbling block

hurry *verb* hurries, hurrying, hurried
1. *If you want to catch the bus, you'd better hurry.* • be quick, hasten, make speed, *(informal)* get a move on, step on it
opposite dawdle
2. *Alice saw the White Rabbit hurrying past.* • rush, dash, fly, speed, hurtle, scurry
opposite amble, stroll

hurt *verb*
1. *Be careful not to hurt yourself with the scissors.* • harm, injure, damage, wound, maim • To hurt someone deliberately is to **torment** or **torture** them.
2. *My feet hurt.* • be sore, be painful, ache, throb, sting, smart
3. *Your letter hurt me deeply.* • upset, distress, offend, grieve

hurtful *adjective*
That was a very hurtful remark. • upsetting, unkind, cruel, mean, painful, spiteful, nasty

hurtle *verb*
The train hurtled along at top speed. • rush, speed, race, dash, fly, charge, tear, shoot, zoom

hush *verb*
The speaker tried his best to hush the crowd.
• silence, quieten, settle, still, calm

hut *noun*
The walkers came across a hut in the forest.
• shed, shack, cabin, den, shelter, shanty, hovel

hysterical *adjective*
1. *The fans became hysterical when the band appeared.* • crazy, frenzied, mad, delirious, raving, wild, uncontrollable
2. *(informal) We laughed at the hysterical jokes in the film.* • hilarious, funny, amusing, comical

a
b
c
d
e
f
g
h
i
j
k
l
m
n
o
p
q
r
s
t
u
v
w
x
y
z

Ii

I is always upper case when talking about yourself.

ice noun

WORD WEB

VARIOUS FORMS OF ICE
• black ice, floe, frost, glacier, iceberg, ice sheet, icicle

WAYS TO DESCRIBE ICE
• brittle, cracked, frozen solid, glacial, glassy, gleaming, glinting, hard, packed, slippery or *(informal)* slippy, smooth, treacherous

THINGS YOU MIGHT DO ON ICE
• glide, skate, skid, slide, slip, slither

SPORTS THAT TAKE PLACE ON ICE
• curling, figure skating, ice skating, ice hockey, speed skating • Ice sports are played on an **ice rink**.

icy *adjective* icier, iciest
1. *You need to dress warmly in icy weather.*
• cold, freezing, frosty, wintry, arctic, bitter, biting
2. *Icy roads are dangerous.* • frozen, slippery, glacial, glassy, *(informal)* slippy

idea *noun*
1. *I've got a great idea!* • plan, scheme, proposal, suggestion, inspiration
2. *She has some funny ideas about life.*
• belief, notion, opinion, view, theory, concept, conception, hypothesis

3. *What's the main idea of this poem?* • point, meaning, intention, thought
4. *Give me an idea of what you are planning.*
• clue, hint, inkling, impression

ideal *adjective*
It's ideal weather for a picnic. • perfect, excellent, the best, faultless, suitable

identical *adjective*
The twins were wearing identical clothes.
• matching, similar, alike, indistinguishable
opposite different

identify *verb* identifies, identifying, identified
1. *The police asked if I could identify the thief.* • recognize, name, distinguish, pick out, single out
2. *The doctor couldn't identify what was wrong.* • diagnose, discover, spot, *(informal)* put a name to

idiotic *adjective*
That was an idiotic thing to do. • stupid, silly, foolish, unwise, senseless, ridiculous, half-witted, unintelligent, crazy, mad, hare-brained, *(informal)* daft
opposite sensible

idle *adjective*
1. *The ogre was an idle, foul-smelling creature.* • lazy, indolent, slothful, work-shy
opposite hard-working
2. *The computers lay idle all week.* • inactive, unused, inoperative **opposite** busy, active

idol *noun*
1. *The floor of the temple was littered with broken idols.* • god, deity, image, statue
2. *He was a pop idol of the fifties.* • star, celebrity, icon, pin-up, favourite

ignorant *adjective*
Trolls are often described as ignorant creatures. • uneducated, simple, stupid

ignore *verb*
Ignoring the weather, Lynn went for a walk.
• disregard, take no notice of, overlook, neglect, spurn, snub, *(informal)* turn a blind eye to

ill *adjective*
1. *I missed school for a week when I was ill.* • sick, unwell, poorly, sickly, ailing, infirm, unfit, indisposed, diseased, infected, nauseous, queasy, off-colour, peaky, *(informal)* under the weather
opposite healthy, well

2. *They suffered no* *ill* *effects from their soaking.* • bad, harmful, adverse, damaging **opposite** good

illegal *adjective*
Stealing is *illegal.* • unlawful, against the law, banned, prohibited, criminal, forbidden, wrong **opposite** legal

illness *noun*
He is suffering from a mystery *illness.*
• disease, infection, affliction, ailment, attack, complaint, condition, disorder, malady, infirmity, sickness, *(informal)* bug • A sudden illness is an **attack** or a **fit**. • A period of illness is a **bout** of it. • A general outbreak of illness in an area is an **epidemic**.

illustrate *verb*
1. *I used some photos to* *illustrate* *my story.*
• depict, picture, portray
2. *The accident* *illustrates* *the importance of road safety.* • show, demonstrate, make clear

illustration *noun*
1. *I like cookery books with lots of* *illustrations.*
• picture, photograph, drawing, sketch, diagram
2. *I'll give you an* *illustration* *of what I mean.*
• example, instance, demonstration, specimen

image *noun*
1. *The film contained frightening* *images of war.* • picture, portrayal, depiction, representation
2. *The temple contained* *images* *of the gods.*
• figure, idol, statue, carving
3. *You can see your* *image* *in the mirror.*
• reflection, likeness

imaginary *adjective*
The story takes place in an *imaginary* *universe.*
• imagined, non-existent, unreal, made-up, invented, fanciful, fictitious, fictional **opposite** real

imagination *noun*
Use your *imagination* *to draw an alien spaceship.* • creativity, inventiveness, ingenuity, inspiration, originality, vision, artistry, fancy

imaginative *adjective*
Roald Dahl wrote highly *imaginative* *stories.* • creative, inventive, inspired, original, artistic, fanciful, ingenious, clever **opposite** unimaginative, dull

imagine *verb*
1. *Imagine* *what it would be like to visit*

Mars. • picture, visualize, pretend, think up, dream up, fancy, conjure up
2. *I* *imagine* *you'd like something to eat.*
• suppose, assume, presume, believe, guess

imitate *verb*
Parrots can *imitate* *the human voice.* • copy, reproduce, mimic, mirror, echo, simulate, impersonate, follow, match, *(informal)* send up, take off

imitation *noun*
This is an *imitation* *of a Viking helmet.* • copy, replica, reproduction, duplicate • An imitation made to deceive someone is a **fake** or a **forgery**.

imitation *adjective*
The coat is made of *imitation* *fur.* • artificial, synthetic, fake, sham, mock **opposite** real, genuine • Imitation jewels are **paste**.
• Imitation money is **counterfeit** money.

immature *adjective*
Tess is quite *immature* *for her age.* • childish, babyish, infantile, juvenile **opposite** mature

immediate *adjective*
1. *Please can I have an* *immediate* *reply.*
• instant, instantaneous, prompt, speedy, swift, urgent, quick, direct, *(informal)* snappy **opposite** slow
2. *Are you friends with your* *immediate* *neighbours?* • closest, nearest, adjacent, next **opposite** distant

immediately *adverb*
You must fetch a doctor *immediately!*
at once, now, straight away, right away, instantly, promptly, directly

immense *adjective*
The giant wiggled one of his *immense* *toes.*
• huge, great, massive, enormous, colossal, vast, giant, gigantic, mighty, mammoth, monumental, *(informal)* whopping, ginormous, humungous **opposite** tiny

immobile *adjective*
The knight stood *immobile* *at the castle gate.*
• motionless, still, unmoving, stationary, static, inert **opposite** mobile

immoral *adjective*
It would be *immoral* *to steal the money.*
• wrong, wicked, bad, sinful, dishonest, corrupt **opposite** moral, right

immortal *adjective*
The ancient Greeks believed their gods

were *immortal*. • undying, ageless, eternal, everlasting **opposite** mortal

impact *noun*
1. *The crater was caused by the impact of a meteor.* • crash, collision, smash, blow, bump, bang, knock, jolt
2. *Computers have a big impact on our lives.* • effect, influence

impair *verb*
Very loud noise can impair your hearing. • damage, harm, injure, weaken

impartial *adjective*
Referees must be impartial. • neutral, detached, objective, unbiased, unprejudiced, disinterested, independent, fair, fair-minded, just, even-handed, open-minded **opposite** biased

impatient *adjective*
1. *As time went on, Henry grew more and more impatient.* • restless, agitated, anxious, edgy, fidgety, irritable, snappy, testy, jumpy **opposite** patient
2. *The crowd were impatient for the show to begin.* • anxious, eager, in a hurry, keen, (informal) itching

important *adjective*
1. *The World Cup is an important sporting event.* • major, significant, big, central, momentous, outstanding, historic
2. *I have some important business to attend to.* • serious, urgent, pressing, weighty, vital, essential, crucial
3. *The prime minister is an important person.* • prominent, powerful, influential, notable, eminent, distinguished

impossible *adjective*
We used to think that space travel was impossible. • impractical, unthinkable, unrealistic, unachievable, unworkable, out of the question **opposite** possible

impress *verb*
Frank impressed the coach with his football skills. • make an impression on, influence, leave its mark on, stick in your mind

impression *noun*
1. *I had the impression that something was wrong.* • feeling, idea, sense, notion, suspicion, hunch
2. *The film made a big impression on them.* • effect, impact, influence, mark
3. *My sister does a good impression of*

the Queen. • imitation, impersonation, (informal) send-up

impressive *adjective*
The film includes some impressive special effects. • striking, effective, powerful, remarkable, spectacular, exciting, inspiring **opposite** unimpressive, uninspiring

imprison *verb*
The thief was imprisoned for two years. • send to prison, jail, lock up, incarcerate, confine, detain, (informal) put away, send down, put under lock and key **opposite** liberate

improve *verb*
1. *Her work improved during the term.* • get better, advance, progress, develop, move on **opposite** deteriorate
2. *Has he improved since his illness?* • get better, recover, recuperate, pick up, rally, revive **opposite** get worse
3. *How can I improve this story?* • make better, enhance, refine, amend, revise, correct, upgrade

improvement *noun*
1. *Your handwriting shows signs of improvement.* • getting better, advance, progress, development, recovery, upturn
2. *The author made some improvements to the book.* • amendment, correction, revision, modification, enhancement

impulsive *adjective*
She regretted her impulsive decision to dye her hair. • hasty, rash, reckless, sudden, spontaneous, thoughtless, unthinking, impetuous **opposite** deliberate

inaccurate *adjective*
That spelling of my surname is inaccurate. • wrong, incorrect, mistaken, false, inexact, untrue **opposite** accurate

inadequate *adjective*
They had brought an inadequate supply of matches. • insufficient, not enough, limited, scarce, scanty, meagre **opposite** adequate

incident *noun*
There was an amusing incident at school this morning. • event, happening, occurrence, episode, affair

include *verb*
Does the cost include postage and packing? • contain, incorporate, comprise, involve, take in, allow for, take into account, cover **opposite** exclude

inconsiderate *adjective*
It's inconsiderate to play the radio so loudly. • selfish, unthinking, thoughtless, insensitive, rude, tactless, unkind, uncaring **opposite** considerate

inconsistent *adjective*
1. *His performance has been inconsistent this season.* • changeable, unreliable, variable, unpredictable, erratic, fickle
2. *The stories of the two witnesses are inconsistent.* • contradictory, conflicting, different **opposite** consistent

inconvenient *adjective*
The guests arrived at an inconvenient moment. • awkward, difficult, unsuitable, unfortunate, untimely, inopportune **opposite** convenient

increase *verb*
1. *They've increased the size of the tennis courts.* • make bigger, enlarge, expand, develop, add to, widen, broaden
2. *She increased the cooking time in the recipe.* • extend, lengthen, prolong
3. *The police increased their efforts to find the murderer.* • intensify, step up
4. *Will you be increasing the bus fares?* • put up, raise
5. *Can you increase the volume of the TV?* • turn up, amplify, boost
6. *The number of cars on the roads continues to increase.* • grow, mount, go up, rise, soar, build up, escalate, multiply

incredible *adjective*
1. *Do you expect us to believe that incredible story?* • unbelievable, unlikely, improbable, far-fetched, absurd, implausible **opposite** credible
2. *The Forth Bridge is an incredible feat of engineering.* • extraordinary, amazing, astounding, magnificent, marvellous, spectacular

independent *adjective*
1. *My granny is a very independent person.* • free, liberated, self-sufficient, self-reliant **opposite** dependent
2. *Luxembourg is an independent country.* • autonomous, self-governing
3. *We need an independent opinion on the matter.* • impartial, neutral, objective, unbiased **opposite** biased

indicate *verb*
A red light indicates danger. • mean, stand for, signal, signify, convey, communicate

indication *noun*
He gave no indication that he felt ill. • sign, signal, hint, clue, inkling, evidence, warning

indifferent *adjective*
1. *I felt indifferent as I watched the game.* • uninterested, detached, uncaring, unenthusiastic, unmoved, uninvolved, unconcerned **opposite** enthusiastic
2. *The food in the restaurant was indifferent.* • mediocre, ordinary, unexciting, average **opposite** excellent

indignant *adjective*
The player was indignant when he was sent off. • annoyed, angry, cross, affronted, offended, outraged, piqued

indirect *adjective*
The bus took an indirect route into town. • roundabout, winding, meandering, rambling, zigzag **opposite** direct

individual *adjective*
Her singing has an individual style. • characteristic, distinct, distinctive, special, unique, personal, singular

industry *noun* **industries**
1. *Many people in the area work in the car industry.* • business, trade, commerce, manufacturing, production
2. *The elves' workshop was a hive of industry.* • hard work, effort, energy, diligence, application, busyness **opposite** laziness

ineffective *adjective*
He was an ineffective captain of the team. • incompetent, inadequate, unsuccessful, inept, (informal) useless, hopeless **opposite** effective

inevitable *adjective*
If it rains, it is inevitable that the pitch will get wet. • certain, sure, definite, unavoidable, inescapable

infect *verb*
A virus may have infected the water supply. • contaminate, pollute, poison

infection *noun*
The infection spread rapidly. • disease, virus, contagion, contamination

infectious *adjective*
Chickenpox is highly infectious. • contagious, catching

inferior adjective
1. *The clothes were of inferior quality.* • poor, bad, second-rate, mediocre, cheap, shoddy
2. *Officers can give orders to those of inferior rank.* • lesser, lower, junior, subordinate

infested adjective
The attic was infested with mice. • swarming, teeming, crawling, overrun, plagued

infinite adjective
You need infinite patience to train a puppy. • endless, limitless, unlimited, boundless, never-ending, unending, inexhaustible **opposite** finite

inflict verb
I hate seeing anyone inflict pain on an animal. • administer, deal out, apply, impose

influence noun
Rock music had a big influence on her life. • effect, impact, power, dominance, guidance, authority, control

influence verb
The money he was offered influenced his decision. • affect, have an effect on, direct, guide, control, motivate

inform verb
Please inform us if you move house. • tell, let you know, notify, advise

informal adjective
1. *The party will be a very informal event.* • casual, relaxed, easygoing, friendly, homely, natural
2. *Emails are usually written in an informal style.* • colloquial, familiar, chatty, personal

information noun
There is more information on our website. • details, particulars, facts, data, advice, guidance, knowledge, (informal) info

inhabit verb
People inhabited the caves thousands of years ago. • live in, occupy, dwell in, reside in, populate, settle in

inherit verb
She inherited the farm from her uncle. • succeed to, be left, come into

inhuman adjective
I think it's inhuman to hunt animals. • barbaric, cruel, inhumane, merciless, heartless **opposite** humane

initially adverb
Initially I didn't like swimming in the sea. • at first, at the start, in the beginning, to begin with, to start with, originally

initiative noun
You must use your initiative on the treasure hunt. • resourcefulness, inventiveness, originality, enterprise

injure verb
Was anyone injured in the accident? • hurt, harm, wound • To injure someone, causing permanent damage, is to **maim** them.

inner adjective
A pasageway led to the inner chamber. • internal, interior, inside **opposite** outer

innocent adjective
1. *The jury found the man innocent.* • guiltless, blameless, free from blame **opposite** guilty
2. *Baby tigers look so innocent.* • angelic, harmless, faultless, virtuous, pure, simple, inexperienced, naive **opposite** wicked

inquire verb
to inquire into
Detectives are inquiring into the robbery. • look into, investigate, examine, explore

inquiry noun inquiries
There will be an official inquiry about the accident. • investigation, inspection, examination

insane adjective
1. *It was rumoured that the king had gone insane.* • mentally ill, mad, crazy, deranged, demented, disturbed, unhinged, (informal) off your head, out of your mind **opposite** sane
2. *It would be insane to swim in the sea in January!* • crazy, mad, daft, senseless, stupid, foolish, idiotic **opposite** sensible, wise

insect noun

WORD WEB

SOME TYPES OF INSECT
• ant, aphid, bee, beetle, bluebottle, bumble-bee, butterfly, cicada, cockroach, crane fly or daddy-long-legs, cricket, dragonfly, earwig, firefly, flea, fly, glow-worm, gnat, grasshopper, greenfly, hornet, horsefly, ladybird, locust, louse, mantis, mayfly, midge, mosquito, moth, stick insect, termite, tsetse fly, wasp, weevil

LIFE STAGES OF SOME INSECTS
• caterpillar, chrysalis, grub, larva, maggot, pupa

PARTS OF INSECTS' BODIES
• head, thorax, abdomen; antennae, legs, wings

SOME CREATURES SIMILAR TO INSECTS
• centipede, earthworm, mite, slug, spider, woodlouse, worm

insecure adjective
1. *Be careful—that scaffolding is insecure.*
• unsafe, unsteady, unstable, loose, shaky, wobbly, dangerous, hazardous, precarious
2. *Colin felt insecure on his first day at school.* • anxious, nervous, worried, apprehensive, uneasy, uncertain, unconfident **opposite** secure

insensitive adjective
I'm sorry if my comments were insensitive.
• thoughtless, tactless, unfeeling, uncaring, unsympathetic, callous **opposite** sensitive

insert verb
Please insert a coin in the slot. • put in, place, push in, stick in, install, implant

inside noun
The inside of the nest was lined with feathers.
• interior, inner surface, centre, core, heart, middle **opposite** outside

insignificant adjective
The author made a few insignificant changes.
• unimportant, minor, trivial, negligible, slight, meaningless **opposite** significant

insincere adjective
The butler welcomed us with an insincere smile. • false, pretended, hypocritical, dishonest, deceitful, deceptive, lying, (informal) two-faced **opposite** sincere

insist verb
Griselda insisted that she was not a witch.
• declare, state, assert, maintain, stress, emphasize, swear, vow, claim
to insist on

The magician insisted on silence before he began. • demand, require

inspect verb
They inspected the damage done by the storm. • check, examine, investigate, look over, study, survey, scrutinize

inspection noun
There will be a safety inspection this afternoon. • check, check-up, examination, review, survey

inspire verb
The crowd inspired the team to play well.
• motivate, prompt, stimulate, encourage, stir, arouse, spur on

install verb
We are getting a new bathroom installed.
• put in, set up, fix, place, position, establish **opposite** remove

instant adjective
Gardeners don't expect instant results.
• immediate, quick, rapid, fast, prompt, snappy, speedy, swift, direct

instant noun
The shooting star was gone in an instant.
• moment, second, split second, flash, (informal) tick, jiffy

instinct noun
The great detective always followed his instincts. • impulse, inclination, intuition, hunch, feeling, urge

instruct verb
1. *All the staff are instructed in first aid.*
• teach, train, coach, tutor
2. *The police officer instructed the cars to wait.* • tell, order, direct, command

instructions plural noun
Please follow the instructions carefully.
• directions, guidelines, orders, commands

instrument noun
Dentists use special instruments to check your teeth. • tool, implement, utensil, appliance, device, gadget, contraption

insult verb
He was insulted not to be invited to the wedding. • offend, outrage, be rude to, hurt, injure, slight, snub

insult noun
It is considered an insult to refuse a gift.
• rudeness, offence, affront, slight, slur, snub

insulting adjective
She made an insulting comment about my
clothes. • offensive, rude, impolite, derogatory,
scornful **opposite** complimentary

intact adjective
The vase has remained intact for centuries.
• unbroken, whole, undamaged, unharmed,
complete, perfect, (informal) in one piece

intelligence noun
1. The robot shows some signs of intelligence.
• cleverness, understanding, comprehension,
reason, sense, wisdom, brainpower, wits,
(informal) brains
2. The spy was sent to gather secret
intelligence. • information, knowledge, data,
facts, reports

intelligent adjective
The aliens from Planet Zog are highly
intelligent. • clever, bright, smart, quick,
sharp, perceptive, shrewd, able, brilliant,
rational, thinking, (informal) brainy
opposite unintelligent, stupid

intense adjective
1. I felt a sudden, intense pain in my chest.
• extreme, acute, severe, sharp, great, strong,
violent **opposite** slight, mild
2. The contest aroused intense feelings.
• deep, passionate, powerful, strong, profound
opposite mild

intent adjective
He read the letter with an intent look on his
face. • concentrating, absorbed, engrossed,
preoccupied, interested
intent on
The detective was intent on solving the
mystery. • determined to, resolved to, eager
to, fixed on, bent on

intention noun
It's his intention to play cricket for Australia.
• aim, objective, target, goal, ambition, plan,
intent

intentional adjective
He was penalized for an intentional foul.
• deliberate, conscious, calculated, planned,
intended, wilful **opposite** accidental

interest verb
Politics doesn't interest me at all. • appeal
to, attract, capture your imagination, excite,
fascinate, stimulate, absorb **opposite** bore

interest noun
1. The dog showed no interest in the bone.
• curiosity, attention, concern, involvement
2. The information was of no interest
to anyone. • importance, significance,
consequence, value
3. My interests include judo and playing the
trombone. • hobby, pastime, pursuit, activity,
diversion

interesting adjective
I found out some very interesting facts
about the solar system. • fascinating,
absorbing, enthralling, intriguing, engrossing,
stimulating, riveting, gripping, entertaining,
diverting **opposite** boring, dull

interfere verb
to interfere in
Don't interfere in other people's affairs.
• intervene in, intrude in, meddle in, pry into,
encroach on, butt in on
to interfere with
The bad weather interfered with our plans.
• hamper, hinder, get in the way of, obstruct

internal adjective
Scoop out the internal parts of the tomato.
• inner, inside, interior **opposite** external

international adjective
Interpol is an international police organization.
• global, worldwide, intercontinental

interrupt verb
1. Please don't interrupt while I am speaking.
• intervene, interject, break in, butt in, cut in
2. Heavy rain interrupted the tennis match.
• stop, suspend, disrupt, break off, cut short

interruption noun
He wrote for an hour without any interruption.
• break, pause, stop, gap, halt, disruption,
suspension

interval noun
1. There will be a short interval after the first
act. • break, pause, wait, delay, lapse, lull
• Another word for an interval in a play or film
is **interlude** or **intermission**. • An interval in
a meeting is a **recess**. • An interval when you
take a rest is a **breather** or **breathing space**.
2. There were signs at regular intervals along
the road. • space, gap, distance

interview verb
He interviewed the author about her new
book. • question, talk to, interrogate, examine

intimate adjective
1. *They have been intimate friends for years.*
• close, cherished, dear, friendly, brotherly, sisterly **opposite** distant
2. *The newspaper printed intimate details about her life.* • personal, private, confidential, secret

intricate adjective
The door was carved with intricate designs.
• complex, complicated, elaborate, sophisticated, involved **opposite** simple

intriguing adjective
The results of the experiment are intriguing.
• interesting, attractive, fascinating, captivating, beguiling

introduce verb
1. *Let me introduce you to my friend.* • present, make known
2. *The director stood up to introduce the film.*
• give an introduction to, announce, lead into
3. *They are introducing a new bus service next year.* • set up, start, begin, create, establish, initiate, bring in

introduction noun
• Something which happens as an introduction to a bigger event is a **prelude**.
• An introduction to a book is a **preface**.
• An introduction to a play is a **prologue**.
• A piece played as an introduction to a concert or opera is an **overture**.

invade verb
The Vikings invaded many parts of Europe.
• attack, enter, occupy, overrun, march into, raid

invaluable adjective
Reena is an invaluable member of the hockey team. • indispensable, irreplaceable, crucial, essential, useful, valuable **opposite** worthless

invent verb
James Dewar invented the thermos flask.
• create, devise, think up, conceive, design, originate

inventor noun
James Dewar was the inventor of the thermos flask. • creator, designer, originator, discoverer

investigate verb
Police are investigating the cause of the accident. • examine, explore, inquire into, look into, study, consider, follow up, probe, research, scrutinize, *(informal)* go into

investigation noun
An investigation showed how the accident happened. • examination, inquiry, inspection, study, review, survey

invisible adjective
The wizard was invisible when he wore his magic cloak. • out of sight, unseen, unnoticed, hidden, concealed, covered, obscured, camouflaged, disguised, undetectable, unnoticeable, inconspicuous **opposite** visible

invite verb
Our neighbours invited us round for tea. • ask, request your company, welcome, summon

involve verb
1. *My job involves a lot of travel.* • include, comprise, require, demand, necessitate, mean
2. *Protecting the environment involves us all.*
• affect, concern, interest, touch

involved adjective
1. *The film has a long and involved plot.*
• complex, complicated, elaborate, intricate, confusing, difficult, convoluted **opposite** simple
2. *Are you involved in the theatre?*
• concerned, participating, engaged, caught up, mixed up

irregular adjective
1. *The bricks were arranged in an irregular pattern.* • varying, erratic, haphazard, random, unpredictable, fitful **opposite** regular
2. *It is highly irregular to eat pizza with a spoon!* • abnormal, unusual, exceptional, unconventional, improper **opposite** normal

irresponsible adjective
It's irresponsible to drive too fast. • reckless, rash, thoughtless, inconsiderate, uncaring, unthinking, negligent **opposite** responsible

irritable adjective
After a bad night, he woke in an irritable mood.
• bad-tempered, grumpy, short-tempered, cross, impatient, snappy, touchy, testy, prickly, peevish, *(informal)* stroppy, shirty **opposite** good-humoured, cheerful

irritate verb
The noise from next door began to irritate me.
• annoy, bother, exasperate, anger, provoke, madden, vex, *(informal)* get on your nerves, bug

island *noun*
• A small island is an **islet**. • An island made of coral is an **atoll**. • A group of islands is an **archipelago**. • An uninhabited island is a **desert island**. • A person who is stranded on a desert island is a **castaway**.

isolated *adjective*
They sheltered in an isolated cave in the mountains. • remote, out-of-the-way, secluded, outlying, inaccessible, cut-off, deserted **opposite** accessible

issue *verb*
1. *They issued blankets to the refugees.* • give out, distribute, supply
2. *They have issued a new set of stamps.* • bring out, put out, produce, publish, release, circulate, print
3. *Green smoke issued from the dragon's nostrils.* • come out, emerge, appear, flow out, gush, erupt

issue *noun*
1. *The new issue of the magazine comes out this week.* • edition, number, instalment, copy
2. *They print stories about local issues in the magazine.* • matter, subject, topic, affair, concern, question, problem

itch *noun*
1. *I had an annoying itch on my foot.* • tickle, tingling, prickle
2. *Olga had a great itch to travel.* • desire, longing, urge, wish, yearning, ache, impulse

item *noun*
1. *I bought a few items in the jumble sale.* • thing, object, article
2. *There was an item about our school in the paper.* • article, piece, report, feature

jab *verb* **jabbing, jabbed**
A passer-by jabbed me in the ribs. • poke, prod, elbow, nudge, stab, thrust

jagged *adjective*
This dinosaur had jagged teeth. • rough, uneven, ragged, spiky, toothed, serrated
opposite smooth

jam *noun*
1. *We got stuck in a jam on the motorway.*
• traffic jam, hold-up, tailback, blockage
2. *(informal) I'm in a bit of a jam.* • difficulty, mess, predicament, plight, *(informal)* fix, tight corner

jam *verb* **jamming, jammed**
1. *Someone had jammed the door open.* • prop, wedge, stick
2. *The roads are jammed at rush hour.* • block, clog, obstruct, congest, *(informal)* bung up
3. *I jammed my things into a backpack.* • cram, pack, stuff, squeeze, squash, crush, ram, crowd

jangle *verb*
Silver bracelets jangled on her wrists. • jingle, chink, clink, tinkle

jar *verb* **jarring, jarred**
1. *He jarred his back badly when he fell.* • jolt, jerk, shake, shock
2. *Those colours jar with each other.* • clash, conflict, be at odds, not go

jealous *adjective*
Cinderella's sisters were jealous of her beauty.
• envious, resentful, grudging

jeer *verb*
Some of the audience whistled and jeered.
• boo, hiss, sneer, taunt, mock, scoff, ridicule
opposite cheer

jerk *verb*
The rider jerked on the horse's reins. • pull, tug, yank, pluck, wrench, tweak

jerky *adjective* **jerkier, jerkiest**
The stagecoach drew to a jerky halt. • jolting, jumpy, shaky, bouncy, bumpy, uneven
opposite steady

jester *noun*
The court jester was a very witty man. • fool, joker, clown

jet *noun*
A jet of water shot high in the air. • spout, spurt, squirt, gush, stream, fountain

jewel *noun*

WORD WEB

SOME ITEMS OF JEWELLERY
• anklet, bangle, beads, bindi, bracelet, brooch, chain, charm, choker, clasp, crown, cufflinks, earring, engagement ring, locket, necklace, pendant, pin, ring, tiara, tie pin, wedding ring

STONES OR GEMS USED TO MAKE JEWELLERY
• agate, amber, amethyst, aquamarine, carnelian or cornelian, coral, diamond, emerald, garnet, jade, jasper, jet, lapis lazuli, onyx, opal, pearl, ruby, sapphire, topaz, turquoise

METALS USED TO MAKE JEWELLERY
• gold, platinum, silver

jingle *verb*
Some coins jingled in his back pocket. • jangle, chink, clink, tinkle

job *noun*
1. *My sister would like a job as a TV reporter.*
• post, position, profession, occupation, employment, trade, work, career
• The job you particularly want to do is your **mission** or **vocation**.
2. *Whose job is it to do the washing-up?*
• duty, task, assignment, chore, errand

jog *verb* jogging, jogged
1. *He jogs round the park every morning.*
• go jogging, run, trot
2. *A boy sitting next to me jogged my elbow.*
• nudge, prod, jolt, knock, bump, jar, jostle
3. *The photograph may jog her memory.*
• prompt, stir, arouse, set off, stimulate

join *verb*
1. *Our families joined together to buy the present.* • combine, come together, merge, unite, amalgamate **opposite** separate
2. *Join one piece of rope to the other.*
• connect, fasten, attach, fix, link, put together, tack on **opposite** detach
3. *The two roads join here.* • meet, merge, converge **opposite** divide
4. *I joined the crowd going into the cinema.* • follow, go with, tag along with **opposite** leave
5. *We have joined a local sports club.*
• become a member of, enrol in, sign up for
• To join the army is to **enlist. opposite** leave, resign from

join *noun*
If you look hard, you can still see the join.
• joint, connection, link, mend, seam

joint *adjective*
The preparation of the meal was a joint effort.
• combined, shared, common, communal, cooperative, united, collective, mutual
opposite individual

joke *noun*
Do you know any good jokes? • jest, quip, crack, witticism, wisecrack, *(informal)* gag

joke *verb*
Those two are always laughing and joking.
• jest, clown, have a laugh, make jokes, lark about or around

jolly *adjective* jollier, jolliest
The old night watchman was a jolly fellow, and everybody liked him. • cheerful, merry, happy, jovial, joyful, lively **opposite** gloomy

jolt *verb*
The car jolted over the bumps in the road.
• jerk, jog, bump, bounce, shake, shudder

journal *noun*
1. *The newsagent sells a few journals.*
• magazine, newspaper, paper, periodical, publication
2. *The captain kept a journal of the voyage.*
• diary, log, record, account, chronicle

journalist *noun*
She started as a journalist on the local paper.
• reporter, correspondent, columnist

journey *noun*
On their journey, the astronauts will pass the Moon. • voyage, trip, expedition, travels, wanderings, tour, route

joy *noun*
I remember the sheer joy of scoring a goal! • happiness, joyfulness, delight, cheerfulness, gladness, mirth, glee, jubilation, gaiety, rejoicing, bliss, ecstasy, elation
opposite sorrow

joyful *adjective*
The wedding was a joyful occasion. • happy, cheerful, merry, joyous, jolly, jovial, good-humoured **opposite** sad

judge *verb*
1. *The umpire judged that the ball was out.*
• rule, decide, decree, adjudicate
2. *Who's judging the flower show this year?*
• decide on, assess, evaluate, appraise
3. *He judged the coin to be about 1000 years old.* • reckon, suppose, consider, gauge, guess, estimate

judgement *noun*
1. *What is the judgement of the court?*
• decision, finding, ruling, verdict, decree
2. *His comments show a lack of judgement.*
• wisdom, common sense, understanding, discrimination
3. *In my judgement, you're making a big mistake.*
• opinion, view, belief, assessment, estimate

jumble *noun*
There was a jumble of clothes on the floor.
• mess, muddle, clutter, chaos, confusion, disorder

jumble *verb*
Please don't jumble the pages. • muddle, mix up, mess up, disorganize, shuffle
opposite arrange

jump *verb*
1. *Suddenly a rabbit jumped in front of us.*
• leap, spring, bound, bounce, hop • When a cat jumps it **pounces**.

2. *All the horses jumped the first hurdle.*
• leap over, vault, clear
3. *The loud bang made them all jump.*
• start, flinch, jolt

jump *noun*
With a jump, the grasshopper landed on the leaf. • leap, spring, bound, vault, hop

jungle *noun*

🕸 WORD WEB

One of my dreams is to be a jungle explorer.
• rainforest, tropical forest

THINGS YOU MIGHT SEE IN THE JUNGLE
• canopy, foliage, forest floor, swamp, undergrowth

SOME ANIMALS WHICH LIVE IN THE JUNGLE
• alligator, ant, anteater, armadillo, bird of paradise, butterfly, chameleon, crocodile, gorilla, hummingbird, jaguar, leopard, macaw, monkey, mosquito, parrot, piranha, porcupine, snake, tarantula, tiger, toucan, tree frog

SOME PLANTS WHICH ARE FOUND IN THE JUNGLE
• banana tree, cacao, creeper or liana, mangrove, orchid, palm tree, rubber tree

---

junior *adjective*
1. *I'm a member of the junior hockey team.*
• younger
2. *He's only a junior employee in the firm.*
• low-ranking, minor, lesser, subordinate

junk *noun*
The garage is full of old junk. • rubbish, clutter, garbage, jumble, trash, waste, scrap, odds and ends

just *adjective*
It was a just punishment, considering the crime. • fair, fitting, appropriate, deserved, proper, reasonable, justified **opposite** unjust, unfair

jut *verb* jutting, jutted
to jut out
A large nail jutted out from the wall.
• stick out, project, protrude, extend, overhang

Kk

Writing about *knights*?
Try using some words like *shield*,
joust and *pennant*.

keen *adjective*
1. *Rhona is a keen hockey player.*
• enthusiastic, eager, fervent, avid, devoted,
committed, motivated • A common simile is
as keen as mustard. opposite unenthusiastic
2. *A carving knife should have a keen edge.*
• sharp, razor-sharp, cutting **opposite** blunt
3. *Owls have very keen eyesight.* • sharp,
acute, piercing **opposites** poor, weak
4. *A keen wind was blowing from the east.*
• bitter, cold, icy, penetrating **opposites** mild,
soft

keep *verb* **keeping, kept**
1. *Let's keep the rest of the cake for later.*
• save, conserve, preserve, retain, hang on to,
hold on to, guard, store
2. *Please keep still.* • stay, remain
3. *A man in the audience kept coughing.*
• persist in, go on, carry on, continue
4. *You're late. What kept you?* • delay, detain,
hold up, keep waiting
5. *Where do you keep the knives and forks?*
• store, house, put, stow
6. *Will the milk keep until tomorrow?* • last, be
usable, stay good
7. *It costs money to keep a pet.* • support,
maintain, provide for, pay for
to keep something up
Keep up the good work! • carry on, continue,
maintain

key *noun*
Have you found the key to the riddle? • answer,
solution, explanation, clue

kick *verb*
1. *The goalkeeper kicked the ball high into the
air.* • strike, hit, boot, drive, send
2. *(informal) Some habits can be hard to kick.*
• give up, quit, break, abandon, cease,
desist from
kick *noun*
1. *Ben closed the gate with a kick.* • boot, hit,
blow, strike

2. *(informal) I get a real kick out of
entertaining people.* • thrill, buzz, excitement

kidnap *verb* **kidnapping, kidnapped**
In the story, a boy is kidnapped by bandits.
• abduct, capture, seize, carry off, snatch

kill *verb*
Several people were killed in the explosion.
(informal) bump off, do away with, *(old
use)* slay • To kill someone deliberately is to
murder them. • To kill someone brutally is
to **butcher** them. • To kill large numbers of
people is to **massacre** or **slaughter** them. • To
kill someone as a punishment is to **execute**
them or **put them to death**. • To kill someone
for political reasons is to **assassinate** them.

kind *noun*
What kind of music do you like to play? • sort,
type, variety, style, category, class, set

kind *adjective*
It was very kind of you to help me.
• good-natured, kind-hearted, kindly, genial,
amiable, caring, affectionate, warm, loving,
sweet, gentle, friendly, generous, giving,
sympathetic, thoughtful, considerate,
obliging, understanding, compassionate,
unselfish, gracious, merciful, benevolent,
charitable, humane, neighbourly
opposite unkind

kit *noun*
I've forgotten my games kit. • gear, outfit,
equipment, paraphernalia, tools, tackle

kitchen *noun*

WORD WEB

EQUIPMENT YOU MIGHT FIND IN A KITCHEN
• apron, blender, bread bin, cooker,
crockery, cutlery, dishwasher, draining
board, food processor, freezer, fridge, grill,
kettle, liquidizer, microwave, mixer, oven,
oven gloves, refrigerator, scales, sink,
toaster

knack *noun*
George has a knack for taking photographs.
• skill, talent, gift, flair

knight *noun*

WORD WEB

THINGS A MEDIEVAL KNIGHT MIGHT WEAR OR CARRY
• armour, baldric (leather belt), coat of arms, falcon or hawk, lance, mace (metal club), pennant, shield, surcoat, sword, tabard, tunic • A fight between knights on horseback was a **joust**. • A series of sporting contests between knights was a **tournament**. • A boy training to be a knight was first a **page** and then a **squire**. • An expedition made by a knight was a **quest**.

knobbly *adjective*
Crocodiles have thick and *knobbly* skin.
• lumpy, bumpy, gnarled

knock *verb*
I *knocked* my head as I got out of the car. • bump, bang, hit, strike, thump, (*informal*) bash

knot *verb* knotting, knotted
The sailors *knotted* the two ropes together.
• tie, bind, fasten, join, entwine, lash
opposite untie

know *verb* knowing, knew, known
1. *Do you know how to mend a puncture?*
• understand, have knowledge of, comprehend
2. *As soon as she saw the unicorn, she knew what it was.* • recognize, realize, appreciate, be aware of
3. *Do you know Stewart well?* • be acquainted with, be familiar with, be a friend of

knowledge *noun*
1. *She has a good knowledge of Italian.*
• understanding, grasp, command, familiarity (with)
2. *He acquired his knowledge from books.*
• information, data, facts, learning, know-how, wisdom, scholarship

There are lots of different words for *like* – try **admire**, **cherish**, **adore** or **dote**.

label *noun*
The washing instructions are on the *label*.
• tag, ticket, sticker

labour *noun*
1. *After hours of hard labour the job was finished.* • work, effort, industry, exertion, toil
2. *The factory took on extra labour.* • workers, employees

lack *noun*
The judge dismissed the case because of a *lack* of evidence. • absence, shortage, scarcity, want • A general lack of food is a **famine**. • A general lack of water is a **drought**. **opposite** abundance

lack *verb*
The game *lacked* excitement. • be short of, be without, want, need, require, miss

lag *verb* **lagging, lagged**
One runner was *lagging* behind the others. • straggle, trail, fall behind, drop behind, dawdle, linger, loiter

lair *noun*
The dragon's *lair* was a deep, dark cave. • den, refuge, shelter, hideout, hiding place • The lair of a fox is a **den** or an **earth**. • The lair of a badger is a **sett**.

lake *noun*
We rowed across the *lake*. • pond, pool, *(Scottish)* loch • A salt-water lake is a **lagoon**. • A lake used to supply water is a **reservoir**.

lame *adjective*
1. *The lame horse had to be withdrawn from the race.* • disabled, handicapped, crippled, limping
2. *I didn't believe her lame excuse.* • feeble, flimsy, poor, unconvincing, inadequate, weak, tame

land *noun*
1. *The castle is surrounded by several acres of land.* • grounds, estate, property
2. *The land here is good for growing strawberries.* • ground, soil, earth
3. *China is a land with an ancient history.* • country, nation, state, region, territory

land *verb*
1. *The plane landed exactly on time.* • touch down, arrive **opposite** take off
2. *The ship will land at Dover.* • dock, berth, come ashore
3. *How did these papers land on my desk?* • arrive, turn up, end up, wind up, settle

landscape *noun*
We sat on the hill and admired the *landscape*. • countryside, scenery, view, scene, outlook, prospect

language *noun*
1. *The scroll was written in an ancient language.* • tongue, speech, dialect
2. *The author uses very poetic language.* • wording, phrasing, vocabulary, expression, style • The words of a language are its **vocabulary**.

lap *noun*
1. *My cat, Snowy, likes to sit on my lap.* • knees, thighs
2. *The cars were on the last lap of the race.* • circuit, round, loop

large *adjective*
1. *Elephants are large animals.* • big, huge, enormous, colossal, giant, gigantic, immense, great, massive, bulky, heavy, hefty, weighty, mighty, towering, *(informal)* whopping, ginormous
2. *The cook gave me a large helping of pudding.* • ample, generous, plentiful, abundant, lavish
3. *Is this room large enough for dancing in?* • spacious, roomy, sizeable
4. *The gales caused damage over a large area.* • wide, broad, extensive, widespread, vast
5. *The meeting was attended by a large number of people.* • considerable, substantial **opposite** small

last *adjective*
1. *Z is the last letter of the alphabet.* • final, closing, concluding, terminating, ultimate **opposite** first
2. *Have you read her last book?* • latest, most recent **opposite** next

last *noun*
at last
*The holidays are here **at last**!* • finally, eventually, in the end

late *adjective*
1. *The bus is **late**.* • delayed, overdue
opposite early, punctual, on time
2. *Mr Pettigrew showed us a portrait of his **late** wife.* • dead, deceased, departed

lately *adverb*
*There has been a lot of snow **lately**.* • recently, latterly, of late

later *adverb*
*I'm busy now, but I'll phone you **later**.* • afterwards, in a while, in a bit, subsequently, next

laugh *verb*
1. *The children all **laughed** when the clown fell over.* • chuckle, chortle, giggle, titter, snigger, cackle, burst out laughing, roar or scream with laughter, roll or fall about laughing, guffaw, *(informal)* have hysterics, be in stitches
2. *It's rude to **laugh** at his singing.* • make fun of, mock, ridicule, scoff at, tease, deride

laugh *noun*
*She heard an evil **laugh** followed by a scream.* • chuckle, chortle, giggle, titter, snigger, cackle, guffaw, *(informal)* belly laugh

laughter *noun*
*We heard bursts of **laughter** coming from the kitchen.* • laughing, amusement, hilarity, mirth, merriment

launch *verb*
1. *The space shuttle will be **launched** tomorrow.* • send off, set off, blast off, fire
2. *The new website was **launched** in the summer.* • begin, start, set up, open, establish, found, initiate

lavish *adjective*
*The king held a **lavish** feast for his birthday.* • generous, extravagant, sumptuous, luxurious, opulent, grand, abundant, copious, plentiful, bountiful **opposite** meagre, paltry

law *noun*
• A law passed by parliament is an **act**.
• A proposed law to be discussed by parliament is a **bill**. • The laws of a game are **regulations** or **rules**. • A regulation which must be obeyed is a **commandment**, **decree**, **edict** or **order**.

lay *verb* **laying, laid**
1. *He **laid** the parchment carefully on his desk.* • put down, set down, place, position, spread, deposit, leave
2. *Please **lay** the table for dinner.* • set, set out, arrange

layer *noun*
1. *Everything was covered in a thick **layer** of dust.* • coat, coating, covering, thickness, film, sheet, skin
2. *You can see various **layers** of rock in the cliff.* • seam, band, stratum

laze *verb*
*We spent the day **lazing** in the garden.* • be lazy, idle, loaf, lounge, lie about, relax, loll

lazy *adjective* **lazier, laziest**
*My **lazy** little brother stayed in bed all day!* • idle, inactive, lethargic, slack, slothful, indolent • An informal name for a lazy person is **lazybones**.

lead *verb* **leading, led**
1. *The rescuers **led** the climbers to safety.* • guide, conduct, escort, usher, steer, pilot, shepherd **opposite** follow
2. *Dr Martez will **lead** the expedition to Peru.* • be in charge of, direct, command, head, manage, supervise
3. *The British cyclist **led** from the start of the race.* • be in front, be in the lead, head the field
4. *The animals in the zoo **lead** a peaceful life.* • have, pass, spend, experience

lead *noun*
1. *The team followed the captain's **lead**.* • example, guidance, leadership, direction
2. *The Australian swimmer is in the **lead**.* • first place, front position
3. *Don't trip over the electrical **lead**.* • cable, flex, wire

leader *noun*
*The **leader** of the pirates was Captain Cutlass.* • head, chief, commander, captain, director, principal, ruler, *(informal)* boss • The leader of a group of wrongdoers is the **ringleader**.

leaf *noun* **leaves**
1. *Deciduous trees lose their **leaves** in autumn.* • A mass of leaves is **foliage** or **greenery**.
2. *A single **leaf** had been torn out of the book.* • sheet, page

a
b
c
d
e
f
g
h
i
j
k
l
m
n
o
p
q
r
s
t
u
v
w
x
y
z

leak noun
The plumber mended a *leak* in the water tank.
• crack, hole, opening, drip • A leak in a tyre is a **puncture**.

leak verb
1. The juice had *leaked* all over my schoolbag.
• escape, drip, seep, ooze, trickle
2. Details of a secret plan were *leaked* to the newspaper. • reveal, disclose, make known, pass on, give away, let out

lean verb **leaning, leaned, leant**
1. I *leaned* against the wall. • recline, rest, prop yourself, support yourself
2. The yacht *leaned* to one side in the wind.
• slope, tilt, tip, incline, slant, list, bank

leap verb **leaping, leapt, leaped**
The dog *leaped* in the air to catch the ball.
• jump, spring, bound, vault

learn verb
1. We are *learning* about the Vikings this term.
• discover, find out, gather, grasp, pick up
2. I've got to *learn* the words of this song.
• learn by heart, memorize, master

learner noun
This swimming session is for *learners* only.
• beginner, starter, novice • Someone learning things at school or college is a **pupil** or **student**. • Someone learning a trade is an **apprentice** or **trainee**. • Someone who learns easily is a **fast** or **quick** learner. • Someone who learns slowly is a **slow** learner.

leave verb **leaving, left**
1. Do you have to *leave* now? • go, go away, depart, withdraw, take your leave, go out, set off, say goodbye, (informal) take off, disappear **opposite** arrive
2. The doctor *left* the room in a hurry.
• exit, go out of, depart from, quit, vacate **opposite** enter
3. Don't *leave* me here on my own! • abandon, desert, forsake
4. The crew *left* the sinking ship. • evacuate, get out of, abandon
5. My sister has *left* her job at the bank. • give up, quit, resign from, give in or hand in your notice, (informal) walk out of
6. *Leave* the milk bottles by the front door.
• place, position, put down, set down, deposit
7. Lady Bigwig *left* all her money to charity.
• bequeath, hand down, will, endow

lecture noun
1. There is a *lecture* about dinosaurs at the museum today. • talk, lesson, speech, address

2. The teacher gave us a *lecture* on how to behave. • reprimand, warning, (informal) telling-off

ledge noun
The climbers rested on a *ledge* of rock.
• shelf, projection • A ledge under a window is a **windowsill**.

leg noun
1. Boris fell and bruised his *leg*.
2. The rowers completed the first *leg* of the race. • part, stage, section, phase, stretch

legal adjective
At what age is it *legal* to drive? • lawful, legitimate, permissible, permitted, allowed **opposite** illegal

legend noun
I like reading *legends* about ancient heroes.
• myth, story, folk tale, fairy tale, fable

legendary adjective
Unicorns are *legendary* beasts. • mythical, fabulous, fabled, fictional, fictitious, invented, made-up **opposite** real

leisure noun
Grandad has plenty of *leisure* since he retired.
• free time, spare time, relaxation, recreation, rest

leisurely adjective
We went for a *leisurely* stroll in the park.
• gentle, relaxed, relaxing, unhurried, restful, slow **opposite** fast, quick

lend verb **lending, lent**
Can you *lend* me some money until the weekend? • loan, advance, let you have **opposite** borrow

length noun
1. My heart sank when I saw the *length* of the queue. • extent, size
2. We only had to wait a short *length* of time.
• space, period, stretch

lengthen verb
1. Is it possible to *lengthen* these curtains?
• extend, make longer, increase, stretch
2. The days *lengthen* in spring. • draw out, get longer, stretch out

lengthy adjective **lengthier, lengthiest**
There was a *lengthy* argument over who was to blame. • long, drawn-out, prolonged, extended, time-consuming, long-drawn-out **opposite** short, brief

lenient *adjective*
The teacher was lenient and let us off.
• easygoing, soft-hearted, tolerant, forgiving, indulgent, kind, merciful **opposite** strict

lessen *verb*
1. *The nurse used ointment to lessen the pain.*
• minimize, reduce, relieve
2. *The strong winds lessened during the night.* • diminish, decrease, dwindle, subside, weaken, ease off, tail off, die away or down **opposite** increase

lesson *noun*
My piano lesson is on Friday afternoon. • class, period, tutorial, instruction

let *verb* letting, let
1. *Abby's parents let her go to the party.*
• allow, give permission to, permit, consent to, agree to **opposite** forbid
2. *Our friends are letting their house for the summer.* • lease, rent out, hire out

lethal *adjective*
The bottle contained a lethal potion.
• deadly, fatal, mortal, poisonous

level *adjective*
1. *You need a level field for playing rounders.* • even, flat, horizontal, smooth **opposite** uneven
2. *At half-time the scores were level.*
• equal, even, the same, matching, (informal) neck-and-neck

level *noun*
1. *The water had reached a high level.* • height
2. *The lift takes you up to the sixth level.* • floor, storey, tier
3. *What level have you reached in judo?*
• grade, standard, stage, rank, degree

liberal *adjective*
1. *We each got a liberal helping of ice cream.*
• generous, ample, plentiful, lavish, abundant, copious, bountiful **opposite** meagre, miserly
2. *She has a liberal attitude towards most things.* • broad-minded, easygoing, lenient, tolerant, permissive **opposite** strict

license *verb*
Are you licensed to drive this vehicle? • permit, allow, authorize, entitle

lid *noun*
Can you help me get the lid off this jar? • cap, cover, covering, top

lie *noun*
He accused the newspaper of printing lies.
• deceit, falsehood, dishonesty, (informal) fib **opposite** truth

lie *verb* lying, lied
1. *It's twelve o'clock and he's still lying in bed!*
• recline, stretch out, lounge, sprawl, rest
• To lie face down is to be **prone**. • To lie face upwards is to be **supine**.
2. *The castle lies in a valley.* • be sited, be situated, be located, be found
3. *I don't trust her—I think she's lying.*
• deceive someone, bluff, (informal) fib

life *noun* lives
1. *My hamster, Fluffy, leads a very easy life.*
• existence, being, way of life
2. *Our lives depended on finding water.*
• survival
3. *Alice was young and full of life.* • energy, liveliness, vigour, vitality, spirit, animation, zest

lift *verb*
1. *The removal men lifted the piano carefully.*
• pick up, raise, elevate, pull up, hoist
2. *The plane lifted off the ground.* • rise, ascend, soar

light *noun*

> ✏️ **WRITING TIPS**
>
> You can use these words to describe **light**.
>
> **TO DESCRIBE HOW LIGHT APPEARS**
> • bright, brilliant, harsh, luminous, lustrous, strong; diffused, dim, muted, soft, warm
>
> **LIGHT MAY**
> • beam, blaze, dazzle, flash, flicker, glare, gleam, glimmer, glint, glisten, glitter, glow, shimmer, shine, sparkle, twinkle

---

light *adjective*
1. *The artist worked in a light and airy studio.*
• bright, well-lit, illuminated **opposite** dim, gloomy
2. *She was wearing light blue jeans.* • pale **opposite** dark
3. *The parcel looks big, but it is quite light.* • lightweight, portable, weightless
• A common simile is **as light as a feather**. **opposite** heavy
4. *A light wind rippled the surface of the water.*
• gentle, faint, slight **opposite** strong
5. *We had a light meal before we went out.* • small, modest, simple, insubstantial **opposite** heavy, substantial

light *verb* **lighting, lit, lighted**
1. *We lit the candles on my birthday cake.*
• ignite, kindle, set alight, set fire to, set light to, switch on **opposite** extinguish, put out
2. *The fireworks lit the sky.* • light up, brighten, illuminate, shed light on, shine on **opposite** darken

like *verb*

> ### ! OVERUSED WORD
>
> Try to vary the words you use for **like**. Here are some other words you could use.
>
> **TO LIKE A PERSON OR ANIMAL**
> • be attached to, be fond of, *(informal)* have a soft spot for
> *Aunt Grace was very fond of her niece.*
>
> **TO LIKE A PERSON OR ANIMAL VERY MUCH**
> • adore, be devoted to, dote on, love, think the world of, *(informal)* love to bits
> *Lauren loves her new puppy to bits*
>
> **TO LIKE A PERSON OR ANIMAL AND TAKE CARE OF THEM**
> • care for, cherish
>
> **TO LIKE AND RESPECT SOMEONE**
> • admire, esteem, look up to
>
> **TO LIKE SOMETHING OR LIKE DOING SOMETHING**
> • appreciate, be fond of, be interested in, be keen on, be partial to, enjoy
> *What sort of films do you enjoy?*
>
> **TO LIKE SOMETHING OR LIKE DOING SOMETHING VERY MUCH**
> • adore, be crazy about, delight in, love, relish, *(informal)* be mad about/on
> *Alex adores reading.*
>
> **TO LIKE SOMETHING OR LIKE DOING SOMETHING BETTER THAN SOMETHING ELSE**
> • prefer, would rather
> *Nicky much prefers skateboarding to skiing.*
> *I'd rather play on my computer than go for a walk.* **opposite** dislike

likely *adjective* **likelier, likeliest**
It's likely that the shops will be closed tomorrow. • probable, expected, anticipated, predictable, foreseeable **opposite** unlikely

limb *noun*
• Your limbs are your **arms** and **legs**. • Birds have **wings**. • Seals, whales and dolphins have **flippers**. • An octopus has **tentacles**. • The limbs of a tree are its **boughs** or **branches**.

limit *noun*
1. *There is a limit of twenty pupils for this class.*
• maximum, restriction, threshold, ceiling, cut-off point • A limit on time is a **deadline** or **time limit**.
2. *The fence marks the limit of the school grounds.* • border, boundary, edge, perimeter, frontier

limit *verb*
I had to limit the invitations to my party. • put a limit on, restrict, control, ration

limited *adjective*
1. *The crew had a limited supply of water.*
• restricted, short, inadequate, insufficient, rationed, finite, fixed **opposite** limitless, endless
2. *It was hard to move about in such a limited space.* • small, cramped, narrow, confined, restricted

limp *adjective*
The leaves on the plant are looking limp.
• drooping, floppy, sagging, wilting, soft, flabby, slack **opposite** rigid

line *noun*
1. *I drew a pencil line across the page.* • stroke, rule, underline, stripe, streak, band, bar, dash
• A line that is cut into a surface is a **groove**, **score** or **scratch**. • A line on a person's skin is a **wrinkle**. • A deep groove or wrinkle is a **furrow**. • A line on fabric is a **crease**
2. *There was a long line of people waiting at the bus stop.* • queue, row, file, column, rank, procession, chain • A line of police officers forming a barrier is a **cordon**. • A line of schoolchildren walking in pairs is a **crocodile**.
3. *The clothes were drying on the washing line.*
• cord, rope, string, thread, wire, cable, flex, lead

linger *verb*
1. *The smell of burning wood lingered in the air.* • continue, remain, stay, last, persist **opposite** disappear
2. *Don't linger outside in this cold weather.*
• hang about, wait about, loiter, dawdle, dally, delay **opposite** hurry

link *noun*
The two schools have close links with each other. • relationship, association, connection, bond, tie

link *verb*
They linked the trailer to the tractor.
• attach, connect, fasten, join, couple **opposite** separate

lion noun
• A female lion is a **lioness**. • A young lion is a **cub**. • A group of lions is a **pride**. • The fur collar on a male lion is its **mane**.

liquid adjective
Pour the liquid jelly into a mould. • runny, watery, fluid, wet, running, sloppy • To make something liquid by heating it is to **melt** it. • Liquid metal or rock is **molten**.

list noun
• A list of people's names is a **roll** or **register**. • A list of people who have tasks to do is a **rota**. • A list of books in the library or of goods for sale is a **catalogue**. • A list of topics mentioned in a book is an **index**. • A list of things to choose from is a **menu**. • A list of things to do or remember is a **checklist**.

list verb
I helped to list the books in the library. • record, write down, catalogue, index, register

listen verb
to listen to something
The spy listened carefully to the instructions. • pay attention to, take notice of, attend to, heed • To listen secretly to a private conversation is to **eavesdrop**.

litter noun
The street was covered with litter. • rubbish, waste, refuse, garbage, junk, clutter, mess, odds and ends

little adjective

> **(!) OVERUSED WORD**
>
> Try to vary the words you use for little. Here are some other words you could use.
>
> **FOR SOMETHING LITTLE IN SIZE**
> • compact, mini, miniature, minute, petite, small, tiny, *(informal)* teeny, *(Scottish)* wee
> *The camera is so tiny it will fit in your pocket.* **opposite** big, large
>
> **FOR SOMEONE LITTLE IN AGE**
> • small, young, *(Scottish)* wee
> *My granny lived in India when she was young.* **opposite** big, old
>
> **FOR A LITTLE TIME OR A LITTLE WHILE**
> • brief, fleeting, passing, short
> *It was a short while before our friends arrived.* **opposite** lengthy, long
>
> **FOR LITTLE FOOD OR LITTLE MONEY**
> • hardly any, insufficient, meagre, paltry,

scarcely any
There was scarcely any food left in the house. **opposite** ample, plenty

live adjective
The fishermen caught a live octopus in their nets. • alive, living, breathing **opposite** dead

live verb
Will these plants live through the winter? • stay alive, survive, exist, flourish, last, continue, remain **opposite** die

lively adjective livelier, liveliest
1. *The toddlers were in a lively mood.*
• active, energetic, animated, spirited, boisterous, excited, vivacious, sprightly, frisky, chirpy, perky **opposite** inactive
2. *The city centre is always lively at night.*
• busy, bustling, crowded, exciting, buzzing **opposite** quiet, dead

living adjective
1. *Miss Millicent had no living relatives.*
• alive **opposite** dead
2. *There are no dinosaurs still living.*
• existing, surviving **opposite** extinct

living noun
1. *He makes a living from painting.*
• income, livelihood
2. *What does she do for a living?* • job, occupation, profession, trade, career

load noun
1. *Camels can carry heavy loads.*
• burden, weight
2. *The lorry delivered its load to the supermarket.* • cargo, consignment, goods, freight

load verb
1. *We loaded the suitcases into the car.*
• pack, pile, heap, stow
2. *He arrived loaded with shopping bags.*
• weigh down, burden, saddle

loathe verb
My brother loathes the colour pink. • hate, detest, dislike, despise, can't bear or stand **opposite** love, adore

local adjective
Our local shop delivers newspapers.
• neighbourhood, nearby, neighbouring

locate verb
1. *I can't locate the book you asked for.*
• find, discover, track down, detect, unearth, lay your hands on **opposite** lose

2. *The art gallery is located in the city centre.*
• place, position, put, situate, set up, build, establish, station

location *noun*
The pilot made a note of his location.
• position, situation, whereabouts, place, spot

lock *noun* **locks**
1. *There was a heavy lock on the lid of the chest.* • fastening, clasp, padlock, bolt, latch
2. *The princess cut a lock from her hair.* • tress, curl, tuft

lock *verb*
Make sure you lock the door when you go out.
• fasten, secure, bolt, close, shut, seal

lodge *verb*
The ball was lodged in a tree. • get caught, get stuck, jam, wedge, fix, embed

logical *adjective*
The robot always gave a logical answer.
• rational, reasonable, sensible, sound, valid, intelligent, clear, lucid, methodical, systematic **opposite** illogical

lone *adjective*
A lone rider galloped past. • single, solitary, unaccompanied, isolated

lonely *adjective* **lonelier, loneliest**
1. *Cara felt lonely while her friends were away.* • alone, friendless, lonesome, solitary, abandoned, neglected, forlorn, forsaken
2. *The climbers sheltered in a lonely hut.*
• deserted, isolated, remote, secluded, out-of-the-way

long *adjective*
It seemed a long time before the bus came.
• lengthy, prolonged, extended, extensive, long-lasting **opposite** short

long *verb*
to long for something
I'm longing for a drink. • yearn for, crave, want, wish for, desire, fancy, hunger for, pine for, hanker after, itch for, *(informal)* be dying for

look *verb*
1. *If you look carefully, you'll see an owl in the tree.* • watch, observe, view, regard, keep your eyes open

2. *My pet snake looks a bit hungry.*
• appear, seem

> **(!) OVERUSED WORD**
>
> Try to vary the words you use for **look**. Here are some other words you could use.
>
> **TO LOOK QUICKLY**
> • glance, glimpse, peek, peep, sneak a look or glance
> *The secret agent glanced at her watch.*
>
> **TO LOOK CAREFULLY OR INTENTLY**
> • stare, peer, study, scrutinize, examine, inspect, take a good look at
> *The fossil hunters examined the rocks.*
>
> **TO LOOK ANGRILY**
> • glare, glower, grimace, frown, scowl
> *The grumpy knight glowered at his servant.*
> • To look steadily is to **gaze**. • To look in amazement is to **gape**. • To look over a wide area is to **scan** or **survey** it.

look *noun*
1. *Did you have a look at what she was wearing?* • glance, glimpse, peep, sight, view
2. *The guard had an unfriendly look.*
• appearance, bearing, manner, air, expression, face

loom *verb*
1. *A figure loomed out of the mist.* • appear, emerge, arise, take shape
2. *The haunted mansion loomed above us.*
• rise, tower, stand out, hang over

loop *noun*
Make a loop in the string and then tie a knot.
• coil, hoop, circle, ring, noose, bend, curl, kink, twist

loop *verb*
The cowboy looped the reins round a fence post. • coil, wind, curl, bend, turn, twist

loose *adjective*
1. *Some of the cobbles on the road are loose.*
• insecure, unsecured, movable, unsteady, shaky, wobbly **opposite** firm, secure
2. *The fire was started by a loose wire.*
• disconnected, unattached, detached
3. *These jeans are loose around the waist.*
• slack, baggy, roomy, loose-fitting, oversized **opposite** tight
4. *The chickens were loose in the farmyard.*
• free, at large, at liberty, on the loose, unconfined, unrestricted **opposite** confined, shut up

loosen verb
Can you loosen these knots? • undo, unfasten, untie, free, loose, slacken, release, ease **opposite** tighten

loot noun
The thieves buried their loot in a safe place. • haul, plunder, takings

loot verb
Rioters looted the shops. • raid, ransack, rob, steal from, pillage, plunder

lose verb losing, lost
1. *Debbie has lost one of her gloves.* • be unable to find, mislay, misplace **opposite** find
2. *Unfortunately, we lost the game on Saturday.* • be defeated, get beaten, suffer a defeat **opposite** win

lot noun
We are having another lot of visitors this weekend. • group, batch, set, crowd, collection
a lot of
My brother needs a lot of help with his spelling. • a large amount of, a good or great deal of, plenty of
lots of
There are lots of toys to choose from in the shop. • a great number of, many, numerous, plenty (of), (informal) loads of, tons of, masses of, oodles of, hundreds of

loud adjective
The whole house was kept awake by the loud music. • noisy, blaring, booming, deafening, rowdy, resounding, thunderous, penetrating, piercing • A noise which is loud enough to hear is **audible. opposite** quiet, soft

lounge verb
They lounged in the garden all day. • relax, be lazy, idle, laze, sprawl, lie around, loll, take it easy, waste time

love noun
She often mentions her love of the outdoors. • liking, fondness, affection, admiration, passion, devotion, adoration, (informal) soft spot (for)

love verb
1. *They love each other and want to get married.* • care for, cherish, hold dear, be in love with, adore, treasure, worship, idolize • A relationship between two people who love each other is a **romance**.
2. *My friend Sally loves skateboarding.* • like, have a passion for, be fond of, be partial to, enjoy

lovely adjective lovelier, loveliest

⚠ OVERUSED WORD

Try to vary the words you use for lovely. Here are some other words you could use.

FOR A LOVELY PERSON
• charming, delightful, likeable, lovable, dear, sweet, enchanting, endearing, adorable
Jemma is a charming girl.

FOR A LOVELY DAY OR LOVELY VIEW
• fine, glorious, gorgeous, beautiful
It's a glorious day for a bike ride.

FOR A LOVELY EXPERIENCE
• pleasant, pleasing, enjoyable
The girls had an enjoyable time camping. **opposite** nasty

FOR SOMETHING THAT LOOKS LOVELY
• appealing, attractive, pretty, beautiful
The roses look beautiful in that vase. **opposite** ugly

low adjective
1. *The garden is surrounded by a low wall.* • short, low-rise
2. *They were soldiers of low rank in the army.* • junior, inferior, lowly, modest, humble
3. *We spoke in low whispers.* • quiet, soft, muted, subdued, muffled
4. *The tuba plays low notes.* • bass, deep **opposite** high

lower verb
1. *The supermarket lowered its prices.* • reduce, cut, bring down, decrease, lessen, (informal) slash
2. *At the end of the Olympic Games, they lower the flag.* • take down, let down, dip

loyal adjective
Sir Valiant had always been a loyal knight. • true, trusty, faithful, steadfast, reliable, dependable, devoted, constant, sincere **opposite** disloyal

luck noun
1. *He found the secret entrance by luck.* • accident, chance, coincidence, fluke, fate, destiny
2. *She had a bit of luck today.* • good fortune, success

lucky adjective luckier, luckiest
1. *I got the right answer by a lucky guess.* • accidental, chance, unintentional, unplanned

2. *Some lucky person won a million pounds.*
• fortunate, favoured, successful

luggage noun
The luggage can go in the boot of the car.
• baggage, cases, suitcases, bags

lumber verb
A rhinoceros lumbered towards them. • move clumsily, trundle, trudge, tramp, blunder, shamble

lump noun
1. *Lumps of sticky clay stuck to his boots.*
• chunk, piece, cluster, clump, wad, mass, hunk, wedge, block • A round lump of something is a **ball**. • A lump of gold is a **nugget**. • A lump of earth is a **clod**. • A lump of blood is a **clot**.
2. *I could feel a lump where I'd bumped my head.* • bump, swelling, bulge, protrusion

lunge verb
Robin lunged at the sheriff with his sword.
• thrust, charge, rush, dive, pounce, throw yourself

lurch verb
1. *The bus passengers lurched from side to side.* • reel, sway, rock, stagger, stumble, totter
2. *The ship lurched as the waves pounded it.*
• pitch, roll, heave, lean, list

lure verb
Spiders lure insects into their webs. • attract, entice, tempt, coax, draw, invite, persuade
• Something used to lure an animal into a trap is **bait**.

lurk verb
The jaguar lurked in wait for its prey. • skulk, loiter, prowl, crouch, hide, lie in wait, lie low

lush adjective
Rainforests have lush vegetation. • rich, dense, thick, rampant, abundant

luxurious adjective
The dress was trimmed with luxurious lace. • grand, lavish, lush, rich, expensive, costly, deluxe, plush, magnificent, splendid, sumptuous **opposite** simple, austere

luxury noun luxuries
The millionaire lived a life of luxury. • affluence, wealth, richness, splendour, comfort, ease **opposite** poverty

Mm

Metaphors use comparisons to create vivid images, e.g. *A white blanket of snow covered the garden.*

machine *noun*
Do you know how this machine works?
• apparatus, appliance, device, engine, contraption

mad *adjective* **madder, maddest**
1. *You must be mad to go out on a day like this.*
• crazy, daft, insane, stupid, foolish, idiotic, (informal) out of your mind, potty, nuts, loopy **opposite** sensible, wise
2. *(informal) Are you still mad at me?* • angry, cross, enraged, furious, infuriated, irate, livid
3. *The emperor was mad with rage.* • crazy, beside yourself, frenzied, hysterical
4. *(informal) Susie is mad about horses.*
• crazy, enthusiastic, mad keen on, fanatical, passionate

magazine *noun*
I bought a magazine to read on the train.
• journal, periodical, paper, comic

magic *adjective*
1. *My uncle taught me some magic tricks.*
• conjuring
2. *The castle was under a magic spell.*
• magical, supernatural

magic *noun*

WORD WEB

Do you believe in magic? • sorcery, witchcraft, wizardry, spells, charms, enchantments

PEOPLE WHO USE MAGIC
• enchanter or enchantress, magician, sorcerer or sorceress, warlock, witch, wizard

THINGS WHICH A SORCERER MIGHT DO
• become invisible or vanish, bewitch, brew a potion, cast or undo a spell, put a curse on you, enchant

magician *noun*
1. *The magician pulled a scarf out of his hat.*
• conjuror
2. *King Arthur was helped by Merlin the magician.* • sorcerer or sorceress, witch, wizard, warlock, enchanter or enchantress

magnificent *adjective*
1. *The mountain scenery was magnificent.*
• beautiful, glorious, splendid, spectacular, impressive, majestic
2. *The film star lived in a magnificent house.*
• grand, imposing, stately, (informal) posh
3. *That was a magnificent meal!*
• excellent, first-class, marvellous, superb, (informal) fabulous, fantastic

magnify *verb* **magnifies, magnifying, magnified**
Objects are magnified when you look through binoculars. • enlarge, make larger, (informal) blow up **opposite** reduce, minimize

main *adjective*
1. *What was the main point of the story?*
• central, chief, most important, basic, essential, fundamental, primary, predominant
2. *This is the main shopping area in the town.*
• major, principal, biggest, foremost, largest, leading, prime **opposite** minor, unimportant

mainly *adverb*
Chimpanzees eat mainly fruit and vegetables.
• largely, mostly, chiefly, principally, predominantly, primarily

maintain *verb*
1. *The referee tried to maintain order.*
• keep, preserve

2. *A team of gardeners maintain the grounds.*
• look after, take care of, keep in order
3. *He still maintains that he's innocent.* • claim, declare, assert, insist, state, contend

major *adjective*
1. *There are delays on all the major roads into the city.* • chief, principal, primary, leading
2. *Writing her first novel was a major achievement.* • big, great, considerable, significant, important **opposite** minor

make *verb* making, made
1. *We made a shelter out of leaves and branches.* • build, construct, assemble, put together, produce, manufacture
2. *Those two are always making trouble.*
• cause, bring about, give rise to, provoke
3. *They made me captain.* • appoint, elect, nominate
4. *They've made the attic into a games room.*
• change, turn, convert, modify, transform, alter
5. *He'll make a good warrior when he's older.*
• become, grow into, turn into, change into
6. *We can't make her go if she doesn't want to.*
• force, compel, order
7. *He made a lot of money last year.* • gain, get, obtain, acquire, receive, earn, win
8. *The ship finally made land.* • reach, arrive at, get to, get as far as
9. *What time do you make it?* • calculate, estimate, reckon
10. *The numbers 2 and 2 make 4.* • add up to, come to, total
11. *I'll make you an offer for your old bike.*
• propose, suggest
12. *Have you made your bed this morning?*
• arrange, tidy
to **make someone** or **something out**
I can't make out why everything went wrong.
• understand, work out, comprehend, fathom, make sense of
to **make up**
I've made up a recipe for a new pudding.
• create, invent, think up, concoct

make *noun*
What make of phone do you have? • brand, model, label

man *noun* men
• A polite word for a man is **gentleman**.
• Informal words are **bloke**, **chap**, **fellow** and **guy**. • A married man is a **husband**. • A man who has children is a **father**. • An unmarried man is a **bachelor**. • A man whose wife has died is a **widower**. • A man on his wedding day is a **bridegroom**. • A man who is engaged

to be married is a **fiancé**. • Words for a young man are **boy**, **lad** and **youth**.

manage *verb*
1. *His eldest son manages the business now.*
• be in charge of, run, direct, lead, control, govern, rule, supervise, oversee, preside over
2. *I can't manage any more work this week.*
• cope with, deal with, take on, carry out
3. *We'll have to manage without the car.*
• cope, make do, get along, get by

manager *noun*
If you have a problem, talk to the manager.
• chief, director, proprietor, supervisor, *(informal)* boss

manner *noun*
1. *They did the work in an efficient manner.*
• way, style, fashion, method
2. *I was put off by her frosty manner.*
• behaviour, conduct, attitude, disposition, air, look, bearing
manners
Trolls have no manners at all! • politeness, courtesy, graces

manufacture *verb*
The factory manufactures pine furniture.
• make, build, assemble, fabricate

many *adjective*
I've been on an aeroplane many times.
• a lot of, plenty of, numerous, frequent, countless, innumerable, untold, *(informal)* umpteen, lots of **opposite** few

map *noun*
The hotel receptionist gave us a free map of Paris. • chart, diagram, plan • A book of maps is an **atlas**. • A person who draws maps is a **cartographer**.

march *verb*
The brass band marched down the High Street.
• parade, file, troop, stride, pace

mark *noun*
1. *There were muddy paw marks all over the kitchen floor.* • spot, stain, blemish, blotch, blot, smear, smudge, streak • A mark left by a pen or pencil is a **scribble**. • A mark left by fingers is a **fingermark**. • A mark on your skin that you are born with is a **birthmark**.
2. *They stood in silence as a mark of respect.*
• sign, token, indication, symbol, emblem
3. *What mark did you get in the spelling test?*
• score, grade

mark *verb*
1. *Please be careful not to* mark *the photographs.* • stain, smudge, dirty, blot
2. *The teacher had a pile of essays to* mark. • correct, grade, assess

marry *verb* marries, marrying, married
In what year did your grandparents marry? • get married, wed, *(informal)* tie the knot, get hitched • A couple who have promised to marry are **engaged** to each other. • A man who is engaged to be married is a **fiancé** and a woman who is engaged to be married is a **fiancée**.

marsh *noun*
Wading birds are found in coastal marshes. • swamp, bog, wetland, marshland, fen

marvel *verb* marvelling, marvelled
to marvel at
The crowd marvelled at *the juggler's skill.* • admire, wonder at, be amazed by, be astonished by

marvellous *adjective*
1. *The professor showed us his* marvellous *inventions.* • amazing, remarkable, extraordinary, incredible, miraculous, astonishing, phenomenal **opposite** ordinary
2. *'I think we're going to have a* marvellous *time,' said Mum.* • excellent, superb, tremendous, wonderful, splendid, *(informal)* brilliant, fantastic, terrific, fabulous **opposite** bad, awful

mash *verb*
Mash *the potatoes until they're smooth.* • crush, pound, pulp, smash, squash • To make something into powder is to **grind** or **pulverize** it.

mask *verb*
The entrance was masked *by an overhanging tree.* • conceal, hide, cover, obscure, screen, veil, shroud, camouflage

mass *noun*
She sifted through the mass *of papers on her desk.* • heap, pile, mound, stack, collection, quantity, accumulation, *(informal)* load

master *noun*
1. *We played a game in which I was* master *of the castle.* • lord, ruler, governor, chief
2. *Sherlock Holmes was a* master *of disguise.* • expert (at), genius, ace, wizard

master *verb*
1. *Chess is a difficult game to* master. • grasp, learn, understand, *(informal)* get the hang of, get to grips with
2. *I've managed to* master *my fear of heights.* • overcome, conquer, defeat, triumph over, get the better of, control, curb, subdue, tame

match *noun*
The semi-final was a really exciting match. • game, contest, competition, fixture, tournament, tie

match *verb*
She was wearing red shoes that matched *her dress.* • go with, suit, complement, fit with, blend with, tone in with **opposite** contrast with

mate *noun (informal)*
Gary is one of my best mates. • friend, *(informal)* pal, chum, buddy, bud

material *noun*
1. *I'm collecting* material *for the school magazine.* • information, facts, data, ideas, notes
2. *The kite is made of lightweight* material. • cloth, fabric
3. *The cleaning* materials *are in the cupboard.* • stuff, substances, things

matter *noun*
1. *The gods held a meeting on Olympus to discuss the* matter. • affair, concern, issue, business, situation, incident, subject, topic, thing
2. *Peat consists mainly of plant* matter. • material, stuff, substance
3. *What's the* matter *with the car?* • problem, difficulty, trouble, worry

matter *verb*
Will it matter *if I'm late?* • be important, count, make a difference

mature *adjective*
1. *The zoo has two* mature *gorillas.* • adult, fully grown, well-developed **opposite** young
2. *He's very* mature *for his age.* • grown-up, responsible, sensible **opposite** immature, childish

maximum *adjective*
What is the maximum *speed of the rocket?* • greatest, top, highest, fullest, biggest, largest **opposite** minimum

maximum *noun* maxima
The heat is at its maximum *at midday.* • highest point, peak, top, upper limit, ceiling

maze

maze *noun*
We were lost in a maze of underground tunnels. • labyrinth, network, web, tangle

mean *adjective*
1. *Scrooge was too mean to buy any presents.* • selfish, miserly, uncharitable, (informal) stingy, tight, tight-fisted, penny-pinching **opposite** generous
2. *That was a mean trick to play.* • unkind, unpleasant, nasty, spiteful, vicious, cruel, malicious **opposite** kind

mean *verb* meaning, meant
1. *A red traffic light means that cars have to stop.* • indicate, signify, denote, express, imply, convey, communicate, stand for, symbolize
2. *I didn't mean to hurt your feelings.* • intend, plan, aim, want

meaning *noun*
Do you know the meaning of the riddle? • sense, significance, explanation, interpretation, definition

means *plural noun*
1. *Email is a popular means of communication.* • method, mode, medium, channel, course, way
2. *They don't have the means to buy a house.* • money, resources, funds, finance, income, wherewithal

measure *verb*
Measure the height of the wall. • calculate, gauge, assess, survey • To measure the weight of something is to **weigh** it.

measure *noun*
They are taking measures to improve the park. • step, action, course, procedure, means

medal *noun*
Our team won a bronze medal in the relay race. • award, prize, trophy • A person who wins a medal is a **medallist**.

meddle *verb*
1. *He is always meddling in other people's affairs.* • interfere, intrude, intervene, pry, (informal) poke your nose in
2. *Don't meddle with my things.* • fiddle about, tinker

medicine *noun*
Did you take your cough medicine? • drug, medication, treatment, remedy • An amount of medicine taken at one time is a **dose**. • Medicine which a doctor gives you is a **prescription**.

medium *adjective*
The man was of medium height. • average, middle, middling, standard, moderate, normal

meek *adjective*
Koalas look meek, but their claws are sharp. • gentle, mild, tame, submissive, modest, docile, quiet, humble **opposite** aggressive

meet *verb* meeting, met
1. *I met an old friend at the party.* • come across, encounter, run into, see, (informal) bump into
2. *My parents met me at the station.* • greet, pick up, welcome
3. *We're meeting outside the cinema at eight.* • gather, assemble, collect, muster, rally
4. *The two roads meet here.* • come together, merge, connect, join, cross, intersect

meeting *noun*
They held a meeting to discuss the problem. • gathering, assembly, council, forum, congress, conference • A large outdoor public meeting is a **rally**. • A formal meeting with a king or queen is an **audience**.

melody *noun* melodies
The pianist played my favourite melody. • tune, air, theme

melt *verb*
The ice began to melt in the sun. • thaw, soften, unfreeze • To melt frozen food is to **defrost** it. • To melt ore to get metal from it is to **smelt** it. • Rock or metal that has melted through great heat is **molten**. **opposite** freeze

memorable *adjective*
The concert should be a memorable event. • unforgettable, notable, noteworthy, impressive, remarkable, outstanding **opposite** ordinary

memory *noun* memories
She has happy memories of her childhood in Wales. • recollection, remembrance, reminiscence, reminder, impression

menace *noun*
1. *Sharks can be a menace to divers.* • danger, threat
2. *That cat is an absolute menace!* • nuisance, annoyance, irritation, inconvenience

mend *verb*
Workmen were mending the pavement. • fix, repair, put right, restore, renovate, patch

mention verb
1. *Please don't mention the idea to anyone.*
• refer to, speak about, touch on, hint at
2. *You mentioned that you spoke Japanese.*
• say, remark, reveal, disclose, (informal) let out
3. *The director mentioned all the cast.* • name, acknowledge, list

mercy noun mercies
The evil queen showed no mercy.
• compassion, humanity, sympathy, pity, leniency, kindness, charity **opposite** cruelty

merge verb
1. *They plan to merge the two schools.* • join together, combine, integrate, put together, unite, amalgamate
2. *Two streams merge here to form a river.*
• come together, converge, join, meet **opposite** separate

merit noun
She's a writer of great merit. • excellence, quality, distinction, worth, talent, virtue, value

merry adjective merrier, merriest
The postman was whistling a merry tune.
• cheerful, happy, jolly, bright, joyful, light-hearted, lively, spirited **opposite** gloomy

mess noun
1. *Please clear up this mess.* • muddle, untidiness, chaos, disorder, confusion, clutter, jumble, litter, dirt, (informal) shambles
2. *Zoe made a mess of her audition.* • disaster, botch, (informal) hash

mess verb
to mess about
We spent the day messing about on the beach.
• play about, fool around, lounge about, (informal) muck about
to mess things up
I hope you haven't messed up my clothes.
• confuse, mix up, muddle, jumble, make a mess of, tangle
to mess something up
I think I messed up my interview. • bungle, botch, (informal) make a hash of

message noun
Did you get my message? • note, letter, communication

messy adjective messier, messiest
Your bedroom is really messy! • muddled, untidy, disorderly, chaotic, dirty, filthy, grubby, mucky, (informal) higgledy-piggledy **opposite** neat

method noun
My granny has a secret method for making jam. • technique, way, procedure, process
• A specially skilful method for doing something is a **knack**.

middle adjective
The middle section of the book is a bit dull.
• central, halfway, mid, midway

middle noun
A scarecrow stood in the middle of the field.
• centre, core, heart, midpoint • The middle of a wheel is the **hub**. • The middle part of an atom or cell is the **nucleus**.

might noun
I banged at the door with all my might.
• strength, power, energy, force, vigour

mighty adjective mightier, mightiest
The dragon let out a mighty roar. • powerful, forceful, vigorous, ferocious, violent, great, enormous, hefty **opposite** weak

mild adjective
1. *He's a mild person who never complains.*
• amiable, docile, easygoing, gentle, good-tempered, harmless, kind, lenient, merciful, placid, soft-hearted
2. *The weather has been mild for this time of year.* • pleasant, warm, temperate **opposite** severe

mind noun
1. *Her mind was as sharp as ever.* • brain, intelligence, intellect, head, sense, understanding, wits, judgement, mental powers, reasoning
2. *Are you sure you won't change your mind?*
• wishes, intention, fancy, inclination, opinion, outlook, point of view

mind verb
1. *Will you mind my bag for a minute?* • guard, look after, watch, care for, (informal) keep an eye on
2. *Mind the step.* • look out for, watch out for, beware of, pay attention to, heed, note
3. *They won't mind if I'm late.* • bother, care, worry, be upset, take offence, object, disapprove

mingle verb
The secret agent mingled with the crowd. • mix in, circulate, blend, combine, merge, fuse

miniature adjective
A piccolo looks like a miniature flute. • tiny, minute, diminutive, small-scale, baby, mini

minimum *adjective*
Set the oven to the minimum temperature.
• least, smallest, littlest, lowest
opposite maximum

minor *adjective*
I only had a minor part in the play. • small, unimportant, insignificant, inferior, subordinate, trivial, petty **opposite** major

minute *adjective*
The crack is so minute you can hardly see it. • tiny, minuscule, microscopic, *(informal)* teeny, teensy **opposite** large

miraculous *adjective*
The patient made a miraculous recovery.
• amazing, astonishing, astounding, extraordinary, incredible, marvellous, unbelievable, wonderful, mysterious, inexplicable

misbehave *verb*
My puppy has been misbehaving again!
• behave badly, be naughty, be disobedient, get up to mischief **opposite** behave

miscellaneous *adjective*
The bag contained miscellaneous balls of wool. • assorted, various, different, mixed

mischief *noun*
The twins are always getting up to mischief.
• naughtiness, bad behaviour, disobedience, playfulness, roguishness

miserable *adjective*
1. *You look miserable—what's the matter?*
• sad, unhappy, sorrowful, gloomy, glum, downhearted, despondent, dejected, depressed, melancholy, mournful, tearful, *(informal)* blue, down, low **opposite** cheerful, happy
2. *The poor animals were living in miserable conditions.* • distressing, uncomfortable, wretched, pitiful, pathetic, squalid **opposite** comfortable

misery *noun*
The slaves must have led a life of misery.
• sadness, sorrow, unhappiness, grief, distress, despair, anguish, wretchedness, suffering, torment, heartache, depression **opposite** happiness

misfortune *noun*
The family has suffered many misfortunes.
• bad luck, trouble, hardship, adversity, affliction, setback, mishap **opposite** good luck

misleading *adjective*
The directions he gave were quite misleading.
• confusing, unreliable, deceptive, ambiguous, unclear

miss *verb*
1. *I missed the bus.* • be too late for
2. *The arrow missed the target.* • fall short of, go wide of
3. *If we leave now, we should miss the traffic.*
• avoid
4. *I missed dad when he was in hospital.*
• long for, yearn for, pine for
to miss something out
I missed out the boring bits of the story.
• leave out, omit, ignore, overlook, skip

mission *noun*
1. *Her mission in life was to help those in need.*
• aim, purpose, objective, task, job, campaign
2. *The astronauts are on a mission to Mars.*
• expedition, journey, voyage, exploration

mist *noun*
We drove slowly through the mist. • fog, haze, cloud, drizzle

mistake *noun*
This piece of writing is full of mistakes.
• error, inaccuracy, blunder, slip, slip-up, lapse • A spelling mistake is a **misspelling**.
• A mistake where something is left out is an **omission**. • A mistake in a printed book is a **misprint**.

misty *adjective* **mistier, mistiest**
1. *If it's misty outside, take a torch.* • foggy, hazy
2. *I can't see through the misty window.*
• steamy, cloudy, smoky, opaque

mix *verb*
Mix the ingredients in a bowl. • combine, blend, mingle, stir in, mix together
to mix something up
Please don't mix up my papers. • muddle, jumble, confuse • To mix up playing cards is to **shuffle** them.

mixed *adjective*
Add a teaspoon of mixed herbs. • assorted, various, different, miscellaneous **opposite** separate

mixture *noun*
1. *Put the cake mixture in a baking tin.* • mix, blend, combination • A mixture of metals is an **alloy**. • A mixture of two different species of plant or animal is a **hybrid**.

2. *There's an odd* mixture *of things in the drawer.* • assortment, collection, variety, jumble • A confused mixture is a **mishmash**.

moan verb
1. *The wounded warrior* moaned *in pain.*
• cry, groan, sigh, wail, howl, whimper
2. *Ned's always* moaning *about the food.*
• complain, grumble, grouse, whine, *(informal)* whinge

mob noun
An angry mob *stormed the gates of the castle.*
• crowd, horde, throng, mass, rabble, gang, pack, herd, bunch

mobile adjective
A mobile *library visits once a fortnight.*
• movable, travelling • Something that you can carry about is **portable**.

mock verb
It was mean of them to mock *his singing.* • jeer at, laugh at, make fun of, scoff at, sneer at, ridicule, scorn, deride, *(informal)* take the mickey out of

model noun
1. *I'm building a* model *of a space rocket.*
• copy, replica, toy
2. *This is the latest* model *of skateboard.*
• design, type, version
3. *She's a* model *of good behaviour.* • example, ideal

moderate adjective
Her first book was a moderate *success.*
• average, fair, modest, medium, reasonable, passable, tolerable **opposite** exceptional

modern adjective
1. *All the equipment in their kitchen was* modern. • up-to-date, contemporary, advanced, the latest **opposite** out-of-date
2. *She always dresses in* modern *clothes.* • fashionable, stylish, modish, *(informal)* trendy, hip **opposite** old-fashioned

modest adjective
1. *He's very* modest *about his success.*
• humble, quiet, reserved, shy, bashful, coy **opposite** conceited
2. *There has been a* modest *increase in sales.*
• moderate, reasonable, average, medium

moist adjective
1. *The walls of the dungeon were* moist.
• damp, wet, watery, clammy, dank
2. *Tropical plants grow well in a* moist *atmosphere.* • humid, muggy, steamy, rainy

moisture noun
There is still a lot of moisture *on the ground.* • wetness, dampness, damp, dew, condensation, humidity

moment noun
1. *I'll be ready in a* moment. • minute, second, instant, flash, *(informal)* jiffy, tick
2. *It was a great* moment *in the history of space travel.* • time, occasion, period

money noun
How much money *do you have with you?* • cash, currency, funds, finance, *(informal)* dough, dosh • A large amount of money is a **fortune**, **riches** or **wealth**.

monster noun
A sea monster *reared its head above the waves.* • beast, giant, ogre, brute

monstrous adjective
1. *The town was engulfed by a* monstrous *wave.* • huge, gigantic, enormous, immense, massive, colossal, great, hulking, mighty, towering, vast
2. *The nation was shocked by the* monstrous *crime.* • horrifying, shocking, wicked, evil, hideous, horrible, terrible, atrocious, dreadful, gruesome, outrageous, scandalous

mood noun
What sort of mood *is he in today?* • temper, humour, state of mind, disposition

moody adjective moodier, moodiest
She's been moody *and withdrawn for weeks.*
• sulky, sullen, grumpy, bad-tempered, temperamental, touchy, miserable, gloomy, glum **opposite** cheerful

moon noun

WORD WEB

FORMS IN WHICH WE SEE THE MOON
• crescent moon, full moon, new moon; moonbeam, moonlight

THINGS YOU MIGHT FIND OR DO ON THE MOON
• crater, moon dust, moon rock, moonscape, moonwalk • A word meaning 'to do with the Moon' is **lunar**.

moral *noun*
The *moral* of this story is that crime doesn't pay. • lesson, message, meaning

more *adjective*
The soup needs *more* pepper. • extra, further, added, additional **opposite** less

mostly *adverb*
I spend my money *mostly* on books and clothes. • mainly, largely, chiefly, primarily, generally, usually, normally, typically, principally, predominantly

motionless *adjective*
The figure lay *motionless* on the ground. • immobile, still, unmoving, stationary, static, inert

motive *noun*
The police can find no *motive* for the crime. • cause, motivation, reason, purpose, grounds

motor *noun*
The toy train had an electric *motor*. • engine

motto *noun* mottoes
Her *motto* has always been, 'keep smiling'. • catchphrase, proverb, saying, slogan, golden rule

mould *verb*
The sculptor *moulded* the figures from clay. • shape, form, fashion, model, cast

mouldy *adjective* mouldier, mouldiest
All I found in the fridge was some *mouldy* cheese. • rotten, rotting, decaying, musty, damp

mound *noun*
1. Her desk was covered with *mounds* of paper. • heap, pile, stack, mass
2. There used to be a castle on top of that *mound*. • hill, hillock, rise, hump
• An ancient mound of earth over a grave is a **barrow**.

mount *verb*
1. She *mounted* the pony and rode off. • get on, jump onto
2. The butler slowly *mounted* the stairs. • go up, climb, ascend
3. The gallery is *mounting* a new exhibition. • put up, set up, display
4. The tension began to *mount* in the crowd. • grow, increase, rise, intensify

mountain *noun*

WORD WEB

• The top of a mountain is the **peak** or **summit**. • A line of mountains is a **range**. • A long, narrow mountain is a **ridge**. • A mountain with a hole at the top caused by an eruption is a **volcano**. • An area of land with many mountains is said to be **mountainous**.

THINGS YOU MIGHT SEE ON OR NEAR A MOUNTAIN
• avalanche, boulder, cave, cliff, crag, crevice, glacier, gorge, ledge, mountain pass, mountain stream, precipice, rocks, slope, valley or (*Scottish*) glen

SOME WORDS TO DESCRIBE A MOUNTAIN
• barren, craggy, forbidding, jagged, lofty, massive, misty, rocky, rugged, snow-capped, soaring, towering, treacherous

mourn *verb*
He was still *mourning* the loss of his friend. • grieve for, lament for

mouth *noun*
1. The crocodile slept with its *mouth* wide open. • jaws • A dog's nose and mouth is its **muzzle**. • A word meaning 'to do with your mouth' is **oral**.
2. They lived in a village at the *mouth* of the river. • outlet • A wide river mouth is an **estuary** or (*Scottish*) **firth**.
3. The *mouth* of the cave was hidden by trees. • entrance, opening

move *noun*
1. Don't make a *move!* • movement
2. The spy was watching their every *move*. • action, step, deed, manoeuvre
3. Is it my *move* next? • turn, go, chance, opportunity

move verb

> **(!) OVERUSED WORD**
>
> Try to vary the words you use for move.
> Here are some other words you could use.
>
> **TO MOVE SOMETHING FROM ONE PLACE TO ANOTHER**
> • carry, remove, transfer, transport, shift
> *They shifted the piano into the front room.*
>
> **TO MOVE FROM A POSITION**
> • go, leave, depart, quit, budge
> *The camel stared and refused to budge.*
>
> **TO MOVE RESTLESSLY**
> • toss, turn, stir, twist, shake, fidget, twitch, flap
> *Please stop twitching in your seat.*
>
> **TO MOVE FROM SIDE TO SIDE**
> • sway, swing, wave, wag, wiggle
> *The knight swung his sword through the air.*
>
> **TO MOVE ALONG**
> • travel, walk, proceed
> *Few people travel on these roads after dark.*
>
> **TO MOVE ALONG QUICKLY**
> • hurry, dash, race, run, rush, hasten, hurtle, career, fly, speed, sweep, shoot, zoom, streak
> *A boy went careering past on a scooter.*
>
> **TO MOVE ALONG SLOWLY**
> • amble, stroll, saunter, dawdle, crawl, drift
> *Gerald the tortoise sauntered down the path.*
>
> **TO MOVE TOWARDS SOMETHING**
> • advance, approach, come, proceed, progress, bear down on
> *The lookout saw a pirate ship approaching.*
>
> **TO MOVE BACK OR MOVE AWAY**
> • back off/away, retreat, reverse, withdraw
> *The serpent retreated, hissing, into its lair.*
>
> **TO MOVE DOWNWARDS**
> • drop, descend, fall, sink, swoop
> *A pair of vultures swooped down from the sky.*
>
> **TO MOVE UPWARDS**
> • rise, ascend, climb, mount, soar, arise
> *A hot-air balloon mounted into the air.*
>
> **TO MOVE GRACEFULLY**
> • flow, float, glide, dance
> *Some swans glided gently across the pond.*
>
> **TO MOVE CLUMSILY**
> • stumble, stagger, flounder, lurch, lumber, shuffle, totter, trundle, trip
> *The ogre stumbled up the narrow steps.*

> **TO MOVE CAREFULLY**
> • creep, crawl, edge, inch
> *They edged carefully along the cliff path.*
>
> **TO MOVE STEALTHILY**
> • creep up on, sneak up on, steal, tiptoe, slink, slither, sidle, skulk
> *I tiptoed downstairs and into the hall.*

movement noun
1. *The robot made a sudden, jerky movement.*
• motion, move, action, gesture
2. *She was involved in the peace movement.*
• organization, group, party, campaign

moving adjective
The story was so moving that I started to cry. • emotional, inspiring, stirring, touching, (informal) tear-jerking

muck noun
They cleared the muck out of the stable. • dirt, filth, grime, mud, sludge, dung, manure

mud noun
The tractor left a trail of mud on the road.
• dirt, muck, mire, sludge, clay, soil

muddle noun
1. *There was a muddle over the date of the party.* • confusion, misunderstanding, (informal) mix-up
2. *There was a muddle of clothes on the floor.*
• jumble, mess, tangle

muddle verb
1. *Who muddled the papers on my desk?*
• mix up, mess up, disorder, jumble up, shuffle, tangle **opposite** tidy
2. *They got muddled and took the wrong turning.* • confuse, bewilder, puzzle, perplex

muffle verb
1. *We muffled ourselves up to play in the snow.*
• wrap, cover
2. *She tried to muffle her sneeze.* • stifle, smother, suppress, silence, deaden, dull

muffled adjective
They heard muffled voices from the next room.
• faint, indistinct, unclear, muted, deadened **opposite** clear

muggy adjective muggier, muggiest
The weather is often muggy before a storm.
• humid, close, clammy, sticky, moist, damp, oppressive **opposite** fresh

multiply *verb* multiplies, multiplying, multiplied
Her problems seemed to be multiplying.
• increase, grow, spread, mount up

mumble *verb*
We couldn't hear the actor as he was mumbling. • mutter, talk indistinctly

munch *verb*
Kim sat munching popcorn all through the film.
• chew, crunch

murky *adjective* murkier, murkiest
A creature loomed out of the murky waters of the loch. • dark, clouded, cloudy, dim, dull, dingy, gloomy, grey, foggy, misty
opposite clear

murmur *verb*
We heard voices murmuring in the room above. • mutter, mumble, whisper

music *noun*

WORD WEB

VARIOUS KINDS OF MUSIC
• blues, classical music, country and western, dance music, disco music, folk music, gospel, hip hop, jazz, orchestral music, pop music, punk, ragtime, rap, reggae, rock, soul, swing

TYPES OF MUSICAL COMPOSITION
• anthem, ballad, carol, concerto, folk song, fugue, hymn, lullaby, march, melody, musical, opera, operetta, sonata, song, symphony, tune

FAMILIES OF MUSICAL INSTRUMENTS
• brass, keyboard, percussion, strings, woodwind

STRINGED INSTRUMENTS THAT CAN BE PLAYED WITH A BOW
• cello, double bass, viola, violin or fiddle

STRINGED INSTRUMENTS PLAYED BY PLUCKING OR STRUMMING
• banjo, cittern, guitar, harp, lute, lyre, mandolin, sitar, ukulele, zither

BRASS INSTRUMENTS
• bugle, cornet, euphonium, flugelhorn, French horn, trombone, trumpet, tuba

OTHER INSTRUMENTS PLAYED BY BLOWING
• bagpipes, bassoon, clarinet, cor anglais, flute, harmonica or mouth organ, oboe, piccolo, recorder, saxophone

KEYBOARD INSTRUMENTS
• accordion, harmonium, harpsichord, keyboard, organ, piano, synthesizer

PERCUSSION INSTRUMENTS
• bass drum, bongo drum, castanets, cymbals, drum, glockenspiel, gong, kettledrum, maracas, marimba, rattle, snare drum, tabor, tambour, tambourine, timpani, tom-tom, triangle, tubular bells, vibraphone, xylophone

PEOPLE WHO PLAY VARIOUS INSTRUMENTS
• bugler, cellist, clarinettist, drummer, fiddler, flautist, guitarist, harpist, lutenist, oboist, organist, percussionist, pianist, piper, timpanist, trombonist, trumpeter, violinist

SOME OTHER MUSICIANS
• accompanist, composer, conductor, instrumentalist, singer, vocalist

GROUPS OF MUSICIANS
• band, choir or chorus, duet or duo, ensemble, group, orchestra, quartet, quintet, trio

TERMS USED IN MUSIC
• chord, counterpoint, discord, harmony, melody, note, octave, pitch, rhythm, scale, semitone, tempo, theme, tone, tune

NAMES OF NOTES AND SIGNS IN WRITTEN MUSIC
• clef, crotchet, flat, key signature, minim, natural, quaver, semibreve, semiquaver, sharp, stave, time signature

musical *adjective*
Helena has a very musical voice. • tuneful, melodic, melodious, harmonious, sweet-sounding

musty *adjective* mustier, mustiest
There was a musty smell in the cellar.
• damp, dank, mouldy, stale, stuffy, airless
opposite fresh

mutiny *noun* mutinies
The crew were plotting a mutiny against the captain. • rebellion, revolt, uprising

mutter *verb*
The goblin sat muttering to himself in the corner. • mumble, murmur, whisper

mutual *adjective*
It is in our mutual interest to work together. • joint, common, shared, reciprocal

mysterious *adjective*
They uncovered a mysterious sign on the wall. • strange, puzzling, baffling, mystifying, perplexing, obscure, unexplained, incomprehensible, inexplicable, curious, weird

mystery *noun* **mysteries**
What really happened was a mystery. • puzzle, riddle, secret

myth *noun*
Have you ever heard of the Greek myth of Theseus and the Minotaur? • legend, story, folk tale, fairy tale, fable

---

WORD WEB

CREATURES FOUND IN MYTHS AND LEGENDS
• basilisk, brownie, chimera, centaur, cyclops, dragon, dwarf, elf, fairy, genie, giant, gnome, goblin, gremlin, gryphon, imp, kelpie, leprechaun, mermaid, nymph, ogre, phoenix, pixie, sea monster, selkie, serpent, sphinx, siren, sprite, troll, unicorn, vampire, werewolf, winged horse, yeti

---

mythical *adjective*
The unicorn is a mythical beast. • fabulous, fanciful, imaginary, invented, fictional, legendary, mythological, non-existent, unreal
opposite real

a
b
c
d
e
f
g
h
i
j
k
l
m
n
o
p
q
r
s
t
u
v
w
x
y
z

Names of people and places start with a capital letter – *Norway*, *Nottingham*, *Nathan* and *Nicky*.

nag *verb* nagging, nagged
He was always nagging her to work harder.
• badger, pester, scold

naked *adjective*
He walked naked into the bathroom. • bare, nude, unclothed, undressed **opposite** clothed

name *noun*
• The official names you have are your **first names** or **forenames** and **surname**. • Names a Christian is given at baptism are **Christian names**. • A false name is an **alias**. • A name people use instead of your real name is a **nickname**. • A false name an author uses is a **pen name** or **pseudonym**. • The name of a book or film is its **title**.

name *verb*
The zoo named the new lion cubs Kiara and Kovu. • call • To name someone at the ceremony of baptism is to **baptize** or **christen** them.

nap *noun*
Granny always takes a nap in the afternoon. • rest, sleep, doze, lie-down, siesta, (*informal*) snooze, forty winks

narrate *verb*
The famous actor narrated the story of his life. • tell, recount, relate

narrow *adjective*
The rabbit squeezed through a narrow opening in the fence. • thin, slender, slim **opposite** wide

nasty *adjective* nastier, nastiest
1. *Ogres have a thoroughly nasty temper.*
• unkind, unpleasant, unfriendly, disagreeable, objectionable, odious, mean, malicious, cruel, spiteful, vicious
2. *A nasty smell wafted from the laboratory.*
• unpleasant, offensive, disgusting, repulsive, revolting, horrible, foul, rotten, sickening **opposite** agreeable, pleasant

3. *The weather suddenly turned nasty.*
• unpleasant, rough, stormy, squally

nation *noun*
People from many nations compete in the Olympic Games. • country, state, land, race, population

national *adjective*
The programme will be broadcast on national television. • nationwide **opposite** local

natural *adjective*
1. *Karen has a natural gift for music.* • born, inborn, instinctive, intuitive, native
2. *It's only natural to be nervous before an exam.* • normal, common, understandable, reasonable, predictable **opposite** unnatural

nature *noun*
1. *I like TV programmes about nature.* • natural history, wildlife
2. *The old sheepdog has a very gentle nature.*
• character, disposition, personality, manner
3. *He collects coins, medals and things of that nature.* • kind, sort, type, description, variety

naughty *adjective* naughtier, naughtiest
The puppies were quite naughty when they were young. • bad, badly behaved, disobedient, mischievous, uncontrollable, unmanageable, troublesome, unruly **opposite** well-behaved

navigate *verb*
The captain navigated his ship between the dangerous rocks. • steer, direct, guide, manoeuvre, pilot

near *adjective*
1. *Their families are near neighbours.*
• next-door, nearby, close, adjacent, surrounding
2. *My birthday is getting near.* • approaching, coming, (*informal*) round the corner
3. *We invited all our nearest relatives.* • close, dear, familiar, intimate **opposite** distant

nearly *adverb*
Thank goodness, it's nearly dinner time!
• almost, practically, virtually, just about, approaching

neat *adjective*
1. *Please leave the room as neat as possible.*
• clean, orderly, tidy, uncluttered, immaculate, (*informal*) spick and span
2. *Craig always looks neat in his school uniform.* • smart, elegant, spruce, trim

3. *Her handwriting is very neat.* • precise, skilful, well-formed **opposite** untidy

necessary *adjective*
The recipe lists all the necessary ingredients. • essential, required, needed, needful, compulsory, obligatory, unavoidable **opposite** unnecessary

need *noun*
There's a need for more sports facilities in our area. • call, demand, requirement

need *verb*
1. *I need a pound coin for the locker.* • require, want, be short of, lack
2. *Charities need our support.* • depend on, rely on

negative *adjective*
He has a very negative attitude. • pessimistic, uncooperative, unenthusiastic, unhelpful, grudging, unwilling **opposite** positive

neglect *verb*
She's been neglecting her work. • forget, ignore, overlook, abandon, disregard, pay no attention to, shirk

neighbourhood *noun*
They live in a very pleasant neighbourhood. • area, district, community, locality

neighbouring *adjective*
The journey will take them to Mexico and neighbouring countries. • nearby, bordering, adjacent, adjoining, surrounding, next-door

nerve *noun*
1. *Acrobats need to have a lot of nerve.* • bravery, courage, daring, pluck, *(informal)* bottle
2. *He had the nerve to ask for more money!* • cheek, impudence, rudeness, impertinence

nervous *adjective*
She always feels nervous before an exam. • anxious, worried, apprehensive, concerned, uneasy, fearful, edgy, fraught, tense, troubled, *(informal)* uptight, jittery **opposite** calm

neutral *adjective*
A referee has to be neutral. • impartial, unbiased, unprejudiced, even-handed **opposite** biased, prejudiced

new *adjective*
1. *Start on a new sheet of paper.* • clean, fresh, unused, brand-new • Something new and unused is **in mint condition**.
2. *They went to the motor show to see the*

new models. • latest, current, modern, recent, up-to-date
3. *They've found a new bug in the computer program.* • additional, extra, unexpected, unfamiliar
4. *Haven't you got any new ideas?* • fresh, original, novel, innovative, creative, different **opposite** old

news *noun*
What's the latest news? • information, word, report, bulletin, *(old use)* tidings

next *adjective*
1. *He lives in the house next to the chip shop.* • adjacent, closest, nearest **opposite** distant
2. *If you miss this bus, you can catch the next one.* • following, subsequent **opposite** previous

nice *adjective*
That's not a very nice thing to say! • pleasant, agreeable **opposite** nasty

> ## ! OVERUSED WORD
>
> Try to vary the words you use for nice. Here are some other words you could use.
>
> **FOR A NICE PERSON**
> • good, kind, friendly, helpful, generous, likeable, amiable, charming, polite, genial
> *Our singing teacher is very likeable.*
>
> **FOR A NICE EXPERIENCE**
> • delightful, enjoyable, wonderful, marvellous, splendid
> *Did you have an enjoyable time in France?*
>
> **FOR SOMETHING THAT LOOKS NICE**
> • beautiful, attractive, pleasing, lovely
> *There is an attractive view from the upstairs window.*
>
> **FOR A NICE SMELL**
> • agreeable, fragrant, sweet-smelling
> *The fragrant scent of lavender filled the garden.*
>
> **FOR NICE FOOD**
> • delicious, tasty, appetizing, satisfying
> *They serve tasty sandwiches in the cafe.*
>
> **FOR NICE WEATHER**
> • fine, sunny, warm
> *The weather has been fine all week.*

night *noun*
Badgers usually come out at night. • night-time, dark • Animals which are active at night are **noctural** animals.

noble *adjective* **nobler**, **noblest**
1. *The knight belonged to an ancient noble family.* • aristocratic, high-born, upper-class
2. *The rescuers were congratulated for their noble efforts.* • brave, heroic, courageous, honourable, worthy, virtuous, gallant
opposite cowardly, unworthy

nod *verb* **nodding**, **nodded**
Simon nodded his head in agreement. • bob, bow, dip, lower
to nod off
He often nods off in front of the television. • fall asleep, doze off, drop off, take or have a nap

noise *noun*
Where is that dreadful noise coming from? • din, racket, row, uproar, commotion, tumult, hullabaloo, pandemonium • If there is a lot of noise, you can say you **can't hear yourself think**.

noisy *adjective* **noisier**, **noisiest**
1. *The people next door were playing noisy music.* • loud, blaring, booming, deafening, ear-splitting, piercing, thunderous
2. *The children are very noisy this morning.* • rowdy, raucous, chattering, talkative

nonsense *noun*
Stop talking nonsense! • rubbish, drivel, garbage, balderdash, piffle, gibberish, claptrap, gobbledegook, *(informal)* rot, tripe, twaddle

non-stop *adjective*
1. *Their non-stop chattering annoyed her.* • constant, continual, continuous, endless, ceaseless, incessant, never-ending
2. *They took a non-stop train from Glasgow to Edinburgh.* • direct, express, fast

normal *adjective*
1. *It was a normal kind of day at school.* • average, common, customary, familiar, habitual, ordinary, predictable, regular, routine, standard, typical, unsurprising, usual
2. *No normal person would sleep on a bed of nails.* • healthy, rational, reasonable, sane
opposite abnormal

nose *noun*
Someone punched Roger on the nose.
• The openings in your nose are your **nostrils**.
• A word meaning 'to do with your nose'

is **nasal**. • Words for an animal's nose are **muzzle** and **snout**.

✎ WRITING TIPS

You can use these words to describe a nose:
• beak-like, bulbous, button, classical or Roman, crooked, hooked, pointed, snub, upturned
The troll had bushy eyebrows and a red, bulbous nose.

---

nosy *adjective* **nosier**, **nosiest** *(informal)*
Stop being so nosy and asking all these questions! • inquisitive, curious, prying, snooping, intrusive • An informal name for a nosy person is a **nosy parker**.

note *noun*
1. *I sent a note thanking him for the present.* • message, letter, communication
2. *There was a note of anger in her voice.* • sound, tone, feeling, quality

note *verb*
1. *The detective noted the address on a scrap of paper.* • jot down, make a note of, write down, record, scribble
2. *Did you note what she was wearing?* • notice, see, take note of, pay attention to, heed, mark, observe

nothing *noun*
Four minus four equals nothing. • nought, zero
• In cricket a score of nothing is a **duck**; in tennis it is **love** and in football it is **nil**.

notice *noun*
Someone put up a notice about the meeting. • sign, advertisement, placard, poster, warning
to take notice of something
They took no notice of the warning. • heed, pay attention to

notice *verb*
1. *Did you notice what he was wearing?* • note, see, take note of, pay attention to, heed, mark, observe
2. *I noticed a funny smell in the room.* • become aware of, detect

notion *noun*
Uncle Ollie has some strange notions about life. • belief, idea, view, thought, opinion, theory, concept

nourish *verb*
Plants are nourished by water drawn up through their roots. • feed, sustain, support

novel *adjective*
The inventor had a novel idea for building a robot. • original, new, innovative, fresh, different, imaginative, creative, unusual, unconventional **opposite** familiar

now *adverb*
1. *My cousins are now living in Melbourne.* • at present, at the moment, currently, nowadays
2. *I'll give them a ring now.* • immediately, at once, straight away, without delay, instantly

nudge *verb*
She nudged me with her elbow. • poke, prod, shove, bump, jog, jolt

nuisance *noun*
The traffic noise is a real nuisance.
• annoyance, irritation, inconvenience, bother, menace, pest, drawback

numb *adjective*
My toes are numb with cold. • unfeeling, deadened, frozen, insensitive, paralysed **opposite** sensitive

number *noun*
1. *Add the numbers together to get the answer.* • figure, numeral • Any of the numbers from 0 to 9 is a **digit**. • A negative or positive whole number is an **integer**. • An amount used in measuring or counting is a **unit**.
2. *A large number of people applied for the job.* • amount, quantity, collection, crowd
3. *The band played some well-known numbers.* • song, piece, tune

a
b
c
d
e
f
g
h
i
j
k
l
m
n
o
p
q
r
s
t
u
v
w
x
y
z

Onomatopoeia can make your writing go with a *bang, splash* and *whizz.*

oath noun
1. *The knights swore an oath of honour.*
• pledge, promise, vow
2. *He banged his head and let out an oath.*
• swear word, curse, blasphemy

obedient adjective
The dog seems very obedient. • well-behaved, disciplined, manageable, dutiful, docile **opposite** disobedient

obey verb
1. *The dog obeyed its owner's commands.*
• follow, carry out, execute, implement, observe, adhere to, heed
2. *The soldiers obeyed without question.* • do what you are told, take orders, be obedient, conform **opposite** disobey

object noun
1. *We saw some strange objects in the museum.* • article, item, thing
2. *What is the object of this exercise?* • point, purpose, aim, goal, intention, objective

object verb
to object to something
Several residents have objected to the plan.
• complain about, be opposed to, disapprove of, take exception to, protest against **opposite** accept, agree to

objection noun
Do you have any objection to my sitting here?
• protest, complaint, disapproval, opposition

objective noun
Their objective was to reach the top of the mountain. • aim, goal, intention, target, ambition, object, purpose

obscure adjective
1. *His point seemed rather obscure.*
• confusing, puzzling, incomprehensible **opposite** obvious

2. *Henry Kirke White is an obscure poet.*
• unknown, unheard-of, unimportant, forgotten, minor **opposite** famous

observant adjective
If you're observant, you might see a badger tonight. • alert, attentive, sharp-eyed, vigilant, watchful **opposite** inattentive

observe verb
1. *Astronomers observed the eclipse last night.*
• watch, look at, view, study
2. *I have observed a change in his behaviour.*
• notice, note, see, detect, spot, discern, perceive, witness
3. *It's important to observe the rules.* • follow, abide by, adhere to, heed, keep to, obey
4. *My aunt observed that I had grown taller.*
• mention, say, comment, remark, declare

obsession noun
Football is Frank's obsession. • passion, fixation, addiction, mania

obstacle noun
1. *I swerved this way and that, dodging all the obstacles.* • obstruction, barrier, barricade
2. *His age proved to be an obstacle.* • problem, difficulty, hindrance, hurdle, snag, catch

obstinate adjective
The obstinate camel refused to budge.
• stubborn, uncooperative, wilful, pig-headed, headstrong

obvious adjective
1. *It was silly to make so many obvious mistakes.* • glaring, noticeable, pronounced
2. *The castle is an obvious landmark.*
• conspicuous, notable, prominent, visible **opposite** inconspicuous
3. *It was obvious that the woman was a spy.*
• clear, evident, apparent, plain, undeniable, unmistakable **opposite** hidden

occasion noun
1. *I've been to Italy on several occasions.*
• time, moment, instance, opportunity, chance
2. *The wedding was a happy occasion.* • affair, event, happening, incident, occurrence

occasional adjective
The weather forecast said there would be occasional showers. • intermittent, odd, scattered, irregular, infrequent **opposite** frequent, regular

occasionally *adverb*
The dragon occasionally lifted its head and roared. • sometimes, now and again, once in a while, every so often **opposite** frequently, often

occupation *noun*
1. *He's not happy with his present occupation.* • job, post, employment, profession, trade, work
2. *Vita's favourite occupation is reading.* • activity, hobby, pastime, pursuit

occupy *verb* occupies, occupying, occupied
1. *A young family occupies the house next door.* • live in, reside in, dwell in, inhabit
2. *The rebel army occupied the town.* • capture, seize, take over, conquer, invade, overrun

occur *verb* occurring, occurred
1. *She told us what had occurred.* • happen, take place, come about, arise
2. *The disease only occurs in certain plants.* • develop, crop up, turn up

odd *adjective*
1. *Her behaviour seemed very odd.* • strange, unusual, abnormal, peculiar, curious, puzzling, unconventional, eccentric, funny, weird **opposite** normal
2. *Harry was wearing odd socks.* • umatched, left over, single, spare
3. *He does odd jobs to earn money.* • occasional, casual, irregular, various

odour *noun*
There's a nasty odour coming from the fridge.
• A nice smell is a **fragrance** or **perfume**.
• A nasty smell is a **reek**, **stench** or **stink**.

offence *noun*
1. *The thief was punished for his offence.* • crime, wrongdoing, misdeed, fault, sin
• In games, an offence is a **foul** or an **infringement**.
2. *I didn't mean to cause any offence.* • hurt, anger, annoyance, displeasure, hard feelings, disgust

offend *verb*
I hope my comments didn't offend you. • give or cause offence to, insult, upset, hurt your feelings, anger, displease, annoy, affront, disgust, vex

offensive *adjective*
1. *The gas produces an offensive smell.* • unpleasant, repellent, disgusting, revolting, nasty **opposite** pleasant

2. *He apologized for his offensive remarks.*
• insulting, impolite, rude, abusive

offer *verb*
1. *A reward was offered for the capture of the outlaws.* • propose, put forward, suggest, make available
2. *He offered to help with the washing-up.* • volunteer

offer *noun*
Their offer of help was gratefully received. • proposal, suggestion

often *adverb*
It often rains in April. • frequently, regularly, repeatedly, time after time, many times, again and again, constantly

old *adjective*

⚠ OVERUSED WORD

Try to vary the words you use for **old**. Here are some other words you could use.

FOR AN OLD PERSON
• elderly, aged, mature, ancient
The bus is free for elderly people.
opposite young

FOR AN OLD BUILDING OR OLD DOCUMENT
• ancient, historic, original
The ancient Norman church is to be restored.
• Something that you respect because it is old is **venerable**.

FOR OLD CLOTHES OR OLD SHOES
• worn, worn-out, scruffy, shabby, threadbare
I put on scruffy jeans to do some gardening.
opposite new

FOR AN OLD MACHINE
• old-fashioned, out-of-date, antiquated, early, obsolete
The museum has a display of early computers.
• Valuable old cars are **veteran** or **vintage** cars. • Other things which are valuable because they are old are **antique**.
opposite up-to-date, current

FOR THE OLD DAYS OR OLD TIMES
• past, former, earlier, previous, bygone, olden
We did a project on how children lived in former times.
• Times before written records were kept are **prehistoric** times.
opposite modern

old-fashioned adjective
Her clothes were old-fashioned and shabby.
• out-of-date, outdated, outmoded, antiquated, obsolete **opposite** modern, up-to-date

omit verb omitting, omitted
1. *His article was omitted from the magazine.*
• exclude, leave out, miss out, cut, eliminate, overlook, skip
2. *They had omitted to inform the police.*
• forget, fail, neglect

ooze verb oozes, oozing, oozed
The filling started to ooze out of my sandwich.
• leak, seep, escape, dribble, drip

opaque adjective
The dirt had turned the window opaque.
• cloudy, obscure, unclear, dull, hazy, muddy, murky **opposite** transparent

open adjective
1. *The puppy escaped through the open door.* • unlocked, unfastened, ajar, gaping **opposite** closed, shut
2. *The jam jar had been left open.* • uncovered, unsealed
3. *There is a view of open country from the back window.* • clear, unrestricted, unenclosed, extensive **opposite** enclosed
4. *He was open about what he had done wrong.* • frank, honest, sincere, straightforward, candid **opposite** deceitful
5. *The captain faced open rebellion from the crew.* • unconcealed, undisguised, obvious, plain **opposite** concealed

open verb
1. *Please open the door.* • unfasten, unlock, unbolt
2. *I can't wait to open my birthday presents!* • undo, unwrap, untie, unseal • To open an umbrella is to **unfurl** it. • To open a wine bottle is to **uncork** it. • To open a map is to **unfold** or **unroll** it.
3. *The jumble sale opens at 10 a.m.* • begin, start, commence, (informal) get going

opening noun
1. *The sheep got out through an opening in the fence.* • gap, hole, breach, break, split
2. *The film has a very dramatic opening.*
• beginning, start, commencement
3. *We are invited to the opening of the new sports centre.* • launch, initiation

operate verb
1. *This watch operates even under water.*
• work, function, go, perform

2. *Do you know how to operate this machine?*
• use, work, drive, handle, manage, deal with

operation noun
1. *He had an operation to remove his appendix.* • surgery
2. *Trying to defuse a bomb is a dangerous operation.* • task, activity, action, exercise, manoeuvre, process, procedure

opinion noun
What was your honest opinion of the film?
• view, judgement, impression, belief, attitude, point of view, thought, conclusion, assessment, notion, feeling, idea

opponent noun
The knight fought bravely against his opponent. • enemy, foe, rival, adversary, challenger • Your opponents in a game are the **opposition. opposite** ally

opportunity noun opportunities
1. *There were few opportunities to relax.*
• chance, occasion, moment, time
2. *The job offers a good opportunity for a keen young person.* • opening, (informal) break • You can **take**, **seize** or **grab** an opportunity.

oppose verb
Many people opposed the building of the new road. • object to, disapprove of, be against, be hostile towards, argue against, fight against, attack, resist **opposite** support, defend

opposite adjective
1. *They have opposite views about politics.*
• contrasting, conflicting, contradictory, opposed, opposing, different, contrary **opposite** similar
2. *My friend lives at the opposite end of the village.* • far, other

opposite noun
She says one thing and then does the opposite.
• contrary, reverse, converse

opposition noun
There was fierce opposition to the new road. • hostility, resistance, disapproval, unfriendliness, scepticism **opposite** support

optimistic adjective
She's optimistic about her chances of success.
• hopeful, positive, confident, expectant, cheerful, buoyant **opposite** pessimistic

option noun
He had the option of staying or leaving.
• choice, alternative, possibility

ordeal noun
The shipwrecked sailor told us about his *ordeal*.
• suffering, troubles, trial, anguish, torment, torture, nightmare

order noun
1. *The captain gave the* *order* *to abandon ship.*
• command, instruction, direction
2. *I've put in an* *order* *for the new book.*
• request, demand, reservation, booking
3. *The police restored* *order* *after the riot.*
• peace, calm, control, quiet, harmony, law and order
4. *The CDs are arranged in alphabetical* *order.*
• arrangement, sequence, series, succession
5. *She keeps her bike in good* *order.* • condition, state

order verb
1. *She* *ordered* *them to be quiet.* • command, instruct, require, tell
2. *He* *ordered* *the new magazine.* • request, reserve, apply for, book

ordinary adjective
1. *It was just an* *ordinary* *sort of day.* • normal, typical, usual, customary, habitual, everyday
2. *This is more than just an* *ordinary* *robot.*
• standard, average, common, conventional, regular
3. *It was a very* *ordinary* *game.* • mediocre, unexceptional, run-of-the-mill, routine, average

organization noun
She works for a charitable *organization*.
• institution, operation, enterprise, company, body, *(informal)* outfit, set-up This word can also be spelled **organisation**.

organize verb
1. *It took her ages to* *organize* *the party.*
• coordinate, plan, make arrangements for, see to, set up, run
2. *The librarian has to* *organize* *the books in the library.* • arrange, put in order, classify, sort out, tidy up This word can also be spelled **organise**.

original adjective
1. *The settlers drove out the* *original* *inhabitants.* • earliest, first, initial, native, aboriginal
2. *The story was very* *original* • inventive, new, novel, creative, fresh, imaginative, unusual, unconventional
3. *Is that an* *original* *painting or a copy?*
• genuine, real, authentic, unique

originally adverb
The ring *originally* belonged to the wizard Sauron. • at first, at the start, in the beginning, to begin with, to start with, initially

ornament noun
The mantelpiece was covered in little *ornaments.* • decoration, adornment, trinket, bauble

ornate adjective
The furniture in the palace was very *ornate.*
• elaborate, fancy, showy, ornamental, decorative **opposite** plain

outbreak noun
1. *The townspeople feared an* *outbreak* *of violence.* • outburst, upsurge (in), flare-up, spate • An outbreak of disease that spreads quickly is an **epidemic**.
2. *The armies prepared for the* *outbreak* *of war.*
• beginning, start, onset

outer adjective
The fishermen wore waterproof *outer* garments. • external, exterior, outside **opposite** inner

outing noun
They've gone on their annual *outing* to London.
• trip, excursion, expedition, jaunt

outlaw noun
A band of *outlaws* held up the train. • bandit, brigand, robber, highwayman, criminal, fugitive

outline noun
1. *We could see the* *outline* *of the church in the distance.* • profile, shape, silhouette
2. *He gave us a brief* *outline* *of his plan.*
• summary, sketch, framework, précis, rough idea

outline verb
The detective *outlined* his plan. • summarize, sketch, describe, set out • To shape something in a mould is to **cast** it.

outrage noun
1. *There was public* *outrage* *at the government's decision.* • anger, fury, disgust, indignation, horror
2. *He said it was an* *outrage* *that so much money has been wasted.* • disgrace, scandal, crime, atrocity

outrageous adjective
1. *The behaviour of the trolls was* *outrageous.*
• disgraceful, scandalous, shocking, atrocious, appalling, monstrous, shameful

2. *They charge* outrageous *prices at that shop.*
• excessive, unreasonable, extortionate, inflated

outside *adjective*
Lookouts were stationed on the outside *wall of the castle.* • exterior, external, outer

outside *noun*
Insects have their skeletons on the outside *of their bodies.* • exterior, shell, surface
opposite inside

outstanding *adjective*
1. *In a few years she will be an* outstanding *tennis player.* • excellent, exceptional, superb, extraordinary, superlative, brilliant, great, fine, distinguished, celebrated, remarkable, superior, striking, notable **opposite** ordinary
2. *There are still some* outstanding *bills to pay.*
• overdue, unpaid, owing

overcome *verb* overcoming, overcame, overcome
He managed to overcome *his fear of flying.*
• conquer, defeat, master, get the better of, get over or past

overpowering *adjective*
I felt an overpowering *urge to giggle.*
• powerful, strong, compelling, overwhelming, irresistible, uncontrollable

overtake *verb* overtaking, overtook, overtaken
We overtook *the car in front.* • pass, go past, leave behind, pull ahead of, outstrip

overthrow *verb* overthrowing, overthrew, overthrown
The rebels overthrew *the president.* • bring down, topple, oust, defeat, drive out, depose

overturn *verb*
1. *The boat* overturned. • capsize, tip over, turn over, turn turtle
2. *She leapt to her feet,* overturning *her chair.*
• knock over, tip over, topple, upset, spill

owe *verb*
• If you owe money to someone, you are **in debt**.

owing *adjective*
owing to
Owing to the rain, the match is cancelled.
• because of, on account of, due to, as a result of, thanks to

own *verb*
It was the first bike she had owned. • be the owner of, have, possess
to own up to
No one owned up to *breaking the window.*
• confess to, admit to, tell the truth about, *(informal)* come clean about

Look out for the Word Web
for things to know about
punctuation.

pace *noun*
1. *Move forward two paces.* • step, stride
2. *The front runner set a fast pace.* • rate,
speed • A formal word is **velocity**.

pack *noun*
There were four candles in each pack.
• package, packet, bundle, bale

pack *verb*
1. *She packed her suitcase and called a taxi.*
• fill, load up
2. *I forgot to pack my hairdryer.* • stow away,
wrap up
3. *They tried to pack too many passengers onto
the train.* • cram, crowd, squeeze, stuff, jam,
wedge

pad *noun*
1. *She put a pad of cotton wool over the
wound.* • wad • A pad to make a chair or bed
comfortable is a **cushion** or **pillow**.
2. *There's a pad for messages next to the
phone.* • jotter, notebook, writing pad

page *noun*
1. *Several pages have been torn out of this
book.* • sheet, leaf
2. *He wrote two pages of notes.* • side

pain *noun*
Dirk felt a sudden jabbing pain in his foot.
• anguish, suffering • A dull pain is an **ache** or
soreness. • Severe pain is **agony**, **torment** or
torture. • A slight pain is **discomfort**. • A slight
pain which doesn't last long is a **twinge**.
• A sudden pain is a **pang** or **stab**. • Pain in
your head is a **headache**. • Pain in your teeth
is **toothache**.

painful *adjective*
1. *My shoulder is still really painful.* • sore,
aching, tender, hurting, smarting, stinging,
throbbing

2. *The conversation brought back many
painful memories.* • unpleasant, upsetting,
distressing, disagreeable, traumatic

paint *verb*
1. *The bedroom walls were painted green.*
• colour, decorate
2. *Samantha painted the flowers in bright
colours.* • depict, portray, represent

painting *noun*
• A picture painted on a wall is a **fresco** or a
mural. • A picture painted by a famous artist
of the past is an **old master**.

pair *noun*
• A pair of people who go out together are a
couple. • Two people who sing or play music
together are a **duet**. • Two people who work
together are **partners** or a **partnership**. • Two
babies born together are **twins**.

pale *adjective*
1. *Are you all right? You're looking a little pale.*
• white, pallid, pasty, wan, ashen, sallow,
anaemic • To go pale with fear is to **blanch**.
opposite ruddy, flushed
2. *That shade of pink is too pale.* • light,
pastel, faded, faint, dim, bleached, colourless
opposite bright

panic *noun*
People fled the streets in panic. • alarm, fright,
terror, frenzy, hysteria

panic *verb* **panicking, panicked**
If a fire starts, don't panic! • be alarmed, take
fright, become hysterical, (informal) lose your
head, get in a flap • To panic is also to be
panic-stricken.

pant *verb*
*Some of the runners were panting by the last
lap.* • breathe quickly, gasp, wheeze, puff

paper *noun*
1. *She started her diary on a fresh sheet of
paper.* • A piece of paper is a **leaf** or a **sheet**.
2. *The doctor had some important papers to
sign.* • document, deed, certificate
3. *The story made the front page of the local
paper.* • newspaper, journal, (informal) rag

parade *noun*
A circus parade passed along the street.
• procession, march, spectacle, show, display
• A parade of vehicles or people or horseback
is a **cavalcade**. • A parade of people in
costume is a **pageant**.

parcel noun
The postman delivered a bulky parcel.
• package, packet

pardon verb
The king decided to pardon the prisoners.
• release, free, set free, let off, spare, excuse, forgive • To pardon someone who is condemned to death is to **reprieve** them.

part noun
1. All the parts of the engine are now working properly. • bit, component, constituent
2. I only saw the first part of the programme.
• section, piece, portion, element
3. Which part of the business do they own?
• branch, department, division
4. Granny lives in another part of the town.
• area, district, region, neighbourhood, sector
5. He's just right to act the part of Peter Pan.
• character, role

part verb
1. It was the first time she'd been parted from her parents. • separate, divide, remove **opposite** join
2. They exchanged a final kiss before parting.
• go away, leave, depart, say goodbye **opposite** meet

participate verb
Our school is participating in the mini marathon. • take part, join in, be involved, cooperate, help, share

particular adjective
1. The tickets must be used on a particular day. • specific, certain, distinct, definite, exact
2. She took particular care not to damage the parcel. • special, exceptional, unusual, extreme, marked, notable
3. The cat's very particular about his food. • fussy, finicky, hard to please, (informal) choosy, picky

partner noun
The two women have been business partners for years. • colleague, associate, ally • In marriage, your partner is your **spouse** or your **husband** or **wife**. • An animal's partner is its **mate**.

party noun parties
1. We had a class party at the end of term.
• celebration, festivity, function, gathering, reception, (informal) get-together, do
2. A party of tourists was going round the museum. • group, band, crowd, gang

pass verb
1. We watched the parade as it passed. • go by, move past
2. She tried to pass the car in front. • overtake, go ahead of
3. We passed over the bridge. • go, advance, proceed, progress
4. Could you pass me the sugar, please? • hand, give, deliver, offer, present
5. Do you think you will pass your music exam?
• be successful in, get through, succeed in
6. How did you pass the time on holiday?
• spend, use, occupy, fill, while away
7. Three years passed before we met again.
• go by, elapse
8. The pain will soon pass. • go away, come to an end, disappear, fade

pass noun
We had a pass to get into the concert for free.
• permit, licence, ticket

passage noun
1. A secret passage led from the chamber to the outside. • passageway, corridor, tunnel
2. The guards forced a passage through the crowd. • path, route, way
3. Our homework is to choose a favourite passage from a book. • episode, excerpt, extract, piece, quotation, section
4. He hadn't changed, despite the passage of time. • passing, progress, advance

passion noun
1. 'Romeo and Juliet' is a story of youthful passion. • love, emotion
2. She has a passion for sports. • enthusiasm, eagerness, appetite, desire, craving, urge, zest, thirst, mania

passionate adjective
1. The captain gave a passionate speech before the battle. • emotional, intense, moving, heartfelt **opposite** unemotional
2. He is a passionate follower of football.
• eager, keen, avid, enthusiastic, fanatical, fervent **opposite** apathetic

past noun
In the past, things were different. • past times, old days, olden days, days gone by • The study of what happened in the past is **history**. • The things and ideas that have come down to us from the past are our **heritage** or **traditions**. **opposite** future

past adjective
Things were very different in past centuries.
• earlier, former, previous, old **opposite** future

pat *verb* patting, patted
Andy patted the Shetland pony on the head.
• tap, touch, stroke, pet • To touch something quickly and lightly is to **dab** it. • To stroke someone with an open hand is to **caress** them.

patch *verb*
I need some material to patch my jeans.
• mend, repair • Another way to mend holes in clothes is to **darn** them or **stitch** them up.

path *noun*
Please keep to the path as you walk through the gardens. • pathway, track, trail, footpath, walk, walkway, lane • A path for horse-riding is a **bridleway**. • A path by the side of a road is a **pavement**. • A path above a beach is an **esplanade** or **promenade**. • A path along a canal is a **towpath**. • A path between buildings is an **alley**.

pathetic *adjective*
1. *The abandoned kittens were a pathetic sight.* • moving, touching, pitiful, distressing, heartbreaking, sad, sorry
2. *The goalie made a pathetic attempt to stop the ball.* • hopeless, useless, weak, feeble, inadequate, incompetent

patience *noun*
She waited with great patience for an hour.
• calmness, tolerance, self-control, endurance, restraint, perseverance, persistence, resignation **opposite** impatience

patient *adjective*
1. *The nurse was very patient with the children.* • calm, composed, even-tempered, easygoing, tolerant, lenient, mild, quiet, uncomplaining, resigned, long-suffering
2. *It took hours of patient work to restore the painting.* • persevering, persistent, unhurried, untiring, steady, determined **opposite** impatient

pause *noun*
There was a pause while the singers got their breath back. • break, gap, halt, rest, lull, stop, wait, interruption, stoppage • A pause in the middle of a performance is an **interlude** or **interval**.

pause *verb*
1. *The stranger paused at the door before knocking.* • hesitate, wait, delay, hang back
2. *The cyclists paused to let the others catch up.* • halt, stop, rest, take a break, break off

paw *noun*
The cat had a mouse under its paw. • foot
• A horse's foot is a **hoof**. • A pig's feet are its **trotters**. • A bird's feet are its **claws**.

pay *verb* paying, paid
1. *How much did you pay for your new bike?*
• spend, give out, hand over, *(informal)* fork out
2. *Who's going to pay the bill?* • pay off, repay, settle, clear, refund
3. *They had to pay for all the damage they caused.* • compensate, pay back
4. *I'll make you pay for this!* • suffer

pay *noun*
We should get an increase in pay next year.
• wages, salary, income, earnings • A payment you get for doing a single job is a **fee**.

peace *noun*
1. *After the war there was a period of peace.*
• agreement, harmony, friendliness
2. *She enjoys the peace of the countryside.*
• calmness, peacefulness, quiet, tranquillity, stillness, serenity, silence

peaceful *adjective*
They enjoyed a peaceful day fishing. • calm, quiet, relaxing, tranquil, restful, serene, undisturbed, untroubled, gentle, placid, soothing, still **opposite** noisy, troubled

peak *noun*
1. *The peak of the mountain was covered in snow.* • summit, cap, crest, crown, pinnacle, top, tip, point
2. *She is at the peak of her career as an athlete.* • top, height, highest point, climax

peculiar *adjective*
1. *What's that peculiar smell?* • strange, unusual, odd, curious, extraordinary, abnormal, funny, weird, bizarre **opposite** ordinary
2. *He recognized her peculiar way of writing.*
• characteristic, distinctive, individual, particular, personal, special, unique, identifiable

people *plural noun*
1. *How many people are you inviting?*
• persons, individuals • People as opposed to animals are **humans** or **human beings** or **humankind**.
2. *The government is elected by the people of the country.* • population, citizens, the public, society, nation, race

perceptive *adjective*
It was very perceptive of you to spot my mistake. • observant, clever, sharp, shrewd, quick, alert **opposite** unobservant

perfect *adjective*
1. *Each petal on the flower was perfect.* • faultless, flawless, ideal, intact, undamaged, complete, whole
2. *The dress is a perfect fit.* • exact, faithful, precise, accurate, correct **opposite** imperfect
3. *I received a letter from a perfect stranger.* • complete, total, absolute, utter

perform *verb*
1. *Is this your first time performing on stage?* • act, appear, play, dance, sing
2. *The children performed a play about Cinderella.* • present, stage, produce, put on
3. *Soldiers are expected to perform their duty.* • do, carry out, execute, fulfil • To perform a crime is to **commit** a crime.

performance *noun*
1. *Tonight's performance is already sold out.* • show, production, presentation
2. *He congratulated the players on their outstanding performance.* • effort, work, endeavour, exertion, behaviour, conduct

permanent *adjective*
1. *Sugar can do permanent damage to your teeth.* • lasting, long-lasting, long-term, everlasting, enduring
2. *Traffic noise is a permanent problem in the city centre.* • never-ending, perpetual, persistent, chronic, perennial
3. *She has been offered a permanent job in the firm.* • stable, steady, fixed, lifelong

permission *noun*
They had the teacher's permission to leave. • consent, agreement, approval, *(informal)* go-ahead

permit *verb* **permitting, permitted**
The council doesn't permit fishing in the lake. • allow, consent to, give permission for, authorize, license, grant, tolerate, admit

permit *noun*
You need a permit to fish in the river. • licence, pass, ticket

persecute *verb*
People were persecuted for their religious beliefs. • oppress, discriminate against, harass, intimidate, bully, terrorize, torment

persevere *verb*
The rescuers persevered despite the bad weather. • continue, carry on, keep going, persist, *(informal)* keep at it, stick at it **opposite** give up

persist *verb*
If your headache persists, you should see a doctor. • continue, carry on, last, linger, remain, endure **opposite** stop
to persist in
He persists in wearing that awful tie! • keep on, insist on

person *noun* **people, persons**
Not a single person has replied to my email. • individual, human being, character, soul

personal *adjective*
1. *The book is based on the writer's personal experience.* • own, individual, particular
2. *The contents of the letter are personal.* • confidential, private, secret, intimate

personality *noun* **personalities**
Like all ogres, he has an ugly personality. • character, nature, disposition, temperament, make-up

persuade *verb*
I persuaded my friend to join the choir. • convince, coax, induce • To persuade someone to do something is also to **talk them into** doing it. **opposite** dissuade

persuasive *adjective*
She used some very persuasive arguments. • convincing, effective, sound, strong, foreceful, compelling, valid **opposite** unconvincing

pessimistic *adjective*
The players are pessimistic about their chances of winning. • negative, unhopeful, gloomy, despairing, resigned, cynical **opposite** optimistic

pest *noun*
1. *I'm trying an organic method to get rid of garden pests.* • Pests in general are **vermin**. • An informal word for insect pests is **bugs**. • A pest which lives on or in another creature is a **parasite**.
2. *Don't be a pest!* • nuisance, bother, annoyance, *(informal)* pain

pester *verb*
Please don't pester me while I'm busy! • annoy, bother, trouble, harass, badger, hound, nag, *(informal)* bug

petrified *adjective*
Jack stood petrified as the monster lumbered towards him. • terrified, horrified, terror-struck, paralysed, frozen

phase *noun*
Going to school is the start of a new phase in your life. • period, time, stage, step

phenomenal *adjective*
The winner of the quiz had a phenomenal memory. • amazing, incredible, outstanding, remarkable, exceptional, extraordinary, *(informal)* fantastic **opposite** ordinary

phenomenon *noun* phenomena
Snow is a common phenomenon in winter. • happening, occurrence, event, fact

phone *verb*
I'll phone you later this evening. • telephone, call, ring, dial

photograph *noun*
I put my holiday photographs in an album. • photo, snap or snapshot, shot
• A photograph for projecting onto a screen is a **slide** or **transparency**.

physical *adjective*
1. *There's a lot of physical contact in rugby.* • bodily • Physical punishment is **corporal** punishment.
2. *Ghosts have no physical presence.* • earthly, material, solid, substantial

pick *verb*
1. *They've picked the players for the hockey team.* • choose, select, decide on, settle on, opt for, single out
2. *Irene picked some flowers from the garden.* • gather, collect, cut
3. *I picked an apple off the tree.* • pluck, pull off, take
to pick up
1. *He was too weak to pick up the box.* • lift, raise, hoist
2. *I'll pick up some milk on the way home.* • get, collect, fetch

picture *noun*
1. *There's a picture of a pyramid in this book.* • illustration, image, print • A picture which represents a particular person is a **portrait**. • A picture which represents the artist himself or herself is a **self-portrait**. • A picture which represents a group of objects is a **still life**. • A picture which represents a country scene is a **landscape**. • Pictures on a computer are **graphics**.
2. *Mum took some pictures of us building a sandcastle.* • photograph, snapshot, snap

picture *verb*
1. *The girl is pictured against a background of flowers.* • depict, illustrate, represent, show, portray
2. *Can you picture what the world will be like in 100 years?* • imagine, visualize

piece *noun*
1. *They collected pieces of wood to build a raft.* • bar, block, length, stick, chunk, lump, hunk, bit, chip, fragment, particle, scrap, shred
2. *I've only got two pieces of chocolate left.* • bit, portion, part, section, segment, share, slice
3. *I've lost one of the pieces of the jigsaw.* • part, element, unit, component, constituent
4. *There's a piece about our school in the local paper.* • article, item, report, feature

pierce *verb*
The arrow had pierced the knight's armour. • enter, go through, make a hole in, penetrate, bore through • To pierce a hole through paper is to **punch** a hole or **perforate** it. • To pierce a hole in a tyre is to **puncture** it. • To pierce someone with a spike is to **impale** or **spear** them.

pig *noun*
• A male pig is a **boar** or **hog**. • A female pig is a **sow**. • A young pig is a **piglet**. • A family of piglets is a **litter**. • An old word for pigs is **swine**. • Meat from a pig is **pork**.

pile *noun*
1. *Where did this pile of rubbish come from?* • heap, mound, mountain, stack, hoard, mass, quantity, collection, assortment
2. *I've still got piles of homework to do.* • plenty, a lot, a great deal, *(informal)* lots, masses

pile *verb*
Pile everything in the corner and we'll sort it out later. • heap, stack, collect, gather, assemble, hoard
to pile up
The bills are beginning to pile up. • build up, mount up, accumulate

pill *noun*
He had to swallow three big pills every day for a week. • tablet, capsule, caplet, lozenge

pillar *noun*
The roof was supported by tall pillars. • column, pier, post, prop, support

pin *noun*
• A decorative pin to wear is a **brooch**.
• A pin to fix something on a noticeboard is a **drawing pin**. • A pin to fix a baby's nappy in place is a **safety pin**.

pinch *verb*
1. *The baby pinched my arm and wouldn't let go.* • nip, squeeze, press, tweak, grip
2. *(informal) Who pinched my calculator?*
• steal, take, snatch, pilfer *(informal)* nick, swipe, make off with

pink *adjective, noun*
Millie was a very small mouse who always wore a pink tutu. Pink is my favourite colour. • rose, rose-coloured, rosy, coral, peach, shocking pink • Something which is rather pink is **pinky** or **pinkish**.

pip *noun*
I got an orange pip stuck in my throat. • seed, stone, pit, kernel

pipe *noun*
The water flows away along this pipe. • tube
• A pipe used for watering the garden is a **hose**. • A pipe in the street which supplies water for fighting fires is a **hydrant**. • A pipe which carries oil, etc., over long distances is a **pipeline**. • The system of water pipes in a house is the **plumbing**.

pirate *noun*

WORD WEB

The ship was overrun by bloodthirsty pirates.
• buccaneer, marauder

THINGS YOU MIGHT FIND ON A PIRATE SHIP
• barrels, cabin, crow's nest, deck, hammock, lantern, mast, plank, pirate flag, rigging, sail, treasure chest, wheel
• A pirate flag is a **Jolly Roger** or **skull-and-crossbones**. • A pirate ship might sail on the **high seas** or the **Spanish Main**.

PEOPLE YOU MIGHT FIND ON A PIRATE SHIP
• cabin boy or girl, captain, captives, cook, crew, first mate, lookout, stowaway

PIRATE TREASURE MIGHT CONTAIN
• doubloons or ducats, gold bullion, pieces of eight • Goods or treasure seized by pirates is **booty**.

WEAPONS A PIRATE MIGHT USE
• cannon, cutlass, dagger, gunpowder, musket, pistol

OTHER THINGS A PIRATE MIGHT WEAR OR CARRY
• bandanna or kerchief, bottle of rum, breeches, cocked hat, earrings, eye patch, hook, parrot or cockatoo, pigtail, sea chart, spyglass or telescope, treasure map, wooden leg or peg leg

SOME WORDS TO DESCRIBE A PIRATE
• barbaric, black-hearted, bloodthirsty, cut-throat, daring, dastardly, fearless, heartless, lawless, merciless, murderous, pitiless, ruthless, savage, swashbuckling, vengeful, vicious, villainous

pit *noun*
1. *They dug a deep pit to bury the treasure.*
• hole, crater, cavity, hollow, depression, pothole, chasm, abyss
2. *Coal used to be mined from the pits in this area.* • mine, coal mine, colliery, quarry

pity *noun*
The pirates showed no pity towards the captives. • mercy, compassion, sympathy, humanity, kindness, concern, feeling **opposite** cruelty

a pity
It's a pity that you have to leave so early.
• a shame, unfortunate, bad luck

pity *verb* pities, pitying, pitied
We pitied anyone who was caught up in the storm. • feel sorry for, feel for, sympathize with, take pity on

place *noun*
1. *This is a good place to park.* • site, venue, spot, location, position, situation
2. *They are looking for a quiet place to live.*
• area, district, locality, neighbourhood, region, vicinity
3. *Save me a place on the bus.* • seat, space

place *verb*
1. *The hotel is placed next to the beach.*
• locate, situate, position, station
2. *You can place your coats on the bed.*
• put down, set down, leave, deposit, lay, *(informal)* dump, plonk

plain *adjective*
1. *The furniture in the room was very* plain. • simple, modest, basic, unelaborate **opposite** elaborate
2. *Some people say she looks* plain *compared with her sister.* • unattractive, ordinary **opposite** attractive
3. *It is* plain *to me that you are not interested.* • clear, evident, obvious, apparent, unmistakable **opposite** unclear
4. *She told us what she thought in very* plain *terms.* • direct, frank, blunt, outspoken, honest, sincere, straightforward
5. *We need to wear a* plain *t-shirt for sports.* • unpatterned

plan *noun*
1. *The captain explained her* plan *to the rest of the team.* • idea, proposal, scheme, strategy, project, suggestion, proposition • A plan to do something bad is a **plot**.
2. *They looked at the* plans *for the new sports centre.* • design, diagram, chart, map, drawing, blueprint

plan *verb* planning, planned
1. *The outlaws* planned *an attack upon the sheriff.* • scheme, design, devise, work out, formulate, prepare, organize • To plan to do something bad is to **plot**.
2. *What do you* plan *to do next?* • aim, intend, propose, mean

planet *noun*

WORD WEB

The new space probe will travel to far-off planets. • world

THE PLANETS OF THE SOLAR SYSTEM (IN ORDER FROM THE SUN) ARE
• Mercury, Venus, Earth, Mars, Jupiter, Saturn, Uranus, Neptune
• The path followed by a planet is its **orbit**.
• Minor planets orbiting the sun are **asteroids**. • Something which orbits a planet is a **satellite**. • The earth's large satellite is the **Moon**.

WRITING TIPS

You can use these words to describe an **alien planet**:
• Earth-like, gaseous, inhospitable, uninhabitable

TO DESCRIBE ITS SURFACE
• barren, desolate, dusty, frozen, icy, molten, rocky, volcanic

TO DESCRIBE ITS ATMOSPHERE OR AIR
• airless, noxious, poisonous, thin, unbreathable

plant *noun*

WORD WEB

• A young plant is a **seedling**. • A piece cut off a plant to form a new plant is a **cutting**.
• A word for plants in general is **vegetation**.
• A word for plants growing thickly under trees is **undergrowth**. • A person who studies plants is a **botanist**.

SOME TYPES OF PLANT
• algae, bush, cactus, fern, grass, herb, lichen, moss, shrub, tree, vine

SOME PARTS OF PLANTS
• bloom, blossom, branch, bud, flower, fruit, leaf, petal, pod, root, shoot, stalk, stem, trunk, twig

platform *noun*
The conductor stood on a platform *to address the audience.* • dias, podium, stage, stand

play *noun*
1. *There was a good* play *on TV last night.* • drama, performance, production
2. *It is important to balance work and* play. • playing, recreation, amusement, fun, games, sport

play verb
1. *The children went out to play.* • amuse yourself, have fun, romp about
2. *Do you like playing basketball?* • take part in, participate in, compete in
3. *We are playing the home team next week.* • compete against, oppose, challenge, take on
4. *Mira played the piano at the school concert.* • perform on
5. *My sister played Goldilocks in the school play.* • act, take the part of, portray, represent

player noun
1. *You need four players for this game.* • contestant, participant, competitor
2. *How many players are in the orchestra?* • performer, instrumentalist, musician
• Someone who plays music on their own is a **soloist**.

playful adjective
The kittens were in a playful mood. • lively, spirited, frisky, mischievous, roguish, impish, joking, teasing **opposite** serious

plead verb
to plead with
The children pleaded with the witch to let them go. • beg, entreat, implore, appeal to, ask, request, petition

pleasant adjective
1. *The owner of the shop is always pleasant to us.* • kind, friendly, likeable, charming, amiable, amicable, cheerful, genial, good-natured, good-humoured, approachable, hospitable, welcoming
2. *We spent a very pleasant evening playing cards.* • pleasing, enjoyable, agreeable, delightful, lovely, entertaining

please verb
1. *I hope my present will please you.* • give pleasure to, make happy, satisfy, delight, amuse, entertain
2. *Do as you please.* • want, wish

pleased adjective
Why do you look so pleased today? • contented, delighted, elated, glad, grateful, happy, satisfied, thankful, thrilled **opposite** annoyed

pleasure noun
1. *Mrs Ramsay gets a lot of pleasure from her garden.* • delight, enjoyment, happiness, joy, satisfaction, comfort, contentment, gladness
• Very great pleasure is **bliss** or **ecstasy**.
2. *He talked about the pleasures of living in the country.* • joy, comfort, delight

pledge noun
The knights swore a pledge of loyalty to the king. • oath, vow, promise, word

plenty noun
Don't buy any milk—there's plenty in the fridge. • a lot, a large amount, an abundance, a profusion • A lot more than you need is a **glut** or **surplus**. **opposite** scarcity
plenty of
We've still got plenty of time. • a lot of, lots of, ample, abundant, *(informal)* loads of, masses of, tons of

plod verb plodding, plodded
The hikers plodded on through the mud. • tramp, trudge, lumber

plot noun
1. *Guy Fawkes was part of a plot against the government.* • conspiracy, scheme, secret plan
2. *It was hard to follow the plot of the film.* • story, storyline, narrative, thread
3. *They bought a plot of ground to build a new house.* • area, piece, lot, patch • A plot of ground for growing flowers or vegetables is an **allotment**. • A large plot of land is a **tract** of land.

plot verb plotting, plotted
1. *The gang were plotting a daring bank raid.* • plan, devise, concoct, hatch, *(informal)* cook up
2. *They were accused of plotting against the queen.* • conspire, intrigue, scheme

plug noun
They removed the plug in the side of the barrel. • stopper, cork, bung

plug verb plugging, plugged
1. *Dad managed to plug the leak in the pipe.* • stop up, block, close, fill, seal, bung up
2. *(informal) We asked the local radio station to plug our concert.* • advertise, publicize, promote, push

plump adjective
The goblin was short and plump, with pointy ears. • chubby, dumpy, fat, tubby, podgy, round, stout, portly **opposite** skinny

plunge verb
1. *One by one, the girls plunged into the pool.* • dive, jump, leap, throw yourself
2. *As the wind died down, the kite plunged to the ground.* • drop, fall, pitch, tumble, plummet, swoop
3. *I plunged my hand in the cold water.* • dip, lower, sink, immerse, submerge

4. *Finn* **plunged** *his spear into the dragon's throat.* • thrust, stab, push, stick, shove, force

poem *noun*
We had to write a **poem** *about the seaside.*
• rhyme • Poems are called **poetry** or **verse**.
• A group of lines forming a section of a poem is a **stanza**. • A pair of rhyming lines within a poem is a **couplet**. • The rhythm of a poem is its **metre**. • Poetry that has no regular rhyme or rhythm is **free verse**.

WORD WEB

SOME KINDS OF POEM
• ballad, clerihew, concrete poem, elegy, epic, haiku, limerick, lyric, narrative poem, nonsense poem, nursery rhyme, ode, tanka, sonnet

poetic *adjective*
The opening chapter is written in a **poetic** *style.*
• expressive, imaginative, lyrical, poetical
• An uncomplimentary synonym is **flowery**.

point *noun*
1. *Be careful—that knife has a very sharp* **point**. • tip, end, spike, prong
2. *The stars looked like* **points** *of light in the sky.* • dot, spot, speck, fleck
3. *He marked on the map the exact* **point** *where the treasure lay.* • location, place, position, site
4. *At that* **point** *the rain started to come down.* • moment, instant, time
5. *I agree with your last* **point**. • idea, argument, thought
6. *His sense of humour is one of his good* **points**. • characteristic, feature, attribute
7. *There is no* **point** *in phoning at this hour.* • purpose, reason, aim, object, use, usefulness
8. *I think I missed the* **point** *of that film.* • meaning, essence, core, gist

point *verb*
1. *She* **pointed** *the way.* • draw attention to, indicate, point out, show, signal
2. *Can you* **point** *me in the right direction for the station?* • aim, direct, guide, lead, steer

pointless *adjective*
It's **pointless** *to argue with him—he's so stubborn.* • useless, futile, vain
opposite worthwhile

poisonous *adjective*
Some of those mushrooms may be **poisonous**. • toxic, venomous, deadly, lethal

poke *verb*
Someone **poked** *me in the back with an umbrella.* • prod, dig, jab, stab, thrust
to poke out
The kitten's head was **poking out** *of the basket.* • stick out, project, protrude

polar *adjective*
The **polar** *expedition will study the marine wildlife.* • The word for referring to the area around the North Pole is **Arctic**. • The word for referring to the area around the South Pole is **Antarctic**.

WORD WEB

THINGS YOU MIGHT SEE IN THE POLAR REGIONS
• glacier, iceberg, ice field, ice floe, moss, pack ice, permafrost, sheet ice, tundra

SOME ANIMALS WHICH LIVE IN POLAR REGIONS
• albatross, arctic fox, arctic tern, narwhal, penguin, polar bear, reindeer, seal, walrus, whale, wolf

THINGS A POLAR EXPLORER MIGHT USE
• goggles, huskies, ice pick, kayak, mittens, parka, ski pole, skis, sledge, snowmobile, snowshoes

pole *noun*
Four poles marked the corners of the field.
• post, bar, rod, stick, shaft • A pole that you use when walking or as a weapon is a **staff**.
• A pole for a flag to fly from is a **flagpole**.
• A pole to support sails on a boat or ship is a **mast** or **spar**. • A pole with a pointed end to stick in the ground is a **stake**. • Poles which a circus entertainer walks on are **stilts**.

polish *verb*
Beeswax is used to polish furniture. • rub down, shine, buff, burnish, wax

polish *noun*
The silverware had been cleaned to give it a good polish. • shine, sheen, gloss, lustre, sparkle, brightness, glaze, finish

polite *adjective*
My aunt is always polite to visitors.
• courteous, well-mannered, respectful, civil, well-behaved, gracious, gentlemanly or ladylike, chivalrous, gallant **opposite** rude, impolite

pollute *verb*
The river has been polluted by chemicals.
• contaminate, infect, poison

poor *adjective*
1. *You can't afford luxuries if you're poor.*
• impoverished, poverty-stricken, penniless, needy, badly off, hard-up **opposite** rich
2. *His handwriting is very poor.* • bad, inferior, inadequate, incompetent, unsatisfactory, shoddy, weak, worthless **opposite** good, superior
3. *They pitied the poor animals standing in the rain.* • unlucky, unfortunate, pitiful, wretched **opposite** lucky

popular *adjective*
1. *Disney has made a lot of popular children's films.* • well-liked, well-loved, celebrated, favourite **opposite** unpopular
2. *Skateboards are very popular just now.* • fashionable, widespread, current, in demand, (informal) trendy **opposite** unpopular

port *noun*
A large cruise ship sailed into the port.
• harbour, dock, anchorage • A harbour for yachts and pleasure boats is a **marina**.

portrait *noun*
There's a portrait of the Queen on every stamp. • picture, image, likeness, representation • A portrait which shows a side view of someone is a **profile**. • A portrait which shows just the outline of someone is a **silhouette**. • A portrait which exaggerates some aspect of a person is a **caricature**.

pose *verb*
The film star posed in front of the camera.
• model, sit
to pose as someone
The spy posed as a newspaper reporter.
• impersonate, pretend to be, pass yourself off as

posh *adjective (informal)*
We went to a posh restaurant for a treat.
• smart, stylish, high-class, elegant, fashionable, up-market, luxurious, luxury, deluxe, plush, (informal) classy, swanky, swish, snazzy

position *noun*
1. *Mark the position on the map.* • location, place, point, spot, site, whereabouts
2. *He shifted his position to avoid getting cramp.* • pose, posture, stance
3. *Losing all her money put her in a difficult position.* • situation, state, condition, circumstances
4. *A referee should adopt a neutral position.*
• opinion, attitude, outlook, view
5. *Being a head teacher is an important position.* • job, post, appointment, function

positive *adjective*
1. *The detective was positive that the cook was lying.* • certain, sure, convinced, assured, confident **opposite** uncertain
2. *Miss Andrews made some positive comments on my singing.* • helpful, useful, worthwhile, beneficial, constructive **opposite** negative

possess *verb*
They don't possess a computer. • have, own

possible *adjective*
1. *Is it possible that life exists on other planets?* • likely, probable, conceivable, credible
2. *It wasn't possible to shift the piano.*
• feasible, practicable, practical

post *noun*
1. *The farmer put up some posts for a new fence.* • pole, pillar, shaft, stake, support, prop
2. *The post was delivered late.* • mail, letters, delivery
3. *Are you thinking of applying for the post?*
• job, position, situation, appointment, vacancy

post *verb*
1. *Did you post those letters?* • mail, send, dispatch
2. *The names of the winners will be posted on the noticeboard.* • display, put up, announce, advertise

postpone *verb*
They postponed the match because of bad weather. • put off, defer, delay • To stop a game or meeting that you intend to start again later is to **adjourn** or **suspend** it.

potion *noun*
A magic potion was brewing in the wizard's cauldron. • drug, medicine, mixture

pounce *verb*
to pounce on
The cat pounced on the mouse. • jump on, leap on, spring on, swoop down on, lunge at, ambush, attack

pound *verb*
Huge waves pounded the stranded ship. • beat, hit, batter, smash • To pound something hard until it is powder is to **crush**, **grind** or **pulverize** it. • To pound something soft is to **knead**, **mash** or **pulp** it.

pour *verb*
1. *Water poured through the hole.* • flow, run, gush, stream, spill, spout
2. *I poured some milk into my cup.* • tip, serve

power *noun*
1. *They were amazed by the power of the robot.* • strength, force, might, energy
2. *The storyteller has the power to enthrall an audience.* • skill, talent, ability, competence
3. *A policeman has the power to arrest someone.* • authority, right
4. *The empress had power over all the people.* • authority, command, control, dominance, domination

powerful *adjective*
1. *Queen Ruby was the most powerful person in the land.* • influential, leading, commanding, dominant, high-powered
2. *The wrestler had a powerful punch.* • strong, forceful, hard, mighty, vigorous, formidable, potent
3. *He used some powerful arguments.* • strong, convincing, effective, persuasive, impressive

practical *adjective*
1. *I'll ask Katie what to do—she is always very practical.* • down-to-earth, matter-of-fact,

sensible, level-headed **opposite** impractical
2. *The robbers' plan was not very practical.* • workable, realistic, sensible, feasible, viable, achievable **opposite** impractical
3. *Do you have any practical experience of childminding?* • real, actual, hands-on **opposite** theoretical

practice *noun*
1. *We have extra football practice this week.* • training, exercises, preparation, rehearsal, drill
2. *Is it the practice among ogres to eat grubs for breakfast?* • custom, habit, convention, routine
in practice
What will the plan involve in practice? • in effect, in reality, actually, really

practise *verb*
1. *My piano teacher asked me to practise for longer.* • do exercises, rehearse, train, drill • To practise just before the start of a performance is to **warm up**.
2. *My sister wants to practise veterinary medicine.* • do, perform, carry out, put into practice, follow, pursue

praise *verb*
The critics praised the actress for her outstanding performance. • commend, applaud, admire, compliment, congratulate, pay tribute to, *(informal)* rave about **opposite** criticize

praise *noun*
She received a lot of praise for her painting. • approval, admiration, compliments, congratulations, applause

prance *verb*
Milly started prancing about in a silly way. • dance, skip, hop, leap, romp, cavort, caper, frolic, gambol

precious *adjective*
1. *Her most precious possession was an old photograph.* • treasured, cherished, valued, prized, dearest, beloved
2. *The throne glittered with precious gems and gold.* • valuable, costly, expensive, priceless **opposite** worthless

precise *adjective*
1. *Can you tell me the precise time, please?* • exact, accurate, correct, true, right **opposite** rough
2. *The map gave precise directions for finding the treasure.* • careful, detailed, specific, particular, definite **opposite** vague

a b c d e f g h i j k l m n o **p** q r s t u v w x y z

predict *verb*
You can't **predict** what may happen in the future. • forecast, foresee, foretell, prophesy

prefer *verb* **preferring, preferred**
Would you **prefer** juice or lemonade? • rather have, go for, opt for, plump for, choose, fancy

prejudice *noun*
The school has a policy against racial **prejudice**. • bias, discrimination, intolerance, narrow-mindedness, bigotry • Prejudice against other races is **racism**. • Prejudice against other nations is **xenophobia**. • Prejudice against the other sex is **sexism**. **opposite** fairness, tolerance

prepare *verb*
The museum staff are **preparing** for the new exhibition. • get ready, make arrangements for, organize, plan, set up • To prepare for a play is to **rehearse**. • To prepare to take part in a sport is to **train**.

present *adjective*
1. Is everyone **present**? • here, in attendance, at hand
2. Who is the **present** world chess champion? • current, existing

present *noun*
What would you like for your birthday **present**? • gift, (informal) prezzie

present *verb*
1. The head **presents** the prizes on sports day. • award, hand over
2. Our class is **presenting** a play about the Vikings. • put on, perform, stage, mount
3. Dr Smart **presented** her amazing invention to the world. • put forward, show, display, exhibit, make known

press *verb*
1. **Press** the fruit through a sieve to get rid of the seeds. • push, force, squeeze, squash, crush, shove, cram, compress
2. She **pressed** her blouse for the party. • iron, flatten, smooth
3. Our friends **pressed** us to stay a bit longer. • beg, urge, entreat, implore

press *noun*
1. We read about the competition in the **press**. • newspapers, magazines
2. The **press** came to the opening of the new arts centre. • journalists, reporters, the media

pressure *noun*
1. The nurse applied **pressure** to the wound. • force, compression, squeezing, weight, load
2. In the final, the home team were under a lot of **pressure**. • stress, strain, tension

presume *verb*
I **presume** you'd like something to eat. • assume, take it, imagine, suppose, think, believe, guess

pretend *verb*
She's not really crying—she's only **pretending**. • put on an act, bluff, fake, sham, pose, (informal) kid, put it on

pretend *adjective*
That's not a real spider—it's just a **pretend** one! • fake, false, artificial, made-up **opposite** real

pretty *adjective* **prettier, prettiest**
The doll was dressed in a **pretty** blue outfit. • attractive, beautiful, lovely, nice, pleasing, charming, dainty, picturesque, quaint, (informal) cute • A common simile is **as pretty as a picture**. **opposite** ugly

prevent *verb*
1. The driver could do nothing to **prevent** the accident. • stop, avert, avoid, head off
2. The police **prevented** an attempted bank raid. • block, foil, frustrate, thwart
3. There's not much you can do to **prevent** colds. • stave off, ward off

price *noun*
What is the **price** of a return ticket to Sydney? • cost, amount, figure, expense, payment, sum, charge, rate • The price you pay for a journey on public transport is a **fare**. • The price you pay to send a letter is the **postage**. • The price you pay to use a private road, bridge or tunnel is a **toll**.

priceless *adjective*
The museum contained many **priceless** antiques. • precious, rare, valuable, costly, expensive, dear

prick *verb*
Jamie burst the balloon by **pricking** it with a pin. • pierce, puncture, stab, jab, perforate

prickle *noun*
A hedgehog uses its **prickles** for defence. • spike, spine, needle, barb, thorn • The prickles on a hedgehog or porcupine are also called **quills**.

prickly *adjective*
Holly leaves are very **prickly**. • spiky, spiny, thorny, bristly, sharp, scratchy

pride noun
1. *Mr Dodds takes great pride in his garden.* • satisfaction, pleasure, delight
2. *The medal winner was a source of great pride to his family.* • self-esteem, self-respect, dignity, honour
3. *Pride comes before a fall.* • arrogance, conceit, bigheadedness, vanity, snobbery
opposite humility

prim adjective **primmer, primmest**
Aunt Jemima is always very prim and proper. • prudish, strait-laced, formal, demure

primary adjective
Their primary aim was to win the match. • main, chief, principal, foremost, major, most important, top, prime

prisoner noun
The prisoner tried to escape from jail. • convict, captive, inmate • A person who is held prisoner until some demand is met is a **hostage**.

private adjective
1. *Everything I write in my diary is private.* • secret, confidential, personal, intimate • Secret official documents are **classified** documents.
2. *Can we go somewhere a little more private?* • quiet, secluded, hidden, concealed

prize noun
Our team won first prize in the relay race. • award, reward, trophy • Money that you win as a prize is your **winnings**. • Prize money that keeps increasing until someone wins it is a **jackpot**.

prize verb
Chrissie prized her grandmother's ring above all else. • treasure, value, cherish, hold dear, esteem, revere **opposite** dislike

probable adjective
A burst pipe was the most probable cause of the flood. • likely, feasible, possible, predictable, expected **opposite** improbable

probe verb
1. *The submarine can probe the depths of the ocean.* • explore, penetrate, see into, plumb
2. *Detectives probed the circumstances surrounding the crime.* • investigate, inquire or enquire into, look into, examine, study

problem noun
1. *Our maths teacher set us a really difficult problem today.* • puzzle, question, (informal) brainteaser, poser
2. *I'm having a problem with my computer.* • difficulty, trouble, snag, worry, (informal) headache

proceed verb
1. *The sheep proceeded slowly along the path.* • go on, advance, move forward, progress
2. *We advised them not to proceed with their plan.* • go ahead, carry on

process noun
The inventor showed us a new process for creating electricity. • method, procedure, operation, system, technique

procession noun
The procession made its way slowly down the hill. • parade, march, column, line

prod verb **prodding, prodded**
Someone prodded me in the back with an umbrella. • poke, dig, jab, nudge, push

production noun
1. *Production at the factory has increased this year.* • output
2. *We went to see a production of 'The Sound of Music'.* • performance, show

professional adjective
1. *The plans were drawn by a professional architect.* • qualified, skilled, trained, experienced
2. *This is a very professional piece of work.* • skilled, expert, proficient, competent, efficient **opposite** incompetent
3. *His ambition is to be a professional footballer.* • paid, full-time **opposite** amateur

programme noun
1. *We worked out a programme for sports day.* • plan, schedule, timetable • A list of things to be done at a meeting is an **agenda**.
2. *There was a really good programme on TV last night.* • broadcast, show, production, transmission

progress noun
1. *I traced their progress on the map.* • journey, route, movement, travels
2. *I'm not making much progress learning Dutch.* • advance, development, growth, improvement, headway • An important piece of progress is a **breakthrough**.

progress *verb*
Work on the new building is progressing well.
• proceed, advance, move forward, make progress, make headway, continue, develop, improve, *(informal)* come along

prohibit *verb*
Skateboarding is prohibited in the school grounds. • ban, forbid, outlaw, rule out, veto **opposite** permit, allow

project *noun*
1. *We did a history project on the Victorians.*
• activity, task, assignment, piece of research
2. *There is a project to create a bird sanctuary in the area.* • plan, proposal, scheme

project *verb*
1. *A narrow ledge projects from the cliff.*
• extend, protrude, stick out, jut out, overhang
2. *The lighthouse projects a beam of light.*
• cast, shine, throw out

promise *noun*
1. *We had promises of help from many people.*
• assurance, pledge, guarantee, commitment, vow, oath, word of honour
2. *That young pianist shows promise.*
• potential, talent

promise *verb*
Dad promised that we'd go camping this summer. • assure someone, give your word, guarantee, swear, take an oath, vow

promote *verb*
1. *Gareth has been promoted to captain.*
• move up, advance, upgrade, elevate
2. *The singer is here to promote her new album.* • advertise, publicize, market, push, sell, *(informal)* plug
3. *The school is trying to promote healthy eating.* • encourage, foster, advocate, back, support

prompt *adjective*
I received a prompt reply to my email.
• punctual, quick, rapid, swift, immediate, instant **opposite** delayed

prompt *verb*
Having a dog prompted her to take more exercise. • cause, lead, induce, motivate, stimulate, encourage, provoke

prone *adjective*
He is prone to exaggerate his health problems.
• inclined, apt, liable, likely

proof *noun*
There is no proof that he is a secret agent.
• evidence, confirmation

proper *adjective*
1. *The nurse showed them the proper way to tie a bandage.* • correct, right, accurate, precise, true, genuine **opposite** wrong, incorrect
2. *It's only proper that he should pay for the broken window.* • fair, just, fitting, appropriate, deserved, suitable **opposite** inappropriate
3. *It's not proper to speak with your mouth full.* • decent, respectable, tasteful **opposite** rude

property *noun* properties
1. *This office deals with lost property.*
• belongings, possessions, goods
2. *The website lists property that is for sale in the city.* • buildings, houses, land, premises
3. *Many herbs have healing properties.*
• quality, characteristic, feature, attribute, trait

prophecy *noun* prophecies
The witch's prophecy came true. • prediction, forecast

proposal *noun*
What do you think of the proposal to build a skate park? • plan, project, scheme, suggestion, recommendation

propose *verb*
1. *He proposed a change in the rules.*
• suggest, ask for, recommend
2. *How do you propose to pay for the holiday?*
• intend, mean, plan, aim

prospect *noun*
What are their prospects of winning the tournament? • chance, hope, expectation, likelihood, possibility, probability

protect *verb*
1. *A sentry was posted outside to protect the palace.* • defend, guard, safeguard, keep safe, secure
2. *I wore a hat to protect myself from the sun.*
• shield, shade, screen, insulate

protest *noun*
1. *There were protests at the plan to close the cinema.* • complaint, objection • A general protest is an **outcry**.
2. *Some streets will be closed for a protest in the city centre.* • demonstration, march, rally, *(informal)* demo

protest *verb*
We wrote a letter protesting about the closure of the cinema. • complain, make a protest, object (to), take exception (to), express disapproval (of)

proud *adjective*
1. *Jennie's father was very proud when she passed her music exam.* • delighted (with) pleased (with) • A common simile is **as proud as a peacock**.
2. *He's too proud to mix with the likes of us!* • conceited, big-headed, arrogant, vain, haughty, self-important, snobbish, superior, *(informal)* stuck-up **opposite** humble

prove *verb*
The evidence will prove that he is innocent. • confirm, demonstrate, establish, verify **opposite** disprove

provide *verb*
1. *We'll provide the juice if you bring the sandwiches.* • bring, contribute, arrange for, lay on • To provide food and drink for people is to **cater** for them.
2. *The ski centre can provide you with boots and skis.* • supply, equip, furnish

provoke *verb*
1. *Don't do anything to provoke the lions!* • annoy, irritate, anger, incense, infuriate, exasperate, tease, taunt, goad, *(informal)* wind up **opposite** pacify
2. *The referee's decision provoked anger from the crowd.* • arouse, produce, prompt, cause, generate, induce, stimulate, spark off, stir up, whip up

prowl *verb*
Guard dogs prowled about the grounds of the palace. • roam, slink, sneak, creep, steal

prudent *adjective*
It would be prudent to start saving some money. • wise, sensible, shrewd, thoughtful, careful, cautious **opposite** reckless, unwise

pry *verb* pries, prying, pried
I didn't mean to pry, but I overheard your conversation. • be curious, be inquisitive, interfere, *(informal)* be nosy, nose about or around, snoop

public *adjective*
1. *The public entrance is at the front of the gallery.* • common, communal, general, open, shared **opposite** private
2. *The name of the author is now public knowledge.* • well-known, acknowledged, published, open, general, universal **opposite** secret

publicity *noun*
1. *Did you see the publicity for the book fair?* • advertising, advertisements, promotion
2. *Famous people don't always enjoy publicity.* • fame, exposure, limelight

publish *verb*
1. *The magazine is published every week.* • issue, print, produce, bring out, release, circulate
2. *When will they publish the results?* • announce, declare, disclose, make known, make public, report, reveal • To publish information on radio, TV or the Internet is to **broadcast** it.

pudding *noun*
Do you want any pudding? • dessert, sweet, *(informal)* afters

puff *noun*
1. *A puff of wind caught his hat.* • gust, breath, flurry
2. *A puff of smoke rose from the chimney.* • cloud, whiff

puff *verb*
1. *The dragon puffed green smoke from its nostrils.* • blow out, send out, emit, belch
2. *By the end of the race I was puffing.* • breathe heavily, pant, gasp, wheeze
3. *The sails puffed out as the wind rose.* • become inflated, billow, swell

pull *verb*
1. *She pulled her chair nearer to the desk.* • drag, draw, haul, lug, trail, tow **opposite** push
2. *Be careful—you nearly pulled my arm off!* • tug, rip, wrench, jerk, pluck
to pull out
1. *The dentist pulled out one of his teeth.* • extract, take out, remove
2. *He had to pull out of the race.* • back out, withdraw, retire
to pull up
The bus pulled up at the traffic lights. • draw up, stop, halt

pump *verb*
The fire brigade pumped water out of the cellar. • drain, draw off, empty • To move liquid from a higher container to a lower one through a tube is to **siphon** it.

punch *verb*
1. *Mrs Rafferty punched the robber on the nose.* • jab, poke, prod, thump
2. *I need to punch a hole through the card.* • bore, pierce

punctuation *noun*

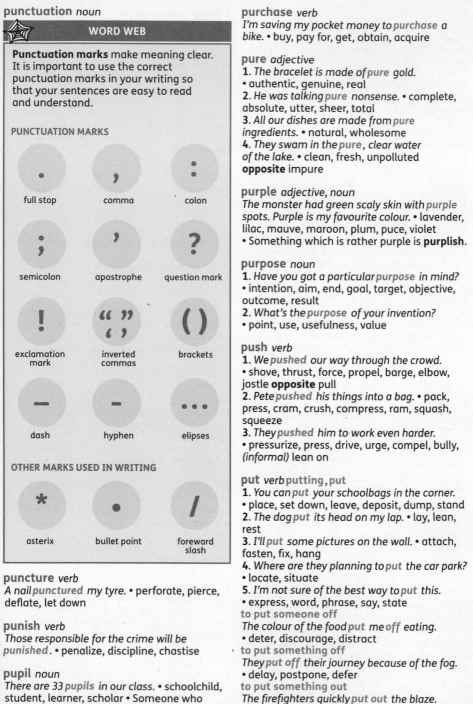

WORD WEB

Punctuation marks make meaning clear. It is important to use the correct punctuation marks in your writing so that your sentences are easy to read and understand.

PUNCTUATION MARKS

full stop

comma

colon

semicolon

apostrophe

question mark

exclamation mark

inverted commas

brackets

dash

hyphen

elipses

OTHER MARKS USED IN WRITING

asterix

bullet point

foreward slash

puncture *verb*
A nail *punctured* my tyre. • perforate, pierce, deflate, let down

punish *verb*
Those responsible for the crime will be *punished*. • penalize, discipline, chastise

pupil *noun*
There are 33 *pupils* in our class. • schoolchild, student, learner, scholar • Someone who follows a great teacher is a **disciple**.

purchase *verb*
I'm saving my pocket money to *purchase* a bike. • buy, pay for, get, obtain, acquire

pure *adjective*
1. The bracelet is made of *pure* gold.
• authentic, genuine, real
2. He was talking *pure* nonsense. • complete, absolute, utter, sheer, total
3. All our dishes are made from *pure* ingredients. • natural, wholesome
4. They swam in the *pure*, clear water of the lake. • clean, fresh, unpolluted
opposite impure

purple *adjective, noun*
The monster had green scaly skin with *purple* spots. Purple is my favourite colour. • lavender, lilac, mauve, maroon, plum, puce, violet
• Something which is rather purple is **purplish**.

purpose *noun*
1. Have you got a particular *purpose* in mind?
• intention, aim, end, goal, target, objective, outcome, result
2. What's the *purpose* of your invention?
• point, use, usefulness, value

push *verb*
1. We *pushed* our way through the crowd.
• shove, thrust, force, propel, barge, elbow, jostle **opposite** pull
2. Pete *pushed* his things into a bag. • pack, press, cram, crush, compress, ram, squash, squeeze
3. They *pushed* him to work even harder.
• pressurize, press, drive, urge, compel, bully, (informal) lean on

put *verb* putting, put
1. You can *put* your schoolbags in the corner.
• place, set down, leave, deposit, dump, stand
2. The dog *put* its head on my lap. • lay, lean, rest
3. I'll *put* some pictures on the wall. • attach, fasten, fix, hang
4. Where are they planning to *put* the car park?
• locate, situate
5. I'm not sure of the best way to *put* this.
• express, word, phrase, say, state
to put someone off
The colour of the food *put* me *off* eating.
• deter, discourage, distract
to put something off
They *put off* their journey because of the fog.
• delay, postpone, defer
to put something out
The firefighters quickly *put out* the blaze.
• extinguish, quench, smother

to put something up
1. *It doesn't take long to put up the tent.*
• set up, construct, erect
2. *I'm going to buy a new bike before they put up the price.* • increase, raise
to put up with something
I don't know how you put up with that noise.
• bear, stand, tolerate, endure

puzzle *noun*
Has anyone managed to solve the puzzle?
• question, mystery, riddle, conundrum, problem, *(informal)* brainteaser, poser

puzzle *verb*
1. *Phil was puzzled by the mysterious message.*
• confuse, baffle, bewilder, bemuse, mystify, perplex, fox
2. *We puzzled over the problem for hours.*
• ponder, think, meditate, worry, brood

puzzled *adjective*
Why are you looking so puzzled? • confused, baffled, bewildered, mystified, perplexed

puzzling *adjective*
There was something puzzling about the signature on the letter. • confusing, baffling, bewildering, mystifying, perplexing, mysterious, inexplicable
opposite straightforward

pyramid *noun*

WORD WEB

THINGS FOUND INSIDE ANCIENT EGYPTIAN PYRAMIDS
• burial chamber, Canopic jar, hieroglyphics, mummy (of a pharaoh), papyrus, sarcophagus. • A pyramid which does not have smooth sides is a **stepped pyramid**.

Quick can have different synonyms: *swift*, *nippy*, *clever* or *snappy*. Can you see the difference in the meanings?

quaint *adjective*
They stayed in a *quaint* thatched cottage. • charming, picturesque, sweet, old-fashioned, old-world

quake *verb*
The ground *quaked* with the thud of the giant's footsteps. • shake, shudder, tremble, quiver, shiver, vibrate, rock, sway, wobble

qualification *noun*
What kind of *qualification* do you need to be a vet? • diploma, certificate, degree, knowledge, training, skill

qualified *adjective*
This job needs a *qualified* electrician. • experienced, skilled, trained, professional **opposite** amateur

qualify *verb* qualifies, qualifying, qualified
1. *The licence* qualifies *him to work as a private detective.* • authorize, permit, allow, entitle
2. *The first three runners will* qualify *to take part in the final.* • get through, pass, be eligible

quality *noun* qualities
1. *We only use ingredients of the highest* quality. • grade, class, standard
2. *The most obvious* quality *of rubber is that it stretches.* • characteristic, feature, property, attribute, trait

quantity *noun* quantities
1. *She receives a huge* quantity *of fan mail every week.* • amount, mass, volume, bulk, weight, (informal) load
2. *We recycled a large* quantity *of empty bottles.* • number • When you add up numbers, you get a **sum** or **total**.

quarrel *noun*
We have *quarrels*, but really we are good friends. • argument, disagreement, dispute, difference of opinion, row, squabble, clash, tiff • Continuous quarrelling is **strife**.
• A long-lasting quarrel is a **feud** or **vendetta**.
• A quarrel in which people become violent is a **brawl** or **fight**.

quarrel *verb* quarrelling, quarrelled
The twins *quarrelled* over who should sit in the front. • disagree, argue, row, squabble, bicker, clash, fight, fall out
to quarrel with something
I can't *quarrel with* your decision. • disagree with, object to, take exception to, oppose

quaver *verb*
The boy's voice *quavered* with fear. • shake, tremble, waver, quake, quiver, falter

quay *noun*
The ship unloaded its cargo onto the *quay*. • dock, harbour, pier, wharf, jetty, landing stage

queer *adjective*
1. *The engine made a* queer *rattling noise.* • curious, strange, unusual, weird, funny, mysterious, puzzling
2. *There's something* queer *going on.* • odd, peculiar, abnormal, suspicious, shady, (informal) fishy

quest *noun*
The knights set out on a *quest* to find the enchanted tower. • search, hunt, expedition, mission

question *noun*
1. *Does anyone have any* questions? • enquiry, query, problem • A question which someone sets as a puzzle is a **brain-teaser** or **conundrum** or **riddle**. • A series of questions asked as a game is a **quiz**. • A set of questions which someone asks to get information is a **questionnaire** or **survey**.
2. *There's some* question *over the player's fitness.* • uncertainty, doubt, argument, debate, dispute

question *verb*
1. *The detective decided to* question *the suspect.* • ask, examine, interview, quiz, interrogate • To question someone intensively is to **grill** them.
2. *He* questioned *the referee's decision.* • challenge, dispute, argue over, quarrel with, object to, query

queue noun
There was a *queue* of people outside the cinema. • line, file, column, string • A long queue of traffic on a road is a **tailback**.

queue verb
Please *queue* at the door. • line up, form a queue

quick adjective
1. You'd better be *quick*—the bus leaves in ten minutes. • fast, swift, rapid, speedy, hasty, (informal) nippy • A common simile is **as quick as a flash**. **opposite** slow
2. Do you mind if I make a *quick* phone call? • short, brief, momentary, immediate, instant, prompt, snappy **opposite** long, lengthy
3. She's very *quick* at mental arithmetic. • bright, clever, sharp, acute, alert, (informal) on the ball **opposite** slow

quiet adjective
1. The deserted house was still and *quiet*. • silent, noiseless, soundless • A common simile is **as quiet as a mouse**. **opposite** noisy
2. The children spoke in *quiet* whispers. • hushed, low, soft • Something that is so quiet that you can't hear it is **inaudible**. **opposite** loud
3. Amy has always been a *quiet* child. • shy, reserved, subdued, placid, uncommunicative, retiring, withdrawn **opposite** talkative
4. We found a *quiet* place for a picnic. • peaceful, secluded, isolated, restful, tranquil, calm, serene **opposite** busy

quietly adverb
I tiptoed *quietly* downstairs and out of the house. • softly, silently, soundlessly, noiselessly, stealthily

quit verb quitting, quitted, quit
1. She *quit* her teaching job to travel round the world. • leave, give up, resign from, (informal) pack in
2. (informal) *Quit* pushing me! • stop, cease, leave off

quite adverb

> Take care how you use **quite**, as the two senses are almost opposites.

1. The two puppies have *quite* different personalities. • completely, totally, utterly, entirely, absolutely, wholly
2. They played *quite* well, but far from their best. • fairly, reasonably, moderately, rather

quiver verb
The jelly *quivered* when the table was banged. • shake, wobble, quake, shiver, quaver, tremble, shudder, vibrate

quiz noun quizzes
Our class took part in a general knowledge *quiz*. • test, competition, questionnaire, exam, examination

a
b
c
d
e
f
g
h
i
j
k
l
m
n
o
p
q
r
s
t
u
v
w
x
y
z

Brick red, cherry red, ruby red or scarlet – there are lots of different shades of red.

race noun
1. We had a race to see who was the fastest runner. • competition, contest, chase • A race to decide who will take part in the final is a **heat**.
2. We belong to different races but we're all humans. • nation, people, ethnic group

race verb
1. We raced each other to the end of the road. • have a race with, run against, compete with
2. She had to race home because she was late. • run, rush, dash, hurry, sprint, fly, tear, whizz, zoom

racket noun
Please stop making that awful racket! • noise, row, din, commotion, disturbance, uproar, rumpus

radiate verb
This fire radiates a lot of heat. • give off, send out, emit

rage noun
Derek slammed the door in a show of rage. • anger, fury, indignation, (old use) wrath • A child's rage is a **tantrum** or **temper**.

rage verb
1. He was still raging about the cost of the meal. • be angry, be fuming, seethe, rant
2. The hurricane raged for three days. • blow, storm, rampage

ragged adjective
They met a traveller wearing ragged clothes. • tattered, tatty, threadbare, torn, frayed, patched, ripped, shabby, worn-out

raid noun
The enemy raid caught them by surprise. • attack, assault, strike, onslaught, invasion, blitz

raid verb
1. Long ago, Vikings raided the towns on the coast. • attack, invade, ransack, plunder, loot, pillage • Someone who raids ships at sea is a **pirate**. • Someone who raids and steals cattle is a **rustler**.
2. Police raided the house at dawn. • descend on, rush, storm, swoop on

rain noun
• A formal word for rain is **precipitation**.
• The rainy season in south and south-east Asia is the **monsoon**. • When there is no rain for a long time you have a **drought**.

raise verb
1. Raise your hand if you need help. • hold up, put up, lift
2. The box was too heavy for him to raise. • lift, pick up, elevate, hoist, jack up
3. The Post Office is raising the price of stamps. • increase, put up
4. The runners hope to raise £1000 for charity. • collect, gather, take in, make
5. He raised some objections to the plan. • bring up, mention, put forward, present, introduce
6. The doctor didn't want to raise their hopes. • encourage, build up, arouse
7. It's hard work trying to raise a family. • bring up, care for, look after, nurture, rear

ram verb ramming, rammed
The car skidded and rammed into a lamp post. • bump, hit, strike, crash into, collide with, smash into

ramble verb
1. They rambled round the country park. • walk, stroll, wander, roam, rove, range, hike, trek
2. The speaker rambled on for hours. • chatter, babble, drift, (informal) rabbit, witter

random adjective
They picked a random selection of pupils. • arbitrary, chance, haphazard, casual, unplanned **opposite** deliberate

range noun
1. There is a range of mountains to the south. • chain, line, row, series, string
2. Supermarkets sell a wide range of goods. • variety, assortment, selection, choice, spectrum
3. The shop caters for all age ranges from toddlers to teenagers. • span, scope

range verb
1. Prices range from 5 to 20 euros. • vary, differ, extend, fluctuate

2. *Rows of jam jars were* ranged *on the shelf.*
• arrange, order, lay out, set out, line up
3. *Wild deer* range *over the hills.* • wander, ramble, roam, rove, stray

rank *noun*
1. *The soldiers formed themselves into* ranks.
• column, line, file, row
2. *A black belt is the highest* rank *in judo.*
• grade, level, position, status • To raise someone to a higher rank is to **promote** them.
• To reduce someone to a lower rank is to **demote** them.

rapid *adjective*
The cyclists set off at a rapid *pace.* • fast, quick, speedy, swift, brisk **opposite** slow

rare *adjective*
1. *These flowers are now very* rare *in the wild.*
• uncommon, unusual, infrequent, scarce, sparse **opposite** common
2. *He has a* rare *ability to make people laugh.*
• exceptional, remarkable, special

rarely *adverb*
Our next-door neighbour rarely *goes out.* • seldom, infrequently, hardly ever **opposite** often

rash *adjective*
Don't make any rash *promises.* • reckless, foolhardy, hasty, hurried, impulsive, unthinking **opposite** careful

rate *noun*
1. *The cyclists were pedalling at a furious* rate.
• pace, speed
2. *What's the usual* rate *for washing a car?*
• charge, cost, fee, payment, price, figure, amount

rate *verb*
How do you rate *their chance of winning?*
• judge, regard, consider, estimate, evaluate

rather *adverb*
1. *It's* rather *chilly today.* • quite, fairly, moderately, slightly, somewhat, a bit, a little
2. *I'd* rather *not go out tonight.* • preferably, sooner

rave *verb*
1. *Connie* raved *about the film she saw last week.* • be enthusiastic, talk wildly
2. *The head* raved *on about their bad behaviour.* • shout, rage, storm, yell, roar

raw *adjective*
1. Raw *vegetables are supposed to be good for you.* • uncooked **opposite** cooked

2. *The factory imports a lot of* raw *materials from abroad.* • crude, natural, unprocessed, untreated **opposite** manufactured, processed
3. *Her knee felt* raw *after she fell off her bike.*
• red, rough, sore, tender, inflamed
4. *There was a* raw *wind blowing from the east.*
• bitter, cold, chilly, biting, freezing, piercing

ray *noun*
A ray *of light shone into the dark cave.* • beam, shaft, stream

reach *verb*
1. *They hoped to* reach *Oxford by lunchtime.*
• arrive at, go as far as, get to, make
2. *The appeal fund has* reached *its target.*
• achieve, attain
3. *I'm not tall enough to* reach *the top shelf.*
• get hold of, grasp, touch
to reach out
Reach out your hands. • extend, hold out, put out, stick out, stretch out

reach *noun*
1. *The shelf was just within his* reach. • grasp
2. *The shops are within easy* reach. • distance, range

react *verb*
How did he react *when he read the letter?*
• respond, behave, answer, reply

reaction *noun*
What was her reaction *when you said you were sorry?* • response, answer, reply

read *verb* reading, read
They couldn't read *the doctor's handwriting.*
• make out, understand, decipher • To read through something very quickly is to **skim through** it. • To read here and there in a book is to **dip into** it. • To read something intently is to **pore over** it.

ready *adjective* readier, readiest
1. *When will tea be* ready? • prepared, set, done, available, in place **opposite** not ready
2. *He's always* ready *to help.* • willing, glad, pleased, happy, keen, eager **opposite** reluctant

real *adjective*
1. *History is about* real *events.* • actual, true, factual, verifiable **opposite** fictitious, imaginary
2. *The necklace was made from* real *rubies.*
• authentic, genuine, bona fide, natural **opposite** artificial, fake

3. She doesn't often show her real feelings.
• true, honest, sincere, genuine, heartfelt
opposite insincere

realistic adjective
1. The portrait of the artist is very realistic.
• lifelike, true-to-life, faithful, convincing,
recognizable
*2. It's not realistic to expect a puppy to be
quiet.* • feasible, practical, sensible, possible,
workable

realize verb
*It took him a long time to realize what she
meant.* • understand, appreciate, grasp,
comprehend, recognize, see, (informal) catch
on to, tumble to, twig This word can also be
spelled **realise**.

really adverb
1. Are you really going to Peru? • actually,
definitely, truly, in fact, certainly, genuinely,
honestly
2. I saw a really good film last night. • very,
extremely, exceptionally

reasonable adjective
1. That seems like a reasonable plan.
• sensible, intelligent, rational, logical, sane,
sound **opposite** irrational
*2. They bought the house for a reasonable
price.* • fair, acceptable, average,
moderate, respectable, normal, proper
opposite excessive

reassure verb
*The doctor reassured her that the wound
was not serious.* • calm, comfort, encourage,
hearten, give confidence to **opposite** threaten

rebel verb rebelling, rebelled
The king feared that the people would rebel.
• revolt, rise up • To rebel against the captain
of a ship is to **mutiny** and someone who does
this is a **mutineer. opposite** obey

rebellion noun
*The protest soon became a widespread
rebellion.* • revolt, revolution, uprising,
resistance • A rebellion on a ship is a **mutiny**.

recent adjective
*We watch the news to keep up with recent
events.* • current, up-to-date, contemporary,
new, the latest, fresh

recently adverb
The family had recently moved into the area.
• lately, latterly, the other day, not long ago,
just now, only just

recite verb
Zoe recited a poem she had written. • say
aloud, read out, narrate

reckless adjective
*A man has been charged with reckless
driving.* • careless, irresponsible, mindless,
thoughtless, negligent, foolhardy, rash, wild
opposite careful

reckon verb
1. I tried to reckon how much she owed me.
• calculate, work out, add up, figure out,
assess, estimate
2. Do you reckon it's going to rain? • think,
believe, guess, imagine, feel

recognize verb
1. I didn't recognize her with her new haircut.
• identify, know, distinguish, make out, recall,
recollect, remember
*2. He refused to recognize that he was to
blame.* • acknowledge, admit, accept, grant,
concede, confess, realize This word can also
be spelled **recognise**.

recommend verb
1. The doctor recommended a complete rest.
• advise, counsel, propose, suggest, advocate,
prescribe, urge
*2. The restaurant was recommended by a
friend of mine.* • approve of, endorse, praise,
commend

record noun
*The zookeepers keep a record of the animals'
diet.* • account, report • A record of daily
events is a **diary** or **journal**. • The record of
a voyage at sea or in space is the **log**. • The
record of what happened at a meeting is
the **minutes**. • A record of people's names is
a **register**. • Records consisting of historical
documents are **archives**.

record verb
1. The concert is being recorded by the BBC.
• tape, video
2. She recorded our interview in a notebook.
• write down, note, set down, put down, enter

recover verb
*1. It took a long time to recover after my
illness.* • get better, heal, improve, recuperate,
pick up, mend, come round, pull through,
revive, rally
*2. The police have recovered the stolen
vehicles.* • get back, retrieve, reclaim,
repossess, find, trace

recovery noun
The doctors were surprised at her speedy recovery. • healing, cure, revival, recuperation, convalescence

recreation noun
What do you do for recreation around here? • fun, enjoyment, pleasure, relaxation, leisure, amusement, diversion, entertainment, play
• A particular activity you do as recreation is a **hobby** or **pastime**.

rectangle noun
• oblong

recur verb **recurring, recurred**
Go to the doctor if the symptoms recur. • happen again, come again, reappear, return

recycle verb
You can recycle glass by putting it in the bottle bank. • reuse, reprocess, salvage, use again

red adjective **redder, reddest**, noun
1. *I chose a red ribbon for my doll. Red is my favourite colour.* • Something which is rather red is **reddish**. • A common simile is **as red as a beetroot**.
2. *My nose and cheeks were red with cold.* • flushed, glowing, rosy, ruddy, blushing
3. *Her eyes were red from lack of sleep.* • bloodshot, inflamed, red-rimmed
4. *The fairy queen had flaming red hair.* • ginger, auburn, coppery, (informal) carroty

---

WORD WEB

SOME SHADES OF RED
• brick-red, cerise, cherry-red, crimson, pillar-box red, rose, ruby, scarlet, vermilion

---

reduce verb
She's reduced the amount of sugar in her diet. • decrease, lessen, lower, cut, cut back, slash
• To reduce something by half is to **halve** it. • To reduce the width of something is to **narrow** it. • To reduce the length of something is to **shorten** or **trim** it. • To reduce speed is to **decelerate**. • To reduce the strength of a liquid is to **dilute** it. **opposite** increase

reel verb
1. *The blow made his head reel.* • spin, whirl
2. *The injured man reeled as if he was drunk.* • stagger, stumble, sway, rock, totter, lurch, roll
to reel off
The chef reeled off a long list of ingredients. • recite, rattle off, fire off

refer verb **referring, referred**
The shop assistant referred me to another department. • hand over, pass on, direct, send
to refer to
1. *Please don't refer to this matter again.* • mention, speak of, make reference to, allude to, bring up
2. *If you can't spell a word, refer to a dictionary.* • look up, consult, go to, turn to

reflect verb
1. *Cat's-eyes reflect the light from car headlights.* • send back, throw back, shine back
2. *Their success reflects their hard work.* • show, indicate, demonstrate, exhibit, reveal
to reflect on
We need time to reflect on what to do next. • think about, contemplate, consider, ponder, mull over

refuse verb
1. *Why did you refuse my offer of help?* • decline, reject, turn down, say no to **opposite** accept
2. *They were refused permission to enter the building.* • deny, deprive of **opposite** allow

region noun
1. *The Arctic and Antarctic are polar regions.* • area, place, land, territory, part of the world
2. *There are two local radio stations serving this region.* • area, district, neighbourhood, locality, vicinity, zone

regret verb **regretting, regretted**
She regretted her decision to leave Ireland. • be sorry for, repent, feel sad about

regular adjective
1. *Signs are placed at regular intervals along the cycle path.* • evenly spaced, fixed **opposite** irregular, uneven
2. *The drummer kept up a regular rhythm.* • constant, consistent, steady, uniform, unvarying • A common simile is **as regular as clockwork. opposite** erratic
3. *Is this your regular route to school?* • normal, usual, customary, habitual, ordinary, routine **opposite** unusual
4. *Craig is a regular customer at the sweet shop.* • frequent, familiar, persistent **opposite** rare, unusual

rehearse verb
We had to rehearse the scene all over again. • go over, practise, try out

reign *verb*
Which British monarch reigned the longest?
• be king or queen, be on the throne, govern, rule

reject *verb*
1. *At first, she rejected their offer of help.*
• decline, refuse, turn down, say no to
2. *As we picked the berries, we rejected any bad ones.* • discard, get rid of, throw out, scrap

rejoice *verb*
The people rejoiced when the wicked queen died. • celebrate, delight, be happy, exult
opposite grieve

relate *verb*
1. *Do you think the two crimes are related?*
• connect, link, associate
2. *The travellers related the story of their adventures.* • tell, narrate, report, describe
relate to
The letter relates to your great grandfather.
• be about, refer to, have to do with, concern

relation *noun*
1. *The stolen car has no relation to the robbery.* • connection, link, association, bond
2. *Are you a relation of hers?* • relative, member of the family, kinsman or kinswoman
For members of a family, see **family**

relationship *noun*
1. *There is a relationship between your diet and health.* • connection, link, association, bond • The relationship between two numbers is a **ratio**.
2. *The twins have a close relationship.*
• friendship, attachment, understanding

relax *verb*
1. *I like to relax by listening to music.* • unwind, rest, take it easy
2. *This exercise will relax your shoulder muscles.* • loosen, ease **opposite** tighten
3. *He relaxed his hold on the dog's leash.*
• slacken, loosen, ease, lessen, reduce
opposite tighten

relaxed *adjective*
They liked the relaxed atmosphere of village life. • informal, casual, carefree, leisurely, easygoing, peaceful, restful, unhurried, calm, *(informal)* laid-back **opposite** tense, stressful

release *verb*
1. *The prisoners were released early.*
• free, let go, discharge, liberate, set free
• To release slaves is to **emancipate** them.
opposite imprison

2. *The dog was tied up—who released him?*
• let loose, set loose, unfasten, unleash, untie
3. *The band will release their new single in April.* • issue, publish, put out

relevant *adjective*
1. *The detective noted everything that was relevant to the case.* • applicable, pertinent, appropriate, suitable, significant, related, connected
2. *Don't interrupt unless your comments are relevant.* • to the point

reliable *adjective*
1. *The king summoned his most reliable knights.* • faithful, dependable, trustworthy, loyal, constant, devoted, staunch, true
2. *The secret agent always sent reliable information.* • dependable, valid, trustworthy, safe, sound, steady, sure

relief *noun*
1. *The pills gave some relief from the pain.*
• comfort, ease, help, release
2. *I watched a film for some light relief after work.* • relaxation, rest

relieve *verb*
The doctor said the pills would relieve the pain.
• ease, help, lessen, diminish, relax, soothe, comfort

religious *adjective*
1. *The choir sang a selection of religious music.*
• sacred, holy, divine **opposite** secular
2. *My grandparents were very religious.*
• devout, pious, reverent, spiritual, godly
opposite ungodly

reluctant *adjective*
The old woman was reluctant to open the door. • unwilling, hesitant, slow, grudging, half-hearted, resistant **opposite** eager

rely *verb* **relies, relying, relied**
Are you sure that we can rely on their help?
• depend on, count on, have confidence in, trust, *(informal)* bank on

remain *verb*
1. *The boys were told to remain behind after school.* • stay, wait, linger, *(informal)* hang about
2. *It will remain warm and sunny all weekend.*
• continue, persist, keep on, carry on
3. *Little remained of the house after the fire.*
• be left, survive

remains *plural noun*
They cleared away the remains of the picnic.
• remnants, leftovers, leavings, fragments, traces, scraps, debris • The remains at the bottom of a cup are **dregs**. • Remains still standing after a building has collapsed are **ruins**. • Historic remains are **relics**.

remarkable *adjective*
1. *He described his remarkable escape from the island.* • amazing, extraordinary, astonishing, memorable, wonderful, incredible, unforgettable, breathtaking
2. *The young violinist shows remarkable skill for her age.* • exceptional, notable, noteworthy, striking, outstanding, impressive, phenomenal

remedy *noun* **remedies**
1. *There is no known remedy for his illness.*
• cure, treatment, medicine, therapy, relief
• A remedy to act against a poison is an **antidote**.
2. *We may have found a remedy for the problem.* • solution, answer

remember *verb*
1. *Can you remember what she looked like?*
• recall, recollect, recognize, place
2. *He was trying to remember his lines for the play.* • learn, memorize, keep in mind
opposite forget
3. *My granny likes to remember the old days.*
• reminisce about, think back to

remind *verb*
Remind me to buy a newspaper. • prompt, jog your memory
to remind you of something
What does this tune remind you of? • make you think of, take you back to

reminder *noun*
1. *They sent him a reminder to pay the bill.*
• prompt, cue, hint, nudge
2. *The photographs are a reminder of our holiday.* • souvenir, memento

remote *adjective*
1. *The tour will explore a remote part of Brazil.* • distant, faraway, isolated, cut-off, inaccessible, out-of-the-way, unfrequented
opposite accessible
2. *The chances of us winning are remote.*
• poor, slender, slight, small, faint, doubtful
opposite likely

remove *verb*
1. *Please remove your rubbish.* • clear away, take away
2. *The rowdy passengers were removed from the bus.* • throw out, turn out, eject, expel, (*informal*) kick out • To remove people from a house where they are living is to **evict** them.
• To remove a monarch from the throne is to **depose** him or her.
3. *The author decided to remove the last paragraph.* • cut out, delete, erase, get rid of, do away with, eliminate
4. *The dentist removed my bad tooth.*
• extract, pull out, take out, withdraw
5. *The divers slowly removed their wetsuits.*
• take off, peel off, strip off, shed, cast off

renew *verb*
1. *The church roof has been completely renewed.* • repair, renovate, restore, replace, rebuild, reconstruct, revamp, refurbish, overhaul, (*informal*) do up
2. *You must renew your passport before you go abroad.* • bring up to date, update

repeat *verb*
1. *The parrot repeated everything he said.*
• say again, copy, duplicate, reproduce, echo
2. *The actors had to repeat the opening scene.*
• do again, redo

repel *verb* **repelling, repelled**
1. *The humans managed to repel the Martian invasion.* • drive back, beat back, push back, fend off, resist
2. *This spray will repel wasps and other insects.*
• keep away, scare off, deter, ward off
3. *They were repelled by the smell of the dragon's lair.* • disgust, revolt, sicken, offend, (*slang*) turn you off

replace *verb*
1. *The spy carefully replaced the missing document.* • put back, return, restore, reinstate
2. *Who will replace the head teacher when she retires?* • follow, succeed, take over from, take the place of
3. *I need to replace one of the tyres on my bike.* • change, renew

replica *noun*
In the garden, there's a replica of a Roman statue. • copy, reproduction, duplicate, model, imitation, likeness • An exact copy of a document is a **facsimile**.

reply noun replies
He has received no replies to his email. • response, answer, reaction, acknowledgement • An angry reply is a **retort**.

reply verb replies, replying, replied to reply to
She took a long time to reply to my letter. • answer, respond to, give a reply to, react to, acknowledge

report verb
1. *The newspapers reported what happened.* • give an account of, record, state, describe, announce, publish
2. *We were told to report to reception when we arrived.* • present yourself, make yourself known, check in
3. *If you cause any damage, I'll report you to the police.* • complain about, inform on, denounce

report noun
There was a report in the paper about the crash. • account, record, story, article, description

reporter noun
The film star was being interviewed by a TV reporter. • journalist, correspondent

represent verb
1. *The picture represents an ancient legend.* • depict, illustrate, portray, picture, show, describe
2. *A dove is often said to represent peace.* • stand for, symbolize
3. *He appointed a lawyer to represent him.* • speak for

reproduce verb
1. *The robot can reproduce a human voice.* • copy, duplicate, imitate, simulate, mimic
2. *Mice reproduce very quickly.* • breed, produce offspring, multiply, procreate • Fish reproduce by **spawning**. • To reproduce plants is to **propagate** them.

reproduction noun
1. *Vets have to know about animal reproduction.* • breeding, procreation
2. *Is that an original painting or a reproduction?* • copy, replica, imitation, likeness, duplicate, print • A reproduction of something which is intended to deceive people is a **fake** or **forgery**. • An exact reproduction of a document is a **facsimile**.

reptile noun

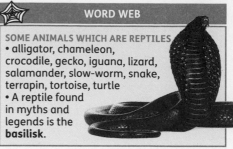

WORD WEB

SOME ANIMALS WHICH ARE REPTILES
• alligator, chameleon, crocodile, gecko, iguana, lizard, salamander, slow-worm, snake, terrapin, tortoise, turtle
• A reptile found in myths and legends is the **basilisk**.

repulsive adjective
We were put off eating by the repulsive smell. • disgusting, revolting, offensive, repellent, disagreeable, foul, repugnant, obnoxious, sickening, hateful, hideous, horrible, loathsome, objectionable, vile **opposite** attractive

reputation noun
The singer's reputation spread throughout the world. • fame, celebrity, name, renown, eminence, standing, stature

request verb
She has requested a transfer to a different job. • ask for, appeal for, apply for, beg for, call for, entreat, implore, invite, pray for, seek

request noun
They have ignored our request for help. • appeal, plea, entreaty, call, cry • A request for a job or membership is an **application**. • A request signed by a lot of people is a **petition**.

require verb
1. *They require a draw to win the championship.* • need, must have
2. *Visitors are required to sign the register.* • instruct, oblige, request, direct, order, command

rescue verb
1. *A helicopter was sent to rescue the trapped climbers.* • free, liberate, release, save, set free • To rescue someone by paying money is to **ransom** them.
2. *The divers rescued some items from the sunken ship.* • retrieve, recover, salvage

reserve verb
1. *The astronauts had to reserve fuel for the return voyage.* • keep, put aside, set aside, save, preserve, retain, hold back
2. *Have you reserved your seats on the train?* • book, order, secure

reserve noun
1. *The climbers kept a reserve of food in their base camp.* • stock, store, supply, hoard, stockpile • A reserve of money is a **fund** or **savings**.
2. *They put him down as a reserve for Saturday's game.* • substitute, standby, stand-in, replacement • Someone who can take the place of an actor is an **understudy**.
3. *The wildlife reserve has a new baby rhino.* • reservation, park, preserve, sanctuary

reserved adjective
1. *These seats are reserved.* • booked, set aside, ordered
2. *She is too reserved to speak up for herself.* • shy, timid, quiet, bashful, modest, retiring, reticent **opposite** outgoing

resign verb
The manager of the football team was forced to resign. • leave, quit, stand down, step down, give in your notice • When a monarch resigns from the throne, he or she **abdicates**.

resist verb
1. *They were too weak to resist the sorcerer's magic.* • stand up to, defend yourself against, withstand, defy, oppose, fend off **opposite** yield to, surrender to
2. *I couldn't resist having another piece of chocolate.* • avoid, hold back from, refuse **opposite** give in, accept

resolve verb
1. *I resolved to try harder next time.* • decide, determine, make up your mind
2. *They held a meeting to try to resolve the dispute.* • settle, sort out, straighten out, end, overcome

resort verb
He didn't want to resort to violence. • start using, turn to, fall back on, rely on, stoop to

resources plural noun
1. *The country is rich in natural resources.* • materials, raw materials, reserves
2. *The library has limited resources for buying computers.* • funds, money, capital, assets, means, wealth

respect noun
1. *Her colleagues have the deepest respect for her.* • admiration, esteem, regard, reverence, honour
2. *Have some respect for other people's feelings.* • consideration, sympathy, thought, concern
3. *In some respects, he's a better player*

than I am. • way, point, aspect, feature, characteristic, detail, particular

respect verb
1. *Everyone respects her for her courage.* • admire, esteem, revere, honour, look up to, value **opposite** scorn, despise
2. *She tried to respect the wishes of her dead husband.* • obey, follow, observe, adhere to, comply with **opposite** ignore

respectable adjective
1. *He came from a very respectable family.* • decent, honest, upright, honourable, worthy
2. *I finished the race in a respectable time.* • reasonable, satisfactory, acceptable, passable, adequate, fair, tolerable

respond verb
to respond to
He didn't respond to my question. • reply to, answer, react to, acknowledge

response noun
Did you get a response to your letter? • reply, answer, reaction, acknowledgement • An angry response is a **retort**.

responsible adjective
1. *Parents are legally responsible for their children.* • in charge **opposite** not responsible
2. *He's a very responsible sort of person.* • reliable, sensible, trustworthy, dependable, conscientious, dutiful, honest **opposite** irresponsible
3. *Looking after people's money is a responsible job.* • important, serious
4. *Who is responsible for all this mess?* • to blame, guilty (of), at fault

rest noun
1. *The actors had a short rest in the middle of the rehearsal.* • break, breather, breathing space, pause, respite, lie-down, nap
2. *The doctor said the patient needed complete rest.* • relaxation, leisure, inactivity, ease, quiet, time off
the rest
Take a few sweets now, but leave the rest for later. • the remainder, the surplus, the others, the remains

rest verb
1. *I think we should stop and rest for a while.* • have a rest, lie down, relax, lounge, have a nap
2. *Rest the ladder against the wall.* • lean, prop, stand, place, support

restaurant noun
Every Christmas my family go to a fancy restaurant for dinner. • buffet, burger bar, cafe, cafeteria, canteen, carvery, chip shop or (informal) chippie, coffee shop, diner, grill, ice cream parlour, snack bar, steakhouse, takeaway, tearoom, wine bar • A restaurant that serves French food is a **bistro** or a **brasserie**. • A restaurant that serves Italian food is a **trattoria**. • A restaurant that serves mainly pizza is a **pizzeria**.

restless adjective
The animals became restless during the storm. • agitated, nervous, anxious, edgy, fidgety, excitable, jumpy, jittery **opposite** relaxed

restore verb
1. *Please restore the book to its proper place on the shelf.* • put back, replace, return
2. *My uncle loves to restore old cars.* • renew, repair, renovate, fix, mend, rebuild
3. *They are going to restore the Sunday bus service.* • bring back, reinstate • To restore someone to health is to **cure** them.

restrain verb
1. *Dogs must be restrained on a lead in the park.* • hold back, keep back, keep under control, subdue, repress, restrict
2. *She tried to restrain her anger.* • control, curb, suppress, stifle

result noun
1. *The water shortage is a result of a long drought.* • consequence, effect, outcome, sequel (to) upshot • The result of a game is the **score**. • The result of a trial is the **verdict**.
2. *If you multiply 9 by 12, what is the result?* • answer, product

result verb
The bruising on his leg resulted from a bad fall. • come about, develop, emerge, happen, occur, follow, ensue, take place, turn out
to result in
Severe flooding resulted in chaos on the roads. • cause, bring about, give rise to, lead to, develop into

retreat verb
1. *The army retreated to a safe position.* • move back, draw back, fall back, withdraw, retire • To retreat in a shameful way is to **run away** or (informal) **turn tail**.
2. *The snail retreated into its shell.* • shrink back, recoil

retrieve verb
I had to climb the fence to retrieve our ball. • get back, bring back, fetch, recover, rescue, salvage

return verb
1. *We hope to return to Paris next summer.* • go back, revisit
2. *My husband returns on Friday.* • get back, come back, come home
3. *I returned the book to its rightful owner.* • give back, restore
4. *Faulty goods may be returned to the shop.* • send back, take back
5. *Please return the money I lent you.* • give back, repay, refund
6. *We hoped that the fever would not return.* • happen again, recur

reveal verb
1. *The spy refused to reveal his real identity.* • declare, disclose, make known, confess, admit, announce, proclaim, publish, tell
2. *She swept aside the curtain to reveal a secret door.* • uncover, unveil, expose

revenge noun
He sought revenge for the killing of his brother. • reprisal, vengeance
to take revenge on someone
He declared that he would take revenge on them all. • get even with, repay, (informal) get your own back on

review noun
1. *They are carrying out a review of after-school clubs.* • study, survey, examination, inspection
2. *We had to write reviews of our favourite books.* • report, criticism, appraisal, critique

review verb
The judge began to review the evidence. • examine, go over, study, survey, consider, assess, appraise, evaluate, weigh up

revise verb
1. *We revised the work we did last term.* • go over, review, study
2. *The new evidence forced me to revise my opinion.* • change, modify, alter, reconsider, re-examine
3. *The last chapter has been revised by the author.* • correct, amend, edit, rewrite, update

revive verb
1. *The patient revived slowly after the operation.* • come round, come to, recover, rally, wake up

2. *A cold drink will* revive *you.* • refresh, restore, invigorate, bring back to life, revitalize

revolt *verb*
1. *The people* revolted *against the cruel king.* • rebel, riot, rise up • To revolt on a ship is to **mutiny**.
2. *They were* revolted *by the stench in the dungeon.* • disgust, repel, sicken, nauseate, offend, appal

revolting *adjective*
What is that revolting *smell?* • disgusting, foul, horrible, nasty, loathsome, offensive, obnoxious, repulsive, repugnant, sickening, nauseating, vile, unpleasant **opposite** pleasant, attractive

revolution *noun*
1. *The* revolution *brought in a new government.* • rebellion, revolt, uprising
2. *Computers brought about a* revolution *in the way people work.* • change, transformation, shift
3. *One* revolution *of the earth takes 24 hours.* • rotation, turn, circuit, cycle

revolve *verb*
The earth revolves *once every 24 hours.* • rotate, turn • To revolve quickly is to **spin** or **whirl**. • To move round something is to **circle** or **orbit** it.

reward *noun*
There is a reward *for finding the missing cat.* • prize, bonus, payment, award, decoration **opposite** punishment

reward *verb*
1. *The firefighters were* rewarded *for their bravery.* • honour, decorate
2. *She was generously* rewarded *for her work.* • compensate, repay

rhythm *noun*
We tapped our feet to the rhythm *of the music.* • beat, pulse • The speed or type of rhythm of a piece of music is the **tempo**. • The type of rhythm of a piece of poetry is its **metre**.

rich *adjective*
1. *They must be* rich *to live in a castle.* • wealthy, affluent, prosperous, well-off, well-to-do **opposite** poor
2. *The palace was full of* rich *furnishings.* • expensive, costly, luxurious, sumptuous, opulent, lavish, splendid, ornate
3. *The dancer wore a dress of a* rich *red colour.* • deep, strong, vivid, intense

riches *plural noun*
They acquired riches *beyond their wildest dreams.* • wealth, money, affluence, prosperity, fortune, treasure

rickety *adjective*
Take care—that ladder looks rickety. • shaky, unsteady, unstable, wobbly, flimsy **opposite** solid

riddle *noun*
They had to solve the riddle *to find the treasure.* • puzzle, mystery, question, conundrum, problem

ride *verb* riding, rode, ridden
My little brother is learning to ride *a bike.* • control, handle, manage, steer

ride *noun*
They took us for a ride *in their new car.* • drive, run, journey, trip, (informal) spin

ridiculous *adjective*
1. *My little sister looked* ridiculous *in Mum's high-heeled shoes.* • silly, stupid, foolish, daft, absurd, funny, laughable
2. *That is a* ridiculous *price for a pair of trainers!* • ludicrous, senseless, nonsensical, preposterous, outrageous, absurd, unreasonable, crazy

right *adjective*
1. *Put up your hand if you got the* right *answer.* • correct, accurate, true, exact **opposite** wrong
2. *She was waiting for the* right *moment to tell him.* • proper, appropriate, fitting, suitable, ideal **opposite** wrong
3. *It's not* right *to steal.* • fair, honest, decent, just, honourable, lawful, moral, upright, virtuous, ethical **opposite** wrong

right *noun*
1. *The post office is on the* right *along the High Street.* **opposite** left
2. *People have the* right *to walk across the common.* • freedom, liberty
3. *You don't have the* right *to tell me what to do.* • authority, power

rim *noun*
Mrs Sharpe peered at us over the rim *of her glasses.* • brim, edge, lip, brink

ring *noun*
1. *The children danced around in a* ring. • circle, round, loop, circuit
2. *The wooden barrel had metal* rings *round it.* • band, hoop

ring *verb* ringing, rang, rung
1. *The whole area was ringed by a high fence.* • surround, encircle, enclose, circle
2. *The doorbell rang.* • chime, peal, toll, jangle, tinkle, sound, buzz
3. *Ring me tomorrow evening.* • phone, call, telephone, ring up, (*informal*) give a buzz

rinse *verb*
After shampooing your hair, rinse it in clean water. • wash, clean, bathe, swill • To rinse out a toilet is to **flush** it.

riot *noun*
The police moved in to stop the riot. • commotion, disorder, disturbance, turmoil, uproar, uprising

riot *verb*
The crowds were rioting in the streets. • run riot, run wild, run amok, rampage, revolt, rise up, rebel

ripe *adjective*
Some of the plums on the tree are ripe now. • mature, ready to eat • To become ripe is to **ripen**.

rise *verb* rising, rose, risen
1. *The kite rose high into the air.* • climb, mount, fly up, ascend, soar • When a plane rises into the air, it **takes off**. • When a rocket rises into the air, it **lifts off**. **opposite** descend
2. *The outer wall of the castle rose before us.* • tower, loom, reach up, stick up
3. *House prices rose again last year.* • go up, increase **opposite** fall
4. *The audience rose and applauded wildly.* • stand up, get up **opposite** sit

rise *noun*
There will be a rise in temperature over the next few days. • increase, jump **opposite** fall

risk *verb*
1. *If you place a bet, you risk losing the money.* • chance, dare, gamble, venture
2. *The firefighter risked his life to save them.* • endanger, put at risk, jeopardize, hazard

risk *noun*
1. *All outdoor activities carry an element of risk.* • danger, hazard, peril
2. *The forecast says there's a risk of snow.* • chance, likelihood, possibility

risky *adjective*
Cycling on icy roads is risky. • dangerous, hazardous, perilous, unsafe **opposite** safe

rival *noun*
He has no serious rival for the championship. • competitor, adversary, challenger, opponent, contender, contestant

river *noun*
• A small river is a **stream** or **rivulet** or (*Scottish*) **burn**. • A small river which flows into a larger river is a **tributary**. • The place where a river begins is its **source**. • The place where a river goes into the sea is its **mouth**. • A wide river mouth is an **estuary** or (*Scottish*) **firth**. • The place where the mouth of a river splits before going into the sea is a **delta**. • A river of ice is a **glacier**.

✏ WRITING TIPS

You can use these words to describe a **river**.

TO DESCRIBE HOW A RIVER FLOWS
• cascade, eddy, flood, gush, plunge, rush, sweep, swirl, flow, glide, meander, snake, twist, wind

TO DESCRIBE HOW A RIVER SOUNDS
• babble, burble, gurgle, murmur, ripple, roar, splash, thunder

---

roar *noun, verb*
The dragon lifted its might head and roared. • bellow, cry, yell, bawl, howl, thunder

rob *verb* robbing, robbed
The thieves planned to rob several banks in the city. • steal from, break into, burgle, hold up, raid, loot, ransack, rifle

rock *verb*
1. *I rocked the baby's cradle to and fro.* • sway, swing
2. *The ship rocked in the storm.* • roll, toss, lurch, pitch, tilt, reel

rod *noun*
The framework is held together by steel rods. • bar, rail, pole, strut, shaft, stick, spoke, staff

role *noun*
1. *Who is playing the lead role in the play?* • character, part
2. *Each player has an important role in the team.* • job, task, function, position

roll *verb*
1. *The wheels of the carriage began to roll.* • move round, turn, revolve, rotate, spin, twirl, whirl
2. *Roll the paper around your finger.* • curl, wind, wrap, twist, coil • To roll up a sail on a yacht is to **furl** it.

3. *Roll the pastry into a large circle.* • flatten, level out, smooth
4. *The ship rolled about in the storm.* • pitch, rock, sway, toss, wallow, lurch

romantic *adjective*
1. *The film had a very romantic ending.*
• sentimental, emotional, tender, (informal) soppy, mushy
2. *The life of an explorer sounds very romantic.*
• exotic, glamorous, exciting

room *noun*
1. *How many rooms are there in your house?*
• An old word for room is **chamber**.
2. *Is there room in the car for another suitcase?*
• space, capacity

WORD WEB

ROOMS YOU MIGHT FIND IN A HOUSE OR FLAT
• bathroom, bedroom, boxroom, conservatory, dining room, drawing room, hall, kitchen or kitchenette, landing, lavatory or toilet or (informal) loo, living room, lounge, nursery, pantry, parlour, scullery, sitting room, spare room or guest room, study, utility room

ROOMS YOU MIGHT FIND IN A SCHOOL
• assembly hall, classroom, cloakroom, corridor, drama room, laboratory, lavatories or toilets or (informal) loos, library, music room, office, sickroom, staffroom, storeroom • A small room in a monastery or prison is a **cell**. • An underground room is a **basement** or **cellar** or **vault**. • The space in the roof of a house is the **attic** or **loft**.
• A room where an artist works is a **studio**.
• A room where you wait to see a doctor or dentist is a **waiting room**. • A room in a boarding school where pupils sleep is a **dormitory**. • A room in a hospital for patients is a **ward**.

root *noun*
We need to get to the root of the problem.
• origin, source, cause, basis, starting point

rope *noun*
The sailors threw a rope to the men in the water. • cable, cord, line • The ropes that support a ship's mast and sails are the **rigging**. • A rope with a loop at one end used for catching cattle is a **lasso**.

rot *verb* **rotting, rotted**
The wooden fence had begun to rot. • decay, decompose, become rotten, crumble, disintegrate • If metal rots it is said to

corrode. • If rubber rots it is said to **perish**.
• If food rots it is said to **go bad** or **putrefy**.

rotten *adjective*
1. *The window frame is rotten.* • decayed, decaying, decomposed, crumbling, disintegrating • Rotten metal is **corroded** or **rusty** metal. **opposite** sound
2. *The fridge smelled of rotten eggs.* • bad, mouldy, mouldering, foul, putrid, smelly **opposite** fresh
3. *(informal) The weather has been rotten all week.* • bad, unpleasant, disagreeable, awful, abysmal, dreadful, nasty, (informal) lousy **opposite** good

rough *adjective*
1. *A rough track led to the farm.* • bumpy, uneven, irregular, rocky, stony, rugged, craggy, jagged **opposite** even, smooth
2. *The sea was rough and the boat lurched from side to side.* • stormy, turbulent, heaving
• If the sea is rough with small waves it is said to be **choppy**. **opposite** calm
3. *The woman wore a rough woollen cloak.*
• coarse, harsh, scratchy, bristly **opposite** soft
4. *The prisoners had suffered rough treatment.*
• harsh, severe, cruel, hard, tough, violent **opposite** gentle, mild
5. *I had only a rough idea of where we were.*
• approximate, vague, inexact, imprecise, hazy **opposite** exact
6. *Our guide made a rough sketch of the route.*
• quick, hasty, crude, basic **opposite** detailed, careful

round *adjective*
Holly bushes have small round berries.
• rounded, spherical • A flat round shape is **circular**.

round *noun*
Our team got through to the second round of the competition. • stage, heat, bout, contest, game

round *verb*
The motorbike rounded the corner at top speed. • go round, travel round, turn
to round something off
They rounded the evening off with some songs. • bring to an end, conclude, end, finish, complete
to round up people or things
The captain rounded up his players.
• assemble, gather, bring together, collect, muster, rally

route *noun*
We drove home by the quickest route. • path, road, way, course, direction, journey

routine *noun*
1. *Brushing my teeth is part of my morning routine.* • pattern, procedure, way, custom, habit, practice, order
2. *The ice skaters practised their new routine.* • act, programme, performance, number

row *noun*
1. *The gardener planted the vegetables in rows.* (rhymes with *go*) • column, line, string, series, sequence • A row of people waiting for something is a **queue**. • A row of people walking behind each other is a **file**. • A row of soldiers standing side by side on parade is a **rank**.
2. *The class next door was making a terrible row.* (rhymes with *cow*) • noise, racket, din, commotion, disturbance, uproar, rumpus
3. *One of the pirates had a row with the captain.* (rhymes with *cow*) • argument, fight, quarrel, squabble, disagreement, dispute

rowdy *adjective* **rowdier, rowdiest**
Later in the evening, the party became rowdy. • noisy, unruly, wild, disorderly, boisterous, riotous **opposite** quiet

royalty *noun*

WORD WEB

SOME MEMBERS OF A ROYAL FAMILY
• king, queen, prince, princess

SOME OTHER WORDS FOR A KING OR QUEEN
• monarch, sovereign • The husband or wife of a king or queen is their **consort**.
• A person who rules when a king or queen is too young or too ill is a **regent**.

rub *verb* **rubbing, rubbed**
1. *Kathy rubbed her sore elbow.* • stroke, knead, massage
2. *I rubbed some suncream on my arms.* • spead, smooth, smear, apply (to)
3. *These boots are rubbing against my ankles.* • graze, scrape, chafe
4. *She rubbed the mirror until it gleamed.* • polish, wipe, shine, buff
to rub something out
Can you rub out those pencil marks? • erase, wipe out, delete, remove

rubbish *noun*
1. *Mike took the rubbish out to the bin.* • refuse, waste, trash, garbage, junk, litter, scrap
2. *Don't talk rubbish!* • nonsense, drivel, balderdash, piffle, gibberish, claptrap, gobbledegook, *(informal)* rot, tripe, twaddle

rude *adjective*
1. *It's very rude to talk with your mouth full.* • impolite, discourteous, disrespectful, impertinent, impudent, insolent, offensive, insulting, bad-mannered, ill-bred • To be rude to someone is to **insult** or **snub** them. • To be rude about sacred things is to be **blasphemous** or **irreverent. opposite** polite
2. *Some of the jokes in the film are rather rude.* • indecent, improper, offensive, coarse, crude **opposite** decent, clean

ruin *verb*
The storm had ruined the farmer's crops. • damage, destroy, spoil, wreck, devastate, demolish, lay waste, shatter

ruin *noun*
When they lost the match, it was the ruin of their dream. • collapse, failure, breakdown • Financial ruin is **bankruptcy**.

ruins *plural noun*
Archaeologists have discovered the ruins of a Roman fort. • remains, remnants, fragments

rule *noun*
1. *Players must stick to the rules of the game.* • law, regulation, principle • A set of rules is a **code**.
2. *The country was formerly under French rule.* • control, authority, command, power, government, reign

rule *verb*
1. *The Romans ruled a vast empire.* • command, govern, control, direct, lead, manage, run, administer
2. *Queen Victoria continued to rule for many years.* • reign, be ruler

3. *The umpire ruled that the batsman was out.* • judge, decree, pronounce, decide, determine, find

ruler *noun*

WORD WEB

SOME KINDS OF RULER
• emperor, empress, governor, king, queen, president, sultan

SOME RULERS IN PAST TIMES
• Caesar, pharaohr, rajah, tsar, tsarina • The leader of a country is the **head of state**.

rumour *noun*
There was a rumour that the queen was a witch in disguise. • gossip, hearsay, talk, *(informal)* tittle-tattle

run *verb* **running, ran, run**
1. *We ran as fast as our legs could carry us.*
• race, sprint, dash, tear, bolt, career, speed, hurry, rush, streak, fly, whiz, zoom, scurry, scamper, scoot • To run at a gentle pace is to **jog**. • When a horse runs, it **gallops, canters** or **trots**
2. *Tears ran down the mermaid's cheeks.*
• stream, flow, pour, gush, flood, cascade, spill, trickle, dribble, leak
3. *That old sewing machine still runs well.*
• function, operate, work, go, perform

4. *My uncle runs a restaurant in Leeds.*
• manage, be in charge of, direct, control, supervise, govern, rule
5. *The High Street runs through the city centre.*
• pass, go, extend, stretch, reach
to run away or **off**
The thieves ran off when they heard footsteps.
• bolt, fly, flee, escape, take off, hurry off, *(informal)* make off, clear off, scarper
to run into
1. *Guess who I ran into the other day?* • meet, come across, encounter, *(informal)* bump into
2. *A cyclist skidded and ran into a tree.* • hit, collide with

run *noun*
1. *She goes for a run in the park every morning.*
• A fast run is a **dash, gallop, race** or **sprint**.
• A gentle run is a **jog**.
2. *We went for a run in the car.* • drive, journey, ride
3. *They've had a run of good luck recently.*
• sequence, stretch, series

runny *adjective* **runnier, runniest**
This custard is too runny. • watery, thin, liquid, fluid **opposite** thick

rural *adjective*
They live in a peaceful rural area. • country, rustic, agricultural, pastoral **opposite** urban

rush *verb*
I rushed home with the good news. • hurry, hasten, race, run, dash, fly, bolt, charge, shoot, speed, sprint, tear, zoom • When cattle or other animals rush along together they **stampede**.

rush *noun*
1. *We've got plenty of time, so what's the rush?*
• hurry, haste, urgency
2. *There was a sudden rush of water.* • flood, gush, spurt, stream, spate

ruthless *adjective*
The pirates launched a ruthless attack. • cruel, brutal, bloodthirsty, barbaric, heartless, pitiless, merciless, callous, ferocious, fierce, savage, vicious, violent **opposite** merciful

Synonyms are words which mean the same or almost the same, as each other. A thesaurus is a treasure trove of synonyms.

sack verb
The manager was *sacked*. • dismiss, discharge, (informal) fire, give you the sack

sacred adjective
The Koran is a *sacred* book. • holy, religious, divine, heavenly

sacrifice verb
I *sacrificed* my lunch break to practise guitar. • give up, surrender, go without

sad adjective sadder, saddest

! **OVERUSED WORD**

Try to vary the words you use for **sad**. Here are some other words you could use.

FOR A SAD MOOD OR SAD PERSON
• unhappy, sorrowful, miserable, depressed, downcast, downhearted, despondent, crestfallen, dismal, gloomy, glum, blue, low, dejected, forlorn, desolate, doleful, wretched, woeful, woebegone, tearful, heartbroken, broken-hearted
Mia felt *miserable* when her best friend moved away. • If you are sad because you are away from home, you are **homesick**.

FOR A SAD STORY OR SAD TUNE
• melancholy, mournful, moving, touching, plaintive, wistful, depressing
He related the *mournful* tale of Billy Bones.

FOR A SAD SITUATION OR SAD NEWS
• grave, grievous, grim, tragic, painful, serious, regrettable, unfortunate, unpleasant
It was a *tragic* accident.

FOR SOMETHING THAT MAKES YOU FEEL SAD
• upsetting, distressing, heartbreaking, heart-rending, pathetic, pitiful
It was *upsetting* to watch the injured bird.
opposite happy

sadden verb
The news of her friend's illness *saddened* her. • distress, upset, depress, grieve, disappoint, (informal) break your heart
opposite cheer up

safe adjective
1. The kitten was found *safe* and well in a neighbour's garden. • unharmed, unhurt, uninjured, undamaged, sound, intact, (informal) in one piece **opposite** hurt, damaged
2. They felt *safe* indoors as the storm raged outside. • protected, guarded, defended, secure **opposite** vulnerable
3. The secret code is in *safe* hands. • reliable, trustworthy, dependable
4. Is the tap water *safe* to drink?
• harmless, uncontaminated, innocuous **opposite** dangerous

safety noun
You must wear a seat belt for your own *safety*. • protection, security, well-being **opposite** danger

sag verb sagging, sagged
The sandwich was so full that it *sagged* in the middle. • sink, dip, droop, flop, slump

sail verb
We *sailed* to Norway rather than going by air. • travel by ship • To have a holiday sailing on a ship is to **cruise**. • To begin a sea voyage is to **put to sea** or **set sail**.

sailor noun
The crew comprised three *sailors* and a cook. • seaman, seafarer, mariner, boatman
• A person who sails a yacht is a **yachtsman** or **yachtswoman**.

salary noun salaries
The job has an annual *salary* of £30,000.
• income, pay, earnings • If your pay is paid week by week, it is called **wages**.

same adjective
the same
1. Each pirate was given *the same* ration of rum. • equal, identical, equivalent
2. Everyone in the choir wore *the same* outfit.
• matching, similar, alike, uniform

3. Her feelings have remained *the same*.
• unaltered, unchanged, constant
opposite different

sarcastic *adjective*
He made a sarcastic remark about my hat.
• mocking, satirical, ironical, sneering, taunting

satisfaction *noun*
My grandfather gets a lot of satisfaction from growing vegetables. • happiness, pleasure, enjoyment, contentment, fulfilment, sense of achievement, pride
opposite dissatisfaction

satisfactory *adjective*
I'm afraid your latest essay is not satisfactory.
• acceptable, adequate, passable, good enough, tolerable, competent, *(informal)* all right, up to scratch **opposite** unsatisfactory

satisfied *adjective*
My teachers said they were extremely satisfied with my progress. • content, contented, pleased, happy

satisfy *verb* satisfies, satisfying, satisfied
Nothing satisfies him—he's always complaining. • please, content, make you happy • To satisfy your thirst is to **quench** or **slake** it. **opposite** dissatisfy

savage *adjective*
1. *The invaders launched a savage attack on the town.* • vicious, cruel, barbaric, brutal, bloodthirsty, pitiless, ruthless, merciless, inhuman **opposite** humane
2. *A savage beast is said to live in the cave.* • untamed, wild, ferocious, fierce
opposite domesticated

save *verb*
1. *They managed to save most of the books from the fire.* • rescue, recover, retrieve, salvage
2. *The knight pledged to save the princess from the witch's curse.* • protect, defend, guard, shield, preserve
3. *She saved him from making a fool of himself.* • stop, prevent, deter
4. *I saved you a piece of my birthday cake.* • keep, reserve, set aside, hold on to
5. *If you share a car, then you can save petrol.* • be sparing with, conserve, use wisely

say *verb* saying, said
1. *He found it hard to say what he meant.* • express, communicate, put into words, convey
2. *I would like to say a few words before we start.* • utter, speak, recite, read

---

! OVERUSED WORD

Try to vary the words you use for **say**, especially in direct speech. Here are some other words you could use.

TO SAY LOUDLY
• call, cry, exclaim, bellow, bawl, shout, yell, roar
'Land ahoy!' bellowed the cabin boy.

TO SAY QUIETLY
• whisper, mumble, mutter
'That woman,' I whispered, 'is a secret agent.'

TO SAY STRONGLY
• state, announce, assert, declare, pronounce, insist, maintain, profess
'I never cut my toenails,' the ogre declared.

TO SAY CASUALLY
• remark, comment, observe, note, mention
'It's very warm for this time of year,' Mr Lewis remarked.

TO SAY ANGRILY
• snap, snarl, growl, thunder, bark, rasp, rant, rave
'Give me that piece of paper!' snapped Miss Crabbit.

TO SAY SUDDENLY
• blurt out
'That's just a pretend dinosaur!' Ben blurted out.

TO SAY UNCLEARLY
• babble, burble, gabble, stammer, stutter
The stranger kept babbling about hidden treasure.

TO SAY IN SURPRISE OR ALARM
• gasp, cry, squeal
'The tunnel is sealed! There's no way out!' gasped Alex.

TO SAY SOMETHING FUNNY
• joke, quip, tease
'Were you singing? I thought it was a cat,' teased my big sister.

TO GIVE AN ORDER
• command, demand, order
A voice outside demanded, 'Open the door at once!'

TO ASK A QUESTION
• enquire, demand, query
'How do you spell your name?' the judge enquired.

TO GIVE A REPLY
• answer, reply, respond, retort
'Certainly not!' retorted Lady Dimsley.

TO MAKE A REQUEST
• beg, entreat, implore, plead, urge
The mouse pleaded, 'Please let go of my tail!'

TO MAKE A SUGGESTION
• suggest, propose
'Let's make them walk the plank,' suggested Captain Hook.

TO SAY AGAIN
• repeat, reiterate, echo
The Martians repeated, 'Take us to your leader!'

saying noun
'Many hands make light work' is a common saying. • expression, phrase, motto, proverb, catchphrase • An overused saying is a **cliché**.

scan verb scanning, scanned
1. *The lookout scanned the horizon, hoping to see land.* • search, study, survey, examine, scrutinize, stare at, eye
2. *I scanned through some magazines in the waiting room.* • skim, glance at, flick through

scandal noun
1. *The waste of food after the party was a scandal.* • disgrace, embarrassment, shame, outrage
2. *Some newspapers like to publish the latest scandal.* • gossip, rumours, dirt

scar noun
The warrior had a scar across his forehead. • mark, blemish, wound

scar verb scarring, scarred
The injuries he received scarred him for life. • mark, disfigure, deface

scarce adjective
Water is very scarce in the desert. • hard to find, in short supply, lacking, sparse, scanty, rare, uncommon, (informal) thin on the ground **opposite** plentiful

scarcely adverb
She was so tired that she could scarcely walk. • barely, hardly, only just

scare noun
The explosion gave them a nasty scare. • fright, shock, alarm

scare verb
My brother tried to scare us by making ghost noises. • frighten, terrify, petrify, alarm, startle, panic **opposite** reassure

scared adjective
When she heard the footsteps, Lily was too scared to move. • frightened, terrified, petrified, horrified, alarmed, fearful, panicky

scary adjective scarier, scariest (informal)
I had to close my eyes at the scary bits in the film. • frightening, terrifying, horrifying, alarming, nightmarish, fearsome, chilling, spine-chilling, hair-raising, bloodcurdling, chilling, eerie, sinister

scatter verb
1. *She scattered the seeds on the ground.* • spread, sprinkle, sow, strew, throw about, shower **opposite** collect
2. *The animals scattered when the children ran towards them.* • break up, separate, disperse, disband **opposite** gather

scene noun
1. *The police arrived quickly at the scene of the crime.* • location, position, site, place, situation, spot
2. *They were rehearsing a scene from the play.* • episode, part, section, act
3. *I gazed out of the window at the moonlit scene.* • landscape, scenery, view, sight, outlook, prospect, spectacle, setting, backdrop
4. *He didn't want to create a scene in the restaurant.* • fuss, commotion, disturbance, quarrel, row

scenery noun
We admired the scenery from the top of the hill. • landscape, outlook, prospect, scene, view, panorama

scent noun
Rowena loves the scent of roses. • smell, fragrance, perfume, aroma

schedule noun
The athletes had a rigorous training schedule. • programme, timetable, plan, calendar, diary • A schedule of topics to be discussed at a meeting is an **agenda**. • A schedule of places to be visited on a journey is an **itinerary**.

scheme noun
They worked out a scheme to raise some money. • plan, proposal, project, procedure, method, system

scheme verb
The smugglers were scheming against each other. • plot, conspire, intrigue

scold *verb*
He scolded the paper boy for being late.
• reprimand, reproach, tell off,
(*informal*) tick off

scoop *verb*
We scooped out a moat for our sandcastle.
• dig, gouge, scrape, excavate, hollow

scope *noun*
1. *The park offers plenty of scope for children to play.* • opportunity, room, space, freedom, liberty
2. *These things are outside the scope of the project.* • range, extent, limit, reach, span

scorch *verb*
The dragon's breath scorched the wizard's beard. • burn, singe, sear, blacken, char

score *noun*
We added up each other's scores. • marks, points, total • The final score is the **result**.

score *verb*
1. *How many goals did you score?* • win, get, make, gain, earn
2. *Some lines were scored into the bark of the tree.* • cut, gouge, mark, scrape, scratch

scorn *noun*
She dismissed my suggestion with scorn.
• contempt, derision, disrespect, mockery, ridicule **opposite** admiration

scowl *verb*
The witch scowled under her floppy black hat.
• frown, glower

scramble *verb*
1. *The smugglers escaped by scrambling over the rocks.* • clamber, climb, crawl, scrabble
2. *The children scrambled to get the best seats.* • push, jostle, struggle, fight, scuffle

scrap *noun*
1. *They fed the scraps of food to the birds.*
• bit, piece, fragment, morsel, crumb, speck, particle
2. *He took a pile of scrap to the tip.* • rubbish, waste, junk, refuse, litter • Scraps of cloth are **rags** or **shreds**.
3. (*informal*) *There was a scrap between the two gangs.* • fight, brawl, scuffle, tussle, squabble

scrap *verb* scrapping, scrapped
The author scrapped the last paragraph.
• discard, throw away, abandon, cancel, drop, give up, (*informal*) dump

scrape *verb*
1. *She scraped her knee when she fell over.*
• graze, scratch, scuff
2. *I tried to scrape the mud off my trainers.*
• rub, scour, scrub, clean

scratch *verb*
1. *Someone scratched the side of the car.*
• mark, score, scrape, gouge, graze
2. *The cat tried to scratch her.* • claw

scratch *noun*
Who made this scratch on the side of the car?
• gash, groove, line, mark, scrape

scream *noun, verb*
A woman ran out of the house screaming.
We heard a woman's scream in the distance.
• shriek, screech, shout, yell, cry, bawl, howl, wail, squeal, yelp

screen *noun*
The room was divided into two by a screen.
• curtain, partition, divider

screen *verb*
Miss Bennett used a parasol to screen her from the sun. • shield, protect, shelter, shade, cover, hide, mask, veil

scribble *verb*
He scribbled his phone number on a scrap of paper. • scrawl, jot down, dash off, write • To scribble a rough drawing, especially when you are bored, is to **doodle**.

scrub *verb* scrubbing, scrubbed
She scrubbed the floor clean. • rub, brush, clean, wash, scour

scruffy *adjective* scruffier, scruffiest
Magnus wore an old jumper and scruffy jeans.
• untidy, messy, ragged, tatty, tattered, worn-out, shabby **opposite** smart

sculpture *noun*
The temple was full of marble sculptures.
• carving, figure, statue

sea *noun*

WORD WEB

• The very large seas of the world are called **oceans**. • An area of sea partly enclosed by land is a **bay** or **gulf**. • A wide inlet of the sea is a **sound**. • A wide inlet where a river joins the sea is an **estuary** or (in Scotland) a **firth**. • A narrow stretch of water linking two seas is a **strait**. • The bottom of the sea is the **seabed**. • The land near the sea is the coast or the **seashore**. • Creatures that live in the sea are **marine** creatures.

THINGS YOU MIGHT SEE ON THE SEA
• breaker, iceberg, sea spray, surf, swell, waves; boat, cruise ship, ocean liner, yacht

SOME CREATURES THAT LIVE IN THE SEA
• dolphin, eel, fish, killer whale, octopus, porpoise, seahorse, seal, sea lion, shark, squid, stingray, turtle, whale

WRITING TIPS

You can use these words to describe the sea.

TO DESCRIBE A CALM SEA
• calm, crystal clear, glassy, sparkling, tranquil, unruffled

TO DESCRIBE A ROUGH SEA
• choppy, raging, rough, stormy, tempestuous, turbulent, wild

WAVES ON THE SEA MIGHT
• billow, break, crash, heave, pound, roll, surge, swell, tumble, wash

seal *verb*
The entrance to the burial chamber had been sealed. • close, fasten, shut, lock, secure • To seal a leak is to **plug** it or **stop** it.

search *verb*
1. *He was searching for the book he had lost.*
• hunt, look, seek • To search for gold or some other mineral is to **prospect**.
2. *The police searched the house but didn't find anything.* • explore; scour, ransack, rummage through, comb
3. *Security staff searched all the passengers.*
• check, inspect, examine, scrutinize, *(informal)* frisk

search *noun*
After a long search, she found her keys. • hunt, look, check • A long journey in search of something is a **quest**.

seashore *noun*

WORD WEB

We explored the seashore, looking for shells and fossils. • seaside, beach, shore, coast

THINGS YOU MIGHT SEE ON THE SEASHORE
• cave, cliff, coral reef, driftwood, dunes, lighthouse, mudflats, pebbles, rock pool, rocks, sand, seashell, seaweed, shingle

CREATURES THAT LIVE ON THE SEASHORE
• barnacle, clam, cockle, coral, crab, cuttlefish, jellyfish, limpet, mussel, oyster, prawn, razor shell, sea anemone, sea bird, seagull, sea urchin, shrimp, sponge, starfish, whelk

seaside *noun*

WORD WEB

If it's sunny tomorrow, we might go to the seaside. • beach, sands, seashore

THINGS YOU MIGHT SEE AT THE SEASIDE
• beach huts, funfair, harbour, ice cream van, jetty, pier, promenade • A town where you go to have fun by the sea is a **seaside resort**.

THINGS YOU MIGHT TAKE TO THE SEASIDE
• beach ball, bucket and spade, deckchair, fishing net, snorkel, suncream, sunglasses, sunhat, sunshade, surfboard, surfsuit, swimming costume, towel, windbreak

THINGS YOU MIGHT DO AT THE SEASIDE
• ball games, beachcombing, building sandcastles, collecting shells, fishing, paddling, scuba diving, snorkelling, sunbathing, surfing, swimming, water-skiing, windsurfing

season *noun*
The hotels are full during the holiday *season*.
• period, time

seat *noun*
We found two empty *seats* at the back of the cinema. • chair, place • A long seat for more than one person is a **bench**. • A long wooden seat in a church is a **pew**. • A seat on a bicycle or horse is a **saddle**. • A special seat for a king or queen is a **throne**.

second *adjective*
Would anyone like a *second* helping of pudding? • another, additional, extra, further

second *noun*
1. *The magic potion only takes a second to work.* • instant, moment, flash, (informal) jiffy, tick
2. *Inga was second in the cross-country race.*
• runner-up

second *verb*
We need someone to *second* the proposal.
• back, support

secret *adjective*
1. *The spy managed to get hold of a secret document.* • confidential, classified, restricted, (informal) hush-hush
2. *The detectives are part of a secret operation.* • undercover, covert
3. *The things I write in my diary are secret.*
• private, confidential, personal, intimate
4. *The cook showed us a secret passageway into the castle.* • hidden, concealed, disguised

secretive *adjective*
Why is she being so *secretive* about her past?
• uncommunicative, tight-lipped, reticent,

reserved, mysterious, quiet, (informal) cagey
opposite communicative, open

section *noun*
The website has a special *section* aimed at children. • part, division, sector, portion, segment, bit, fragment • A section of a book is a **chapter**. • A section from a piece of classical music is a **movement**. • A section taken from a book or a long piece of music is a **passage**.
• A section of a journey is a **stage**.

secure *adjective*
1. *The ladder was not very secure.* • steady, firm, solid, fixed, fast, immovable
2. *She is still trying to find a secure job.*
• permanent, regular, steady
3. *They bolted the doors to make the castle secure.* • safe, guarded, protected, defended

see *verb* seeing, saw, seen
1. *If you look closely, you might see a dragonfly.* • catch sight of, spot, notice, observe, make out, distinguish, note, perceive, recognize, sight, spy • To see something briefly is to **glimpse** it. • To see an accident or some unusual event is to **witness** it.
2. *Did you see the news yesterday?* • watch, look at, view
3. *You may see me in my office after work.*
• go to, report to
4. *I didn't expect to see you here!* • meet, run into, encounter, (informal) bump into
5. *Will we have time to see them on the way home?* • visit, call on, drop in on
6. *I see what you mean.* • understand, appreciate, comprehend, follow, grasp, realize, take in
7. *I find it hard to see him in the role of Peter Pan.* • imagine, picture, visualize
8. *Please see that the windows are shut.*
• make sure, make certain, ensure
9. *I'll see what I can do.* • think about, consider, ponder, reflect on, weigh up
10. *I'll see you to the door.* • conduct, escort, accompany, guide, lead, take

seek *verb* seeking, sought
1. *For many years he sought his long-lost brother.* • search for, hunt for, look for
2. *The king sought only to make his daughter happy.* • try, attempt, strive, want, wish, desire

seem *verb*
Everything *seems* to be all right. She is far more friendly than she *seems*. • appear, look, give the impression of being

segment noun
Divide the orange into segments. • section, portion, piece, part, bit, wedge, slice

seize verb
1. *The climber stretched out to seize the rope.* • grab, catch, snatch, take hold of, grasp, grip, clutch
2. *The police seized the robbers as they left the bank.* • arrest, capture, (informal) collar, nab • To seize someone's property as a punishment is to **confiscate** it. • To seize someone's power or position is to **usurp** it. • To seize an aircraft or vehicle during a journey is to **hijack** it.

seldom adverb
It seldom rains in the desert. • rarely, infrequently **opposite** often

select verb
They had to select a new captain. • choose, pick, decide on, opt for, settle on, appoint, elect

selection noun
The shop has a wide selection of phones. • choice, range, variety, assortment

selfish adjective
He's so selfish that he kept all the chocolate to himself. • greedy, mean, miserly, grasping, self-centred, thoughtless **opposite** unselfish, generous

sell verb selling, sold
The corner shop sells newspapers and sweets. • deal in, trade in, stock, retail • Uncomplimentary synonyms are **peddle** and **hawk**. **opposite** buy

send verb sending, sent
1. *I sent each of my friends a postcard.* • post, mail, dispatch
2. *They plan to send a rocket to Mars.* • launch, propel, direct, fire, shoot
to send for someone
I think we should send for a doctor. • call, summon, fetch
to send something out
The device was sending out weird noises. • emit, issue, give off, discharge

sensation noun
1. *She had a tingling sensation in her fingers.* • feeling, sense
2. *The unexpected news caused a sensation.* • excitement, thrill • A sensation caused by something bad is an **outrage** or a **scandal**.

sensational adjective
1. *The newspaper printed a sensational account of the murder.* • shocking, horrifying, startling, lurid
2. *(informal) Did you hear the sensational result of yesterday's match?* • amazing, extraordinary, remarkable, fantastic, spectacular, stupendous

sense noun
1. *A baby learns about the world through its senses.* • Your five senses are **hearing**, **sight**, **smell**, **taste** and **touch**.
2. *A drummer needs to have a good sense of rhythm.* • awareness, consciousness, perception, feeling (for)
3. *If you had any sense you'd stay at home.* • common sense, intelligence, wisdom, wit, brains
4. *The sense of the word is not clear.* • meaning, significance, import
to make sense of something
They couldn't make sense of the garbled message. • understand, make out, interpret, follow

sense verb
1. *He sensed that she didn't like him.* • be aware, realize, perceive, feel, guess, notice, suspect
2. *The device senses any change of temperature.* • detect, respond to

sensible adjective
1. *It would be sensible to wait until the weather improves.* • wise, intelligent, shrewd, rational, reasonable, careful, prudent, logical, sane, sound **opposite** stupid
2. *You will need sensible shoes for the hiking trip.* • comfortable, practical **opposite** impractical

sensitive adjective
1. *She has sensitive skin which gets sunburnt.* • delicate, tender, fine, soft
2. *Take care what you say—he's very sensitive.* • easily offended, easily upset, touchy
3. *She's very sensitive towards other people.* • tactful, considerate, thoughtful, sympathetic, understanding

sentence verb
The judge sentenced him to five years in prison. • pass judgement on, pronounce sentence on, condemn

sentimental adjective
1. *He gets sentimental looking at old photographs.* • emotional, nostalgic, tearful

2. *I hate sentimental messages on birthday cards.* • romantic, tender, (informal) soppy, mushy

separate *adjective*
1. *The zoo kept the male lions separate from the cubs.* • apart, separated, distinct, independent **opposite** together
2. *They slept in separate rooms.* • different, detached, unattached **opposite** attached, joined

separate *verb*
1. *The sheepdog separated the sheep from the lambs.* • cut off, divide, fence off, isolate, keep apart, remove, segregate, set apart, take away • To separate something which is connected to something else is to **detach** or **disconnect** it. • To separate things which are tangled together is to **disentangle** them. **opposite** combine, mix
2. *They walked along together until their paths separated.* • split, branch, fork **opposite** merge
3. *Her friend's parents have separated.* • split up, break up, part company • To end a marriage legally is to **divorce**.

sequence *noun*
The detective tried to piece together the sequence of events. • order, progression, series, succession, string, chain, train

series *noun* series
1. *We had to answer a series of questions in our exam.* • succession, sequence, string, set, chain, train
2. *Are you watching the new series on TV?* • serial

serious *adjective*
1. *His serious expression told them something was wrong.* • solemn, sombre, unsmiling, grave, grim **opposite** cheerful
2. *She is writing a serious book about global warming.* • learned, intellectual, scholarly, (informal) heavy **opposite** light
3. *Are you serious about wanting to learn to ski?* • sincere, genuine, in earnest
4. *This hospital ward is for people with serious injuries.* • severe, acute, critical, bad, terrible, appalling, dreadful, major, grave **opposite** minor, trivial

servant *noun*
This part of the house was where the servants lived. • attendant, retainer, helper, domestic, manservant, maid • The chief manservant in a private house is a **butler**. • The servant of a medieval knight was a **page** or **squire**.

serve *verb*
1. *The shopkeeper was busy serving customers.* • help, assist, aid
2. *When everyone had sat down they served the first course.* • give out, dish up, pass round, distribute

service *noun*
1. *The genie bowed and said he was glad to be of service.* • help, assistance, aid, use, usefulness, benefit
2. *Their marriage service was held in the local church.* • ceremony, ritual, rite • A service in church is a meeting for **worship**.
3. *Mum says her car needs a service.* • a check-over, maintenance, servicing

service *verb*
The garage serviced her car. • maintain, check, repair, mend, overhaul

session *noun*
We have a training session on Saturday mornings. • period, time

set *verb* setting, set
1. *The removal men set the piano on the floor.* • place, put, stand, position
2. *I helped Dad to set the table.* • arrange, lay, set out
3. *Have they set a date for the wedding yet?* • appoint, specify, name, decide, determine, choose, fix, establish, settle
4. *The jelly will set quicker in the fridge.* • become firm, solidify, harden, stiffen
5. *The sun was just beginning to set.* • go down, sink
to set off
1. *The knights set off on their quest.* • depart, get going, leave, set out, start out
2. *The burnt toast set off the smoke alarm.* • activate, start, trigger
to set something out
The information is clearly set out on the page. • lay out, arrange, display, present
to set something up
They're trying to set up an after-school club. • establish, create, start, begin, introduce, organize

set *noun*
1. *There is a set of measuring spoons in the drawer.* • collection, batch, kit
2. *Our class painted the set for the play.* • scenery, setting

setting *noun*
The house stood in a rural setting. • surroundings, location, place, position, site, background

settle verb

1. *The brothers tried to settle their differences.*
• resolve, sort out, deal with, end
2. *The cat had just settled on the sofa.*
• sit down, relax, rest
3. *A robin settled on a nearby branch.* • land, alight
4. *The family is planning to settle in Canada.*
• emigrate (to), move (to), set up home
5. *You can see lots of fish when the mud settles.* • sink to the bottom, clear, subside
6. *We'll settle the hotel bill in the morning.*
• pay, clear, square

to settle on
Have you settled on a date for the wedding?
• agree on, decide on, choose, name, fix

settler noun

The film is about early European settlers in America. • colonist, immigrant, pioneer

severe adjective

1. *The jailer was very severe with the prisoners.*
• harsh, strict, hard, stern **opposite** lenient
2. *The traffic warden gave him a severe look.*
• unkind, unsympathetic, disapproving, grim
opposite kind
3. *Ruby has a severe case of chickenpox.* • bad, serious, acute, grave **opposite** mild
4. *The Arctic has a severe climate.* • extreme, tough, harsh, hostile • A severe frost is a **sharp** frost. • Severe cold is **intense** cold.
• A severe storm is a **violent** storm.

shabby adjective shabbier, shabbiest

The witch disguised herself in a shabby cloak.
• ragged, scruffy, tattered, worn, worn-out, threadbare, frayed, tatty, seedy, dingy
opposite smart

shade noun

1. *They sat in the shade of a chestnut tree.*
• shadow
2. *The porch had a shade to keep out the sun.*
• screen, blind, canopy • A type of umbrella used as a sun shade is a **parasol**.
3. *The bathroom walls are a pale shade of blue.*
• hue, tinge, tint, tone, colour

shade verb

Wearing a cap will shade your eyes from the sun. • shield, screen, protect, hide, mask

shadow noun

Her face was deep in shadow. • shade, darkness, gloom

shadow verb

The detective was shadowing the suspect.
• follow, pursue, tail, stalk, track, trail

shady adjective shadier, shadiest

1. *They found a shady spot under a tree.*
• shaded, shadowy, sheltered, dark, sunless
opposite sunny
2. *He took part in some shady business deals.*
• dishonest, disreputable, suspicious, dubious, suspect, untrustworthy, (informal) fishy, dodgy **opposite** honest

shaggy adjective shaggier, shaggiest

Llamas have long shaggy coats. • bushy, woolly, fleecy, hairy, thick

shake verb shaking, shook, shaken

1. *The hurricane made the whole house shake.*
• quake, shudder, shiver, rock, sway, totter, wobble, quiver, vibrate, rattle
2. *He was so upset that his voice was shaking.*
• tremble, quaver
3. *The giant shook his fist and growled angrily.*
• wave, brandish, flourish, wag, waggle, joggle
4. *They were shaken by the terrible news.*
• shock, startle, distress, upset, disturb, alarm, frighten

shaky adjective shakier, shakiest

1. *Be careful—the table is rather shaky.*
• unsteady, wobbly, insecure, rickety, flimsy, weak
2. *He was so nervous that his hands were shaky.* • shaking, trembling, quivering
3. *He spoke in a shaky voice.* • quavering, faltering, nervous, tremulous **opposite** steady

shallow adjective

The children paddled about in the shallow water. **opposite** deep

shame noun

The guilty man hung his head in shame.
• disgrace, dishonour, humiliation, embarrassment, guilt

a shame
It's a shame that you can't stay for longer.
• a pity, unfortunate

shape verb

The potter shaped the clay into a tall vase.
• form, mould, fashion • To shape something in a mould is to **cast** it.

shape noun

The cake was in the shape of a star. • form, figure • A line showing the shape of something is an **outline**. • A dark outline seen against a light background is a **silhouette**.
• A container for making things in a special shape is a **mould**.

share *noun*
Each of the pirates got a share of rum. • ration, allowance, portion, quota, helping, division, part, (informal) cut

share *verb*
The robbers shared the loot between them.
• divide, split, distribute, allot, allocate, deal out, ration out

shatter *verb*
1. *The ball shattered a window.* • break, smash, destroy, wreck
2. *The windscreen shattered when a stone hit it.* • break, splinter, disintegrate

shed *noun*
They kept their lawnmower in the garden shed.
• hut, shack, outhouse

shed *verb* **shedding, shed**
A lorry shed its load on the motorway. • drop, let fall, spill, scatter

sheen *noun*
He waxed the table to give it a nice sheen.
• shine, polish, gloss, gleam, lustre

sheep *noun* **sheep**
• A male sheep is a **ram**. • A female sheep is a **ewe**. • A young sheep is a **lamb**. • The woolly coat of a sheep is its **fleece**. • Meat from a sheep is **lamb** or **mutton**.

sheer *adjective*
1. *The story he told was sheer nonsense.*
• complete, total, utter, absolute, pure
2. *Don't try to climb that sheer cliff.* • vertical, perpendicular

sheet *noun*
1. *She started her diary on a fresh sheet of paper.* • page, leaf, piece
2. *The pond was covered with a thin sheet of ice.* • layer, film, covering, surface
3. *The glazier came to fit a new sheet of glass.* • panel, pane, plate

shelf *noun* **shelves**
She put the books back on the shelf.
• ledge, rack • A shelf above a fireplace is a **mantelpiece**.

shell *noun*
Tortoises have hard shells. • covering, case, casing, outside, exterior

shelter *noun*
They reached shelter just before the storm broke. • cover, protection, safety, refuge, sanctuary

shelter *verb*
1. *The hedge shelters the garden from the wind.* • protect, screen, shield, guard, defend, safeguard
2. *We sheltered from the rain under the trees.* • hide, take refuge

shield *noun*
The trees act as an effective wind shield.
• screen, barrier, defence, guard, protection
• The part of a helmet that shields your face is the **visor**.

shield *verb*
The mother bear shielded her cubs from danger. • protect, defend, guard, safeguard, keep safe, shelter

shift *verb*
1. *I need some help to shift the furniture.*
• move, rearrange, reposition
2. *It was hard work shifting the mud off the tyres.* • remove, dislodge, budge

shine *verb* **shining, shone, shined**
1. *A light shone from an upstairs window.*
• beam, glow, blaze, glare, gleam
2. *He shines his shoes every morning.* • polish, rub, brush

shiny *adjective* **shinier, shiniest**
She polished the mirror until it was shiny.
• shining, bright, gleaming, glistening, glossy, polished, burnished, lustrous **opposite** dull

ship *noun*
• Ships that travel long distances at sea are **ocean-going** or **seagoing** ships. • People who work on ships at sea are **nautical** or **seafaring** people.

shiver *verb*
Ali waited outside, shivering with cold.
• tremble, quiver, shake, shudder, quake

shock *noun*
1. *The news of his death came as a great shock.* • blow, surprise, fright, upset
2. *People felt the shock of the explosion miles away.* • bang, impact, jolt
3. *The driver involved in the accident was in a state of shock.* • distress, trauma

shock *verb*
The whole town was shocked by the news.
• horrify, appal, startle, alarm, stun, stagger, shake, astonish, astound, surprise, dismay, upset • A formal synonym is **traumatize**.

shocked *adjective*
Ellie was shocked at the sight that met her eyes. • startled, horrified, appalled, staggered, shaken, dismayed, upset

shoe *noun*

WORD WEB

SOME TYPES OF SHOE OR BOOT
• ballet shoes, baseball boots, football boots, gym shoes, plimsolls, tap shoes; ankle boots, brogues, clogs, court shoes, espadrilles, flats, flip-flops, high heels, high tops, kitten heels, platform shoes, pumps, sandals, slip-ons, slippers, sneakers, stilettoes, trainers, wellington boots or (*informal*) wellies

shoot *verb* **shooting, shot**
1. *Robin Hood shot an arrow into the air.* • fire, discharge, launch, aim
2. *It is now illegal to hunt and shoot tigers.* • fire at, hit, open fire on, gun down
3. *They watched the racing cars shoot past.* • race, speed, dash, rush, streak, hurtle, fly, whiz, zoom
4. *Part of the film was shot in Canada.* • film, photograph

shop *noun*

WORD WEB

VARIOUS TYPES OF SHOP
• boutique, convenience store, corner shop, department store, hypermarket, kiosk, market, minimart, outlet, shopping arcade, shopping centre, shopping mall, supermarket

SPECIALIST SHOPS
• antique shop, baker, bookshop, butcher, cheesemonger, chemist, clothes shop, confectioner, delicatessen, DIY or do-it-yourself shop, fishmonger, florist, garden centre, greengrocer, grocer, haberdasher, health-food shop, ironmonger, jeweller, music shop, newsagent, off-licence, pharmacy, post office, shoe shop or shoemaker, stationer, toyshop, watchmaker

PEOPLE WHO WORK IN SHOPS
• cashier, salesman or saleswoman, shop assistant, shopkeeper or storekeeper

short *adjective*
1. *They live a short distance from the shops.* • little, small **opposite** long
2. *It was a very short visit.* • brief, quick, fleeting, hasty, temporary **opposite** long
3. *The troll was very short and fat.* • small, tiny, little, squat, dumpy, diminutive, petite **opposite** tall
4. *The supply of water was getting short.* • low, meagre, scant, limited, inadequate, insufficient **opposite** plentiful
5. *There is no need to be short with me!* • abrupt, rude, sharp, curt, impolite, snappy **opposite** patient, polite

shortage *noun*
The shortage of water is worrying. • scarcity, deficiency, lack, want, dearth • A shortage of water is a **drought**. • A shortage of food is a **famine**.

shorten *verb*
She had to shorten the essay because it was too long. • cut down, reduce, cut, trim, abbreviate, abridge, condense, compress, curtail **opposite** lengthen

shortly *adverb*
The post should arrive shortly. • soon, before long, presently

shot *noun*
1. *I heard a noise like the shot of a pistol.* • bang, blast, crack
2. *The striker had an easy shot at the goal.* • hit, strike, kick
3. *The photographer took some unusual shots.* • photograph, picture, snap, snapshot
4. *(informal) We each had a shot at solving the riddle.* • try, go, attempt, *(informal)* bash

shout *verb*
The ogre was shouting and stamping with rage. • call, cry out, bawl, yell, bellow,

roar, howl, yelp, scream, screech, shriek
opposite whisper

shove verb
A man ran past and shoved me to the side.
• push, thrust, force, barge, elbow, jostle,
shoulder

show verb showing, showed, shown
1. *My uncle showed us his coin collection.*
• present, reveal, display, exhibit
2. *The photo shows my grandparents on
holiday.* • portray, picture, depict, illustrate,
represent
3. *The dance tutor showed them what to do.*
• explain to, make clear to, instruct, teach, tell
4. *The evidence shows that he was right.*
• prove, demonstrate
5. *A nurse showed them into the waiting room.*
• direct, guide, conduct, escort, usher
6. *The signpost shows the way.* • indicate,
point out
7. *His vest showed through his shirt.* • be seen,
be visible, appear
to show off
Walter is always showing off. • boast, brag,
crow, gloat, swagger, *(informal)* blow your
own trumpet • A person who shows off is a
show-off.

show noun
1. *There is a show of artwork at the end of
term.* • display, exhibition, presentation
2. *There's a good show on at the theatre.*
• performance, production, entertainment

showy adjective showier, showiest
She was wearing very showy earrings. • gaudy,
flashy, bright, loud, garish, conspicuous
opposite plain

shriek noun, verb
'Quick!' shrieked Alice. 'Open the door!'
• cry, scream, screech, shout, howl, bawl,
squeal, wail, yell

shrill adjective
They heard the shrill sound of a whistle.
• high, high-pitched, piercing, sharp, screechy
opposite low, soft

shrink verb shrinking, shrank, shrunk
My jeans have shrunk in the wash. • become
smaller, contract **opposite** expand

shrivel verb shrivelling, shrivelled
The plants shrivelled in the heat. • wilt, wither,
droop, dry up, wrinkle, shrink

shudder verb
*They shuddered with fear when they heard the
creature roar.* • tremble, quake, quiver, shake,
shiver

shuffle verb
1. *She shuffled along the corridor in her
slippers.* • shamble, scuffle, hobble, scrape
2. *Did you remember to shuffle the cards?*
• mix, mix up, jumble

shut verb shutting, shut
Please shut the door behind you. • close,
fasten, seal, secure, lock, bolt, latch • To shut
a door with a bang is to **slam** it.
to shut someone up
*He had been shut up in a dungeon for five
years.* • imprison, confine, detain
shut up *(informal)*
I wish those people behind us would shut up!
• be quiet, be silent, stop talking, hold your
tongue

shy adjective
The little girl was too shy to say anything.
• bashful, timid, coy, reserved, hesitant,
self-conscious, inhibited, modest **opposite** bold

sick adjective
1. *Katie is off school because she's sick.* • ill,
unwell, poorly, sickly, ailing, indisposed,
off-colour, peaky **opposite** healthy
2. *The sea was rough and the cabin boy felt
sick.* • nauseous, queasy
to be sick of
I'm sick of this miserable weather! • be fed up
with, be tired of, have had enough of

side noun
1. *A cube has six sides.* • face, surface
2. *The path runs along the side of the field.*
• edge, border, boundary, fringe, perimeter
• The side of a page is the **margin**. • The side
of a road is the **verge**.
3. *I could see both sides of the argument.*
• point of view, view, angle, aspect
4. *The football club has a strong side this year.*
• team

sift verb
Sift the flour to get rid of any lumps. • sieve,
strain, filter
to sift through something
*The detective began to sift through the
evidence.* • examine, inspect, sort out,
analyse, scrutinize, review

sight noun
1. *Weasels have sharp sight and excellent
hearing.* • eyesight, vision

2. *The woods in autumn are a lovely sight.*
• spectacle, display, show, scene
3. *By the third day, the ship was in sight of land.* • view, range
4. *We went to London to see the sights.*
• attraction, landmark

sign *noun*
1. *A sign pointed to the exit.* • notice, placard, poster, signpost • The sign belonging to a particular business or organization is a **logo**.
• The sign on a particular brand of goods is a **trademark**.
2. *The witch gave no sign that she was angry.*
• indication, clue, hint, warning
3. *The guard gave us a sign to pass through the gates.* • signal, gesture, cue, reminder

sign *verb*
1. *Please sign your name on the form.* • write, inscribe
2. *The club signed a new player last week.*
• take on, engage, recruit, enrol

signal *noun*
The spy waited for the signal that all was clear.
• sign, indication, prompt, cue • A signal that tells you not to do something is a **warning**.

signal *verb* signalling, signalled
The pilot signalled that he was going to descend. • give a sign or signal, gesture, indicate, motion

significance *noun*
What's the significance of that symbol?
• importance, meaning, message, point, relevance

significant *adjective*
1. *The book describes the significant events of last century.* • important, major, noteworthy, influential
2. *Global warming is having a significant effect on wildlife.* • noticeable, considerable, perceptible, striking

signify *verb* signifies, signifying, signified
A red light signifies danger. • represent, stand for, symbolize, indicate, denote, mean

silence *noun*
There was silence while we sat the exam.
• quiet, quietness, hush, stillness, calm, peace
opposite noise

silence *verb*
He silenced the audience by ringing a gong. • deaden, muffle, quieten, suppress
• To silence someone by putting something in or over their mouth is to **gag** them.

silent *adjective*
1. *At night, the desert was cold and silent.*
• quiet, noiseless, soundless, still, hushed
• Something you can't hear is **inaudible**.
• A common simile is **as silent as the grave**.
opposite noisy
2. *Morris kept silent throughout the meeting.*
• quiet, speechless, mute, *(informal)* mum
• To be too shy to speak is to be **tongue-tied**.
opposite talkative

silly *adjective* sillier, silliest
It was silly of me to lock myself out of the house. • foolish, stupid, idiotic, senseless, thoughtless, brainless, unwise, unintelligent, half-witted, hare-brained, scatterbrained, *(informal)* daft **opposite** sensible

similar *adjective*
The puppies are similar in appearance. • alike, identical, indistinguishable, matching, the same **opposite** dissimilar, different
similar to
The new book is similar to the previous one. • alike, close to, comparable to
opposite unlike, different from

similarity *noun*
It's easy to see the similarity between the twins. • likeness, resemblance
opposite difference

simple *adjective*
1. *Can you answer this simple question?* • easy, elementary, straightforward **opposite** difficult
2. *The help file is written in simple language.*
• clear, plain, uncomplicated, understandable, intelligible **opposite** complicated
3. *The girl wore a simple cotton dress.* • plain, undecorated **opposite** elaborate
4. *He enjoys simple pleasures like walking and gardening.* • ordinary, unsophisticated, humble, modest, homely
opposite sophisticated

sin *noun*
Some people believe that lying is a sin.
• wrong, evil, wickedness, wrongdoing

sincere *adjective*
Please accept my sincere apologies. • genuine, honest, true, truthful, real, earnest, wholehearted, frank **opposite** insincere

single *adjective*
1. *We saw a single house high on the moors.*
• solitary, isolated • When only a single example of something exists, it is **unique**.
2. *Miss Dempster was quite content to stay single.* • unmarried • An unmarried man is

a **bachelor**. • An old-fashioned name for an unmarried woman is a **spinster**.

sinister *adjective*
He looked up with a sinister smile on his face.
• menacing, threatening, malevolent, evil, disturbing, unsettling, eerie, *(informal)* creepy

sink *verb* **sinking, sank, sunk, sunk**
1. *The ship hit the rocks and sank.* • go down, become submerged, founder, capsize • To let water into a ship to sink it deliberately is to **scuttle** it.
2. *The sun began to sink below the horizon.*
• drop, fall, descend, subside, dip • When the sun sinks to the horizon it **sets**.

sit *verb* **sitting, sat**
1. *Rachel sat on the sofa reading a magazine.*
• have a seat, settle down, rest, perch • To sit on your heels is to **squat**. • To sit to have your portrait painted is to **pose**.
2. *My brother is sitting his driving test next week.* • take, *(informal)* go in for

site *noun*
This is the site of an ancient burial ground.
• location, place, position, situation, setting, plot

situated *adjective*
The house is situated next to the park.
• located, positioned

situation *noun*
1. *The house is in a pleasant situation.*
• location, locality, place, position, setting, site, spot
2. *I found myself in an awkward situation.*
• position, circumstances, condition, state of affairs • A bad situation is a **plight** or **predicament**.

size *noun*
1. *What size is the garden?* • dimensions, proportions, area, extent
2. *They were amazed by the sheer size of the pyramids.* • scale, magnitude, immensity

sketch *noun*
1. *She drew a quick sketch of her cat.*
• drawing, picture, outline • A sketch you do while you think of other things is a **doodle**.
2. *The actors performed a comic sketch.*
• scene, turn, routine

sketch *verb*
He sketched a rough design for the poster
• draw, draft, outline, rough out

skid *verb* **skidding, skidded**
The postman skidded on the icy pavement.
• slide, slip

skilful *adjective*
Dickens was a skilful writer. • expert, skilled, accomplished, able, capable, talented, brilliant, clever, masterly, deft • If you are skilful at a lot of things, you are **versatile**.
opposite incompetent

skill *noun*
It takes a lot of skill to build a boat. • expertise, ability, aptitude, capability, competence, accomplishment, talent, proficiency, deftness

skim *verb* **skimming, skimmed**
The stone skimmed across the surface of the pond. • glide, slide, skid, slip
to skim through
Luke skimmed through the newspaper. • scan, look through, skip through, flick through

skin *noun*
The cave people were dressed in animal skins.
• coal, fur, hide, pelt • The type of skin you have on your face is your **complexion**. • Skin on fruit or vegetables is **peel** or **rind**. • Skin that might form on top of a liquid is a **coating**, **film** or **membrane**.

skinny *adjective* **skinnier, skinniest**
A skinny girl in bare feet answered the door.
• thin, lean, bony, gaunt, lanky, scrawny, scraggy **opposite** plump

skip *verb* **skipping, skipped**
1. *The children skipped along the pavement.*
• hop, jump, leap, bound, caper, dance, prance
2. *I skipped the boring bits in the book.* • pass over, miss out, ignore, omit, leave out

slam *verb* **slamming, slammed**
Don't slam the door! • bang, shut loudly

slant *verb*
Her handwriting slants backwards. • lean, slope, tilt, incline, be at an angle

slant *noun*
The floor of the caravan was at a slant.
• slope, angle, tilt, incline, gradient • A slant on a damaged ship is a **list**. • A slanting line joining opposite corners of a square, etc., is a **diagonal**. • A surface slanting up to a higher level is a **ramp**.

slap *verb* **slapping, slapped**
He slapped his hand against his thigh and laughed. • smack, strike, spank, hit, clout, *(informal)* whack

slaughter *noun*
The battle ended in terrible slaughter.
• bloodshed, killing, massacre, butchery

slave *verb*
They slaved all day to get the job done. • work hard, labour, toil, grind, sweat

slavery *noun*
The prisoners were sold into slavery.
• captivity, bondage **opposite** freedom

sleek *adjective*
Otters have sleek coats. • smooth, glossy, shiny, silky, soft, velvety **opposite** coarse

sleep *verb* sleeping, slept
The baby is sleeping in the next room. • be asleep, take a nap, doze, *(informal)* snooze • To go to sleep is to **drop off** or **nod off**.

sleep *noun*
Mr Khan had a short sleep after lunch. • nap, rest, doze, catnap, *(informal)* snooze, forty winks, shut-eye • An afternoon sleep is a **siesta**. • The long sleep some animals have through the winter is **hibernation**.

sleepy *adjective* sleepier, sleepiest
The giant was usually sleepy after dinner.
• drowsy, tired, weary, heavy-eyed, lethargic, ready to sleep, *(informal)* dopey **opposite** wide awake

slender *adjective*
1. *The ballerina had a slender figure.* • slim, lean, slight, graceful, trim, svelte **opposite** fat
2. *The spider dangled on a slender thread.*
• thin, fine, fragile, delicate **opposite** thick
3. *They only had a slender chance of winning.*
• poor, slight, slim, faint, negligible, remote **opposite** good
4. *The team won by a slender margin.*
• narrow, small, slim **opposite** wide

slice *verb*
• To slice meat is to **carve** it.

slide *verb* sliding, slid
I like sliding down the chute in the playground.
• glide, skid, slip, slither

slight *adjective*
1. *There's a slight problem with the computer.*
• minor, unimportant, insignificant, negligible, superficial, trifling, trivial **opposite** important
2. *The fairy was a slight creature, barely two inches tall.* • delicate, fragile, frail, slender, slim, small, spare, thin, tiny **opposite** stout

slim *adjective* slimmer, slimmest
1. *A tall, slim figure appeared out of the fog.*
• graceful, lean, slender, spare, thin, trim **opposite** fat
2. *Their chances of winning are slim.* • faint, poor, slight, slender, negligible, remote **opposite** good
3. *They won by a slim margin.* • narrow, small, slender **opposite** wide

slimy *adjective*
The floor of the tunnel was covered with slimy mud. • slippery, slithery, sticky, oozy, *(informal)* gooey, icky

sling *verb* slinging, slung
Robin Hood slung his quiver over his shoulder.
• throw, cast, fling, hurl, pitch, heave, toss, lob, *(informal)* chuck

slink *verb* slinking, slunk
The spy slunk away without being seen.
• slip, sneak, steal, creep, edge, sidle

slip *verb* slipping, slipped
1. *The paper boy slipped on the ice.*
• skid, slither, skate
2. *The lifeboat slipped into the water.*
• glide, slide
3. *Marion slipped out while everyone was talking.* • sneak, steal, slink, tiptoe, creep, edge, sidle

slippery *adjective*
Take care—the floor is slippery. • slithery, slippy, smooth, glassy • A surface slippery with frost is **icy**. • A surface slippery with grease is **greasy** or **oily**. • A common simile is **as slippery as an eel**.

slit *noun*
The archers shot arrows through the slits in the castle wall. • opening, chink, gap, slot, split, tear, cut

slit
For ways to cut things, see **cut**.

slither *verb*
The rattlesnake slithered through the long grass. • slide, slip, glide, slink, snake

slope *verb*
The beach slopes gently down to the sea.
• fall or rise, incline, bank, shelve

slope *noun*
1. *It was hard work pushing my bike up the slope.* • hill, rise, bank, ramp • An upward slope is an **ascent**. • A downward slope is a **descent**.

2. *Rain runs down the roof because of the slope.* • incline, slant, tilt, gradient

sloppy adjective **sloppier, sloppiest**
1. *For breakfast, there was a bowl of steaming, sloppy porridge.* • runny, slushy, watery, liquid, wet, *(informal)* gloopy
2. *His handwriting is very sloppy.*
• untidy, messy, careless, slovenly, slapdash, slipshod

slot noun
To use the phone, put a coin into the slot.
• slit, chink, hole, opening

slouch verb
Enid sat at her desk, slouched over the computer. • hunch, stoop, slump, droop, flop

slow adjective
1. *Tortoises move at a slow but steady pace.*
• unhurried, leisurely, gradual, plodding, dawdling, sluggish
2. *They took the train to London, followed by a slow bus journey.* • lengthy, prolonged, drawn-out, tedious
3. *The prisoner was slow to answer.* • hesitant, reluctant, tardy

slow verb
to slow down
Slow down—you're driving too fast!
• go slower, brake, reduce speed
opposite accelerate

slowly adverb
They heard footsteps slowly creeping closer.
• unhurriedly, gradually, at a snail's pace, inch by inch, slowly but surely

sly adjective
The chess player knew several sly moves. • crafty, cunning, artful, clever, wily, tricky, sneaky, devious, furtive, secretive, stealthy, underhand
• A common simile is **as sly as a fox**.
opposite straightforward

smack verb
He smacked the other player on the head by accident. • slap, strike, hit, cuff, *(informal)* whack

small adjective

> ## ! OVERUSED WORD
>
> Try to vary the words you use for small. Here are some other words you could use.
>
> **FOR A SMALL OBJECT**
> • little, tiny, minute, compact, miniature, microscopic, minuscule, mini, baby, *(informal)* teeny, titchy, dinky, weeny, *(Scottish)* wee **opposite** big, large
> *Moles have incredibly tiny eyes and ears.*
>
> **FOR A SMALL PERSON**
> • little, short, petite, slight, dainty, diminutive, *(informal)* pint-sized, titchy
> *A diminutive elf was standing on a toadstool.* **opposite** big, tall, large
>
> **FOR A SMALL HELPING OR SMALL PORTION**
> • meagre, inadequate, insufficient, paltry, scanty, stingy, skimpy, *(informal)* measly
> **opposite** large, generous, ample
> *For breakfast there was stale bread with a meagre scraping of butter.*
>
> **FOR A SMALL CHANGE OR SMALL PROBLEM**
> • minor, unimportant, insignificant, trivial, trifling, negligible **opposite** major, substantial
> *The writers made some minor changes to the script.*

smart adjective
1. *Everyone looked smart at the wedding.*
• elegant, well-dressed, well-groomed, stylish, spruce, fashionable, chic, neat, trim
• To make yourself smart is to **smarten up**.
opposite scruffy
2. *They booked a table in a very smart restaurant.* • fashionable, high-class, exclusive, fancy, *(informal)* posh
3. *The detective made a very smart move.*
• clever, ingenious, intelligent, shrewd, crafty
opposite stupid
4. *The cyclists set off at a smart pace.* • fast, quick, rapid, speedy, swift, brisk **opposite** slow

smart verb
The smoke from the barbecue made our eyes smart. • hurt, sting, prick, prickle, tingle

smash verb
A vase fell off the table and smashed to pieces on the floor. • break, crush, shatter, crack
• When wood smashes it **splinters**. • To smash something completely is to **demolish** or **destroy** or **wreck** it.
to smash into
A lorry had smashed into the side of a bus.
• crash into, collide with, bang into, bump into

a b c d e f g h i j k l m n o p q r s t u v w x y z

smear verb
The chef smeared butter over the cooking dish.
• spread, wipe, plaster, rub, dab, smudge, daub

smell noun
1. *The air was filled with the smell of roses.*
• scent, aroma, perfume, fragrance
2. *The smell of mouldy cheese was unbearable.* • odour, stench, stink, reek, whiff, (informal) pong, niff

smell verb smelling, smelt, smelled
1. *I could smell something baking in the oven.*
• scent, sniff, (informal) get a whiff of
2. *After being in boots all day, my feet smelled awful.* • stink, reek, (informal) pong

---

✏ WRITING TIPS

You can use these words to describe how something smells.

TO DESCRIBE SOMETHING WHICH SMELLS GOOD
• fragrant, aromatic, perfumed, scented, sweet-smelling
The whole garden was planted with sweet-smelling herbs.

TO DESCRIBE SOMETHING WHICH SMELLS BAD
• smelly, stinking, evil-smelling, foul-smelling, musty, fusty, odorous, reeking, rotten, fetid, foul, rank, pungent, putrid, (informal) stinky, pongy, whiffy
The witch stirred the evil-smelling brew.

---

smile verb, noun
The stranger smiled and introduced himself.
• grin, beam • To smile in a silly way is to **simper**. • To smile in a self-satisfied way is to **smirk**. • To smile in an insulting way is to **sneer**.

smoke noun
Puffs of green smoke came from the dragon's nostrils. • fumes, gas, steam, vapour
• The smoke given out by a car is **exhaust**.
• A mixture of smoke and fog is **smog**.

smooth adjective
1. *This part of the road is smooth and good for cycling.* • flat, even, level **opposite** uneven
2. *In the early morning, the lake was perfectly smooth.* • calm, still, unruffled, undisturbed, glassy **opposite** rough
3. *Otters have smooth and shiny coats.* • silky, sleek, velvety **opposite** coarse
4. *The journey by train is very quick and smooth.* • comfortable, steady **opposite** bumpy

5. *Stir the cake mixture until it is smooth.*
• creamy, flowing, runny **opposite** lumpy

smooth verb
Charlotte stood up and smoothed her dress.
• flatten, level, even out • To smooth cloth you can **iron** or **press** it. • To smooth wood you can **plane** or **sand** it.

smother verb
1. *Pythons smother their prey to death.*
• suffocate, choke, stifle
2. *The pudding was smothered with cream.*
• cover, coat

smudge noun
There were smudges of ink all over the page.
• smear, blot, streak, stain, mark

smudge verb
Don't smudge the icing on the cake! • smear, blur, streak

snap verb snapping, snapped
1. *A twig snapped under one of my boots.*
• break, crack
2. *The dog snapped at the postman's ankles.*
• bite, nip
3. *Mr Baker was in a bad mood and snapped at everyone.* • snarl, bark

snatch verb
The thief snatched the jewels and ran off.
• grab, seize, grasp, pluck, wrench away, wrest away

sneak verb
I managed to sneak in without anyone seeing.
• slip, steal, creep, slink, tiptoe, sidle, skulk

sneaky adjective sneakier, sneakiest
That was a really sneaky trick. • sly, underhand, cunning, crafty, devious, furtive, untrustworthy **opposite** honest

sneer verb
to sneer at
He sneered at my first attempts to ice-skate.
• make fun of, mock, ridicule, scoff at, jeer at, deride

snivel verb snivelling, snivelled
For goodness' sake, stop snivelling! • cry, sob, weep, sniff, whimper, whine

snobbish adjective
She's too snobbish to mix with us.
• arrogant, pompous, superior, haughty, (informal) stuck-up, snooty, toffee-nosed **opposite** humble

snoop *verb*
They caught a man snooping round the office.
• sneak, pry, poke, rummage, spy

snub *verb* **snubbing, snubbed**
She snubbed the neighbours by not inviting them to the party. • insult, offend, be rude to, brush off, *(informal)* put down

snug *adjective* **snugger, snuggest**
Lucy was tucked up snug in bed. • cosy, comfortable, warm, relaxed, *(informal)* comfy
• A common simile is **as snug as a bug in a rug**. **opposite** uncomfortable

soak *verb*
1. *Days of rain had soaked the cricket pitch.*
• wet thoroughly, drench, saturate
2. *Leave the beans to soak in water overnight.*
• steep, immerse, submerge

soaking *adjective*
My socks are absolutely soaking! • wet through, drenched, dripping, wringing, saturated, sodden, sopping, soggy • Ground that has been soaked by rain is **waterlogged**.

soar *verb*
The seagull spread its wings and soared into the air. • climb, rise, ascend, fly, wing

sob *verb* **sobbing, sobbed**
Tina threw herself on the bed, sobbing loudly.
• cry, weep, bawl, blubber, shed tears, snivel

sober *adjective*
1. *He drank a little wine, but he stayed sober.*
• clear-headed **opposite** drunk
2. *The funeral was a sober occasion.* • serious, solemn, sombre, grave, dignified, sedate **opposite** light-hearted, frivolous

society *noun* **societies**
1. *Ancient Egypt was a society ruled by pharaohs.* • community, civilization
2. *Mrs Burns is head of the local music society.*
• association, group, organization, club

soft *adjective*
1. *The kittens can only eat soft food.*
• pulpy, spongy, squashy, *(informal)* squidgy **opposite** hard, dry
2. *My head sank into the soft pillow.*
• supple, pliable, springy, yielding, flexible **opposite** firm, rigid
3. *The rabbit's fur felt very soft.* • smooth, silky, sleek, velvety, downy, feathery **opposite** coarse
4. *A soft breeze stirred the leaves.* • gentle, light, mild, delicate **opposite** rough, strong

5. *The smugglers spoke in soft whispers.*
• quiet, low, faint **opposite** loud
6. *It was hard to see clearly in the soft light.* • subdued, muted, pale, dim, low **opposite** bright, dazzling
7. *You are being too soft with that puppy.*
• lenient, easygoing, tolerant, indulgent **opposite** strict, tough

soggy *adjective* **soggier, soggiest**
1. *The pitch was soggy after all the rain.*
• wet, drenched, soaked, saturated, sodden, waterlogged
2. *The bread in my sandwich had become soggy.* • moist, soft, pulpy, squelchy, *(informal)* squidgy

solemn *adjective*
1. *The butler always had a solemn expression on his face.* • serious, grave, sober, sombre, unsmiling, glum **opposite** cheerful
2. *The coronation was a solemn occasion.*
• formal, dignified, grand, stately, majestic, pompous **opposite** frivolous

solid *adjective*
1. *A cricket ball is solid.* **opposite** hollow
2. *The water turned into solid ice.* • hard, firm, dense, compact, rigid, unyielding • A common simile is **as solid as a rock**. **opposite** soft
3. *The bars of the climbing frame are quite solid.* • firm, robust, sound, strong, stable, sturdy **opposite** weak, unstable
4. *The crown was made of solid gold.* • pure, genuine
5. *He got solid support from his team-mates.*
• firm, reliable, dependable, united, unanimous **opposite** weak, divided

solve *verb*
The professor was trying to solve an ancient riddle. • interpret, explain, answer, work out, find the solution to, unravel, decipher

soon *adverb*
Dinner will be ready soon. • before long, in a minute, shortly, presently, quickly

soothe *verb*
1. *The quiet music soothed her nerves.* • calm, comfort, relax, pacify
2. *This cream will soothe the pain.* • ease, lessen, relieve

soothing *adjective*
They played soothing music. • calming, relaxing, restful, peaceful, gentle, pleasant

sore *adjective*
My feet are still sore from the walk. • painful, aching, hurting, smarting, tender, sensitive, inflamed, raw, red

sorrow *noun*
1. *He felt great sorrow at leaving his children behind.* • sadness, unhappiness, misery, woe, grief, anguish, despair, distress, heartache, heartbreak, melancholy, gloom, depression, desolation, wretchedness • Sorrow because of someone's death is **mourning**. • Sorrow at being away from home is **homesickness**. **opposite** happiness
2. *She expressed her sorrow for what she had done.* • regret, remorse, repentance, apologies

sorry *adjective* **sorrier, sorriest**
1. *Scott said he was sorry for losing my football.* • apologetic, regretful, remorseful, ashamed (of), repentant **opposite** unapologetic
2. *We felt sorry for the villagers who had lost their homes.* • sympathetic, pitying, understanding, compassionate **opposite** unsympathetic

sort *noun*
What sort of music do you like? • kind, type, variety, form, nature, style, genre, category, order, class • A sort of animal is a **breed** or **species**.

sort *verb*
The books are sorted according to their subjects. • arrange, organize, class, group, categorize, classify, divide **opposite** mix
to sort something out
They managed to sort out their disagreement. • settle, resolve, clear up, cope with, deal with

sound *noun*

WORD WEB

We heard the sound of footsteps approaching. • noise, tone • A loud, harsh sound is a **din** or **racket**.

SOUNDS MADE BY PEOPLE
• bawl, bellow, boo, boom, cackle, chortle, clap, croak, cry, gasp, groan, gurgle, hiccup, hiss, howl, hum, moan, murmur, puff, scream, shout, shriek, sigh, sing, sniff, snore, snort, sob, splutter, stammer, stutter, wail, wheeze, whimper, whine, whisper, whistle, whoop, yell, yodel

SOUNDS MADE BY THINGS
• bang, blare, beep, bleep, boom, buzz, chime, chink, chug, clang, clank, clash, clatter, click, clink, clunk, crack, crackle, crash, creak, crunch, ding, drone, drum, fizz, grate, gurgle, jangle, jingle, patter, peal, ping, plop, pop, purr, putter, rattle, ring, rumble, rustle, scrunch, sizzle, slam, snap, squeak, squelch, swish, throb, thud, thunder, tick, ting, tinkle, twang, whirr, whoosh, whistle, whiz, zoom

WRITING TIPS

You can use these words to describe a sound.

TO DESCRIBE A PLEASANT SOUND
• dulcet, harmonious, mellifluous, melodious, sweet
I heard the sweet strains of a harp playing.

TO DESCRIBE AN UNPLEASANT SOUND
• grating, harsh, jarring, piercing, rasping, raucous, shrill, thin, tinny
A raucous fight was going out outside.

sound *adjective*
1. *The walls of the fortress seemed sound.* • firm, solid, stable, safe, secure, intact, undamaged **opposite** unsound, unstable
2. *She gave us some sound advice.* • good, sensible, wise, reasonable, trustworthy **opposite** unwise
3. *The travellers returned safe and sound.* • strong, well, fit, healthy **opposite** weak, unfit

sour *adjective*
1. *These apples are a bit sour.* • tart, bitter, sharp, acid **opposite** sweet
2. *The guard opened the door with a sour look on his face.* • cross, bad-tempered, grumpy, disagreeable, peevish

source noun
The vet has found the source of the infection.
• origin, start, starting point, head, root, cause
• The source of a river or stream is usually a
spring.

space noun
1. *There wasn't much space to move about.*
• room, freedom, scope
2. *He peered through the tiny space in the
curtains.* • gap, hole, opening, break • A space
without any air in it is a **vacuum**. • A space of
time is an **interval** or **period**.
3. *The astronauts will spend ten days in space.*
• outer space

WORD WEB

• Everything that exists in space is the
universe or **cosmos**. • Distances in space
stretch to **infinity**. • Travel to other planets
is **interplanetary** travel. • Travel to other
stars is **interstellar** travel. • Travel to other
galaxies is **intergalactic** travel. • A traveller
in space is an **astronaut**. • In stories, beings
from other planets are **aliens** or
extraterrestrials.

NATURAL OBJECTS FOUND IN SPACE
• asteroid, black hole, comet, constellation,
galaxy, meteor, meteorite, Milky Way,
moon, nebula, nova, planet, red dwarf, red
giant, shooting star, solar system, star, sun,
supernova

WORDS TO DO WITH TRAVEL IN SPACE
• blast-off, countdown, launch, mission,
orbit, re-entry, rocket, satellite, spacecraft,
spaceship, space shuttle, space station,
spacesuit, spacewalk • A robot spacecraft is
a **probe**. • A vehicle which can travel on the
surface of a planet is a **buggy** or **rover**.

THINGS YOU MIGHT FIND ON A SPACESHIP
• booster rocket, bridge, cargo bay, capsule,
computer, docking bay, fuel tank, heat
shield, instrument panel, life-support
system, module, pod, solar panel

THINGS A SPACESHIP MIGHT DO
• blast off, burn up, drift off-course, land, lift
off, malfunction, orbit, re-enter the earth's
atmosphere, splash down, touch down

span noun
The bridge has a span of 200 metres.
• breadth, extent, length, width, distance,
reach • A span of time is a **period** or **stretch**.

span verb
A rickety footbridge spanned the river. • cross,
stretch over, extend across, straddle, bridge,
traverse

spare verb
1. *Can you spare any money for a good cause?*
• afford, part with, give, provide, do without
2. *Gretel begged the witch to spare her brother.*
• show mercy to, pardon, reprieve, let off,
release, free

spare adjective
1. *The spare tyre is in the boot.* • additional,
extra, reserve, standby
2. *Have you any spare change?* • leftover,
surplus, odd, remaining, unused, unwanted

spark noun
*There was a spark of light as he struck the
match.* • flash, gleam, glint, flicker, sparkle

sparkle verb
The diamond ring sparkled in the sunlight.
• glitter, glisten, glint, twinkle

speak verb speaking, spoke, spoken
*The robot opened its mouth and began to
speak.* • communicate, express yourself,
say something, talk, utter

special adjective
1. *Are you keeping the champagne
for a special occasion?* • important,
significant, memorable, noteworthy,
momentous, exceptional, extraordinary,
out-of-the-ordinary **opposite** ordinary
2. *My granny has her own special way
of making porridge.* • unique, individual,
characteristic, distinctive, different, peculiar
3. *You need a special camera to film
underwater.* • particular, specific, proper,
specialized

specific adjective
The treasure map gave specific directions.
• detailed, precise, exact, definite, particular,
clear-cut **opposite** general, vague

specimen noun
The police asked for a specimen of his

handwriting. • sample, example, illustration, instance

speck noun
She brushed a *speck* of dust from her shoes. • bit, dot, spot, fleck, grain, particle, trace, mark

spectacle noun
The fireworks for Diwali will be a great *spectacle*. • display, show, performance, exhibition, extravaganza

spectacular adjective
1. The acrobats gave a *spectacular* performance. • dramatic, exciting, impressive, thrilling, magnificent, sensational
2. The tulips are *spectacular* at this time of year. • eye-catching, showy, splendid, breathtaking, colourful

spectator noun
• The spectators at a show are the **audience**.
• The spectators at a football match are the **crowd**. • A person watching TV is a **viewer**.
• If you see an accident or a crime you are an **eyewitness** or **witness**. • If you just happen to see something going on you are a **bystander** or **onlooker**.

speech noun
1. His *speech* was slurred and he looked tired. • speaking, talking, articulation, pronunciation
2. She was invited to give an after-dinner *speech*. • talk, address, lecture, oration • A talk in church is a **sermon**. • Speech between actors in a play is **dialogue**. • A speech delivered by a single actor is a **monologue**.

speed noun
1. Could a spaceship travel faster than the *speed* of light? • pace, rate • A formal synonym is **velocity**. • The speed of a piece of music is its **tempo**. • To increase speed is to **accelerate**. • To reduce speed is to **decelerate**.
2. They finished clearing up with amazing *speed*. • quickness, rapidity, swiftness
opposite slowness

speed verb speeding, sped, speeded
The skiers *sped* down the mountain. • race, rush, dash, dart, hurry, hurtle, career, fly, streak, tear, shoot, zoom, zip

spell noun
1. A magic *spell* had turned the knight into a toad. • charm, incantation • Making magic spells is **sorcery**, **witchcraft** or **wizardry**.
2. We're hoping for a *spell* of dry weather. • period, interval, time, stretch, run

spend verb
1. Have you *spent* all your pocket money already? • pay out, use up, get through, exhaust, (informal) fork out, shell out • To spend money unwisely is to **fritter** or **squander** it.
2. She *spends* a lot of time working in the garden. • pass, occupy, fill • To spend time doing something useless is to **waste** it.

sphere noun
1. The earth has the shape of a *sphere*. • ball, globe, orb
2. He's an expert in the *sphere* of photography. • subject, area, field

spill verb spilling, spilt, spilled
1. Katie *spilled* her juice all over the table. • overturn, upset, tip over
2. Milk *spilled* onto the floor. • overflow, pour, slop, slosh, splash
3. The treasure chest fell open, *spilling* gold coins everywhere. • shed, tip, scatter, drop

spin verb spinning, spun
The rear wheels of the jeep *spun* round. • turn, rotate, revolve, whirl, twirl

spine noun
1. Your *spine* runs down the middle of your back. • backbone, spinal column • The bones in your spine are your **vertebrae**.
2. A porcupine has sharp *spines*. • needle, quill, point, spike, bristle

spirit noun
1. He carried a charm to keep evil *spirits* away. • ghost, ghoul, phantom, spectre, demon
2. The orchestra played the piece with great *spirit*. • energy, liveliness, enthusiasm, vigour, zest, zeal, fire
3. There is a real *spirit* of cooperation in the team. • feeling, mood, atmosphere

spite noun
I believe that she ripped my book out of *spite*. • malice, spitefulness, ill will, ill feeling, hostility, bitterness, resentment, venom

spiteful adjective
He made some really *spiteful* comments. • malicious, malevolent, ill-natured, hostile, venomous, vicious, nasty, unkind
opposite kind

splash verb
1. The bus *splashed* water over us. • shower, spray, spatter, sprinkle, squirt, slop, slosh, spill, (informal) splosh

2. *The children splashed about in the playing pool.* • paddle, wade, dabble, bathe

splendid *adjective*
1. *There was a splendid banquet on the eve of the wedding.* • magnificent, lavish, luxurious, impressive, imposing, grand, great, dazzling, glorious, gorgeous, elegant, rich, stately, majestic
2. *That's a splendid idea!* • excellent, first-class, admirable, superb, wonderful, marvellous

splendour *noun*
They admired the splendour of the cathedral. • magnificence, glory, grandeur, majesty, richness, brilliance, spectacle

splinter *verb*
The glass splintered into pieces. • shatter, smash, fracture, chip, crack, split

split *verb* **splitting, split**
1. *He split the log in two.* • chop, cut up, crack open, splinter
2. *He split his trousers climbing over the fence.* • rip open, tear
3. *The pirates split the gold between them.* • distribute, share out
4. *The path splits here.* • branch, fork, separate
to split up
The search party decided to split up. • break up, part, separate, divide • If a married couple splits up, they may **divorce**.

split *noun*
He had a split in the seat of his trousers. • rip, tear, slash, slit

spoil *verb* **spoiling, spoilt, spoiled**
1. *Bad weather spoiled the holiday.* • ruin, wreck, upset, mess up, mar, scupper
2. *The grafitti spoils the look of the new building.* • damage, harm, hurt, disfigure, deface
3. *His parents have spoiled him since he was a baby.* • indulge, pamper, make a fuss of

spooky *adjective* **spookier, spookiest**
At dusk they came to a spooky house on the edge of the forest. • scary, eerie, chilling, creepy, menacing

sport *noun*

WORD WEB

I enjoy playing sport at the weekend. • exercise, games

TEAM SPORTS INCLUDE
• American football, baseball, basketball, bowls, cricket, football or soccer, hockey, lacrosse, netball, polo, rounders, rugby, volleyball, water polo

INDIVIDUAL SPORTS INCLUDE
• angling, archery, athletics, badminton, billiards, boxing, bowling, canoeing, climbing, croquet, cross-country running, cycling, darts, diving, fencing, golf, gymnastics, horse racing, jogging, judo, karate, motor racing, mountaineering, orienteering, pool, rowing, sailing, show jumping, snooker, squash, surfing, swimming, table tennis, tae kwon do, tennis, waterskiing, weightlifting, windsurfing, wrestling

WINTER SPORTS INCLUDE
• bobsleigh, curling, ice hockey, ice skating, skiing, snowboarding, speed skating, tobogganing

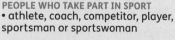

PEOPLE WHO TAKE PART IN SPORT
• athlete, coach, competitor, player, sportsman or sportswoman

PLACES WHERE SPORT TAKES PLACE
• arena, field, ground, park, pitch, pool, ring, rink, run, slope, stadium, track

SOME ATHLETIC EVENTS
• cross-country, decathlon, discus, heptathlon, high jump, hurdles, javelin, long jump, marathon, pentathlon, pole vault, relay race, running, shot, sprinting, steeplechase, triathlon, triple jump

spot noun

1. *There were several spots of paint on the carpet.* • mark, stain, blot, blotch, smudge, dot, fleck, speck • Small brown spots on your skin are **freckles**. • A small dark spot on your skin is a **mole**. • A mark you have had on your skin since you were born is a **birthmark**. • A small round swelling on your skin is a **pimple**. • A lot of spots is a **rash**.
2. *We felt a few spots of rain.* • drop, blob, bead
3. *Here's a nice spot for a picnic.* • place, position, location, site, situation, locality

spot verb spotting, spotted

1. *Nina spotted her friend in the crowd.* • see, sight, spy, catch sight of, notice, observe, make out, recognize, detect
2. *The tyres were spotted with mud.* • mark, stain, blot, spatter, fleck, speckle, mottle

spotty adjective

It was a spotty dinosaur. • spottled, mottled, speckly, flecked

spout verb

Molten lava and ash spouted from the volcano. • gush, spew, pour, stream, spurt, squirt, jet

sprawl verb

1. *We sprawled on the lawn.* • flop, lean back, lie, loll, lounge, recline, relax, slouch, slump, spread out, stretch out
2. *New houses have started to sprawl across the countryside.* • spread, stretch

spray verb

A passing bus sprayed mud over us. • shower, spatter, splash, sprinkle, scatter

spread verb spreading, spread

1. *I spread the map on the table.* • lay out, open out, fan out, unfold, unfurl, unroll
2. *The milk spilled and spread all over the floor.* • expand, extend, stretch, broaden, enlarge, swell
3. *The school website is a good way of spreading news.* • communicate, circulate, distribute, transmit, make known, pass on, pass round
4. *She spread jam on a piece of toast.* • smear
5. *He spread the seeds evenly over the ground.* • scatter, strew

spring verb springing, sprang, sprung

Suddenly a rabbit sprang over the fence. • jump, leap, bound, hop, vault • When a cat springs at a mouse, it **pounces**.

to spring up

Weeds spring up quickly in damp weather. • appear, develop, emerge, shoot up, sprout

sprinkle verb

She sprinkled flakes of chocolate over the cake. • scatter, shower, spray, dust, powder

sprout verb

The seeds will sprout if they are warm and damp. • grow, germinate, shoot up, spring up, develop, emerge

spurt verb

Water spurted from the hole in the pipe. • gush, spout, shoot out, stream, squirt, jet

spy noun spies

WORD WEB

The spy was on a top-secret mission. • agent, secret agent • The work of a spy is **spying** or **espionage**. • A spy who works for two rival countries or organizations is a **double agent** • An informal name for a spy who works undercover is a **mole**.

THINGS A SPY MIGHT DO
• adopt a disguise or cover, assume a secret identity, carry out a secret mission, crack or decipher a code, gather intelligence, keep someone under surveillance, report to headquarters, uncover an enemy agent, work undercover

THINGS A SPY MIGHT USE OR CARRY
• coded message, false passport, hidden camera or microphone, listening device, motion detector, night-vision goggles, password, torch, walkie talkie

A SPY'S MISSION MIGHT BE
• clandestine, covert, secret, stealthy, surreptitious, top-secret, undercover, (*informal*) cloak-and-dagger, hush-hush

squabble *verb*
The twins are always squabbling in the car.
• argue, fight, quarrel, bicker, wrangle

squander *verb*
He squandered his money on an expensive watch. • waste, fritter away, misuse, (informal) blow **opposite** save

squash *verb*
1. *My sandwich got squashed at the bottom of my schoolbag.* • crush, flatten, press, compress, mangle • To squash food deliberately is to **mash** or **pulp** or **purée** it.
2. *We squashed our sleeping bags into our rucksacks.* • squeeze, stuff, force, cram, pack, ram

squat *verb* squatting, squatted
We squatted on the ground to watch the puppet show. • crouch, sit

squat *adjective*
The alien had a squat little body on three short legs. • dumpy, stocky, plump, podgy, portly

squeeze *verb*
1. *She squeezed the water out of the sponge.*
• press, wring, compress, crush
2. *Five of us squeezed into the back of the car.*
• squash, cram, crowd, stuff, push, ram, shove, wedge
3. *Holly squeezed her sister affectionately.*
• clasp, hug, embrace, cuddle • To squeeze something between your thumb and finger is to **pinch** it.

squirt *verb*
My little brother made the tap water squirt all over me. • spurt, spray, gush, spout, shoot, jet

stab *verb* stabbing, stabbed
1. *He stabbed the sausage with his fork.*
• spear, jab, pierce, impale
2. *She stabbed a finger at him.* • stick, thrust, push, jab

stab *noun*
Jake felt a sudden stab of pain in his chest.
• pang, prick, sting

stable *adjective*
1. *The ladder doesn't look very stable.*
• steady, secure, firm, fixed, solid, balanced **opposite** wobbly, shaky
2. *He's been in a stable relationship for years.*
• steady, established, lasting, durable, strong **opposite** temporary

stack *noun*
There were stacks of books all over the floor.
• pile, heap, mound, tower • Another word for a stack of hay is a **rick** or **hayrick**.

stack *verb*
Stack the papers on the desk. • gather, assemble, collect, heap up, pile up

staff *noun*
There was a party at the hospital for all the staff. • workers, employees, personnel, workforce, team • The staff on a ship or aircraft are the **crew**.

stage *noun*
1. *They went up on the stage to collect their prizes.* • platform
2. *The final stage of the journey was made by coach.* • leg, step, phase, portion, stretch
3. *At this stage in her life, she wants to try something new.* • period, point, time, juncture

stagger *verb*
1. *The wounded knight staggered and fell.*
• reel, stumble, lurch, totter, sway, falter, waver, wobble
2. *We were staggered at the size of the pyramid.* • amaze, astonish, astound, surprise, flabbergast, stupefy, startle, stun

stain *noun*
There were several coffee stains on the tablecloth. • mark, spot, blot, blotch, blemish, smear, smudge

stain *verb*
Her trainers were stained with mud.
• discolour, mark, soil, dirty, blacken, tarnish

stairs *plural noun*
The stairs up to the front door were worn with age. • steps • A set of stairs taking you from one floor to another is a **flight of stairs** or a **staircase** or **stairway**. • A moving staircase is an **escalator**. • A handrail at the side of a staircase is a **banister**.

stale *adjective*
The bread had gone stale. • dry, hard, old, mouldy, musty **opposite** fresh

stalk *noun*
The recipe requires half a stalk of celery.
• stem, shoot, twig

stalk *verb*
1. *The cheetah stalked its prey.* • hunt, pursue, track, trail, follow, shadow, tail
2. *Miss Foster turned and stalked out of the room.* • stride, strut

stall *verb*
The man was stalling to give his friends time to escape. • play for time, delay, hesitate, hedge

stammer *verb*
Angela went red and started stammering. • stutter, falter, stumble, splutter

stamp *verb*
1. *He stamped on the flower by mistake.* • step, tread, trample
2. *The librarian stamped my library book.* • mark, print • To stamp a postmark on a letter is to **frank** it. • To stamp a mark on cattle with a hot iron is to **brand** them.

stampede *noun*
When the bell went, there was a stampede towards the door. • charge, rush, dash, rout

stand *verb* **standing, stood**
1. *The newborn pup was too weak to stand.* • get to your feet, get up, rise
2. *They stood the ladder against the wall.* • put, place, set, position, station, erect
3. *The offer still stands.* • remain valid, be unchanged, continue
4. *I can't stand the smell any longer.* • bear, abide, endure, put up with, tolerate, suffer
to stand for something
1. *She won't stand for any nonsense.* • put up with, tolerate, accept, allow, permit
2. *What do these initials stand for?* • mean, indicate, signify, represent
to stand out
Among all the photographs, this one really stood out. • catch your eye, stick out, be prominent
to stand up for someone
He always stands up for his friends. • support, defend, side with, speak up for, *(informal)* stick up for

standard *noun*
1. *Their writing is of a very high standard.* • grade, level, quality
2. *He considered the book good by any standard.* • guidelines, ideal, measurement, model
3. *The soldiers carried their standard proudly.* • colours, flag, banner

standard *adjective*
The teacher showed us the standard way to write a letter. • normal, usual, common, conventional, typical, customary, accepted, approved, established, orthodox, regular, traditional **opposite** abnormal

star *noun*
1. *Astronomers study the stars.* • A word meaning 'to do with stars' is **stellar**. • A night sky in which you can see stars is **starry** or **star-studded**. • A mark in the shape of a star in a piece of writing is an **asterisk**.
2. *Several Hollywood stars attended the premiere of the film.* • celebrity, idol, superstar

stare *verb*
The guard stared straight ahead, not blinking. • gaze, gape, peer, look
to stare at someone
The wolf was staring hungrily at us. • gaze at, gawp at, goggle at, eye, ogle, scrutinize, watch • To stare angrily at someone is to **glare** at them.

start *verb*
1. *The new course will start in the autumn.* • begin, commence, *(informal)* get going, get cracking, kick off **opposite** finish, end
2. *We are planning to start a book club.* • create, set up, establish, found, institute, originate, introduce, initiate, open, launch **opposite** close
3. *The horses started when the gun went off.* • jump, flinch, jerk, twitch, recoil, wince

start *noun*
1. *Try not to miss the start of the film.* • beginning, opening, introduction, commencement **opposite** end, close, finish
2. *She has been with the theatre company right from the start.* • beginning, outset, creation, inception, birth, dawn, launch
3. *The explosion gave us all a nasty start.* • jump, jolt, shock, surprise

startle *verb*
The sudden noise startled the deer. • alarm, panic, frighten, scare, make you start, make you jump, surprise, take you by surprise

starving *adjective (informal)*
What's for dinner? I'm starving! • hungry, famished, ravenous • To be slightly hungry is to be **peckish**.

state *noun*
1. *The roof of the cottage is in a bad state.* • condition, shape • The state of a person or animal is their **fitness** or **health**.
2. *He gets into a terrible state before an exam.* • panic, fluster, *(informal)* flap
3. *The queen is the head of state.* • country, nation

state verb
Her passport states that she is an Australian citizen. • declare, announce, report, say, proclaim, pronounce, communicate

stately adjective
The royal banquet will be a stately occasion. • grand, dignified, formal, imposing, majestic, noble, splendid

statement noun
The prime minister made a statement to the press. • announcement, declaration, communication, report, testimony

station noun
1. *Does the train stop at the next station?* • The station at the end of a line is the **terminus**.
2. *He was taken to the police station for questioning.* • depot, headquarters
3. *There are two local radio stations.* • channel

stationary adjective
The bus was stuck behind a stationary vehicle. • still, static, unmoving, immobile, motionless, standing, at rest **opposite** moving

status noun
Slaves had a very low status in ancient Rome. • rank, level, position, grade, importance, prestige

stay verb
1. *Can you stay there while I park the car?* • wait, hang about, remain **opposite** leave, depart
2. *We tried to stay warm by stamping our feet.* • keep, carry on being, continue
3. *Do you plan to stay in America for long?* • live, reside, dwell, lodge, settle, stop

stay noun
Our friends came for a short stay. • visit, stopover, holiday, break

steady adjective steadier, steadiest
1. *You need a steady hand to be a surgeon.* • stable, balanced, settled, secure, fixed, firm, fast, solid • A common simile is **as steady as a rock. opposite** unsteady, shaky
2. *The plants need a steady supply of water.* • continuous, uninterrupted, non-stop, consistent **opposite** intermittent
3. *The runners kept up a steady pace.* • regular, constant, even, smooth, rhythmic, unvarying **opposite** irregular

steal verb stealing, stole, stolen
1. *The thieves stole several valuable paintings.* • rob, thieve, take, lift, make off with, *(informal)* pinch, nick, swipe, snaffle
2. *The children stole quietly upstairs.* • creep, sneak, tiptoe, slip, slink

stealing noun
The police have accused him of stealing. • robbery, theft • Stealing from someone's home is **burglary** or **housebreaking**. • Stealing from a shop is **shoplifting**. • Stealing small things is **pilfering**.

stealthy adjective stealthier, stealthiest
We heard stealthy footsteps going upstairs. • furtive, secretive, surreptitious, sly, sneaky, underhand **opposite** conspicuous, open

steep adjective
The bus inched its way slowly up the steep slope. • abrupt, sudden, sharp • A cliff or drop which is straight up and down is **sheer** or **vertical. opposite** gradual, gentle

steer verb
She steered the car into the parking space. • direct, guide • To steer a vehicle is to **drive** it. • To steer a boat is to **navigate** or **pilot** it.

stem noun
The gardener pulled out the dead stems. • stalk, shoot, twig, branch • The main stem of a tree is its **trunk**.

stem verb stemming, stemmed
Chloe blinked, trying to stem the flow of her tears. • stop, check, hold back, restrain, curb

step noun
1. *The baby took her first steps yesterday.* • footstep, pace, stride
2. *Be careful not to trip on the step.* • doorstep, stair • A set of steps going from one floor of a building to another is a **staircase**. • A folding set of steps is a **stepladder**. • The steps of a ladder are the **rungs**.
3. *The first step in making a cake is to weigh the ingredients.* • stage, phase, action

step verb stepping, stepped
Don't step in the puddle! • put your foot, tread, walk, stamp, trample
to step something up
They have stepped up security at the airport. • increase, intensify, strengthen, boost

stern adjective
The coach gave each of the players a stern look. • disapproving, unsmiling, severe, strict, hard, harsh, grim **opposite** lenient

stick noun
1. *They collected sticks to make a fire.* • twig, branch, stalk
2. *The elderly patient walked with a stick.* • cane, rod, staff, pole • A stick used by a conductor is a **baton**. • A stick carried by a police officer is a **truncheon**. • A magic stick used by a witch or fairy is a **wand**.

stick verb sticking, stuck
1. *He stuck his fork into the potato.* • poke, prod, stab, thrust, dig, jab
2. *She tried to stick the broken pieces of china together.* • glue, paste, cement, bond, join, fasten
3. *The stamp wouldn't stick to the envelope.* • adhere, attach, cling
4. *The wheels of the caravan stuck fast in the mud.* • jam, wedge, become trapped
to stick out
The shelf sticks out too far. • jut out, poke out, project, protrude
to stick up for someone (informal)
She stuck up for him when he was in trouble. • support, defend, side with, stand up for, speak up for

sticky adjective stickier, stickiest
1. *Someone had left a blob of sticky toffee on the chair.* • tacky, gummy, gluey, (informal) gooey, icky
2. *I don't like hot sticky weather.* • humid, muggy, clammy, close, steamy, sultry
opposite dry

stiff adjective
1. *Stir the flour and water to a stiff paste.* • firm, hard, solid • A common simile is **as stiff as a poker. opposite** soft
2. *He mounted the picture on stiff card.* • rigid, inflexible, thick **opposite** pliable
3. *Her muscles were stiff after the long walk.* • aching, achy, painful, taut, tight **opposite** supple
4. *The team will face stiff competition in the final.* • strong, powerful, tough, difficult **opposite** easy
5. *His stiff manner made him hard to talk to.* • unfriendly, cold, formal, awkward, wooden **opposite** relaxed
6. *The judge imposed a stiff penalty.* • harsh, severe, strict, hard **opposite** lenient
7. *A stiff breeze was blowing.* • strong, brisk, fresh **opposite** gentle

stifle verb
1. *We were almost stifled by the fumes from the exhaust pipe.* • choke, suffocate, smother • To kill someone by stopping their breathing is to **strangle** or **throttle** them.
2. *She tried to stifle a yawn.* • suppress, muffle, hold back, repress, restrain

still adjective
1. *The prisoner sat still and said nothing.* • motionless, unmoving, stationary, static, inert
2. *It was a beautiful still evening.* • calm, peaceful, quiet, tranquil, serene, hushed, silent, noiseless, windless

stimulate verb
1. *Her travels stimulated her to write a book.* • encourage, inspire, spur
2. *The exhibition stimulated my interest in painting.* • arouse, rouse, stir up, kindle, excite, provoke, trigger

sting verb stinging, stung
The smoke made our eyes sting. • smart, hurt, prick, prickle, tingle

stingy adjective stingier, stingiest (informal)
He's too stingy to give anyone a birthday card. • mean, miserly, selfish, uncharitable, (informal) tight-fisted, penny-pinching
opposite generous

stink verb stinking, stank, stunk, stunk
The dungeon stank of unwashed bodies. • reek, smell

stink noun
The mouldy cheese gave off a dreadful stink. • odour, stench, reek, bad smell

stir verb stirring, stirred
1. *Stir the mixture until it is smooth.* • mix, beat, blend, whisk
2. *The giant stirred in his sleep.* • move slightly, shift, toss, turn
to stir something up
The bandits were always stirring up trouble. • arouse, encourage, provoke, set off, trigger, whip up

stir noun
The news caused quite a stir. • fuss, commotion, excitement, hullabaloo

stock noun
1. *Stocks of food were running low.* • supply, store, reserve, hoard, stockpile
2. *The shopkeeper arranged his new stock.* • goods, merchandise, wares

stock verb
Most supermarkets now stock organic food. • sell, carry, trade in, deal in, keep in stock

stocky *adjective* stockier, stockiest
The wrestler had a strong stocky body.
• dumpy, squat, thickset, solid, sturdy
opposite thin

stodgy *adjective* stodgier, stodgiest
1. *The pudding was rich and stodgy.* • heavy, solid, starchy, filling **opposite** light
2. *I'm finding the book a bit stodgy.*
• boring, dull, uninteresting, slow, tedious **opposite** lively

stomach *noun*
He rolled over and lay on his stomach. • belly, gut, paunch, *(informal)* tummy • The part of the body that contains the stomach is the **abdomen**.

stone *noun* stones, stone
The columns of the temple were carved from stone. • A large lump of stone is a **rock**.
• A large rounded stone is a **boulder**. • Small rounded stones are **pebbles**. • A mixture of sand and small stones is **gravel**. • Pebbles on the beach are **shingle**. • Round stones used to pave a path are **cobbles**.

stoop *verb*
We had to stoop to go through the tunnel.
• bend, duck, bow, crouch

stop *verb* stopping, stopped
1. *I'll go into town when the rain stops.*
• end, finish, cease, conclude, terminate **opposite** start
2. *Can you stop talking for a minute?*
• give up, cease, suspend, quit, leave off, break off, *(informal)* knock off, pack in **opposite** continue, resume
3. *Guards, stop that man!* • hold, detain, seize, catch, capture, restrain
4. *You can't stop me from going.* • prevent, obstruct, bar, hinder
5. *How do you stop this machine?* • turn off, immobilize
6. *The bus will stop at the school gates.* • come to a stop, halt, pull up, draw up
7. *If you tighten the valve, it will stop the leak.*
• close, plug, seal, block up, bung up

stop *noun*
1. *Everything suddenly came to a stop.* • end, finish, conclusion, halt, standstill
2. *They drove down through France, with a short stop in Paris.* • break, pause, stopover, rest

store *verb*
Squirrels need to store food for the winter.
• save, set aside, stow away, hoard, reserve, stockpile, *(informal)* stash

store *noun*
1. *The building is now used as a grain store.*
• storeroom, storehouse, repository, vault
• A store for food is a **larder** or **pantry**.
• A store for weapons is an **armoury** or **arsenal**.
2. *He kept a large store of wine in the cellar.*
• hoard, supply, quantity, stock, stockpile, reserve
3. *He's the manager of the local grocery store.*

storm *noun*
1. *Crops were damaged in the heavy storms.*
• squall, blizzard, gale, thunderstorm, hurricane, typhoon • An old word for storm is **tempest**. • When a storm begins to develop it is **brewing**.
2. *Plans to close the library caused a storm of protest.* • outburst, outcry, uproar, clamour

storm *verb*
The soldiers stormed the castle. • charge at, rush at

stormy *adjective* stormier, stormiest
1. *It was a dark, stormy night.* • blustery, squally, tempestuous, wild, windy, rough, choppy, gusty, raging **opposite** calm
2. *Fighting broke out at the end of a stormy meeting.* • bad-tempered, quarrelsome, turbulent, violent

story *noun* stories
1. *Peter Pan is a story about a boy who never grew up.* • tale • A story of a person's life is a **biography**. • The story of your life told by you is your **autobiography**. • Invented stories are **fiction**.
2. *It was the front page story in all the newspapers.* • article, item, feature, piece, report

WORD WEB

VARIOUS KINDS OF STORY
• adventure story, bedtime story, crime story, detective story, fable, fairy tale, fantasy, folk tale, ghost story, horror story, legend, love story, mystery, myth, narrative poem, novel, parable, romance, saga, science fiction or SF, short story, spy story, thriller

a
b
c
d
e
f
g
h
i
j
k
l
m
n
o
p
q
r
s
t
u
v
w
x
y
z

stout *adjective*
1. *The doctor was a stout man with grey hair.*
• fat, plump, chubby, dumpy, tubby, portly, stocky, beefy, burly **opposite** thin
2. *You will need a pair of stout walking boots.*
• strong, sturdy, tough, robust, sound, substantial **opposite** weak
3. *The enemy put up a stout resistance.*
• brave, courageous, spirited, plucky, determined, staunch, resolute, firm **opposite** cowardly

straight *adjective*
1. *They walked in a straight line.* • direct, unswerving • A common simile is **as straight as an arrow. opposite** crooked
2. *It took a long time to get the room straight.* • neat, orderly, tidy **opposite** untidy
3. *She found it difficult to get a straight answer from him.* • honest, plain, frank, straightforward **opposite** indirect, evasive

straightforward *adjective*
The cake recipe is fairly straightforward.
• simple, plain, uncomplicated, easy, clear, direct **opposite** complicated

strain *verb*
1. *The dog was straining at its lead.* • pull, tug, stretch, haul
2. *People were straining to see what was going on.* • struggle, strive, make an effort, try, attempt
3. *Take it easy and don't strain yourself.* • weaken, exhaust, wear out, tire out, tax

strain *noun*
The strain of her job was making her ill.
• stress, tension, worry, anxiety, pressure

stranded *adjective*
1. *A whale lay stranded on the beach.* • run aground, beached, marooned
2. *He was stranded in London without any money.* • abandoned, deserted, helpless, lost, stuck, (informal) high and dry

strange *adjective*
1. *A strange thing happened this morning.* • funny, odd, peculiar, unusual, abnormal, curious, extraordinary, remarkable, singular, uncommon **opposite** ordinary, everyday
2. *Did you hear strange noises in the night?* • mysterious, puzzling, baffling, mystifying, perplexing, bewildering, inexplicable
3. *The professor showed us his strange inventions.* • weird, eccentric, peculiar, bizarre, (informal) oddball, wacky

4. *I find it hard to get to sleep in a strange bed.* • unfamiliar, unknown, new, alien **opposite** familiar

strangle *verb*
The victim had been strangled. • throttle

strap *noun*
The trunk was fastened with a leather strap.
• belt, band

stray *verb*
Some sheep had strayed onto the road.
• wander, drift, roam, rove, straggle, meander, ramble

streak *noun*
1. *The horse had a white streak on its muzzle.*
• band, line, stripe, strip, smear, stain
2. *There is a streak of meanness in his character.* • element, trace

streak *verb*
1. *Rain had begun to streak the window.*
• smear, smudge, stain, line
2. *A group of motorbikes streaked past.* • rush, speed, dash, fly, hurtle, flash, tear, zoom

stream *noun*
1. *The climbers dipped their feet in a cool mountain stream.* • brook, rivulet, (Scottish) burn
2. *The raft was carried along with the stream.*
• current, flow, tide
3. *A stream of water poured through the hole.*
• cataract, flood, gush, jet, rush, torrent
4. *The museum had a steady stream of visitors.*
• series, string, line, succession

stream *verb*
Warm sunlight streamed through the window.
• pour, flow, flood, issue, gush, spill

strength *noun*
1. *Hercules was said to have enormous strength.* • power, might, muscle, brawn, toughness, force, vigour
2. *The main strength of the team is in scoring goals.* • strong point, asset, advantage **opposite** weakness

strengthen *verb*
1. *Regular exercise strengthens your muscles.*
• make stronger, build up, toughen, harden
2. *Concrete was used to strengthen the tunnel.*
• fortify, reinforce, bolster, prop up

stress *noun*
1. *The hospital staff were working under a lot of stress.* • strain, pressure, tension, worry, anxiety

2. *My piano teacher puts great* **stress** *on the need to practise.* • emphasis, importance, weight

stress *verb*
She **stressed** *the need for absolute secrecy.* • emphasize, draw attention to, highlight, underline

stretch *verb*
1. *He* **stretched** *the rubber band until it snapped.* • expand, extend, draw out, pull out, elongate, lengthen
2. *She* **stretched** *her arms wide.* • extend, open out, spread out
3. *The road* **stretched** *into the distance.* • continue, extend

stretch *noun*
1. *He had a two-year* **stretch** *in the army.* • spell, period, time, stint
2. *There are often accidents on this* **stretch** *of road.* • section, length, piece
3. *It's a beautiful* **stretch** *of countryside.* • area, tract, expanse, sweep

strict *adjective*
1. *The club has* **strict** *rules about who can join.* • rigid, inflexible, *(informal)* hard-and-fast **opposite** flexible
2. *The sergeant was known for being* **strict** *with his men.* • harsh, severe, stern, firm **opposite** lenient
3. *He used the word in its* **strict** *scientific sense.* • exact, precise, correct **opposite** loose

stride *noun*
The robot took two **strides** *forward.* • pace, step

strike *verb* **striking, struck**
1. *Roy* **struck** *his head on the low ceiling.* • bang, bump, hit, knock, thump, collide with, *(informal)* wallop, whack
2. *The enemy could* **strike** *again at any time.* • attack

striking *adjective*
The most **striking** *feature of the mermaid was her iridescent tail.* • conspicuous, noticeable, prominent, remarkable, memorable, extraordinary, outstanding, impressive **opposite** inconspicuous

string *noun*
1. *She tied some* **string** *round the parcel.* • rope, cord, twine
2. *They have received a* **string** *of complaints.* • series, succession, chain, sequence

string *verb* **stringing, strung**
We **strung** *the fairy lights on the Christmas tree.* • hang, arrange, thread

strip *verb* **stripping, stripped**
1. *Lottie* **stripped** *the paper off her present.* • peel, remove **opposite** cover, wrap
2. *He* **stripped** *and got into the bath.* • get undressed, undress **opposite** dress

strip *noun*
In front of the house was a narrow **strip** *of grass.* • band, length, ribbon, piece, bit

stripe *noun*
The tablecloth was white with blue **stripes***.* • line, strip, band, bar

strive *verb* **striving, strove, striven**
Each athlete **strives** *to do his or her best.* • try hard, aim, attempt, endeavour

stroke *noun*
1. *He split the log with a single* **stroke***.* • blow, hit, action, movement, effort
2. *She added a few quick pencil* **strokes** *to her drawing.* • line, mark

stroke *verb*
Jess was curled up on the sofa, **stroking** *the cat.* • pat, caress, rub, touch, fondle, pet

stroll *verb*
The children **strolled** *quietly home.* • walk slowly, amble, saunter

strong *adjective*

(!) OVERUSED WORD

Try to vary the words you use for **strong**. Here are some other words you could use.

FOR A STRONG PERSON OR STRONG BODY
• powerful, muscular, mighty, well-built, beefy, brawny, burly, strapping
Crocodiles have **powerful** *jaws.* • A common simile is **as strong as an ox. opposite** weak, puny

FOR STRONG MATERIAL
• robust, sturdy, tough, hard-wearing, durable, stout, substantial
The tent is made from **hard-wearing** *material.* **opposite** thin, flimsy

FOR A STRONG LIGHT OR STRONG COLOUR
• bright, brilliant, dazzling, glaring
The fugitive was caught in the **glaring** *beam of a searchlight.* **opposite** weak, pale

---

FOR A STRONG FLAVOUR OR STRONG SMELL
• overpowering, pronounced, pungent, piquant
I smelled the *pungent* aroma of roasting coffee. **opposite** faint, slight

FOR A STRONG ARGUMENT OR STRONG CASE
• convincing, persuasive, effective, sound, solid, valid
The police have *solid* evidence of his guilt. **opposite** weak, feeble, flimsy

FOR A STRONG INTEREST OR STRONG SUPPORTER
• enthusiastic, keen, passionate, fervent, avid, zealous
Zelda takes a *keen* interest in fashion. **opposite** slight

---

structure *noun*
1. *The pagoda is a magnificent* structure.
• building, construction, framework
2. *Can you explain the* structure *of the poem?* • design, plan, shape, arrangement, organization

struggle *verb*
1. *The captives* struggled *to get free.* • strain, strive, wrestle, writhe about, tussle, fight, battle
2. *The expedition had to* struggle *through a snowstorm.* • stagger, stumble, flounder, labour

struggle *noun*
The rebels surrendered without a struggle.
• fight, battle, combat, clash, contest

stubborn *adjective*
She's too stubborn *to admit that she was wrong.* • obstinate, pig-headed, strong-willed, uncooperative, inflexible, wilful
• A common simile is **as stubborn as a mule.**
opposite compliant

stuck-up *adjective (informal)*
Nobody likes Ernest—he's so stuck-up.
• arrogant, conceited, haughty, proud, snobbish, superior, *(informal)* snooty, toffee-nosed **opposite** humble

studious *adjective*
Sadiq is a quiet, studious *boy.* • hard-working, diligent, scholarly, academic, bookish

study *verb* **studies, studying, studied**
1. *He went to university to* study *medicine.*
• learn about, read, research into
2. *The spy* studied *the document carefully.*
• examine, inspect, analyse, investigate, look closely at, scrutinize, survey

3. *She has to* study *for her exams.* • revise, cram, (informal) swot

stuff *noun*
1. *What's that sticky* stuff *on the carpet?*
• matter, substance
2. *You can put your* stuff *in one of the lockers.*
• belongings, possessions, things, gear

stuff *verb*
1. *We managed to* stuff *everything into the boot of the car.* • pack, push, shove, squeeze, ram, compress, force, cram, jam
2. *The cushions are* stuffed *with foam rubber.*
• fill, pad

stuffy *adjective* **stuffier, stuffiest**
1. *Open a window—it's* stuffy *in here.*
• airless, close, muggy, humid, stifling, musty, unventilated **opposite** airy
2. *I found the book a bit* stuffy. • boring, dull, dreary, pompous, stodgy **opposite** lively

stumble *verb*
1. *He* stumbled *on a tree root and twisted his ankle.* • trip, stagger, totter, flounder, lurch
2. *The actress* stumbled *over her words.*
• stammer, stutter, falter, hesitate
to stumble across something
I stumbled across *some old photos.* • come across, encounter, find, unearth, discover

stump *verb*
The detective was stumped *by the case.*
• baffle, bewilder, perplex, puzzle, fox, mystify, outwit, defeat, *(informal)* flummox

stun *verb* **stunning, stunned**
1. *The pilot was alive but* stunned. • daze, knock out, knock senseless, make unconscious
2. *The whole town was* stunned *by the news.*
• amaze, astonish, astound, shock, stagger, stupefy, bewilder, dumbfound

stunt *noun*
The acrobats performed breathtaking stunts.
• feat, exploit, act, deed, trick

stupid *adjective*
1. *Trolls are often very* stupid. • foolish, unintelligent, dense, dim, dim-witted, brainless, dumb, slow, thick, feeble-minded, half-witted, simple, simple-minded, dopey, dull
2. *It would be* stupid *to go snowboarding without a helmet.* • senseless, mindless, idiotic, unwise, foolhardy, silly, daft, crazy, mad **opposite** intelligent

sturdy adjective **sturdier, sturdiest**
1. *Shetland ponies are short and sturdy.*
• stocky, strong, robust, athletic, brawny, burly, healthy, hefty, husky, muscular, powerful, vigorous, well-built **opposite** weak
2. *She bought some sturdy walking boots.*
• durable, solid, sound, substantial, tough, well-made **opposite** flimsy

stutter verb
He tends to stutter when he's nervous.
• stammer, stumble, falter

style noun
1. *I don't like that style of jeans.* • design, pattern, fashion
2. *The book is written in an informal style.*
• manner, tone, way, wording
3. *The actress always dresses with great style.*
• elegance, stylishness, taste, sophistication

subdue verb
1. *The army managed to subdue the rebels.*
• beat, conquer, defeat, overcome, overpower, crush, vanquish
2. *Jason tried hard to subdue his anger.*
• suppress, restrain, repress, check, hold back, curb, control

subject noun
1. *Do you have any strong views on the subject?* • matter, issue, question, point, theme, topic
2. *Her passport shows that she is a British subject.* • citizen, national

submit verb **submitting, submitted**
1. *The swordsman finally submitted to his opponent.* • give in, surrender, yield
2. *You need to submit a membership form to join the club.* • give in, hand in, present

subside verb
1. *One side of the old cottage has started to subside.* • sink, settle
2. *After three days, the flood waters began to subside.* • go down, fall, recede, decline, ebb
3. *The pain will eventually subside.* • decrease, diminish, lessen, die down, dwindle

substance noun
1. *The spaceship was made from an alien substance.* • material, matter, stuff
2. *What was the substance of the book?*
• theme, essence, gist, subject matter

substantial adjective
1. *They have made substantial improvements to the city.* • considerable, significant, sizeable, worthwhile, big, large, generous **opposite** small
2. *There is a substantial fence to keep out wild animals.* • strong, sturdy, solid, robust, hefty, durable, sound, well-built **opposite** flimsy

substitute verb
You can substitute margarine for butter in the recipe. • exchange, swap, switch

You can also say: *margarine can* **take the place of** *butter or you can* **replace** *butter with margarine.*

substitute noun
The manager brought on a substitute during extra time. • replacement, reserve, standby, stand-in • A substitute for a sick actor is an **understudy**.

subtle adjective
1. *There was a subtle smell of roses in the air.*
• faint, slight, mild, delicate
2. *His jokes are too subtle for most people.*
• ingenious, sophisticated
3. *I tried to give her a subtle hint.* • gentle, tactful, indirect

subtract verb
If you subtract 5 from 20, you will have 15 left.
• take away, deduct, remove **opposite** add

succeed verb
1. *You have to work hard if you want to succeed.* • be successful, do well, prosper, flourish, thrive, (informal) make it
2. *Everyone hoped that the plan would succeed.* • be effective, produce results, work, (informal) catch on **opposite** fail
3. *Edward VII succeeded Queen Victoria.*
• come after, follow, take over from, replace

success noun
1. *She talked about her success as an actress.*
• achievement, attainment, fame
2. *They congratulated the team on their success.* • victory, win, triumph
3. *The success of the mission depends on the astronauts.* • effectiveness, successful outcome, completion

successful adjective
1. *She owns a very successful chain of restaurants.* • thriving, flourishing, booming, prosperous, profitable, popular
2. *The supporters cheered the successful team.* • winning, victorious, triumphant **opposite** unsuccessful

succession noun
Arthur received a succession of mysterious emails. • series, sequence, run, string, chain

suck verb
to suck something up
A sponge will suck up water. • soak up, draw up, absorb

sudden adjective
1. *Maria felt a sudden urge to burst into song.* • unexpected, unforeseen, impulsive, rash, quick **opposite** expected
2. *The bus came to a sudden halt.* • abrupt, sharp, swift **opposite** gradual

suffer verb
1. *He suffers terribly with his back.* • feel pain, hurt
2. *He will suffer for his crime.* • be punished, pay
3. *The home team suffered a humiliating defeat.* • experience, undergo, go through, endure, stand, bear, tolerate

suffering noun
The people endured great suffering during the war. • hardship, deprivation, misery, anguish, pain, distress

sufficient adjective
The castaways had sufficient food for five days. • enough, adequate, satisfactory **opposite** insufficient

suffocate verb
The firefighters were nearly suffocated by the fumes. • choke, stifle • To stop someone's breathing by squeezing their throat is to **strangle** or **throttle** them. • To stop someone's breathing by covering their nose and mouth is to **smother** them.

suggest verb
1. *Mum suggested going to the zoo.* • propose, advise, advocate, recommend
2. *Her comments suggest that she's not happy.* • imply, hint, indicate, signal

suggestion noun
They didn't like his suggestion. • proposal, plan, idea, proposition, recommendation

suit verb
1. *Would it suit you to stay here overnight?* • be convenient for, be suitable for, please, satisfy **opposite** displease
2. *His new haircut doesn't suit him.* • look good on, become, flatter

suitable adjective
1. *Please wear clothes suitable for wet weather.* • appropriate, apt, fitting, suited (to), proper, right **opposite** unsuitable
2. *Is this a suitable time to have a chat?* • convenient, acceptable, satisfactory **opposite** inconvenient

sulk verb
I was sulking because I wasn't allowed to play outside. • be sullen, mope, brood, pout

sulky adjective sulkier, sulkiest
Ron had turned into a sulky teenager. • moody, sullen, brooding, moping, mopey

sullen adjective
Beth slouched on the sofa, looking sullen. • sulky, moody, bad-tempered, mopey, morose, surly, sour **opposite** cheerful, good-tempered

sum noun
1. *The sum of 2 and 2 is 4.* • total, result
2. *They lost a large sum of money.* • amount, quantity
sums
Desmond is good at doing sums. • adding up, arithmetic, (informal) maths

sum verb summing, summed
to sum up
See **summarize**.

summarize verb
Can you summarize the main points of the story? • sum up, outline, review, (informal) recap This word can also be spelled **summarise**.

summary noun summaries
We each wrote a summary of the poem. • synopsis, précis, outline

summon verb
The king summoned his knights from far and wide. • call, send for, order to come, bid to come • To ask someone politely to come is to **invite** them.

sunny adjective sunnier, sunniest
It was a beautiful sunny day. • fine, clear, cloudless **opposite** cloudy

sunrise noun
The magic spell wears off at sunrise. • dawn, daybreak **opposite** sunset

sunset noun
They arranged to meet in the churchyard at sunset. • sundown, dusk, twilight, evening, nightfall **opposite** sunrise

superb adjective
Brazil scored another superb goal. • excellent, outstanding, exceptional, remarkable, impressive, magnificent, marvellous, splendid, tremendous, wonderful, (informal) brilliant, fantastic, terrific, fabulous, sensational, super

superficial adjective
1. *The scratch on his leg was only superficial.* • on the surface, shallow, slight **opposite** deep
2. *The book gives a very superficial view of history.* • simple, trivial, lightweight, shallow, frivolous, casual **opposite** thorough, profound

superior adjective
1. *A colonel is superior in rank to a captain.* • senior, higher, greater
2. *They only sell chocolate of superior quality.* • first-class, first-rate, top, top-notch, choice, select, better
3. *I don't like her superior attitude.* • arrogant, haughty, snobbish, stuck-up, self-important, (informal) snooty **opposite** inferior

supervise verb
Children must be supervised by an adult in the park. • oversee, superintend, watch over, be in charge of, be responsible for, direct, manage • To supervise candidates in an exam is to **invigilate**.

supple adjective
The moccasins are made of supple leather. • flexible, pliable, soft **opposite** stiff, rigid

supply verb supplies, supplying, supplied
The art shop can supply you with brushes and paints. • provide, equip, furnish

supply noun supplies
They had a good supply of fuel for the winter. • quantity, stock, store, reserve
supplies
We bought supplies for the camping trip. • provisions, stores, rations, food, necessities

support noun
1. *She thanked them for their support.* • assistance, backing, aid, cooperation, encouragement, help
2. *The cinema was reopened with support from local businesses.* • donations, contributions, sponsorship
3. *The supports prevented the wall from collapsing.* • prop, brace • A support for a shelf is a **bracket**. • A support built against a wall is a **buttress**. • A support for someone with an injured leg is a **crutch**. • A bar of wood or metal supporting a framework is a **strut**. • A support put under a board to make a table is a **trestle**.

support verb
1. *The rope couldn't support his weight.* • bear, carry, stand, hold up
2. *The beams support the roof.* • prop up, strengthen, reinforce
3. *His friends supported him when he was in trouble.* • aid, assist, help, back, encourage, stand by, stand up for, rally round
4. *She had to work to support her family.* • maintain, keep, provide for
5. *He supports several local charities.* • donate to, contribute to, give to
6. *Which team did you support in the World Cup?* • be a supporter of, follow

supporter noun
1. *The home supporters cheered their team.* • fan, follower
2. *She is a well-known supporter of animal rights.* • champion, advocate, backer, defender

suppose verb
1. *I suppose you want to borrow some money.* • expect, presume, assume, guess, believe, think
2. *Suppose a spaceship landed in your garden!* • imagine, pretend, fancy
to be supposed to do something
The bus is supposed to leave at 9 o'clock. • be meant to, be due to, be expected to, ought to

suppress verb
1. *He managed to suppress his anger.* • check, hold back, contain, control, repress, restrain, curb, bottle up, stifle • To suppress ideas for political or moral reasons is to **censor** them.
2. *The army suppressed the rebellion.* • crush, quash, quell, put down, stamp out, stop, subdue

supreme adjective
Her supreme achievement was winning a gold medal. • greatest, highest, best, outstanding, top

sure adjective
1. *I'm sure that I'm right.* • certain, convinced, confident, definite, positive **opposite** unsure, uncertain
2. *He's sure to phone tonight.* • bound, certain **opposite** unlikely

surface noun
1. *The surface of Mars is barren and rocky.*
• exterior, outside • The surface of something may be covered with a **crust** or **shell** or **skin**. • A thin surface of expensive wood on furniture is a **veneer**. **opposite** centre
2. *A dice has dots on each surface.* • face, side **opposite** inside
3. *Oil floated on the surface of the water.* • top **opposite** bottom

surge verb
1. *Massive waves surged around the tiny raft.*
• rise, roll, swirl, heave, billow
2. *The crowd surged forward.* • rush, push, sweep

surpass verb
It will be hard to surpass last year's performance. • beat, exceed, do better than, outdo

surprise noun
The news that Sara was married came as a surprise. • amazement, astonishment, revelation, shock, wonder, (informal) bombshell

surprise verb
1. *I was surprised by how well she could sing.* • amaze, astonish, astound, stagger, startle, stun, take aback, take by surprise, dumbfound, (informal) bowl over, flabbergast
2. *He surprised the burglars as they came through the window.* • discover, come upon, catch unawares, catch off guard, catch red-handed

surprised adjective

WRITING TIPS

SOMEONE WHO FEELS SURPRISED MIGHT
• have eyes bulging out of their head, have eyes on the end of stalks, jump out of their skin, stare wide-eyed

SOMETHING WHICH SURPRISES YOU MIGHT
• knock you for six, knock your socks off, knock you sideways, make your eyes pop

---

surprising adjective
There are a surprising number of errors in the book. • amazing, astonishing, astounding, extraordinary, remarkable, incredible, staggering, startling, stunning, unexpected **opposite** predictable

surrender verb
1. *The band of outlaws refused to surrender.*
• admit defeat, give in, yield, submit, capitulate
2. *Please surrender your ticket to the driver.*
• give, hand over

surround verb
1. *The garden was surrounded by a stone wall.*
• enclose, fence in, wall in
2. *The pack of wolves surrounded its prey.*
• encircle, ring, hem in, besiege

surroundings plural noun
The hotel is set in very pleasant surroundings.
• setting, location, environment

survey noun
They did a survey of local leisure facilities.
• review, investigation, study • A survey to count the population of an area is a **census**.

survey verb
1. *You can survey the whole valley from the top of the tower.* • view, look over, look at, observe
2. *They surveyed the damage done by the storm.* • inspect, examine, scrutinize, study

survive verb
1. *He managed to survive alone on the island for six months.* • stay alive, last, live, keep going, carry on, continue **opposite** die
2. *Will the birds survive this cold weather?*
• endure, withstand, live through, weather

suspect verb
1. *The police suspected his motives.* • doubt, mistrust, have suspicions about
2. *I suspect that the shop will be closed on Sundays.* • expect, imagine, presume, guess, sense, fancy

suspend verb
1. *The meeting was suspended until the next day.* • adjourn, break off, discontinue, interrupt
2. *For the party, we suspended balloons from the ceiling.* • hang, dangle, swing

suspense noun
The film was a thriller, full of action and suspense. • tension, uncertainty, anticipation, expectancy, drama, excitement

suspicion noun
I have a suspicion that he is lying. • feeling, hunch, inkling, intuition, impression

suspicious adjective
1. *There is something about him which makes me suspicious.* • doubtful, distrustful,

mistrustful, unsure, uneasy, wary
opposite trusting
2. *What do you make of his suspicious behaviour?* • questionable, suspect, dubious, shady, (informal) fishy

swagger verb
The lead actor swaggered about on stage.
• strut, parade

swallow verb
The bread was so dry that it was hard to swallow. • gulp down
to swallow something up
As it climbed higher, the rocket was swallowed up by the clouds. • envelop, engulf, cover over, absorb

swamp verb
A huge wave threatened to swamp the ship. • overwhelm, engulf, inundate, flood, submerge

swamp noun
Much of the land near the coast is swamp.
• marsh, bog, mire, fen, quicksand, quagmire

swap or **swop** verb swapping, swapped or swopping, swopped
We swapped seats so I could sit by the aisle.
• change, exchange, switch, substitute

swarm verb
Hundreds of people swarmed around the film star. • crowd, flock
to swarm with
The garden is swarming with ants. • be overrun by, be crawling with, be infested with, teem with

sway verb
The tall grass swayed in the breeze. • wave, swing, rock, bend, lean

swear verb swearing, swore, sworn
1. *The knight swore that he would protect the unicorn.* • pledge, promise, vow, give your word, take an oath
2. *The player swore when he bashed his knee.*
• curse

sweat verb
He sweats a lot in hot weather. • perspire

sweep verb sweeping, swept
1. *She swept the floor with an old broom.*
• brush, clean, dust
2. *The bus swept past.* • shoot, speed, zoom

sweet adjective
1. *The pudding is too sweet for me.*
• sickly, sugary, sweetened, syrupy
opposites acid, bitter, savoury
2. *The sweet smell of roses filled the room.*
• fragrant, pleasant
opposite foul
3. *Fergus heard the sweet sound of a harp.*
• melodious, pleasant, soothing, tuneful
opposite ugly
4. *What a sweet little cottage!*
• attractive, charming, dear, lovely, pretty, quaint
opposite unattractive

sweet noun

WORD WEB

SOME KINDS OF SWEET
• barley sugar, boiled sweet, bull's-eye, butterscotch, candyfloss, caramel, chewing gum, chocolate, fruit pastille, fudge, humbug, liquorice, lollipop, marshmallow, marzipan, mint or peppermint, nougat, rock, tablet, toffee, Turkish delight

swerve verb
The car swerved to avoid a hedgehog. • turn aside, veer, dodge, swing

swift adjective
1. *They set off at a swift pace.*
• fast, quick, rapid, speedy, brisk, lively
2. *She received a swift reply to her email.*
• quick, fast, immediate, instant, prompt, speedy, snappy

swim verb swimming, swam, swum
We swam in the sea on our holiday.
• go swimming, bathe, take a dip

WORD WEB

VARIOUS SWIMMING STROKES
• backstroke, breaststroke, butterfly, crawl, doggy-paddle

PLACES WHERE YOU CAN SWIM
• baths, leisure pool, lido, paddling pool, swimming baths or swimming pool

CLOTHING FOR SWIMMING
• bathing costume, bathing suit, bikini, swimming cap, swimming costume, swimsuit, trunks

OTHER EQUIPMENT FOR SWIMMING
• armbands, flippers, float, goggles, nose-clip, rubber ring, snorkel

swing *verb* **swinging, swung**
1. *A glass chandelier swung from the ceiling.*
• hang, dangle, sway, flap, wave about
2. *She swung round when I called her name.*
• turn, twist, veer, swerve

swirl *verb*
Clouds of dust swirled up in the desert wind.
• spin, twirl, whirl, churn

switch *verb*
1. *Please remember to switch off the light.*
• turn
2. *The teams will switch ends at half-time.*
• change, swap, exchange, shift

swoop *verb*
The owl swooped and caught the mouse.
• dive, drop, plunge, plummet, descend, pounce

symbol *noun*
The dove is a symbol of peace. • sign, emblem, image • The symbols we use in writing are **characters** or **letters**. • The symbols used in ancient Egyptian writing were **hieroglyphics**. • The symbol of a club or school is their **badge**. • The symbol of a firm or organization is their **logo**.

sympathetic *adjective*
They were sympathetic when my mother was ill. • understanding, compassionate, concerned, caring, comforting, kind, supportive **opposite** unsympathetic

sympathize *verb*
to sympathize with
We sympathized with those who had lost their homes. • be sympathetic towards, be sorry for, feel for, commiserate with This word can also be spelled **sympathise**.

sympathy *noun* **sympathies**
Did you feel any sympathy for the characters in the story? • understanding, compassion, pity, fellow-feeling, tenderness

synonym *noun*
'Cheerful' is a synonym of 'happy'.
opposite antonym

synthetic *adjective*
Nylon is a synthetic material. • artificial, man-made, manufactured, imitation
opposite natural

system *noun*
1. *The city has an archaic transport system.*
• organization, structure, network, framework, (informal) set-up
2. *Do you understand the new cataloguing system?* • procedure, process, scheme, arrangement, method, routine

Look at the *Writing Tips* in this thesaurus to inspire you.

tablet *noun*
1. *The doctor prescribed some tablets for the pain.* • pill, capsule, pellet
2. *There was a stone tablet above the entrance to the tomb.* • slab, plaque
3. *He put a tablet of powder in the washing machine.* • block, piece, bar, chunk

tactful *adjective*
She gave him a tactful reminder about her birthday. • subtle, discreet, diplomatic, sensitive, thoughtful **opposite** tactless

tag *verb* tagging, tagged
Every item is tagged with a price label. • identify, label, mark
to tag along with someone
She tagged along with them when they left. • accompany, follow, go with, join
to tag something on
He tagged on a PS at the end of his letter. • add, attach, tack on

tail *noun*
He joined the tail of the queue. • end, back, rear

tail *verb*
The detective tailed the suspect to this address. • follow, pursue, track, trail, shadow, stalk
to tail off
The number of tourists tails off in October. • decrease, decline, lessen, diminish, dwindle, wane

take *verb* taking, took, taken
1. *Naomi took her sister's hand.* • clutch, clasp, take hold of, grasp, grip, seize, snatch, grab
2. *The soldiers took many prisoners.* • catch, capture, seize, detain
3. *Someone has taken my pen.* • steal, remove, make off with, (informal) swipe, pinch
4. *The guide will take you to the edge of the forest.* • conduct, escort, lead, accompany
5. *The bus took us right to the station.* • bring, carry, convey, transport

6. *It'll take two people to lift that table.* • need, require
7. *The caravan can take six people.* • hold, contain, accommodate, have room for
8. *He couldn't take the heat of the midday sun.* • bear, put up with, stand, endure, tolerate, suffer, stomach
9. *He took their names and addresses.* • make a note of, record, write down
10. *The magician asked me to take a card.* • pick, choose, select
11. *Take 2 from 8 and you get 6.* • subtract, take away, deduct

tale *noun*
Pinocchio is a tale about a boy made of wood. • story, narrative, account, (informal) yarn

talent *noun*
She has a great talent for music. • gift, ability, aptitude, skill, flair, knack • Unusually great talent is **genius**.

talented *adjective*
He's a very talented dancer. • gifted, able, accomplished, capable, skilled, skilful, clever, brilliant • If you are talented in several ways, you are **versatile**.

talk *verb*
1. *Doug was trying to teach his parrot to talk.* • speak, say things, communicate, express yourself
2. *The two old friends had a lot to talk about.* • discuss, converse, chat, chatter, gossip, (informal) natter

talk *noun*
1. *I need to have a talk with you soon.* • conversation, discussion, chat • The talk between characters in a story is the **dialogue**.
2. *There is a talk about Egyptian art at lunchtime.* • lecture, presentation, speech, address • A talk in church is a **sermon**.

talkative *adjective*
You're not very talkative this morning. • chatty, communicative, vocal, forthcoming, articulate • An informal name for a talkative person is a **chatterbox**.

tall *adjective*
1. *Jasmine is tall for her age.* • big **opposite** short
2. *Singapore has many tall buildings.* • high, lofty, towering, soaring, giant • Buildings with many floors are **high-rise** or **multi-storey** buildings. **opposite** low

a b c d e f g h i j k l m n o p q r s t u v w x y z

tame *adjective*
1. *The guinea pigs are tame and used to people.* • domesticated, broken in, docile, gentle, obedient, manageable **opposite** wild
2. *The film seems very tame nowadays.* • dull, boring, tedious, bland, unexciting, uninteresting **opposite** exciting

tamper *verb*
to tamper with something
Someone has been tampering with the lock. • meddle with, tinker with, fiddle about with, interfere with

tap *verb* tapping, tapped
Someone tapped three times on the door. • knock, rap, strike

tape *noun*
The stack of old letters was tied up with tape. • ribbon, braid, binding

target *noun*
1. *Her target was to swim thirty lengths.* • goal, aim, objective, intention, purpose, hope, ambition
2. *She was the target of his jokes.* • object, victim, butt

task *noun*
1. *The robot was given a number of tasks to do.* • job, chore, exercise, errand
2. *The soldiers' task was to capture the hill.* • assignment, mission, duty, undertaking

taste *verb*
Taste the soup to see if it needs salt. • sample, try, test, sip

taste *noun*
1. *I love the taste of ginger.* • flavour
2. *Can I have a taste of the cheese?* • mouthful, bite, morsel, nibble, bit, piece, sample
3. *Her taste in clothes is a bit odd.* • choice, preference, discrimination, judgement

tasteless *adjective*
1. *He apologized for making a tasteless remark.* • crude, tactless, indelicate, inappropriate **opposite** tasteful
2. *The sprouts were overcooked and tasteless.* • flavourless, bland, insipid **opposite** flavourful

tasty *adjective* tastier, tastiest
That pie was very tasty. • delicious, appetizing **opposite** unappetizing

taunt *verb*
The gladiator taunted his opponent. • barrack, insult, jeer at, laugh at, make fun of, mock, ridicule, sneer at

taut *adjective*
Make sure the rope is taut. • tight, tense, stretched **opposite** slack

teach *verb* teaches, teaching, taught
My dad is teaching me to play the guitar. • educate, inform, instruct • To teach people to play a sport is to **coach** or **train** them. • To teach one person at a time or a small group is to **tutor** them.

teacher *noun*
We have a new ballet teacher. • tutor, instructor, trainer • Someone who teaches you to play a sport is a **coach**. • In the past, a woman who taught children in a private household was a **governess**.

team *noun*
She's been picked for the junior hockey team. • side

tear *verb* tearing, tore, torn
1. *The tree branch tore a hole in our kite.* • rip, snag, gash, shred, split, slit
2. *He tore home to watch his favourite TV programme.* • run, rush, dash, hurry, race, sprint, speed

tear *noun*
There was a tear in one of the sails. • cut, rip, rent, split, gash, hole, opening, slit, gap

tease *verb*
They teased him about his new haircut. • taunt, make fun of, poke fun at, mock, ridicule, laugh at

tedious *adjective*
It was a tedious journey by bus. • boring, dreary, dull, tiresome, monotonous, unexciting, uninteresting **opposite** exciting

television *noun*
Jay was in the front room watching television. • TV, home cinema, *(informal)* telly, the box, the tube, the goggle box • The part of a television where the images appear is the **screen**.

tell *verb* telling, told
1. *Tell us what you can see.* • describe, explain, reveal, report, say, state
2. *Tell me when you are ready.* • let you know, inform, notify, announce, communicate

3. *He told them to stop making so much noise.* • order, command, direct, instruct

4. *We told each other scary ghost stories.*
• narrate, relate
5. *He told me he would buy the tickets.*
• assure, promise
6. *She couldn't tell where she was in the dark.*
• make out, recognize, identify, perceive
7. *Can you tell one twin from the other?*
• distinguish, separate
to tell someone off
She told them off for being late. • scold, reprimand, reproach, (informal) tick off

temper *noun*
1. *Mr Black had been in a bad temper all morning.* • mood, humour, state of mind
2. *The chef is always flying into a temper.*
• rage, fury, fit of anger, tantrum
to lose your temper
When she loses her temper, her cheeks go red.
• get angry, get annoyed, fly into a rage

temporary *adjective*
They made a temporary shelter for the night.
• makeshift, provisional **opposite** permanent

tempt *verb*
Can I tempt you to have more pudding? • coax, entice, persuade, attract • To tempt someone by offering them money is to **bribe** them. • To tempt an animal into a trap is to **lure** it.

tend *verb*
1. *One of the campers was left to tend the fire.*
• mind, watch over, maintain
2. *Ned spends a lot of time tending his garden.*
• take care of, cultivate, manage
3. *Nurses tended those who were injured.*
• care for, attend to, look after, nurse, treat
to tend to do something
She tends to worry too much. • be inclined to, be liable to, be apt to

tender *adjective*
1. *Frost may damage tender plants.* • delicate, fragile **opposite** hardy, strong
2. *Cook the meat slowly until it is tender.* • soft, succulent, juicy **opposite** tough
3. *The bruise is still tender.* • painful, sensitive, sore
4. *She gave him a tender smile.* • affectionate, kind, loving, caring, warm-hearted, compassionate, sympathetic, fond
opposite uncaring

tense *adjective*
1. *The muscles in her shoulders were tense.*
• taut, tight, strained, stretched
2. *The crowd were tense as they waited to hear the results.* • anxious, nervous, apprehensive, edgy, on edge, fidgety, jumpy, jittery, (informal) uptight
3. *It was a tense moment for all of us.*
• nerve-racking, stressful, worrying
opposite relaxed

tension *noun*
The tension of waiting was almost unbearable.
• stress, strain, anxiety, nervousness, suspense, worry

term *noun*
1. *He was sentenced to a term in prison.*
• period, time, spell, stretch, session
2. *The book has a glossary of technical terms.*
• word, name, expression

terrible *adjective*
We heard there had been a terrible accident.
• awful, dreadful, horrible, appalling, shocking, ghastly, horrific, frightful

terrific *adjective (informal)*
1. *The footprint of the yeti was a terrific size.*
• big, huge, immense, enormous, giant, gigantic, colossal, massive
2. *She's a terrific tennis player.* • excellent, first-class, first-rate, superb, marvellous, wonderful, (informal) brilliant, fantastic, fabulous

terrify *verb* terrifies, terrifying, terrified
The dogs were terrified by the thunder.
• frighten, scare, startle, alarm, panic, horrify, petrify

territory *noun* territories
We had now entered uncharted territory.
• land, area, ground, terrain, country, district, region, sector, zone • A territory which is part of a country is a **province**.

terror *noun*
Her eyes filled with terror as she described the ghost. • fear, fright, horror, panic, alarm, dread

test *noun*
How did you do in the maths test? • exam, examination, assessment, appraisal, evaluation • A set of questions you answer for fun is a **quiz**. • A test for a job as an actor or singer is an **audition**. • A test to find the truth about something is an **experiment** or **trial**.

test *verb*
1. *I made an appointment to have my eyes tested.* • examine, check, evaluate, assess, screen
2. *He is testing a new formula for invisibile ink.*
• experiment with, try out, trial

a b c d e f g h i j k l m n o p q r s t u v w x y z

texture *noun*
Silk has a smooth texture. • feel, touch, quality, consistency

thankful *adjective*
to be thankful for something
The travellers were thankful for our help.
• grateful for, appreciative of, pleased about, relieved about **opposite** ungrateful

thanks *plural noun*
She sent them a card to show her thanks.
• gratitude, appreciation

thaw *verb*
1. *The snowman gradually began to thaw.*
• melt, dissolve
2. *Leave frozen food to thaw before cooking it.*
• defrost, unfreeze

theft *noun*
He was found guilty of theft. • robbery, stealing

theme *noun*
What is the theme of the poem? • subject, topic, idea, gist, argument

theory *noun* **theories**
1. *The detective has a theory about the case.*
• explanation, hypothesis, view, belief, idea, notion, suggestion
2. *She bought a book about musical theory.*
• laws, principles, rules

thick *adjective*
1. *The Roman wall was about two metres thick.*
• wide, broad
2. *The cabin was made from thick logs of wood.* • stout, chunky, heavy, solid, substantial **opposite** thin, slender
3. *The explorers hacked their way through the thick jungle.* • dense, close, compact
4. *His boots got stuck in a thick layer of mud.*
• deep, heavy **opposite** thin, shallow
5. *The guide spoke with a thick Polish accent.*
• heavy, noticeable **opposite** slight
6. *(informal) Fortunately, the giant was rather thick.* • stupid, brainless, foolish **opposite** intelligent

thief *noun* **thieves**
The police managed to catch the thief. • robber
• Someone who steals from people's homes is a **burglar** or **housebreaker**. • Someone who steals from people in the street is a **pickpocket**. • Someone who steals from shops is a **shoplifter**. • In the past, someone who stole from travellers was a **highwayman**.

thin *adjective* **thinner, thinnest**
1. *The prisoners were dreadfully thin.* • lean, skinny, bony, gaunt, underweight, spare, slight • Someone who is thin and tall is **lanky**.
• Someone who is thin but strong is **wiry**.
• Someone who is thin but attractive is **slim** or **slender**. • Thin arms or legs are **spindly**.
• A common simile is **as thin as a rake**. **opposite** fat
2. *The fairy wore a thin cloak of spider's silk.*
• fine, light, delicate, flimsy, sheer, wispy
• A thin line is a **fine** or **narrow** line. • A thin book is a **slim** book. **opposite** thick
3. *The icing should be thin enough to spread.*
• runny, watery **opposite** thick

thing *noun*
1. *What's that green thing on the floor?* • item, object, article
2. *We had a lot of things to talk about.*
• matter, affair, detail, point, factor
3. *A lot of things had happened since we spoke.* • event, happening, occurrence, incident
4. *I have only one thing left to do.* • job, task, act, action
things
Put your things in one of the lockers.
• belongings, possessions, stuff, equipment, gear

think *verb* **thinking, thought**
1. *Think before you do anything rash.*
• consider, contemplate, reflect, deliberate, reason • To think hard about something is to **concentrate** on it. • To think quietly and deeply about something is to **meditate**.
• To keep thinking anxiously about something is to **brood** on it.
2. *Do you think this is a good idea?* • believe, feel, consider, judge, conclude
3. *What do you think this ring is worth?*
• reckon, suppose, imagine, estimate, guess, expect
to think about something
I need some more time to think about it.
• consider, reflect on, ponder, muse on, mull over
to think something up
They thought up a good plan. • invent, make up, conceive, concoct, devise

thirsty *adjective* **thirstier, thirstiest**
They were thirsty after their long walk. • dry, parched • If someone is ill through lack of fluids, they are **dehydrated**.

thorn *noun*
The florist cut the thorns off the rose stems.
• prickle, spike, needle, barb

thorough *adjective*
1. *The doctor gave him a thorough examination.* • comprehensive, full, rigorous, careful, methodical, systematic, meticulous, painstaking, conscientious **opposite** superficial
2. *He's made a thorough mess of things!*
• complete, total, utter, absolute, downright

thought *noun*
1. *She gave a lot of thought to the problem.*
• consideration, deliberation, study
2. *The detective spent some time in thought.*
• thinking, contemplation, reflection, meditation
3. *What are your thoughts on the matter?*
• opinion, belief, idea, notion, conclusion

thoughtful *adjective*
1. *Mr Levi had a thoughtful expression on his face.* • pensive, reflective, absorbed, preoccupied **opposite** blank, vacant
2. *She added some thoughtful comments in the margin.* • well-thought-out, careful, conscientious, thorough **opposite** careless
3. *It was very thoughtful of you to visit me in hospital.* • caring, considerate, kind, friendly, good-natured, unselfish **opposite** thoughtless

thoughtless *adjective*
It was thoughtless of him to mention her dead husband. • inconsiderate, insensitive, uncaring, unthinking, negligent, ill-considered, rash **opposite** thoughtful

thrash *verb*
1. *The rider thrashed his horse to make it go faster.* • hit, beat, whip, flog, (informal) whack, wallop
2. *The crocodile thrashed its tail in the mud.*
• swish, flail, jerk, toss
3. *(informal) The visitors thrashed the home side 6–0.* • beat, defeat, trounce, hammer, smash

threat *noun*
1. *She made a threat about phoning the police.*
• warning
2. *Earthquakes are a constant threat in California.* • danger, menace, hazard, risk

threaten *verb*
1. *The bandits threatened him when he tried to escape.* • make threats against, menace, intimidate, terrorize, bully, browbeat
2. *The forecast threatened rain.* • warn of

3. *Wild tigers are threatened with extinction.*
• endanger, put at risk

thrill *noun*
Kim loves the thrill of rock climbing.
• adventure, excitement, sensation, tingle, (slang) buzz, kick

thrill *verb*
The thought of seeing a real shark thrilled him no end. • excite, exhilarate, electrify, rouse, stir, stimulate **opposite** bore

thrilled *adjective*
I was thrilled to be invited to the wedding.
• delighted, pleased, excited, overjoyed, ecstatic

thrive *verb* thriving, thrived, throve, thrived, thriven
Tomato plants thrive in greenhouses. • do well, flourish, grow, prosper, succeed

throb *verb* throbbing, throbbed
She could feel the blood throbbing through her veins. • beat, pound, pulse, pulsate

throw *verb* throwing, threw, thrown
1. *I threw some bread into the pond for the ducks.* • fling, cast, pitch, sling, toss, (slang) bung, chuck • To deliver the ball in cricket or rounders is to **bowl**. • To throw the shot in athletics is to **put** the shot. • To throw something high in the air is to **lob** it.
• To throw something heavy is to **heave** it.
• To throw something with great force is to **hurl** it. • If someone throws a lot of things at you, they **pelt** you.
2. *The horse threw its rider.* • throw off, shake off, dislodge
to throw away
We threw away a pile of old junk. • get rid of, dispose of, discard, scrap, (informal) dump, ditch

thrust *verb*
1. *Drew thrust his hands into his pockets.*
• push, force, shove
2. *The bandit thrust at him with a dagger.*
• lunge, jab, prod, stab, poke

thump *verb*
'Silence!' he rasped, thumping his fist on the table. • bang, bash, pound, hit, strike, knock, rap, (informal) whack, wham

tidy *adjective* tidier, tidiest
Mr Rackham likes to keep his office tidy. • neat, orderly, uncluttered, trim, smart, spruce, straight **opposite** untidy

tie *verb* **ties**, **tying**, **tied**
1. *Zoe tied a pink ribbon round the parcel.*
• bind, fasten, hitch, knot, loop, secure • To tie up a boat is to **moor** it. • To tie up an animal is to **tether** it. **opposite** untie
2. *The two teams are still tied.* • be equal, be level, draw

tight *adjective*
1. *The lid was too tight for him to unscrew.*
• firm, fast, secure • If it is so tight that air cannot get through, it is **airtight**. • If it is so tight that water cannot get through, it is **watertight**. **opposite** loose
2. *They squeezed into the tight space.*
• cramped, compact, small, narrow, poky, snug **opposite** spacious
3. *Make sure that the ropes are tight.* • taut, tense, stretched, rigid • A common simile is **as tight as a drum**. **opposite** slack

tighten *verb*
1. *She tightened her grip on his hand.*
• increase, strengthen, tense, stiffen
2. *You need to tighten the guy ropes.* • make taut, pull tighter, stretch
3. *He tried to tighten the screw.* • make tighter, screw up **opposite** loosen

tilt *verb*
The caravan tilted to one side. • lean, incline, tip, slant, slope, angle • When a ship tilts to one side, it **lists**.

time *noun*
1. *Is this a convenient time to talk?* • moment, occasion, opportunity
2. *Autumn is my favourite time of the year.*
• phase, season
3. *He spent a short time living in China.*
• period, while, term, spell, stretch
4. *Shakespeare lived in the time of Elizabeth I.*
• era, age, days, epoch, period
5. *Please try to keep time with the music.*
• tempo, beat, rhythm

WORD WEB

UNITS FOR MEASURING TIME
• second, minute, hour, day, week, fortnight, month, year, decade, century, millennium

INSTRUMENTS USED TO MEASURE TIME
• clock, eggtimer, hourglass, pocket watch, stopwatch, sundial, timer, watch, wristwatch

---

on time
Please try to be on time. • punctual, prompt

timid *adjective*
At first, the mermaid was too timid to say anything. • shy, bashful, modest, nervous, fearful, shrinking, retiring, sheepish
• A common simile is **as timid as a mouse**.
opposite brave, confident

tingle *verb*
My ears were tingling with the cold. • prickle, sting, tickle

tingle *noun*
1. *She felt a tingle in her foot.* • prickling, stinging, tickle, tickling, pins and needles
2. *He felt a tingle of excitement.* • thrill, sensation, quiver, shiver

tinker *verb*
He tinkered with the computer to get it to work. • fiddle, play about, dabble, meddle, tamper

tint *noun*
The paint was white with a faint tint of blue.
• colour, hue, shade, tone

tiny *adjective* **tinier**, **tiniest**
The ladybird was so tiny that you could hardly see it. • little, minute, miniature, microscopic, minuscule, *(informal)* teeny, titchy
opposite big, large

tip *noun*
1. *The tip of his nose felt cold.* • end, point
• The tip of an ink pen is the **nib**.
2. *The tip of the mountain was covered in snow.* • cap, peak, top, summit, pinnacle, crown
3. *He gave them some useful tips on first aid.* • hint, piece of advice, suggestion, clue, pointer
4. *They took a load of rubbish to the tip.*
• dump, rubbish heap

tip *verb* **tipping**, **tipped**
1. *The caravan tipped to one side.* • lean, tilt, incline, slope, slant • When a ship tips slightly to one side, it **lists**. • When a ship tips right over, it **capsizes**.
2. *Sophie tipped the box of crayons onto the table.* • empty, turn out, dump, unload
to tip over
He tipped the milk jug over by accident.
• knock over, overturn, topple, upset

tire *verb*
to tire someone out
Running in the playground had tired us all out. • exhaust, wear out **opposite** refresh, invigorate

tired *adjective*
Lie down if you're tired. • exhausted, fatigued, weary, worn out, listless, sleepy, drowsy, *(informal)* all in
to be tired of something
I'm tired of watching TV. • bored with, fed up with, sick of • If you are not interested in anything, you are **apathetic**.

title *noun*
1. *She couldn't think of a title for the story.*
• name, heading • The title above a newspaper story is a **headline**. • A title or brief description next to a picture is a **caption**.
2. *The form asks you to fill in your name and title.* • form of address, designation, rank • The ordinary title used before a man's name is **Mr**.
• The ordinary title used before a woman's name is **Miss, Mrs or Ms**. • A polite way to address someone whose name you don't know is **sir** or **madam**.

token *noun*
1. *You can exchange this token for a free drink.*
• voucher, coupon, ticket, counter
2. *They gave her a card as a token of their thanks.* • sign, symbol, mark, expression, indication, proof, reminder

tolerant *adjective*
Molly was very tolerant towards other people.
• understanding, easygoing, open-minded, sympathetic, charitable, forgiving, lenient, indulgent, long-suffering **opposite** intolerant

tolerate *verb*
1. *He won't tolerate sloppy writing.* • accept, permit, put up with
2. *Cactus plants can tolerate extreme heat.*
• bear, endure, stand, abide, suffer, stomach, *(informal)* stick

tomb *noun*
Inside the tomb were several ancient skeletons. • burial chamber, crypt, grave, mausoleum, sepulchre, vault • An underground passage containing several tombs is a **catacomb**. • A tomb is often marked by a **tombstone**, **gravestone** or **headstone**.

tone *noun*
1. *There was an angry tone to her voice.* • note, sound, quality, intonation, manner
2. *The room is painted in subtle tones.* • colour, hue, shade, tint

3. *Eerie music created the right tone for the film.* • feeling, mood, atmosphere, spirit, effect

tooth *noun* **teeth**

✏️ WRITING TIPS

You can use these words to describe **teeth** or **jaws**:
• jagged, serrated, razor-sharp, pincer-like, needle-sharp

TEETH MAY
• bite, chew, grind, munch, chomp, gnash, snap, tear, rip, puncture

---

top *noun*
1. *They climbed to the top of the hill.*
• peak, summit, tip, crown, crest, head **opposite** bottom, base
2. *The desk top was covered with newspapers.*
• surface
3. *The top of the jar was screwed on tightly.*
• lid, cap, cover, covering

top *adjective*
1. *Their office is on the top floor.* • highest, topmost, uppermost, upper **opposite** bottom, lowest
2. *She got top marks in her exam.* • most, best, highest
3. *The skiers set off at top speed.* • greatest, maximum
4. *He is one of Europe's top chefs.* • best, leading, finest, foremost, principal, superior **opposite** junior

top *verb* **topping, topped**
1. *Mum topped the cake with fudge icing.*
• cover, decorate, garnish, crown
2. *The athlete is hoping to top her personal best.* • beat, better, exceed, outdo, surpass

topic *noun*
What was the topic of the conversation?
• subject, talking-point, issue, matter, question

topical *adjective*
The website often discusses topical issues.
• current, recent, up-to-date

topple *verb*
1. *The books were piled too high and toppled over.* • fall, tumble, overbalance, collapse
2. *The gale toppled their TV aerial.* • knock down, overturn, upset
3. *The rebels plotted to topple the king.*
• overthrow, bring down, remove from office

torrent *noun*
A torrent of water flowed down the hill. • flood, gush, rush, stream, cascade

toss *verb*
1. *He tossed a coin into the wishing-well.* • throw, cast, hurl, fling, pitch, sling, (*informal*) chuck
2. *Let's toss a coin to see who'll go first.* • flip, spin
3. *The little boat tossed about in the storm.* • lurch, pitch, roll, heave, rock, bob
4. *She tossed and turned, unable to get to sleep.* • thrash about, flail, writhe, wriggle

total *noun*
A total of 15 million people live in Tokyo. • sum, whole, entirety, amount

total *adjective*
1. *The bill shows the total amount due.* • full, complete, whole, entire
2. *The party was a total disaster.* • complete, utter, absolute, thorough, downright, sheer

total *verb* **totalling, totalled**
The donations total almost 300 euros. • add up to, amount to, come to, make

totally *adverb*
I totally forgot to do my homework. • completely, utterly, fully, absolutely

totter *verb*
The child tottered across the floor. • stagger, stumble, reel, wobble

touch *verb*
1. *Some animals don't like to be touched.* • feel, handle, stroke, fondle, caress, pat, pet
2. *The car just touched the gatepost.* • brush, graze, contact
3. *The speed of the racing car touched 200 miles per hour.* • reach, rise to
4. *I was touched by the poem that she wrote.* • move, affect, stir

touch *noun*
1. *I felt a light touch on my arm.* • pat, stroke, tap, caress, contact
2. *There's a touch of frost in the air.* • hint, trace, suggestion

touchy *adjective* **touchier, touchiest**
Be careful what you say—he's very touchy. • easily offended, sensitive, irritable, quick-tempered

tough *adjective*
1. *You'll need tough shoes for hiking.* • strong, sturdy, robust, durable, stout, hard-wearing, substantial • Common similes are **as**

tough as nails and **as tough as old boots**. **opposite** flimsy
2. *The meat was very tough.* • chewy, leathery, rubbery **opposite** tender
3. *They played against tough opposition.* • strong, stiff, powerful, resistant, determined, stubborn **opposite** weak, feeble
4. *The police deal with some tough criminals.* • rough, violent, vicious, hardened
5. *It was a tough job to clean the oven.* • demanding, laborious, strenuous, gruelling, tiring, exhausting **opposite** easy
6. *The crossword puzzle was too tough for him.* • difficult, hard, puzzling, baffling, knotty, thorny **opposite** easy

tour *noun*
They went on a sightseeing tour. • journey, trip, excursion, expedition, outing, drive, ride

tournament *noun*
She reached the semi-final of the chess tournament. • championship, competition, contest, series

tow *verb*
Horses used to tow barges up and down the river. • pull, tug along, drag, haul, draw

tower *noun*
• A small tower on a castle or other building is a **turret**. • A church tower is a **steeple**. • The pointed structure on a steeple is a **spire**. • The top part of a steeple with a bell is a **belfry**. • The tall tower of a mosque is a **minaret**.

tower *verb*
to tower above something
The castle towers above the village. • rise above, stand above, dominate, loom over

toy *noun*

WORD WEB

SOME TOYS YOU MIGHT PLAY WITH
• ball, balloon, bicycle, board game, building bricks, computer or video game, construction kit, doll, doll's house, frisbee, hoop, jigsaw, kaleidoscope, kite, marbles, model, playing cards, puppet, puzzle, rattle, rocking horse, (trademark) Rollerblades, roller skates, skateboard, skipping rope, teddy bear, top, train set, yo-yo

trace *noun*
1. *The burglar left no trace of his presence.* • evidence, sign, mark, indication, hint, clue, track, trail, • A trace left by an animal might be its **footprint** or **scent** or **spoor**.

2. *They found traces of blood on the carpet.*
• tiny amount, drop, spot

trace *verb*
She is trying to trace her distant ancestors.
• track down, discover, find, uncover, unearth

track *noun*
1. *A rough track leads past the farm.* • path, pathway, footpath, trail
2. *They followed the deer's tracks for miles.*
• footprint, footmark, trail, scent
3. *They are laying the track for a new railway.*
• line, rails
4. *The athletes are warming up on the track.*
• racetrack, circuit, course

track *verb*
Astronomers are tracking the path of the comet. • follow, trace, pursue, chase, tail, trail, hunt, stalk
to track someone or **something down**
They tracked down the owner of the car. • find, discover, trace, hunt down, sniff out, run to ground

trade *noun*
1. *The trade in antiques has been booming recently.* • business, dealing, buying and selling, commerce, the market
2. *He is still learning his trade as a plumber.*
• craft, skill, occupation, profession, business

trade *verb*
to trade in something
The company trades in second-hand computers. • deal in, do business in, buy and sell

tradition *noun*
It's a tradition to sing 'Auld Lang Syne' on New Year's Eve. • custom, convention, habit, routine, fashion

traditional *adjective*
1. *The African drummers wore traditional costumes.* • national, regional, historical
2. *They chose to have a traditional wedding.*
• conventional, customary, established, time-honoured, habitual, typical, usual

tragedy *noun* **tragedies**
The accident at sea was a terrible tragedy.
• disaster, catastrophe, calamity, misfortune

tragic *adjective*
He died in a tragic accident. • catastrophic, disastrous, calamitous, terrible, appalling, dreadful, unfortunate, unlucky

trail *noun*
1. *We walked along a trail through the woods.*

• path, pathway, track, route
2. *The police were on the trail of the bank robbers.* • track, chase, hunt, pursuit • The trail left in the water by a ship is its **wake**.

trail *verb*
1. *The detective trailed the suspect all day.*
• follow, chase, tail, track, pursue, shadow, stalk, hunt
2. *She trailed her suitcase behind her.* • pull, tow, drag, draw, haul
3. *He is already trailing behind the front runners.* • fall behind, lag, straggle, dawdle

train *verb*
1. *He trains the football team every Saturday.*
• coach, instruct, teach, tutor
2. *They are training hard for the Commonwealth Games.* • practise, exercise, prepare yourself, (informal) work out

tramp *verb*
They tramped across the muddy fields.
• march, hike, trek, trudge, plod, stride

trample *verb*
Don't trample the flowers! • crush, flatten, squash, tread on, walk over, stamp on

transfer *verb* **transferring, transferred**
Some paintings have been transferred to the new gallery. • move, remove, shift, relocate, convey, hand over

transform *verb*
They transformed the attic into an office.
• change, alter, turn, convert, adapt, modify

transmit *verb* **transmitting, transmitted**
1. *The spy transmitted her messages in code.*
• send, communicate, relay, emit, broadcast
• To transmit a programme on radio or TV is to **broadcast** it. **opposite** receive
2. *Can the disease be transmitted to humans?*
• pass on, spread, carry

transparent *adjective*
The box had a transparent lid. • clear, (informal) see-through • Something which is not fully transparent, but allows light to shine through, is **translucent**.

transport *verb*
The goods are transported to Europe by sea.
• take, carry, convey, ship, transfer, move, bring, fetch, haul, shift

transport noun

TRANSPORT BY AIR
• aeroplane, airship, helicopter, hot-air balloon

TRANSPORT BY ROAD
• bicycle, bus, car, coach, horse, jeep, lorry, minibus, taxi, van

TRANSPORT BY RAIL
• monorail, train, tram, underground

TRANSPORT BY WATER
• barge, boat, canoe, ferry, punt, raft, ship, yacht

VEHICLES WHICH CARRY PEOPLE
• bus, cab, camper, car or motor car, caravan, coach, jeep, minibus, minicab, people carrier, rickshaw, taxi, train, tram, trolleybus

VEHICLES USED FOR WORK
• ambulance, bulldozer, dustcart, fire-engine, hearse, HGV or heavy goods vehicle, horsebox, lorry, milkfloat, removal van, pick-up truck, police car, steamroller, tank, tanker, tractor, truck, van

VEHICLES WHICH TRAVEL ON SNOW OR ICE
• sled or sledge, sleigh, skidoo, snowplough, toboggan

OLD HORSE-DRAWN VEHICLES
• carriage, cart, chariot, coach, gig, stagecoach, trap, wagon

trap noun

1. *The animal was caught in a* **trap**. • snare, net, noose, booby trap
2. *The police set up a* **trap** *to catch the robbers.* • ambush

trap verb trapping, trapped

They tried to **trap** *the mouse.* • capture, catch, snare, corner

travel verb travelling, travelled

She prefers to **travel** *to work by bus.* • go, journey, move along, proceed, progress

VARIOUS WAYS TO TRAVEL
• cruise, cycle, drive, fly, go by rail, hike, hitch-hike, motor, pedal, ramble, ride, roam, row, sail, tour, trek, voyage, walk, wander
• When birds travel from one country to another they **migrate**. • When people travel to another country to live there they **emigrate**.

PEOPLE WHO TRAVEL AS A WAY OF LIFE
• itinerant, nomad, traveller

OTHER PEOPLE WHO TRAVEL
• astronaut, commuter, cyclist, driver or motorist, explorer, hitch-hiker, holidaymaker, motorcyclist, passenger, pedestrian, pilot or aviator, rambler or walker, sailor, tourist • A person who travels to a religious place is a **pilgrim**. • A person who travels illegally on a ship or plane is a **stowaway**. • A person who likes travelling round the world is a **globetrotter**.

treacherous adjective

1. *His* **treacherous** *plan was to ambush them as they escaped.* • disloyal, traitorous, deceitful, double-crossing, faithless, false, unfaithful, untrustworthy • A treacherous person is a **traitor**. **opposite** loyal
2. *The roads are often* **treacherous** *in winter.* • dangerous, hazardous, perilous, unsafe, risky **opposite** safe

tread verb treading, trod, trodden

Please **tread** *carefully.* • step, walk, proceed
to tread on
Don't **tread** *on the wet cement!* • walk on, step on, stamp on, trample, crush, squash

treasure *noun*
The treasure was buried somewhere on the island. • hoard, riches, wealth, fortune
• A hidden store of treasure is a **cache**.

treasure *verb*
She treasures the photograph of her grandmother. • cherish, prize, value

treat *verb*
1. *The old woman had always treated him kindly.* • behave towards, deal with
2. *She is being treated for minor injuries.* • give treatment to • To treat a wound is to **dress** it.
• To treat an illness or wound successfully is to **cure** or **heal** it.

treatment *noun*
1. *The hospital is for the treatment of sick animals.* • care, nursing, healing
2. *He is trying a new treatment for back pain.*
• remedy, therapy, medication • Emergency treatment at the scene of an accident is **first aid**.
3. *The sculpture has been damaged by careless treatment.* • handling, use, care, management

treaty *noun* **treaties**
The two sides signed a peace treaty.
• agreement, pact, contract

tree *noun*

WORD WEB

• Trees which have leaves all year round are **evergreen**. • Trees which lose their leaves in winter are **deciduous**. • Trees which grow cones are **conifers**. • A young tree is a **sapling**. • Miniature trees grown in very small containers are **bonsai**.

SOME TYPES OF TREE THAT GROW IN COOL PLACES
• alder, ash, beech, birch, chestnut, elder, elm, fir, holly, larch, lime, maple, oak, pine, plane, poplar, spruce, sycamore, willow, yew

SOME TYPES OF TREE THAT GROW IN HOT PLACES
• banyan, baobab, cedar, cypress, eucalyptus, jujube, olive, palm

PLACES WHERE TREES GROW
• forest, grove, jungle, spinney, thicket, wood, woodland
• A small group of trees is a **copse** or **coppice**. • An area covered with trees is **wooded** or **forested**. • An area planted with fruit trees is an **orchard**. • An area planted with crops or with trees grown for their wood, is a **plantation**. • An area of open ground in the middle of a wood or forest is a **clearing**.

tremble *verb*
The little fairy was trembling with cold.
• shake, shiver, quake, quiver, shudder

tremendous *adjective*
1. *They heard a tremendous roar issue from the cave.* • big, enormous, great, huge, immense, massive, mighty, fearful
2. *Winning the cup was a tremendous achievement.* • marvellous, magnificent, wonderful, superb, terrific, sensational, spectacular, stupendous, extraordinary, outstanding

trend *noun*
1. *There is a general trend towards healthier eating.* • tendency, movement, shift, leaning
2. *This type of computer game is the latest trend.* • fashion, style, craze, fad, vogue

trial *noun*
1. *Scientists are conducting trials on a new space probe.* • test, experiment
2. *The trial will be heard in a crown court.*
• case, hearing • A military trial is a **court martial**.

trick *noun*
1. *Stephie played a trick on her brother.* • joke, practical joke, prank • Tricks which a magician performs are **conjuring tricks**.
2. *The Trojans never guessed that the wooden horse was a trick.* • deception, pretence, fraud, cheat, hoax, (informal) con

trick *verb*
He tricked them into believing he was a police officer. • deceive, dupe, fool, hoodwink, cheat, swindle, (*informal*) con

trickle *verb*
Water trickled from the tap. • dribble, drip, leak, seep, ooze **opposite** gush

tricky *adjective* trickier, trickiest
There were a couple of tricky questions in the exam. • difficult, complicated, awkward, intricate, involved, ticklish **opposite** straightforward, easy

trim *adjective* trimmer, trimmest
Mr Stanley always keeps his garden trim. • neat, orderly, tidy, well-kept, smart, spruce **opposite** untidy

trim *verb* trimming, trimmed
1. *He asked the barber to trim his beard.* • cut, clip, shorten, crop, neaten, tidy
2. *The cuffs of the blouse are trimmed with lace.* • edge, decorate, adorn

trip *noun*
They went on a trip to the seaside. • journey, visit, outing, excursion, jaunt, expedition

trip *verb* tripping, tripped
He tripped on the loose carpet. • catch your foot, stumble, fall, slip, stagger

triumph *noun*
The team celebrated their triumph at the Olympic Games. • victory, win, success, conquest

triumphant *adjective*
1. *They cheered the triumphant team.* • winning, victorious, conquering, successful **opposite** unsuccessful
2. *'I've solved the riddle!' said Nat with a triumphant smile.* • elated, exultant, joyful, gleeful, jubilant

trivial *adjective*
Don't bother me with trivial details. • unimportant, minor, insignificant, trifling, negligible, petty, silly, slight, frivolous **opposite** important

troop *verb*
The children trooped along the road. • march, parade, walk, proceed • To walk one behind the other is to **file** along.

trophy *noun* trophies
My friend Marnie won a trophy for gymnastics. • award, prize, cup, medal

trouble *noun*
1. *The family has had a lot of trouble recently.* • difficulty, hardship, suffering, unhappiness, distress, misfortune, pain, sadness, sorrow, worry
2. *The police dealt with trouble in the crowd.* • disorder, unrest, disturbance, commotion, fighting, violence
3. *The trouble with this computer is that it's very slow.* • problem, difficulty, disadvantage, drawback
to take trouble
He took trouble to remember all our names. • bother, make an effort, take pains

trouble *verb*
1. *What's troubling you?* • distress, upset, bother, worry, concern, pain, torment, vex
2. *I don't want to trouble her if she's busy.* • disturb, interrupt, bother, pester
3. *Nobody troubled to tidy up the room.* • bother, make an effort, take trouble

true *adjective* truer, truest
1. *Do you think the newspaper report is true?* • accurate, correct, right, factual, authentic, undeniable **opposite** untrue, false
2. *This is a true copy of my birth certificate.* • genuine, real, actual, faithful, exact **opposite** false
3. *Esther has always been a true friend.* • faithful, loyal, constant, devoted, sincere, steady, trustworthy, dependable, reliable **opposite** unreliable

trust *verb*
I trusted her to keep my identity a secret. • rely on, depend on, count on, bank on, believe in, be sure of, have confidence in, have faith in

trust *noun*
1. *The director has trust in her acting ability.* • belief, confidence, faith
2. *They put their lives in the trust of the pilot.* • responsibility, safe-keeping, hands

trustworthy *adjective*
Sir Boldwood was a trustworthy ally of the king. • reliable, dependable, loyal, trusty, true, honourable, responsible **opposite** untrustworthy

truth *noun*
1. *The detective doubted the truth of her story.* • accuracy, authenticity, correctness, genuineness, reliability, truthfulness, validity **opposite** inaccuracy or falseness
2. *Are you sure you're telling the truth?* • facts **opposite** lies

truthful *adjective*
1. *She is normally a truthful person.* • honest, frank, sincere, straight, straightforward, reliable, trustworthy
2. *He gave a truthful answer.* • accurate, correct, proper, right, true, valid
opposite dishonest

try *verb* **tries**, **trying**, **tried**
1. *I'm going to try to beat my dad at chess.* • aim, attempt, endeavour, make an effort, strive, struggle
2. *Would you like to try a larger size?* • test, try out, evaluate, experiment with

try *noun* **tries**
1. *We may not succeed, but it's worth a try!* • attempt, effort, go, shot
2. *Would you like a try of my mango smoothie?* • trial, test, taste

trying *adjective*
The way he keeps asking questions is very trying. • tiresome, irritating, annoying, wearing, wearisome

tuck *verb*
He tucked his t-shirt into his jeans. • push, insert, stuff

tug *verb* **tugging**, **tugged**
1. *It annoys me when my brother tugs my hair.* • pull, yank, jerk, pluck, wrench
2. *We tugged the sledge up the hill.* • drag, pull, tow, haul, lug, draw, heave

tumble *verb*
The boy slipped and tumbled into the water. • topple, drop, fall, pitch, flop, stumble, plummet

tune *noun*
Can you play the tune to 'Happy Birthday'? • melody, song, air, theme

turn *verb*
1. *A wheel turns on its axle.* • go round, revolve, rotate, roll, spin, swivel, pivot, twirl, whirl
2. *The van turned into a side street.* • change direction, corner • To turn unexpectedly is to **swerve** or **veer** off course. • If you turn to go back in the direction you came from, you **do a U-turn**. • If marching soldiers change direction, they **wheel**.
3. *He turned a curious shade of green.* • become, go, grow
4. *They turned the attic into a spare bedroom.* • convert, adapt, change, alter, modify, transform, develop

to turn something down
She turned down the offer of a part in the play. • decline, refuse, reject
to turn something on or **off**
He turned on the radio. • switch on or off
to turn out
Everything turned out well in the end. • end up, come out, happen, result
to turn over
The boat turned over. • capsize, overturn, turn upside-down, flip over, keel over

to turn up
A friend turned up unexpectedly. • arrive, appear, drop in

turn *noun*
1. *She gave the handle a turn.* • twist, spin, whirl, twirl • A single turn of wheel is a **revolution**. • The process of turning is **rotation**.
2. *The house is just past the next turn in the road.* • bend, corner, curve, angle, junction • A sharp turn in a country road is a **hairpin bend**.
3. *It's your turn to do the washing-up.* • chance, opportunity, occasion, time, slot, go
4. *(informal) Seeing the skeleton gave her quite a turn.* • fright, scare, shock, start, surprise

twilight *noun*
In the gathering twilight her face looked thin and wistful. • dusk, nightfall, sunset, sundown

twinkle *verb*
The stars twinkled in the sky. • sparkle, shine, glitter, glisten, glimmer, glint

twirl *verb*
1. *The dancers twirled faster and faster.* • spin, turn, whirl, revolve, rotate, pirouette
2. *He paced up and down, twirling his umbrella.* • twiddle, twist

twist *verb*
1. *She twisted a bandage round her wrist.* • wind, loop, coil, curl, entwine
2. *Twist the handle to open the door.* • turn, rotate, revolve, swivel
3. *The road twists through the hills.* • wind, weave, curve, zigzag
4. *He twisted and turned in his sleep.* • toss, writhe, wriggle
5. *I tried to twist the cap off the bottle.* • unscrew
6. *Heat can twist metal out of shape.* • bend, buckle, warp, crumple, distort

twisted *adjective*
The trunk of the olive tree was twisted with age. • knarled, warped, buckled, misshapen, deformed

twitch *verb*
The dog twitched in his sleep. • jerk, jump, start, tremble

type *noun*
1. *What type of films do you like to watch?* • kind, sort, variety, category, class, genre
2. *The book was printed in large type.* • print, lettering, letters, characters

typical *adjective*
1. *The weather is typical for this time of year.* • normal, usual, standard, ordinary, average, predictable, unsurprising **opposite** unusual
2. *The pointed arch is typical of Gothic architecture.* • characteristic, representative **opposite** uncharacteristic

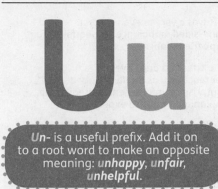

Uu

Un- is a useful prefix. Add it on to a root word to make an opposite meaning: **un**happy, **un**fair, **un**helpful.

ugly *adjective* **uglier, ugliest**
1. *The princess had to kiss a fat, ugly toad.* • grotesque, hideous, unattractive, repulsive, revolting, monstrous **opposite** beautiful
2. *The room was filled with ugly furniture.* • unattractive, unsightly, displeasing, tasteless, horrid, nasty **opposite** beautiful
3. *The crowd was in an ugly mood.* • unfriendly, hostile, menacing, threatening, angry, dangerous **opposite** friendly

ultimate *adjective*
Her ultimate goal is to be a writer. • eventual, final **opposite** initial

un- *prefix*

✏ WRITING TIPS

To find synonyms for words beginning with **un-** which are not listed below, try the following. Look up the word to which **un-** has been added, then add **un-** or the word *not* to its synonyms. For example, to find synonyms for *unable*, you would look up *able* and then work out the synonyms *not allowed, unwilling*, etc.

unavoidable *adjective*
The accident was unavoidable. • inevitable, bound to happen, certain, destined

unaware *adjective*
unaware of
They were unware of the dangers that lay ahead. • ignorant of, oblivious to, unconscious of

unbearable *adjective*
The stench in the cave was unbearable. • unendurable, intolerable, impossible to bear

unbelievable *adjective*
1. *The account of the UFO sighting was* *unbelievable.* • unconvincing, unlikely, far-fetched, improbable, incredible
2. *She scored an unbelievable goal.* • amazing, astonishing, extraordinary, remarkable, sensational, phenomenal

uncertain *adjective*
1. *I was uncertain what to do next.* • unsure, doubtful, in two minds, unclear
2. *They are facing an uncertain future.* • indefinite, unknown, undecided, unpredictable

uncomfortable *adjective*
1. *She complained that her shoes were* *uncomfortable.* • restrictive, cramped, hard, stiff, tight, tight-fitting
2. *He spent an uncomfortable night sleeping on the floor.* • restless, troubled, disagreeable, uneasy

unconscious *adjective*
1. *The patient had been unconscious for two days.* • If you are unconscious because of a hit on the head, you are **knocked out**. • If you are unconscious for an operation, you are **anaesthetized**. • If you are unconscious because of an accident or illness, you are **in a coma**.
2. *She's unconscious of the effect she has on other people.* • ignorant, unaware
3. *They laughed at her unconscious slip of the tongue.* • accidental, unintended, unintentional **opposite** conscious
unconscious of
He's unconscious of all the trouble he's caused. • unaware of, ignorant of, oblivious to

uncover *verb*
1. *Archaeologists have uncovered two more skeletons.* • dig up, unearth, expose, reveal, show, disclose • To uncover your body is to **strip** or **undress**.
2. *He uncovered the truth about his family's past.* • detect, discover, come across **opposite** cover up, hide

undergo *verb* **undergoes, undergoing, underwent, undergone**
Wizards have to undergo rigorous training. • go through, be subjected to, experience, put up with, endure

understand *verb*
1. *I don't understand what you mean.* • comprehend, grasp, follow, see, take in, realize, appreciate, recognize, work out, fathom

2. *Can you* understand *this writing?* • read, interpret, make out, make sense of
• To understand something in code is to **decode** or **decipher** it.
3. *I* understand *they're moving to Sydney.*
• believe, hear

understanding *noun*
1. *The robot has limited powers of* understanding. • intelligence, intellect, sense, judgement
2. *The course will increase your* understanding *of science.* • appreciation, awareness, knowledge, comprehension, grasp,
3. *The two sides reached an* understanding.
• agreement, deal, settlement, arrangement, accord
4. *She treats her patients with* understanding.
• sympathy, compassion, consideration

undertake *verb* undertaking, undertook, undertaken
1. *She was asked to* undertake *a secret mission.* • take on, accept, tackle, handle
2. *He* undertook *to pay all the costs.* • agree, consent, promise, guarantee, commit yourself

undo *verb* undoes, undoing, undid, undone
1. *I'll have to* undo *this row of knitting.*
• unfasten, untie, unravel, loosen, release
• To undo stitching is to **unpick** it.
2. *Sue* undid *the wrapping on the parcel.*
• open, unwrap, unfold, unwind, unroll, unfurl
3. *The good witch tried to* undo *the spell.*
• reverse, cancel out, wipe out

undoubtedly *adverb*
She is undoubtedly *our best player.* • certainly, definitely, surely, doubtless, without doubt, of course, unquestionably

uneasy *adjective* uneasier, uneasiest
I had an uneasy *feeling that something was wrong.* • anxious, nervous, apprehensive, tense, troubling, upsetting, worrying
opposite confident

unemployed *adjective*
Since the factory closed, he has been unemployed. • out of work, jobless, (*informal*) on the dole • To be unemployed because there is not enough work to do is to be **redundant. opposite** employed, working

uneven *adjective*
1. *The ground was very* uneven *in places.*
• rough, bumpy, rutted **opposite** smooth
2. *Their performance has been* uneven *this season.* • erratic, inconsistent, irregular, variable, unpredictable **opposite** consistent

3. *It was a very* uneven *contest.*
• one-sided, unbalanced, unequal, unfair
opposite balanced

unexpected *adjective*
Her reaction was totally unexpected.
• surprising, unforeseen, unpredictable, unplanned **opposite** expected

unfair *adjective*
1. *Do you think that the umpire's decision was* unfair? • unjust, unreasonable, wrong, one-sided, imbalanced, impartial, biased **opposite** fair, just
2. *I felt that her criticism of my work was* unfair. • undeserved, unmerited, uncalled-for, unjustified **opposite** fair, deserved

unfamiliar *adjective*
The astronauts looked on an unfamiliar *landscape.* • stange, unusual, curious, novel, alien
unfamiliar with
They were unfamiliar with *the local customs.*
• unaccustomed to, unused to, unaware of

unfortunate *adjective*
1. *The* unfortunate *couple had lost all their possessions.* • unlucky, poor, unhappy, hapless, wretched, ill-fated
2. *The goalkeeper made one* unfortunate *error.* • disastrous, calamitous, unwelcome **opposite** fortunate, lucky
3. *He made an* unfortunate *remark about her cooking.* • regrettable, inappropriate, tactless, unsuitable, untimely

unfortunately *adverb*
Unfortunately by the time we got there the fair was nearly over. • regrettably, sadly, sad to say, I'm sorry to say

unfriendly *adjective* unfriendlier, unfriendliest
The housekeeper greeted us with an unfriendly *glare.* • unwelcoming, inhospitable, unsympathetic, unkind, impolite, uncivil, unhelpful, hostile, cold, cool, distant, standoffish, aloof, unsociable, unneighbourly **opposite** friendly, amiable

ungrateful *adjective*
Don't be so ungrateful. • unappreciative, unthankful **opposite** grateful

unhappy *adjective* unhappier, unhappiest
You look unhappy—*what's the matter?*
• brokenhearted, dejected, depressed, desolate, despairing, dismal, distressed, downcast, downhearted, forlorn, gloomy,

glum, grave, heartbroken, in low spirits, miserable, regretful, sad, sorrowful, sorry, tearful, troubled, upset, wistful, woeful, wretched, *(informal)* down, down in the dumps **opposite** happy

unhealthy *adjective* unhealthier, unhealthiest
1. *One of the calves has been unhealthy since birth.* • unwell, ill, sick, diseased, infirm, sickly, poorly, weak, delicate, feeble, frail **opposite** healthy, strong
2. *He eats an unhealthy diet of junk food.* • unwholesome, unnatural, harmful, unhygienic **opposite** healthy, wholesome

unhelpful *adjective*
The shop assistant was most unhelpful. • uncooperative, unfriendly, inconsiderate, reluctant to help **opposite** helpful

uniform *noun*
The guards at the Tower of London wear fancy uniforms. • costume, outfit, regalia, livery

unimportant *adjective*
Don't worry about unimportant details. • insignificant, minor, trivial, trifling, irrelevant, secondary, slight, small, negligible, worthless, petty **opposite** important

unique *adjective*
Each person's fingerprints are unique. • distinctive, different, individual, special, peculiar, *(informal)* one-off

unite *verb*
1. *King Bluetooth united the kingdoms of Denmark and Norway.* • combine, join, merge, link, integrate, unify, amalgamate, bring together **opposite** separate
2. *People of all ages united to celebrate Chinese New Year.* • collaborate, cooperate, join forces • To unite to do something bad is to **conspire. opposite** compete

universal *adjective*
Scientists have made a discovery of universal importance. • general, widespread, global, worldwide

unkind *adjective*
It was a thoughtless and unkind remark. • callous, hard-hearted, cruel, thoughtless, heartless, uncaring, unfeeling, inconsiderate, unsympathetic, unfriendly, uncharitable, harsh, mean, nasty, selfish, spiteful, vicious, malicious **opposite** kind

unknown *adjective*
1. *The letter was in an unknown hand.* • unidentified, unrecognized **opposite** known
2. *The author of the story is unknown.* • anonymous, nameless, unnamed, unspecified **opposite** named
3. *The explorers entered unknown territory.* • unfamiliar, alien, foreign, undiscovered, unexplored, uncharted **opposite** familiar
4. *The part was played by an unknown actor.* • little known, unheard of, obscure **opposite** famous

unlikely *adjective* unlikelier, unlikeliest
No one believed her unlikely excuse. • unbelievable, unconvincing, improbable, implausible, incredible, far-fetched **opposite** likely

unlucky *adjective* unluckier, unluckiest
1. *Some people think that 13 is an unlucky number.* • unfavourable, ill-omened, ill-starred, jinxed
2. *By an unlucky chance, their plan was discovered.* • unfortunate, unwelcome, untimely

unmistakable *adjective*
There was an unmistakable smell of burnt toast. • distinct, distinctive, clear, obvious, plain

unnatural *adjective*
It's unnatural for it to snow in July. • unusual, abnormal, odd, strange, weird, bizarre, freakish

unnecessary *adjective*
I'm deleting unnecessary files from my computer. • inessential, non-essential, uncalled for, unwanted, needless, excessive, superfluous, surplus, extra, redundant **opposite** necessary

unpleasant *adjective*
1. *Mr Smallweed was a thoroughly unpleasant man.* • disagreeable, unfriendly, unkind, bad-tempered, nasty, malicious, spiteful, hateful
2. *Being lost in the jungle had been an unpleasant experience.* • uncomfortable, disagreeable, awful
3. *The smell from the drain was very unpleasant.* • disgusting, foul, repulsive, revolting, horrible, horrid, repellent, offensive, objectionable

unpopular *adjective*
The new manager was unpopular at first. • disliked, hated, despised, unloved **opposite** popular

untidy *adjective* untidier, untidiest
1. *Our house is the one with the untidy garden.* • messy, disorderly, cluttered, jumbled, tangled, littered, chaotic, *(informal)* higgledy-piggledy, topsy-turvy

2. *His work was untidy and full of mistakes.* • careless, disorganized, slapdash, *(informal)* sloppy
3. *She arrived looking untidy and flustered.* • dishevelled, bedraggled, rumpled, unkempt, scruffy, slovenly

unusual *adjective*
1. *The weather was unusual for the time of year.* • abnormal, out-of-the-ordinary, exceptional, remarkable, extraordinary, odd, peculiar, singular, strange, unexpected, irregular, unconventional, unheard-of **opposite** ordinary
2. *Ebenezer is an unusual name.* • uncommon, rare, unfamiliar **opposite** common

unusually *adverb*
The postman was carrying an unusually large load of parcels. • exceptionally, extraordinarily, distinctly, extremely, incredibly

unwillingly *adverb*
I dragged myself unwillingly up the steep, rocky hill. • reluctantly, grudgingly, with a heavy heart, under protest **opposite** willingly

uphill *adjective*
1. *The last part of the road is uphill.* • upward, ascending, rising
2. *Finding a job proved to be an uphill struggle.* • hard, difficult, tough, strenuous, laborious, arduous, exhausting, gruelling, taxing

upkeep *noun*
The upkeep of a car can be expensive. • care, maintenance, running

upper *adjective*
My bedroom is on the upper floor. • higher, upstairs **opposite** lower

upright *adjective*
1. *The car seat should be in an upright position.* • erect, perpendicular, vertical **opposite** horizontal
2. *He is an upright member of the local community.* • honest, honourable, respectable, reputable, moral, virtuous,

upstanding, principled, trustworthy **opposite** corrupt

uproar *noun*
The meeting ended in uproar. • chaos, confusion, disorder, commotion, turmoil, pandemonium, mayhem, rumpus, furore

upset *verb* upsetting, upset
1. *Something in the letter had upset her.* • distress, trouble, disturb, displease, unsettle, offend, dismay, grieve, fluster, perturb
2. *Bad weather upset the train timetable.* • disrupt, interfere with, interrupt, affect, throw out
3. *The baby upset a whole bowl of cereal.* • knock over, spill, tip over, topple
4. *A fallen tree branch upset the canoe.* • overturn, capsize

upside-down *adjective*
1. *I can't read the writing if it's upside-down.* • wrong way up, inverted, *(informal)* topsy-turvy
2. *(informal) Everything in her life seemed to be upside-down.* • in a mess, chaotic, disorderly, jumbled, *(informal)* higgledy-piggledy **opposite** orderly

up-to-date *adjective*

> Note that you write **up-to-date**, with hyphens, immediately before a noun.

1. *The spacecraft uses up-to-date technology.* • new, modern, present-day, recent, current, the latest, advanced, cutting-edge **opposite** out of date or out-of-date
2. *Her clothes are always up to date.* • fashionable, stylish, contemporary, *(informal)* trendy, hip **opposite** old-fashioned

urge *verb*
He urged her to reconsider her decision. • advise, counsel, appeal to, beg, implore, plead with, press • To urge someone to do something is also to **advocate** or **recommend** it. **opposite** discourage

urge *noun*
I had a sudden urge to burst into song. • impulse, compulsion, longing, wish, yearning, desire, itch, *(informal)* yen

urgent *adjective*
1. *She had urgent business in New York.* • pressing, immediate, essential, important, top-priority **opposite** unimportant
2. *He spoke in an urgent whisper.* • anxious, insistent, earnest

use verb
1. *She used a calculator to add up the figures.*
• make use of, employ, utilize • To use your knowledge is to **apply** it. • To use your muscles is to **exercise** them. • To use a musical instrument is to **play** it. • To use an axe or sword is to **wield** it. • To use people or things selfishly is to **exploit** them.
2. *Can you show me how to use the photocopier?* • operate, work, handle, manage
3. *You've used all the hot water.* • use up, go through, consume, exhaust, spend

use noun
1. *Would these books be any use to you?* • help, benefit, advantage, profit, value
2. *A sonic screwdriver has many uses.* • function, purpose, point

useful adjective
1. *A flask is useful for keeping food warm.* • convenient, handy, effective, efficient, practical
2. *The website offers some useful advice.* • good, helpful, valuable, worthwhile, constructive, invaluable **opposite** useless

useless adjective
1. *This old vacuum cleaner is useless.* • ineffective, inefficient, impractical, unusable **opposite** useful, effective
2. *Her advice was completely useless.* • worthless, unhelpful, pointless, futile, unprofitable, fruitless **opposite** useful
3. *(informal) I'm useless at drawing.* • bad, poor, incompetent, *(informal)* rubbish, hopeless **opposite** good

usual adjective
1. *I'll meet you at the usual time.* • normal, customary, familiar, habitual, regular, standard
2. *It's usual to knock before entering.* • common, accepted, conventional, traditional

utensil noun
A row of cooking utensils hung on the wall. • tool, implement, device, gadget, instrument, appliance

utter adjective
They stared at the unicorn in utter amazement. • complete, total, absolute, sheer, downright, out-and-out

utter verb
The robot could only utter a few phrases. • say, speak, express, pronounce, put into words

Build your *vocabulary* by using synonyms to describe things more accurately or vividly.

vacant *adjective*
1. *The house over the road is still vacant.*
• unoccupied, uninhabited, deserted **opposite** occupied
2. *The receptionist gave me a vacant stare.* • blank, expressionless, mindless, absent-minded, deadpan **opposite** alert

vague *adjective*
1. *The directions she gave me were rather vague.* • indefinite, imprecise, inexact, broad, general, hazy, ill-defined, unclear, woolly **opposite** exact, detailed
2. *A vague shape could be seen through the mist.* • blurred, blurry, indistinct, obscure, dim, hazy, shadowy **opposite** definite

vain *adjective*
1. *The duchess was vain about her appearance.* • arrogant, proud, conceited, haughty, self-satisfied, superior, big-headed **opposite** modest
2. *He made a vain attempt to tidy the room.* • unsuccessful, ineffective, useless, worthless, fruitless, futile, pointless, failed **opposite** successful

valid *adjective*
1. *The ticket is valid for three months.* • current, legal, approved, authorized, official, permitted, suitable, usable
2. *She made several valid points.* • acceptable, reasonable, sound, convincing, genuine, legitimate

valley *noun* **valleys**
A rocky path meandered through the valley. • vale, dale, dell, gorge, gully, hollow, pass, ravine, canyon, *(Scottish)* glen

valuable *adjective*
1. *Apparently the painting is very valuable.* • expensive, costly, dear, precious, priceless

2. *He gave her some valuable advice.* • useful, helpful, constructive, good, worthwhile, invaluable **opposite** worthless

> Notice that *invaluable* is not the opposite of valuable.

value *noun*
1. *Her paintings have increased greatly in value.* • price, cost, worth
2. *He stressed the value of taking regular exercise.* • advantage, benefit, merit, use, usefulness, importance

value *verb*
1. *He had always valued her advice.* • appreciate, respect, esteem, have a high opinion of, set great store by • To value something highly is to **prize** or **treasure** it.
2. *An expert has valued the paintings.* • price, cost, rate, evaluate, assess

vanish *verb*
With a flick of his wand, the wizard vanished into thin air. • disappear, go away, fade, dissolve, disperse **opposite** appear

vanity *noun*
His vanity is such that he never admits he's wrong. • arrogance, pride, conceit, self-esteem, self-importance

variety *noun* **varieties**
1. *The centre offers a variety of leisure activities.* • assortment, mixture, array, range, choice
2. *The supermarket has over thirty varieties of pasta.* • kind, sort, type, make, brand
• A variety of animal is a **breed** or **species**.
3. *There is not much variety in her choice of words.* • variation, change, difference, diversity

vast *adjective*
1. *The miser accumulated a vast fortune.* • large, huge, enormous, great, immense, massive
2. *A vast stretch of water lay between them and dry land.* • broad, wide, extensive, sweeping

vault *verb*
to vault over something
He vaulted over the fence. • jump over, leap over, bound over, spring over, clear, hurdle

vault *noun*
The gold was stored in the vaults of the bank. • strongroom, treasury • An underground part of a house is a **cellar**. • A room underneath a church is a **crypt**.

vehicle *noun*

⊕ WORD WEB

VEHICLES WHICH CARRY PEOPLE
• bus, cab, camper (van) car or motor car, caravan, coach, minibus, minicab, people carrier, rickshaw, taxi, train, tram, trolleybus

VEHICLES USED FOR WORK
• ambulance, bulldozer, dustcart, fire-engine, hearse, HGV or heavy goods vehicle, horsebox, lorry, milkfloat, removal van, pick-up truck, police car, steamroller, tank, tanker, tractor, truck, van

VEHICLES WHICH TRAVEL ON SNOW OR ICE
• sled or sledge, sleigh, skidoo, snowplough, toboggan

OLD HORSE-DRAWN VEHICLES
• brougham, buggy, carriage, cart, chariot, coach, covered wagon, gig, hansom, stagecoach, trap, wagon

vengeance *noun*
The knight swore *vengeance* on his enemies. • revenge, retribution, retaliation **opposite** forgiveness

venomous *adjective*
The adder is Britain's only *venomous* snake. • poisonous **opposite** harmless

vent *noun*
A *vent* in the roof lets the smoke out. • gap, hole, opening, outlet, slit
to give vent to
She *gave vent to* her anger. • express, let go, release

verdict *noun*
What was the jury's *verdict?* • conclusion, decision, judgement, opinion

verge *noun*
Don't park on the *verge* of the road. • side, edge, margin • A stone or concrete edging beside a road is a **kerb**. • The flat strip of road beside a motorway is the **hard shoulder**.

verse *noun*
1. Most of the play is written in *verse*. • rhyme
• The rhythm of a line of verse is its **metre**.
• Something written in verse is **poetry** or a **poem**.
2. We need to learn the first two *verses* of the poem by heart. • stanza

version *noun*
1. The papers gave different *versions* of the accident. • account, description, story, report

2. It's an English *version* of a French play.
• adaptation, interpretation • A version of something which was originally in another language is a **translation**.
3. A new *version* of the game will be released in May. • design, model, form, variation

vertical *adjective*
The fence posts must be *vertical*. • erect, perpendicular, upright • A vertical drop is a **sheer** drop. **opposite** horizontal

very *adverb*
Carl is a *very* talented juggler. • highly, really, truly, extremely, enormously, exceedingly, immensely, intensely, especially, particularly, remarkably, unusually, uncommonly, extraordinarily, outstandingly, *(informal)* terribly **opposite** slightly

vessel *noun*
1. A fishing *vessel* has gone missing in the North Sea. • boat, ship, craft
2. Archaeologists found clay *vessels* at the site.
• pot, dish, bowl, jar, bottle, container

vibrate *verb*
I pulled a lever and the whole engine began to *vibrate*. • shake, shudder, tremble, throb, judder, quake, quiver, rattle

vicious *adjective*
1. This was once the scene of a *vicious* murder.
• brutal, barbaric, violent, bloodthirsty, cruel, merciless, pitiless, ruthless, callous, inhuman, malicious, sadistic, atrocious, barbarous, murderous, villainous, wicked
2. Male baboons can be *vicious* if provoked.
• fierce, ferocious, violent, savage, wild

victim *noun*
1. Ambulances took the *victims* to hospital.
• casualty • Victims of an accident are also **the injured** or **the wounded**. • A person who dies in an accident is a **fatality**.
2. The hawk carried its *victim* in its talons.
• prey

victorious *adjective*
A trophy was presented to the *victorious* team.
• winning, triumphant, conquering, successful, top, first **opposite** defeated

victory *noun* victories
Hannibal won several *victories* over the Romans. • win, success, triumph, conquest **opposite** defeat

view *noun*
1. There's a good *view* from the top of the hill.

- outlook, prospect, scene, panorama, scenery
2. *What are your views on animal testing?*
- opinion, thought, attitude, belief, conviction, idea, notion

view *verb*
1. *Thousand of tourists come to view Niagara Falls each year.* • look at, see, watch, observe, regard, contemplate, gaze at, inspect, survey, examine, eye
2. *Wanda viewed her cousin with extreme dislike.* • think of, consider, regard

vigilant *adjective*
A lookout has to be vigilant at all times.
- alert, watchful, attentive, wary, careful, observant, on the lookout, on your guard
opposite negligent

vigorous *adjective*
1. *She does an hour of vigorous exercise every week.* • active, brisk, energetic, enthusiastic, lively, strenuous
2. *I gave the door a vigorous push.* • forceful, powerful, mighty
3. *He was a vigorous man in the prime of life.*
- healthy, strong

vigour *noun*
When they sighted land, they began to row with vigour. • energy, force, spirit, vitality, gusto, verve, enthusiasm, liveliness, zeal, zest

vile *adjective*
1. *The professor gave us a vile concoction to drink.* • disgusting, repulsive, revolting, foul, horrible, loathsome, offensive, repellent, sickening, nauseating **opposite** pleasant
2. *Murder is a vile crime.* • dreadful, despicable, appalling, contemptible, wicked, evil

villain *noun*
Detectives are on the trail of an infamous villain. • criminal, offender, rogue, wrongdoer, (*informal*) crook • An informal word for the villain in a story is **baddy**. **opposite** hero

violence *noun*
1. *The marchers protested against the use of violence.* • fighting, might, war, brute force, barbarity, brutality, cruelty, savagery **opposite** non-violence, pacifism
2. *The violence of the storm uprooted trees.* • force, power, strength, severity, intensity, ferocity, fierceness, fury, rage **opposite** gentleness, mildness

violent *adjective*
1. *There were violent clashes in the streets.*
- aggressive, forceful, rough, fierce, frenzied,

vicious, brutal **opposite** gentle, mild
2. *The bridge was washed away in a violent storm.* • severe, strong, powerful, forceful, raging, tempestuous, turbulent, wild **opposite** weak, feeble

virtue *noun*
1. *She has the virtue of a saint!* • goodness, decency, honesty, integrity, righteousness, uprightness, worthiness, morality
2. *One virtue of living in the country is that it's quiet.* • advantage, benefit, asset, good point, merit, strength

virtuous *adjective*
She had always tried to lead a virtuous life.
- good, honest, honourable, innocent, just, law-abiding, moral, praiseworthy, pure, righteous, trustworthy, upright, worthy
opposite wicked

visible *adjective*
There were no visible signs that the door had been forced. • noticeable, obvious, conspicuous, clear, distinct, evident, apparent, perceptible, recognizable, detectable
opposite invisible

vision *noun*
1. *He began to have problems with his vision.*
- eyesight, sight
2. *The soothsayer saw a vision of the future.*
- apparition, dream, hallucination • Something travellers in the desert think they see is a **mirage**.

visit *verb*
They're visiting friends in Toronto for a few days. • call on, drop in on, look in on, pay a call on, come to see, go to see, stay with

visit *noun*
1. *My grandmother is coming for a visit.*
- call, stay • A very short visit is a **flying visit**.
2. *We are planning a short visit to Paris.*
- trip, excursion, outing, jaunt

visitor *noun*
1. *They've got some Polish visitors staying with them.* • guest, caller
2. *Rome welcomes millions of visitors every year.* • tourist, holidaymaker, sightseer, traveller

vivid *adjective*
1. *Gauguin often painted in vivid colours.*
- bright, colourful, strong, intense, vibrant, dazzling, brilliant, glowing, striking, showy
2. *He gave a vivid description of his travels in Mexico.* • lively, clear, powerful, evocative,

imaginative, dramatic, lifelike, realistic, graphic **opposite** dull

voice noun
The robot spoke with a slow, metallic voice.
• speech, tone, way of speaking

✎ WRITING TIPS

You can use these words to describe a **voice**:
• high, high-pitched, shrill, squeaky, croaky, gruff, hoarse, husky, throaty, low, low-pitched, soft, droning
A gruff voice cried, 'Who dares to enter my cave?'

---

volcano noun volcanoes
• Molten rock that builds up inside a volcano is **magma**. • Molten rock that pours from a volcano is **lava**. • Lava and ash pouring from a volcano is an **eruption**. • A volcano that often erupts is an **active** volcano. • A volcano that can no longer erupt is an **extinct** volcano.
• A scientist who studies volcanoes is a **vulcanologist**.

volume noun
1. *We had to measure the volume of the jug.*
• capacity, size, dimensions
2. *They struggle to cope with the volume of fan mail they receive.* • amount, quantity, bulk, mass
3. *The full encyclopedia consists of twenty volumes.* • book, tome

voluntary adjective
She does voluntary work for a charity.
• optional, unpaid **opposite** compulsory

vomit verb
The rough sea made him want to vomit. • be sick, heave, retch, (informal) throw up, hurl

vote verb
Everyone has a right to vote in the election.
• cast your vote
to vote for someone or **something**
I haven't decided whom to vote for. • choose, opt for, nominate, elect

vote noun
The results of the vote will be known tomorrow.
• ballot, election, poll, referendum

vow verb
He vowed never to reveal the genie's name.
• pledge, promise, guarantee, swear, give your word, take an oath

vow noun
The mermaid took a vow to leave the sea forever. • pledge, promise, oath, word

voyage noun
• A holiday voyage is a **cruise**. • A voyage across a channel or sea is a **crossing**. • A long voyage is a **sea passage**.

vulgar adjective
1. *The book sometimes uses vulgar language.* • indecent, offensive, rude, coarse **opposite** decent
2. *The new shopping centre just looks vulgar to me.* • tasteless, unsophisticated, cheap, tawdry, (informal) tacky **opposite** tasteful

vulnerable adjective
As night fell, the outlaws were in a vulnerable position. • defenceless, exposed, unguarded, unprotected, at risk **opposite** safe

a b c d e f g h i j k l m n o p q r s t u **v** w x y z

Look out for the **Word Webs** – they provide related words and are useful for topic work.

waddle verb
A pair of geese waddled along the path.
• toddle, totter, shuffle, shamble, wobble

wade verb
1. *Is it safe to wade in the river?*
• paddle, wallow
2. *She had piles of paperwork to wade through.*
• toil, labour, work, plough

wag verb wagging, wagged
The dog was eagerly wagging its tail. • move to and fro, shake, swing, wave, waggle, wiggle

wage noun
How much is your weekly wage? • earnings, income, pay, pay packet • A fixed regular amount you are paid for work is a **salary**.

wage verb
The Greeks waged a long war against Troy.
• carry on, conduct, fight

wail verb
Upstairs, the baby began to wail. • cry, howl, bawl, cry, moan, shriek

wait verb
Please wait here until I get back. • stay, remain, remain or stay where you are, stay behind, stop, rest, pause, linger, *(informal)* hang about or around, hold on, stick around

wait noun
There was a long wait before the show began.
• interval, pause, delay, hold-up

wake or waken verb waking, woke, woken
1. *Hagor the giant woke from a deep sleep.*
• awake, awaken, become conscious, come round, rise, arise, stir, wake up
2. *The alarm clock woke me at 6 a.m.* • rouse, arouse, awaken, disturb

walk verb

> **! OVERUSED WORD**
>
> Try to vary the words you use for walk. Here are some other words you could use.
>
> **TO WALK SLOWLY**
> • amble, crawl, creep, dodder, plod, saunter, stroll, wander
> *I sauntered down the lane, humming a tune.*
>
> **TO WALK UNSTEADILY**
> • hobble, limp, lurch, shamble, shuffle, stagger, stumble, toddle, totter, waddle
> *A squat little troll shuffled towards the forest.*
>
> **TO WALK HEAVILY OR LOUDLY**
> • clump, pound, stamp, stomp, traipse, tramp, trudge, wade
> *The robot clumped its way up the stairs.*
>
> **TO WALK QUIETLY**
> • pad, patter, prowl, slink, stalk, steal, tiptoe
> *The burglar slunk away into the shadows.*
>
> **TO WALK SMARTLY OR PROUDLY**
> • march, parade, strut, swagger
> *Captain Flint swaggered on board the ship.*
>
> **TO WALK A LONG DISTANCE**
> • hike, trek, ramble
> *They are planning to trek across the Himalayas.*
>
> **TO WALK WITH LONG STEPS**
> • lope, stride, bound, lollop
> *The astronauts loped along with huge strides.*
>
> **TO WALK IN A GROUP**
> • file, troop
> *The children trooped into the classroom.*

walk noun
1. *We went for a walk in the country.* • stroll, saunter, ramble, hike, trek, tramp, trudge
2. *There are some lovely walks through the forest.* • path, route

wallow verb
1. *Hippos like to wallow in mud.* • roll about, flounder, wade, lie, loll
2. *He is wallowing in all the attention.* • revel, take delight, bask

wander verb
1. *Sheep wandered about the hills.* • stray, roam, rove, range, ramble, meander, travel, walk
2. *We must have wandered off the path.*
• stray, turn, veer, swerve

want *verb*
1. *He desperately wants to win a medal.* • wish, desire, long, hope
2. *Gayle had always wanted a pony of her own.* • wish for, desire, fancy, crave, long for, yearn for, hanker after, pine for, set your heart on, hunger for, thirst for
3. *That floor wants a good scrub.* • need, require

war *noun*
The war between the two countries lasted many years. • fighting, warfare, conflict, strife, hostilities

ward *verb*
to ward off someone or **something**
1. *He put up his shield to ward off the blow.* • avert, block, check, deflect, turn aside, parry
2. *The charm was intended to ward off bad luck.* • fend off, drive away, repel, keep away, push away

warm *adjective*
1. *It was a warm September evening.* • Weather which is unpleasantly warm is **close** or **sultry**. • Water or food which is only just warm is **lukewarm** or **tepid**. • A common simile is **as warm as toast**. **opposite** cold
2. *Sandy put on a warm jumper.* • cosy, thick, woolly **opposite** thin
3. *The local people gave them a warm welcome.* • friendly, welcoming, warm-hearted, kind, affectionate, genial, amiable, loving, sympathetic
opposite unfriendly

warm *verb*
She sat by the fire, warming her hands and feet. • heat, warm up, make warmer, thaw out
• To heat food until all of it is warm is to **warm it through**. **opposite** chill

warn *verb*
The guide warned us to keep to the path. • advise, caution, alert, remind • To warn people of danger is to **raise the alarm**.

warning *noun*
1. *There was no warning of the danger ahead.* • sign, signal, indication, advance notice
2. *The traffic warden let him off with a warning.* • caution, reprimand

warp *verb*
The wheel is slightly warped with age. • bend, buckle, twist, curl, bend out of shape, distort

wash *verb*
1. *It took Rapunzel a long time to wash her hair.* • clean • To wash something with a cloth is to **mop**, **sponge** or **wipe** it. • To wash something with a brush is to **scrub** it. • To wash something in clean water is to **rinse**, **sluice** or **swill** it. • To wash yourself all over is to **bath** or **shower**.
2. *Waves washed over the sea wall.* • flow, splash

waste *verb*
Let's not waste any more time. • squander, misuse, throw away, fritter away
opposite save

waste *noun*
A lot of household waste can be recycled. • rubbish, refuse, trash, garbage, junk, litter • Waste food is **leftovers**. • Waste metal is **scrap**.

wasteful *adjective*
It's wasteful to cook more food than you need. • extravagant, uneconomical, prodigal, lavish, spendthrift **opposite** economical, thrifty

watch *verb*
1. *I could sit and watch the sea for hours.* • gaze at, look at, stare at, view, contemplate
2. *Watch how the batsman holds the bat.* • observe, take notice of, keep your eyes on, pay attention to, attend to, heed, note
3. *Could you watch my bag for a few minutes?* • keep an eye on, keep watch over, guard, mind, look after, safeguard, supervise, tend

watch *noun*
He checked his watch repeatedly. • clock, eggtimer, hourglass, pocket watch, stopwatch, sundial, timer, watch, wristwatch

watchful *adjective*
She kept a watchful eye on the baby. • alert, attentive, observant, vigilant, careful, sharp-eyed, keen

water *noun*

> ✎ **WRITING TIPS**
>
> You can use these words to describe **how water moves**:
> • bubble, cascade, dribble, drip, flood, flow, froth, gurgle, gush, jet, ooze, overflow, ripple, roll, run, seep, shower, spatter, spill, splash, spout, spray, sprinkle, spurt, squirt, stream, surge, sweep, swirl, swish, trickle, well up

wave *verb*
1. *The tall grass waved in the breeze.* • move to and fro, sway, swing, flap, flutter
2. *I tried to get their attention by waving a newspaper.* • shake, brandish, flourish, twirl, wag, waggle, wiggle

wave *noun*
1. *We watched the waves break on the shore.* • breaker, roller, billow • A very small wave is a **ripple**. • A huge wave caused by an earthquake is a **tidal wave** or **tsunami**. • A number of white waves following each other is **surf**. • Waves that are white on top are sometimes called **white horses**. • The top of a wave is the **crest** or **ridge**. • The low part between two waves is a **trough**.
2. *A wave of anger spread through the crowd.* • surge, upsurge, outbreak

waver *verb*
1. *She wavered about whether to send the letter.* • hesitate, dither, falter, be uncertain, think twice
2. *The candle flame wavered in the draught.* • flicker, quiver, tremble, shake, shiver

wavy *adjective* **wavier, waviest**
The mermaid combed her long wavy hair. • curly, curling, rippling, winding, zigzag **opposite** straight

way *noun*
1. *Can you show me the way to the bus station?* • direction, route, road, path
2. *Is your house a long way from here?* • distance, journey
3. *This is the best way to make porridge.* • method, procedure, process, system, technique
4. *What a childish way to behave!* • manner, fashion, style
5. *In some ways, the brothers are very alike.* • respect, particular, feature, detail, aspect
6. *Things are in a bad way.* • state, condition

weak *adjective*
1. *The footbridge was old and weak in places.* • fragile, flimsy, rickety, shaky, unsound, unsteady, unsafe, decrepit
2. *The patient was too weak to walk very far.* • feeble, frail, ill, sickly, infirm, delicate, puny
3. *The nobles plotted against the weak king.* • timid, spineless, ineffective, powerless, useless
4. *The film was fun, but the plot was a bit weak.* • feeble, lame, unsatisfactory, unconvincing
5. *He asked for a mug of weak tea.* • watery,
diluted, tasteless, thin, *(informal)* wishy-washy **opposite** strong

weaken *verb*
1. *Too much water will weaken the flavour.* • reduce, lessen, diminish, sap, undermine

2. *The storm had weakened overnight.* • decrease, decline, die down, fade, dwindle, ebb away, wane **opposite** strengthen

weakness *noun*
1. *He pointed out the weakness in their plan.* • fault, flaw, defect, imperfection, weak point
2. *Eve has a weakness for toffee apples.* • liking, fondness, *(informal)* soft spot

wealthy *adjective* **wealthier, wealthiest**
They say that he comes from a very wealthy family. • rich, well-off, affluent, prosperous, moneyed, well-to-do, *(informal)* flush, loaded **opposite** poor

wear *verb* **wearing, wore, worn**
1. *Can I wear my new dress to the party?* • dress in, be dressed in, have on
2. *The rug in the hallway is starting to wear.* • fray, wear away, wear out
3. *Those tyres have worn well.* • last, endure, survive

weather *noun*

WORD WEB

• The typical weather in a particular area is the **climate**. • A person who studies and forecasts the weather is a **meteorologist**.

SOME TYPES OF WEATHER

FOG
• mist, *(Scottish)* haar, haze, smog

ICE AND SNOW
• blizzard, frost, hail, ice, sleet, snowstorm

LIGHT RAIN
• drizzle, shower

HEAVY RAIN
• cloudburst, deluge, downpour, monsoon, torrent

SUN
• drought, heatwave, sunshine

STORM
• squall, tempest

LIGHT WIND
• breeze, gust

STRONG WIND
• cyclone, gale, hurricane, strong wind, tornado, typhoon, whirlwind

WRITING TIPS

You can use these words to describe weather.

TO DESCRIBE CLOUDY WEATHER
• dull, grey, overcast, sunless

TO DESCRIBE COLD WEATHER
• arctic, bitter, chilly, frosty, icy, nippy, freezing, perishing, raw, snowy, wintry

TO DESCRIBE SNOW
• crisp, powdery, slushy

TO DESCRIBE HOT WEATHER
• baking, humid, melting, roasting, sizzling, sticky, sultry, sweltering

TO DESCRIBE STORMY WEATHER
• rough, squally, tempestuous, turbulent, violent, wild

THUNDER MAY
• boom, crash, resound, roar, rumble

TO DESCRIBE SUNNY WEATHER
• bright, cloudless, fair, fine, springlike, summery, sunny, sunshiny

TO DESCRIBE WET WEATHER
• damp, drizzly, showery, spitting, raining cats and dogs, torrential

RAIN MAY
• pour, teem, lash or pelt down, (informal) bucket, tip down

TO DESCRIBE WINDY WEATHER
• blowy, blustery, breezy, gusty, biting

WIND MAY
• batter, blast, buffet, howl, moan, wail

weep verb weeping, wept
Malika buried her face in her hands and began to weep. • cry, sob, shed tears • To weep noisily is to **bawl** or **blubber**. • To weep in an annoying way is to **snivel** or **whimper**.

weigh verb
to weigh someone down
1. Many troubles weighed him down. • bother, worry, trouble, distress, burden
2. She was weighed down with shopping. • load, burden, lumber
to weigh something up
The detective weighed up the evidence. • consider, assess, evaluate, examine, study, ponder

weight noun
Take care when lifting heavy weights. • load, mass, burden

weird adjective
1. Weird noises have been heard in the tower at midnight. • eerie, ghostly, unearthly, mysterious, uncanny, unnatural, (informal) spooky, creepy **opposite** ordinary, natural
2. My big sister has a weird taste in music. • strange, odd, peculiar, bizarre, curious, quirky, eccentric, outlandish, unconventional, unusual, (informal) wacky, way-out **opposite** conventional

welcome noun
The landlady gave us a friendly welcome. • greeting, reception

welcome adjective
1. A cup of tea would be very welcome. • pleasant, pleasing, agreeable, appreciated, desirable, acceptable **opposite** unacceptable
2. You're welcome to use my bike. • allowed, permitted, free **opposite** forbidden

welcome verb
An elderly butler welcomed us at the door. • greet, receive, meet, hail

welfare noun
Her only concern was the welfare of her children. • well-being, good, benefit, interests

well adverb better, best
1. The whole team played well on Saturday. • ably, skilfully, expertly, effectively, efficiently, admirably, marvellously, wonderfully **opposite** badly
2. It's cold outside, so you'd better wrap up well. • properly, suitably, correctly, thoroughly, carefully
3. I know her brother well. • closely, intimately, personally

well adjective
You're looking very well. • healthy, fit, strong, sound, robust, vigorous, lively, hearty **opposite** ill, unwell

well-known *adjective*
A well-known local athlete is going to open the new sports shop. • famous, celebrated, prominent, notable, renowned, distinguished, eminent **opposite** unknown, obscure

wet *adjective* wetter, wettest
1. *Archie took off his wet clothes and had a hot bath.* • damp, soaked, soaking, drenched, dripping, sopping, wringing wet
2. *The pitch was too wet to play on.*
• waterlogged, saturated, sodden, soggy, muddy, boggy, dewy
3. *Take care—the paint is still wet.* • runny, sticky, tacky
4. *It was cold and wet all afternoon.* • rainy, showery, drizzly, pouring

whiff *noun*
I caught a whiff of coffee as I walked past the cafe. • smell, scent, aroma

whip *verb* whipping, whipped
1. *The jockey whipped his horse to make it go faster.* • beat, hit, lash, flog, thrash
2. *Whip the cream until it is thick.* • beat, whisk

whirl *verb*
The snowflakes whirled in the icy wind. • turn, twirl, spin, twist, circle, spiral, reel, pirouette, revolve, rotate

whisk *verb*
Whisk the egg yolks together in a bowl. • beat, whip, mix, stir

whisper *verb*
What are you two whispering about?
• murmur, mutter, mumble **opposite** shout

white *adjective, noun*
White puffy clouds drifted lazily across the sky. White is my favourite colour. • cream, ivory, lily-white, off-white, silvery, snow-white, snowy • When coloured things become whiter they become **bleached** or **faded**. • When someone turns white with fear they **blanch** or **turn pale**. • Common similes are **as white as chalk** and **as white as snow**.

whole *adjective*
1. *I haven't read the whole book yet.*
• complete, entire, full, total, unabbreviated **opposite** incomplete
2. *The dinosaur skeleton appears to be whole.*
• in one piece, intact, unbroken, undamaged, perfect **opposite** broken, in pieces

wicked *adjective*
1. *Cinderella had a wicked stepmother.*
• evil, cruel, vicious, villainous, detestable, mean, corrupt, immoral, sinful, foul, vile **opposite** good, virtuous
2. *They hatched a wicked scheme to take over the world.* • evil, fiendish, malicious, malevolent, diabolical, monstrous, deplorable, dreadful, shameful
3. *The goblin had a wicked grin on his face.*
• mischievous, playful, impish, naughty

wide *adjective*
1. *The hotel is close to a wide sandy beach.*
• broad, expansive, extensive, large, spacious **opposite** narrow
2. *She has a wide knowledge of classical music.* • comprehensive, vast, wide-ranging, encyclopedic **opposite** limited

widespread *adjective*
The storm caused widespread damage.
• general, extensive, universal, wholesale
• Something which spreads over the whole world is **global** or **worldwide**. **opposite** uncommon

wield *verb*
The lumberjack was wielding his axe.
• brandish, flourish, hold, use

wild *adjective*
1. *I don't like seeing wild animals in captivity.*
• undomesticated, untamed **opposite** tame
2. *The hedgerow was full of wild flowers.*
• natural, uncultivated **opposite** cultivated
3. *To the west is a wild and mountainous region.* • rough, rugged, uncultivated, uninhabited, desolate **opposite** cultivated
4. *The crowd were wild with excitement.*
• riotous, rowdy, disorderly, unruly, boisterous, excited, noisy, uncontrollable, hysterical **opposite** calm, restrained
5. *The weather looked wild outside.* • blustery, windy, gusty, stormy, turbulent, tempestuous **opposite** calm

willing *adjective*
1. *She is always willing to help.* • eager, happy, pleased, ready, prepared
2. *I need a couple of willing volunteers.*
• enthusiastic, helpful, cooperative, obliging **opposite** unwilling

willingly *adverb*
The witch willingly accepted the king's invitation. • gladly, readily, happily, freely **opposite** unwillingly

wilt verb
The flowers wilted in the heat. • become limp, droop, flop, sag, fade, shrivel, wither **opposite** flourish

win verb winning, won
1. Who do you think will win? • come first, be victorious, succeed, triumph, prevail • To win against someone is also to **beat**, **conquer**, **defeat** or **overcome** them. **opposite** lose
2. She won first prize in the poetry competition. • get, receive, gain, obtain, secure, (informal) pick up, walk away with

wind verb
1. She wound the wool into a ball. • coil, loop, roll, turn, curl
2. The road winds up the hill. • bend, curve, twist and turn, zigzag, meander

windy adjective windier, windiest
It was a cold, windy day. • breezy, blustery, gusty, squally, stormy **opposite** calm

wink verb
The lights winked on and off. • flash, flicker, sparkle, twinkle

winner noun
The winner was presented with a silver cup. • victor, prizewinner, champion, conqueror **opposite** loser

winning adjective
The winning team returned home in triumph. • victorious, successful, conquering **opposite** losing

wipe verb
I wiped the table with a cloth. • rub, clean, polish, mop, swab, sponge
to wipe something out
Pompeii was wiped out by the eruption of Mount Vesuvius. • destroy, annihilate, exterminate, get rid of

wire noun
Several wires protruded from the robot's head. • cable, lead, flex • A system of wires is **wiring**.

wisdom noun
She's a woman of great wisdom. • sense, judgement, understanding, intelligence, common sense, good sense, insight, reason

wise adjective
1. The soothsayer was very old and wise. • sensible, reasonable, intelligent, perceptive, knowledgeable, rational, thoughtful
2. I think you made a wise decision. • good, right, proper, sound, fair, just, appropriate **opposite** foolish

wish noun
Her greatest wish was to visit the Amazon rainforest. • desire, want, longing, yearning, hankering, craving, urge, fancy, hope, ambition, (informal) yen

wish verb
I wish that everyone would sit still for a minute! • If you wish something would happen, you can say that you **want** or **would like** it to happen.

withdraw verb withdrawing, withdrew, withdrawn
1. The general withdrew his troops. • call back, recall **opposite** send in
2. She withdrew her offer of help. • take back, cancel, retract **opposite** make, present
3. The wolves withdrew into the forest. • retire, retreat, draw back, fall back, back away **opposite** advance
4. He withdrew his hands from his pockets. • draw back, pull back, take away, remove **opposite** put out, extend
5. Some competitors withdrew at the last minute. • pull out, back out, drop out **opposite** enter

wither verb
The flowers had withered and died. • shrivel, dry up, shrink, wilt, droop, sag, flop **opposite** flourish

withstand verb withstanding, withstood
Penguins can withstand extreme cold. • bear, endure, stand up to, tolerate, cope with, survive, resist, weather

witness noun
A witness said that the car was going too fast. • bystander, observer, onlooker, eyewitness, spectator

witty adjective wittier, wittiest
He gave a witty account of his schooldays. • humorous, amusing, comic, comical, funny, sparkling, clever, entertaining **opposite** dull

wizard noun
1. The wizard cast a spell over the whole palace. • magician, sorcerer, enchanter
2. My sister is a wizard with computers. • expert, specialist, genius, (informal) whizz

wobble verb
1. *The cyclist was wobbling all over the road.*
• sway, totter, teeter, waver, rock
2. *The jelly wobbled as I carried it on the plate.*
• shake, tremble, quake, quiver, vibrate

wobbly adjective
1. *The baby giraffe was a bit wobbly on its legs.*
• shaky, tottering, unsteady
2. *This chair is a bit wobbly.* • loose, rickety, rocky, unstable, unsafe

woman noun women
• A polite word for a woman is **lady**.
• A married woman is a **wife**. • A woman who has children is a **mother**. • A woman whose husband has died is a **widow**. • A woman on her wedding day is a **bride**. • A woman who is engaged to be married is a **fiancée**.
• Words for a young woman are **girl** and **lass**.
• An old-fashioned word for an unmarried woman is a **spinster**. • Old words for a young woman are **maid** and **maiden**.

wonder noun
The sight of the Taj Mahal filled them with wonder. • admiration, awe, reverence, amazement, astonishment

wonder verb
I wonder why she left in such a hurry. • be curious about, ask yourself, ponder, think about

wonderful adjective
1. *It's wonderful how much you can see if you really look.* • amazing, astonishing, astounding, incredible, remarkable, extraordinary, marvellous, miraculous, phenomenal
2. *We had a wonderful time in Spain.*
• excellent, splendid, great, superb, delightful, (informal) brilliant, fantastic, terrific, fabulous, super **opposite** ordinary

wood noun
1. *All the furniture in the room was made of wood.* • timber, lumber, planks, logs
2. *We followed a nature trail through the wood.*
• woodland, woods, forest, trees

woolly adjective woollier, woolliest
1. *He wore a woolly hat with a bobble on top.*
• wool, woollen • Clothes made of wool, such as hats and scarves, are **woollens**.
2. *Mammoths were like elephants with woolly coats.* • thick, fleecy, furry, downy, fuzzy, hairy, shaggy, soft, cuddly

3. *Some parts of the plot were rather woolly.*
• vague, confused, unclear, unfocused, hazy, indefinite, uncertain

word noun
1. *What's the French word for 'birthday'?*
• expression, term • All the words you know are your **vocabulary**.
2. *You gave me your word.* • promise, assurance, guarantee, pledge, vow
3. *There has been no word from him for several weeks.* • news, message, information

work noun
1. *Digging the garden involves a lot of hard work.* • effort, labour, toil, exertion
2. *Do you have any work to do this weekend?*
• task, assignment, chore, job, homework, housework
3. *What kind of work does she do?*
• occupation, employment, job, profession, business, trade, vocation

work verb
1. *She's been working in the garden all day.*
• be busy, exert yourself, labour, toil, slave
2. *He works in a cafe on Saturdays.* • be employed, have a job, go to work
3. *My watch isn't working.* • function, go, operate
4. *Do you know how to work the washing machine?* • operate, run, use, control, handle

world noun
1. *Antarctica is a remote part of the world.*
• earth, globe
2. *Scientists are searching for life on other worlds.* • planet

worried adjective
You look worried. Is something the matter?

> ### WORD WEB
>
> **IF YOU ARE WORRIED ABOUT SOMETHING THAT HAS HAPPENED, YOU MIGHT BE**
> • troubled, distressed, disturbed, bothered, upset, strained
>
> **IF YOU ARE WORRIED ABOUT SOMETHING THAT MIGHT HAPPEN, YOU MIGHT BE**
> • anxious, uneasy, apprehensive, concerned, tense, nervous **opposite** relaxed

worry verb worries, worrying, worried
1. *There's no need to worry.* • be anxious, be troubled, be disturbed, brood, fret
2. *It worried her that he hadn't replied to her letter.* • trouble, distress, upset, concern, disturb, bother

worry *noun* **worries**
1. *He's been a constant source of worry to her.*
• anxiety, distress, unease, concern
2. *I don't want to add to your worries.*
• trouble, concern, burden, care, problem

worship *verb* **worshipping, worshipped**
1. *Ancient Egyptians worshipped the sun god, Ra.* • pray to, glorify, praise
2. *She adores her sons and they worship her.*
• adore, be devoted to, look up to, love, revere, idolize

worth *noun*
This ring was once an object of great worth. • value, merit, quality, significance, importance

worthless *adjective*
It's nothing but a worthless piece of junk. • useless, unusable, valueless, (informal) trashy **opposite** valuable

worthwhile *adjective*
It may be worthwhile to get a second opinion. • helpful, useful, valuable, beneficial, profitable **opposite** useless

worthy *adjective* **worthier, worthiest**
They gave the money to a worthy cause.
• good, worthwhile, deserving, praiseworthy, admirable, commendable, respectable **opposite** unworthy

wound *noun*
He is being treated in hospital for a head wound. • injury, cut, gash, graze, scratch, sore

wound *verb*
The fox was wounded in the leg and bleeding.
• injure, hurt, harm

wrap *verb* **wrapping, wrapped**
1. *She wrapped the presents in shiny gold paper.* • cover, pack, enclose, enfold, swathe
• To wrap water pipes is to **insulate** or **lag** them.
2. *The mountain was wrapped in mist.* • cloak, envelop, shroud, surround, hide, conceal

wreck *verb*
1. *His bicycle was wrecked in the accident.*
• demolish, destroy, crush, smash, shatter, crumple, write off
2. *The injury wrecked her chances of becoming a dancer.* • ruin, spoil

wreckage *noun*
Divers have discovered the wreckage of an old ship. • debris, fragments, pieces, remains • The wreckage of a building is **rubble** or **ruins**.

wretched *adjective*
I lay in bed with flu feeling wretched.
• miserable, unhappy, woeful, pitiful, unfortunate, sorry for yourself

wriggle *verb*
The prisoner managed to wriggle out of his bonds. • twist, writhe, squirm, worm your way

wring *verb* **wringing, wrung**
1. *She wrung the water out of her skirt.* • press, squeeze, twist
2. *He wrung her hand enthusiastically.* • shake, clasp, grip, wrench

wrinkle *noun*
The old hag's face was covered in wrinkles.
• crease, fold, furrow, line, ridge, crinkle, pucker, pleat • A small hollow on someone's skin is a **dimple**.

wrinkle *verb*
The creature wrinkled its nose and sniffed.
• pucker up, crease, crinkle, crumple, fold **opposite** smooth

write *verb* **writing, wrote, written**
1. *My granny wrote a diary when she was a girl.* • compile, compose, draw up, set down, pen • To write letters or emails to people is to **correspond** with them. • To write a rough version of a story is to **draft** it.
2. *He wrote his address on the back of an envelope.* • jot down, note, print, scrawl, scribble • To write on a hard surface is to **inscribe** it. • To write your signature on something is to **sign** or **autograph** it.

writer *noun*
• A person who writes books is an **author**.
• A person who writes novels is a **novelist**.
• A person who writes plays is a **dramatist** or **playwright**. • A person who writes scripts for films or television is a **scriptwriter** or **screenwriter**. • A person who writes poetry is a **poet**. • A person who writes about someone else's life is a **biographer**. • A person who writes for newspapers is a **correspondent**, **journalist** or **reporter**. • A person who writes a blog is a **blogger**. • A person who writes a diary is a **diarist**. • A person who writes music is a **composer**.

writing *noun*
1. *Can you read the writing on the envelope?*
• handwriting • Untidy writing is a **scrawl** or **scribble**. • The art of beautiful handwriting is **calligraphy**.
2. *The writing on the stone was very faint.*
• inscription
3. *(often plural) She introduced me to the writings of Roald Dahl.* • literature, works

---

⭐ **WORD WEB**

VARIOUS FORMS OF WRITING AND LITERATURE
• autobiography, biography, children's literature, comedy, crime or detective story, diary, drama or play, essay, fable, fairy story or fairy tale, fantasy, fiction, film or TV script, folk tale, ghost story, graphic novel, historical fiction, history, journalism, legend, letters or correspondence, lyrics, memoir, myth, newspaper or magazine article, non-fiction, novel, parody, philosophy, play, poetry or verse, prose, romance, satire, science fiction or sci-fi, spy story, thriller, tragedy, travel writing, western

✏️ **WRITING TIPS**

You can use these words to describe **a piece of writing.**

TO DESCRIBE THE LANGUAGE OR STYLE IN A POSITIVE WAY
• elegant, literary, ornate, poetic, colloquial, informal, slangy, formal, spare, concise, vivid, lively
The author uses poetic words and vivid imagery.

TO DESCRIBE THE LANGUAGE OR STYLE IN A NEGATIVE WAY
• dull, dry, tedious, insipid, lacklustre, prosaic

TO DESCRIBE A CHARACTER
• believable, convincing, lifelike, realistic, strong, well-drawn, thin, unbelievable, feeble, unconvincing, weak
Mr Scruggs is a thoroughly convincing villain.
• The main character is the **protagonist**.
• The person who tells the story is the **narrator**. • The main female character is the **heroine** and the main male character is the **hero**. • The main bad character is the **villain**.

TO DESCRIBE THE SETTING
• atmospheric, alien, exotic, imaginary, strange, unfamiliar, eerie, spooky, weird, familiar, recognizable
The story is set on an imaginary planet far away. • The ending of a story is the **climax** or the **conclusion**. • An exciting ending to part of a story is a **cliffhanger**.

TO DESCRIBE THE PLOT IN A POSITIVE WAY
• action-packed, dramatic, eventful, fast-paced, gripping, hair-raising, imaginative, intriguing, moving, thought-provoking, amusing, entertaining, hilarious, humorous
Finn's adventures are dramatic and at times moving. • The ending of a story is the **climax** or the **conclusion**. • An exciting ending to part of a story is a **cliffhanger**.

---

wrong *adjective*
1. *It was wrong to take the book without asking.* • bad, dishonest, irresponsible, immoral, sinful, wicked, criminal, unfair, unjust
2. *His calculations were all wrong.* • incorrect, mistaken, inaccurate
3. *Did I say the wrong thing?* • inappropriate, unsuitable, improper
4. *There's something wrong with the TV.*
• faulty, defective, not working, out-of-order
opposite right
to go wrong
The professor's plan began to go wrong. • fail, backfire, *(informal)* flop, go pear-shaped
opposite succeed

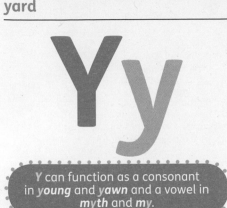

Y can function as a consonant in *young* and *yawn* and a vowel in *myth* and *my*.

yard *noun*
A solitary tree stood in the middle of the yard. • courtyard, court, enclosure

yell *verb*
I yelled to attract their attention. • call out, cry out, shout, bawl, bellow

yellow *adjective, noun*
The bright yellow taxi pulled up outside. Yellow is my favourite colour. • amber, chrome-yellow, cream, gold, golden, lemon, lemony, saffron, sandy, straw-coloured, tawny • Something which is rather yellow is **yellowish**.

young *adjective*
1. *A lot of young people went to the concert.* • youthful, juvenile **opposite** older, mature
2. *I think this book is a bit young for you.* • childish, babyish, immature, infantile **opposite** adult, grown-up • A young person is a **child** or **youngster**. • A young adult is an **adolescent** or **youth**. • A very young child is a **baby** or **infant**. • A young bird is a **chick**, **fledgling** or **nestling**. • Young fish are **fry**. • A young plant is a **cutting** or **seedling**. • A young tree is a **sapling**.

young *plural noun*
The mother bird returned to feed her young. • offspring, children, young ones, family • A family of young birds is a **brood**. • A family of young cats or dogs is a **litter**.

youth *noun*
1. *In her youth, she had been a keen tennis player.* • childhood, boyhood or girlhood, adolescence, teens
2. *The fight was started by a group of youths.* • adolescent, youngster, juvenile, teenager, young adult

youthful *adjective*
The queen appeared youthful but she had been alive for hundreds of years. • young, youngish, vigorous, sprightly, young-looking

The word *zero* comes from French, Italian and Spanish words that in turn come from an Arabic word, *sifr*.

zero *noun* zeros
Four minus four makes zero. • nothing, nought • A score of zero in football is **nil**; in cricket it is a **duck** and in tennis it is **love**.

zigzag *verb* zigzagging, zigzagged
The road zigzags up the hill. • wind, twist, twist and turn, snake, meander

zone *noun*
No one may enter the forbidden zone. • area, district, region, sector, locality, neighbourhood, territory, vicinity

Top tips

to help you get writing

Things to know about
writing

Each of type of writing has its own style and features.

fiction

non-fiction

poetry

mystery story

report

crime

blog

funny story

sports match report

thriller

newspaper article

fairy tale

diary

advertisement

love story

10 things to know about writing fiction

There are lots of different types of stories. You can even mash up different types to make a completely new type of story.

| mysteries | fantasies | fairy tales |

funny stories   mash ups

traditional tales   historical stories

love and romance stories

1 Characters can be heroes or villains, goodies and baddies, children, animals, adults or even things like a sock whose partner has gone mysteriously missing. Who – or what – will yours be?

> See the entries for attractive, bad, dishonest, good, repulsive or sad to get some inspiration for describing your characters.

2 Lost the plot? What happens in your story is the **plot**. If the plot is confusing, try taking out a twist here or there. Look at the entry writing for lots of other words about writing stories.

3 Adjectives can describe characters – how they move, speak and sound. This thesaurus is full of new ones to discover. Here, for example, are some words you could use instead of boring:

> dull, dreary, tedious, tiresome, unexciting, uninteresting, dry, humdrum

A thesaurus is a treasure trove of alternative words. Have a look at these entries for more interesting adjectives:

> sad scary sensible sensitive
> serious shabby slim small smart
> snobbish stout strange

4 Where is your story **set**? Look at the list of nearly 80 **Word Webs**, such as **alien**, **clothes**, **detective**, **dinosaur**, **polar** or **reptile** given at the beginning of this thesaurus. Each of these entries will give you ideas for writing about your setting. For example,

> **astronauts** – jet packs, moonboots and starbases.
>
> **dance** – mazurkas, foxtrots and choreographers.
>
> **travel** – hitchhikers or ramblers, nomads, aviators, and stowaways.

5 Have a look at your favourite book. Find all the full stops on a particular page. This will help you to look at the **sentences**. Short sentences can build suspense; long sentences can be descriptive; **paragraphs** can separate big ideas.

6 **Metaphors** and **similes** will create great images that will stick with your readers, for example,

> a lion, the king of beasts   **(metaphor)**
>
> as wobbly as a chair with three legs   **(simile)**

7 **Direct speech** (the actual words that the characters say) lets your characters speak for themselves. Punctuation at the end of the sentence (comma, full stop, question mark or exclamation mark) comes before the closing inverted comma.

> 'Watch out for the tracker-jackers, Elinor!'
>
> 'I'll see you at home later.'
>
> 'Did you notice anything unusual about the head teacher today?'

8 Some words are used a lot. This book has lots of **alternatives** for overused words like big, good, say and many more. You could try **burly, vast, ginormous** or **important** instead of big. Here are some other examples,

> Inside, the spaceship was surprisingly **roomy**.
>
> The **mighty** robot clanked as it moved.
>
> A **vast** stretch of road opened out in front of them. The road trip had begun!
>
> Today looked like it would be the **most significant** day of my life.

You could try **excellent, lovely** or **great** instead of good. Here are some other examples,

> The **virtuous** knight defeated the evil queen.
>
> My dog Rusty is a **loyal** companion.
>
> I hope you have a **valid** excuse for being late.

9 Asking **questions**, making **statements** and **exclamations** are different sentence types to choose from.

10 If you set your story in the past, the **tense** (when things happened) should be consistent.

Keep your reader guessing what will happen next!

things to know about writing non-fiction

Persuasive writing tries to convince or persuade us of something with evidence and facts.

Explanatory text explains a process or tells us how something works.

Non-chronological reports are organized by topic or theme.

Instructions tell us how to do or make something and often have bullet points or numbered points.

1 Non-fiction gives **information** so it often involves researching key facts and dates.

2 Textbooks, travel books, user manuals and essays are all non-fiction.

3 Non-fiction often uses **formal language** rather than **informal language**. There are labels in this book to help you choose the right word.

> an informal word for **friend** is mate
>
> an informal word for **money** is dosh

4 Each **paragraph** can cover a different part of the topic or answer a different question.

5 Some non-fiction writing uses **headings**. **Paragraphs** could have **sub-headings**. Sometimes headings can be **questions**.

6 If you need to explain a difficult word you can put your explanation in brackets or include a **diagram with labels** or a **picture with captions**.

7 Non-fiction uses **conjunctions** to join sentences or lead from one idea into the next.

> after although as before
> for if since so unless
> when though until therefore
> however

8 When you give more information you often use **adverbs**.

> later twice noisily
> fortunately perhaps terribly

9 Non-fiction reports are often written in the **present tense**. Check the tense stays the same through the report.

> There are hundreds of species of frogs living in the rainforests. The frogs like the tropical conditions.

10 Use the last paragraph to write your **conclusion** or summing up.

5 things to know about writing media reports

1 An eye-catching **headline** grabs attention and gives clues as to what the story is about. The more unusual the story, the better the headline!

> Blazing Inferno Burns in Bradbury!
>
> Man bites dog!

2 Look at a newspaper and read the **first paragraph** of any story – it summarizes the whole story.

3 Newspapers include a mixture of **real facts** and **people's opinions**.

4 **Quoting** people who were there makes readers feel as though it could have happened to them.

> "The building just burst into flames!" reported Edna Blythe, an 80-year old woman from the village.

5 You can even say what happens after the story finishes.

> Edna returns every day to check on the progress of her thatched roof being repaired. She's hopeful that she'll be back home soon!

5 things to know about writing a formal letter

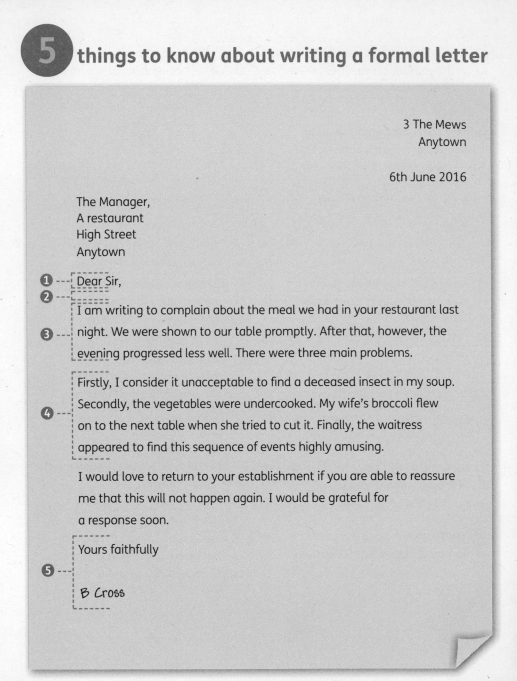

3 The Mews
Anytown

6th June 2016

The Manager,
A restaurant
High Street
Anytown

❶ Dear Sir,

❷

❸ I am writing to complain about the meal we had in your restaurant last night. We were shown to our table promptly. After that, however, the evening progressed less well. There were three main problems.

❹ Firstly, I consider it unacceptable to find a deceased insect in my soup. Secondly, the vegetables were undercooked. My wife's broccoli flew on to the next table when she tried to cut it. Finally, the waitress appeared to find this sequence of events highly amusing.

I would love to return to your establishment if you are able to reassure me that this will not happen again. I would be grateful for a response soon.

❺ Yours faithfully

B Cross

1 Dear Sir or Madam. This is the **salutation**. If you know the name of the person you are writing to this would be, for example, Dear Mr Smith.

2 Miss a line before you start the first paragraph.

3 Now explain the **reason for your letter**.

> I am writing to complain about the meal we had in your restaurant last night. We were shown to our table promptly. After that however, the evening progressed less well. There were three main problems.

4 Use **formal vocabulary** and use adverbs to **make your point clearly**.

> **Firstly,** I consider it unacceptable to find a deceased insect in my soup.
>
> **Secondly**, the vegetables were undercooked.
>
> **Finally,** the waitress appeared to find this sequence of events highly amusing.

5 Close your letter with a formal ending. If you know the name of the person you are writing to, it will be 'Yours sincerely'. If you don't know the name, it will be 'Yours faithfully'. Leave a line space and then sign your name.

Check your letter for spelling and correct punctuation before you send it.

5 things to know about writing informal letters

You can use language that is friendly and more like the way that you speak.
If you were writing a postcard to a friend, it might look like this:

❶——Hi!

❷——It's great to be here. I'm having an amazing time and the
sea's a dazzling blue. How are
❸——you? I hope you're back to
your usual fun-lovin' self now
school's finished!

❹——Bye for now – see ya!
Janey

G. Walker

The Mews

Anytown

❶ You can start by simply saying, 'Hello' or 'Hi'.

❷ Use contractions [it's, sea's, school's] to keep it chatty.

❸ Feel free to write as though you are really speaking.

❹ Sign off informally.

Bye for now!　　Can't wait to see you soon!　　Love from . . .

❺ Read your letter or postcard to check its meaning is clear.

5 things to know about writing emails

Writing an email is much like writing a letter – it can be **formal** or **informal** depending on who you are writing to.

1 Be sure to enter the **email address** of the person you are writing to carefully and correctly.

2 Sending an email is quicker than sending a letter by post.

3 You can **attach documents** or **pictures** and send them at the same time.

4 You can also **cc** or **bcc** other people in to your email: **cc** stands for 'carbon copy' and **bcc** for 'blind carbon copy'. If you **bcc** someone, the person receiving the email does not know that they have been copied in. Here, for example, Mrs Phillips does not know that Carey has copied her mum in to the email.

5 Remember **only press 'send'** when you are sure you are ready!

File	Message	Insert	Options	Format Text	Review		
	Clipboard		Basic Text			Names	Include

	To...	bookshop@townsville.co.uk
Send	Cc...	headteacher
	Bcc...	mum
	Subject:	Summer Fair

Dear Mrs Phillips,

I have been asked to run a stall at the Summer Fair and I am trying to collect items to sell. I'm writing to ask if you have anything you would consider donating. As you know, the Summer Fair raises funds for local charities so any money raised will go to a good cause.

I hope to hear from you soon,

Thank you,

Carey Jones

 **things to know about writing poetry**

A **shaped poem** is a poem where the words are shaped to look like a picture on the page.

A **limerick** is a funny poem of five lines.

A **rhyming couplet** is a poem where pairs of lines rhyme.

A **tanka** is a poem with a special syllable pattern of 5, 7, 5, 7, 7.

A **haiku** is a short poem of three lines with a syllable pattern of 5, 7, 5.

A **riddle** is a puzzle that needs to be solved.

A **list poem** is a poem that uses a list structure.

A **cinquain** is a poem with the syllable pattern 2, 4, 6, 8, 2.

1 Poems do not need to **rhyme**, but many do! The words at the end of every line can rhyme, the lines can rhyme in pairs and every other line can rhyme as can other combinations.

2 **Figurative language** compares two things.
Simile and **metaphor** are figurative language.
A **simile** compares two things that have something in common:

> Catherine's eyes are as blue as the sky.

A **metaphor** describes something as if it is something else:

> My dad is a star!

3 **Alliteration** can be a good choice for a poem. This is when words that start with the same sound are used close together in a phrase or sentence. It can also be funny!

> Lips of **ruby red**, cheeks of **palest pink**. A **spotty skin** and a **smelly stink**.

4 **Personification** is when you give human qualities to an object or animal.

> The cat danced a jig across the floor.
> The car complained when I tried to start it.
> My alarm clock yells at me every morning!

5 A **chorus** is when the lines of a poem are repeated.

> a. **Look, look at me!**
> b. I can run and jump.
> a. **Look, look at me!**
> d. I can dance and spin.

6 Some poems have a set number of syllables in each line. If you are following a certain structure, keep checking your choice of words and their syllables.

7 Use strong and exciting vocabulary – vivid and descriptive language is called **imagery**.

8 Try using another poem as a model. Remember to use your own words, though!

9 Punctuation can work differently in poems.

10 Read your poem aloud – poems are meant to be read aloud and listened to.

5 things to know about writing a script

1 If your story is going to go on **stage** or be on **television** or be made in to a **film**, it needs to be written as a script.

2 **Characters** are key – think of your characters and what they are like. Look up some words in this thesaurus to describe them. Look at the synonyms and see if they make your description even more accurate.

> Sophie Missprint (*a small schoolgirl*)
>
> Sophie Missprint (*a slight, wiry girl who often wears odd shoes to school*)

3 Your characters' names should be written on the left, with their **lines** following. There's no need for inverted commas to show what they are saying. This is how the actors know when it is their turn to speak.
You can include an adverb to help them understand how you want them to speak.

> **Ben** (*guiltily*) It wasn't me, Mum. I didn't eat the cake!
>
> **Mum** (*crossly*) Tell the truth, Ben! The cake was on the table and no-one else has been in the kitchen.

4 **Directions** can be in italics and in brackets. There is no need for lots of description. The actors' words tell the story. Stage directions tell us where each scene is happening and give a small description to help the actors.

> (*The kitchen. Mum enters from the left. Ben has crumbs around his mouth.*)

5 A play is divided into **scenes** and **acts**. They are a bit like paragraphs and chapters. You can use them to help you tell your story through the script.

5 things to know about writing a diary or blog

Lots of writers keep a **diary**. It can be like a secret best friend. You can write about things that you do, such as going on holiday, or just how you feel. A diary is usually just for you to read.

A **blog** is similar to a diary but it is online on the Internet. Lots of people write about their interests in a blog and people follow the blog because they share the same interests.

1 In a diary, it is all about you – you can **write as you think or speak** and be yourself.

2 In a diary, you can write **every day**, every other day or once a week, or maybe only once a month!

3 In a blog, **followers** want to hear news regularly so a blogger needs to think about how often they might want to write.

4 Diaries and blogs are written in the **first person**. This means using first person pronouns, such as **I**, **we**, **us**, **my** and **our**.

5 When writing a diary or a blog, you will use **different tenses**. You may write about things that happened in the past and things that are happening now, in the present. Keep a close eye on your tenses to make sure they make sense.

> Today we are going on a boat ride.
>
> We were standing at the top of a castle when the wind blew our hats off.

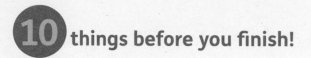 **10 things before you finish!**

Read through what you have written and check you are happy with your finished piece. Become an expert editor and proofreader!

☑ The punctuation is working.

☑ I checked the spellings of tricky words in my dictionary.

☑ It is easy to tell who says what.

☑ It has the right amount of description.

☑ It has the right amount of action.

☑ It is formal enough or informal enough.

☑ The plot is interesting.

☑ I'm happy with my writing.

☑ I have read it to a friend and they like it too.

☑ I have finished!